DAVID H. COPE

New Directions in Music

FOURTH EDITION

New Directions in Music

p. 64 - L. Nono
p. 66-67
p. 98-101

p 207

p 220

improvisation
indeterminacy
serialism
minimalism
(cluster textures
(sound mass
microtones
alternate scales/tunings
electronic
fusion w/traditional developments

p 231/345 ff.

p 256

p 273

D A V I D   H.   C O P E

University of California, Santa Cruz

New Directions in Music

FOURTH EDITION

wcb

Wm. C. Brown Publishers, Dubuque, Iowa

Consulting Editor
 Frederick W. Westphal
 Sacramento State College

Copyright © 1971, 1976, 1981, 1984 by Wm C. Brown Company Publishers. All rights
reserved

Library of Congress Catalog Number: 83–71324

ISBN 0–697–03607–03

Second Printing, 1984

Printed in the United States

2-03607-02

Music

*Dedicated to my wife, without whom
this book would not have been written; and to my parents, whose faith
started it all.*

Contents

Foreword

Most music history or literature courses beginning with 1750 proceed to Prokofieff (or perhaps to Penderecki, if the course is given by an enlightened professor). Twenty-five years ago this course would have culminated with Debussy. Due in part to the considerable volume of recent writing about the new music (by way of periodicals such as *Source, The Composer,* and *Perspectives of New Music*), and to its vastly expanded availability through various media and recordings, it has become a matter of urgent necessity to present relevant updated information about the subject, in textbook form. No longer can the new music of our time be disregarded, particularly since so many of the techniques of the *avant-garde* of the 1940s and 1950s are now part of the mainstream! My study of the manuscript of this book makes it clear that David Cope presents the music of the recent decades in a most articulate and balanced manner. In fact, much of this material existed for some time "underground," and we owe to this book a debt of gratitude for moving that material out into the open and presenting it in a vital way to students, educators, and professional musicians.

Is it presumptuous to write a book about 1950 to 1982 when the latter year is only partially spent? Where is the perspective that is a by-product of time and research? Frankly, it isn't always in evidence, *nor should it be,* as the author (a composer and not a musicologist or critic) does not seek to present definitive judgments, and therefore does not need such time-honored perspective. One of the great joys of this book is that it does not "sit in judgment," but reports what happened: how and why. The author's avoidance of partisanship and pomposity help make this text eminently readable. It contains, moreover, so much information for its size that it can and will, I am sure, function as a valuable source book. This is a rare combination, readability and reference value, and *New Directions in Music* combines both attributes with style, empathy, and lucidity.

As an American musician, I cherish these years during which we stepped into the international music scene, not as the "noble savage" but as a leader. The influence of Ives, Cowell, Cage, and Varèse (who considered himself a composer of the "New World") have been felt and heard so markedly and repeatedly that I feel the so-called "international" style is in large part a Europeanization of the American style. This notion is easily documented by the influence of John Cage alone, for one. Add Ives, Cowell, and the others and the picture becomes quite clear. The missing part of the picture is post-Webern serialism, which has been a dead issue for some time and a small part of the total scene. In considering any recent movement or tendency, the origin is almost always American. This is quite the reverse of the musical scene at the beginning of the century!

Some of the concepts and music discussed may take many readers to personal limitations of what music means. All these controversial ideas are presented with clarity, balance, and understanding. The restraint of the author is most commendable, and I am often amazed at the way he adroitly sidesteps main "traps" and too-often fought battles.

If this foreword seems more in the style of a positive review, please consider these words as a recommendation for a most important book that will, I hope, inform students, educators, and professional musicians alike about some of the more adventuresome movements in the music of our time.

Bertram Turetzky
Del Mar, California

Preface

This, the fourth edition of *New Directions in Music,* contains three major additions. A new chapter "The Challenge to Tonality" attempts to bridge possible gaps between the reader's experience and the origins of dodecaphonic techniques. The only prerequisite for readers is the ability to read and comprehend traditional notation and some acquaintance with late Romantic classical music. This chapter also contextualizes music at the turn of the century by referencing other art forms (painting in particular). Secondly, a number of works receive more in-depth analysis within the chapters themselves (vis à vis the *vectoral* analysis). Finally, additions to chapter contents (particularly jazz, rock, computer music and the new tonality) and an updating of chapter bibliographies (both reading and listening) bring the book more to date.

The annotated chapter bibliographies include not only materials discussed in the chapters but supplemental materials which would be of use to the reader seeking out specifics in greater detail. Each chapter bibliography is divided into two categories.

1. Readings: books and articles relevant to the subject matter of the chapter (listed alphabetically by author, or subject). Also included are reference materials for in-depth biographical study of the composers mentioned in the chapter.
2. Recordings and Publishers: these include record numbers and publishers (when available) of works referred to in the chapter as well as other works the author feels demonstrate chapter content (listed by composer alphabetically).

Though by no means all-inclusive, these bibliographies are sufficiently comprehensive to serve the reader quite adequately. They are intended to be used as lists of information selected for importance and relevance to chapter material, and as *sources* in themselves for bibliographical information to support more intensive research. The bibliographies have been extensively updated and their scope broadened since the first edition. This, combined with the updating of the composer biographies (Appendix 2), the expansions of terms and their definitions (Appendix 1), and the source addresses of Appendix 4, should make the materials discussed more easily understood by and accessible to the reader. Composition or publication dates are included if available. They are mentioned with the first appearance of the name of the work and not thereafter (i.e., if the work is discussed and date listed in the body of the chapter the date will not be included in the chapter bibliography under *Recordings and Publishers*).

When on tour, one is ofttimes confronted by readers holding a variety of misconceptions, two of which this composer-author would like to dispel with brevity and singular decisiveness. First of all, just as writing about Greek mythology does not make one either a Greek or a believer in myths, so writing about various types of *avant-garde* musics does not *necessarily* make one a composer of those selfsame musics. Secondly, due to the volatile nature of much of the subject matter under discussion, one must weigh carefully a most important statement in the *Preface* to the first edition:

The lack of material related herein to more traditional (mainstream) techniques is not intended to reflect or suggest their unimportance (they are *most* important), but is rather due to both the fact that there is a wealth of material already available on these subjects, and to the necessarily limited scope of this text to reasonable length and coverage of the material discussed.

Whether one agrees or disagrees with the concepts, philosophies, and resultant sound activities and/or silences discussed herein is simply beside the point. These musics *do* exist and to avoid either their manifestations or significance is simply playing ostrich.

It is quite possible that more compositions have been brought into the world during the past 50 years than during the entire previous 120-year period. A large part of these works are experimental, some destined to become, like P.D.Q. Bach, "hopelessly lost," others perhaps to help found a broader and more creative base for artistic endeavor. In any event, they can no longer be considered external to the history of this era, or to its future existence.

Directions seem as numerous or as diverse as composers or works. And yet there exists behind these directions historical motives and constant aesthetic values, traceable and uniquely observable due to their singularly radical nature. Electronic instruments and techniques, aleatoric methods, adoption of scientific procedures and theatrical participation, once held as highly controversial and innovative, have entered a large number of current mainstream compositions, due in part to the recent sophistication of international communications media. It was not always so. Berlioz's innovations in orchestration waited half a century for recognition and acceptance. Charles Ives' experiments took many years to be discovered—many more to be considered even rational.

The purpose of this book, then, is to explore the history, philosophies, materials, composers, and works pertaining to those directions of music since the late 1940s which express a radical departure from tradition in concept and/or production, with special emphasis on the relationship of these to significant and realistic directions of style and thought.

New Directions in Music is intended as an introduction and general survey of *avant-garde* and post *avant-garde* music in the twentieth century to the present, in the hope that it will serve to stimulate the reader to further listening and research. Designed for music students at the college and graduate level, it may be suitably integrated into any course incorporating the study of various aspects of twentieth-century composition: forms, techniques, philosophy. It can be a valuable supplement to the well-rounded education of any serious musician. By the very fact that most of the years discussed have not yet become "history" in the academic sense, the author has intentionally avoided the standard historical approach and rhetoric in order to develop *concepts* and *interest* in the *New Directions in Music*.

David Cope

Introduction

As work neared completion on this, the 4th Edition of *New Directions in Music,*
I was struck with the notion of including an original Cage mesostic (text arranged to create names and ideas in vertical simultaneity). I wrote to John in
New York half suspecting he wouldn't even receive my letter before the dead-
line passed. He wrote back in less than ten days (he is amazing in keeping up
on correspondence) and promised something as soon as he could get to it. He
had just returned from Europe and now must fly to Oakland. Since I had
thought to send a copy of the 3rd Edition with my request, I was overjoyed
to think that he would now be able to contribute a mesostic on the text.

After a few days had passed, John phoned from Oakland. He was quite
apologetic. It seems that he had placed *New Directions in Music* in a drawer
in New York City. When he went to retrieve it for creating the mesostic, the
drawer would not open; something was stuck between the upper shelf and the
contents (probably *New Directions in Music*) and no subsequent pulling and
tugging would pry it open. John called a carpenter. Time passed, however;
and since he had to get to the airport to fly to Oakland, he left the book "locked"
in the drawer.

I, of course, was aghast at this trick of fate but more than understanding
of John's plight. In fact, I guess I was so overjoyed that he would *think* of
doing a mesostic, I momentarily forgot that I was not going to receive same.

I quickly mailed John a new copy of the 3rd Edition (actually not "new"
since the only copy I had was the one in which I had made editorial changes
for Edition IV). But time was getting short and my optimism was fast re-
treating. I did have hope, however, since it could have been worse: John could
have read the will of fate into my book's active reluctance to allow his drawer
to act normally.

Finally, John wrote a lovely note and attached the following correspondence. While nothing could truly surpass a personal Cage mesostic, as far as
I was concerned, this serial came close. The articulate and perceptive dialogue
present speaks for itself. It does, I hope, give the reader a spirit of inquiry
which accompanies the soul bent on these kinds of exploratory journeys. Mr.
Berry's kind permission to use his letters is gratefully appreciated.

1 November, 1982

Dear Mr. Cage,

What follows is the angry cry of a young composer demanding explanation and justification for what he perceives as folly in an older colleague. It is offered as a tossed gauntlet. I challenge you to defend yourself so I may understand you better. And be assured I sincerely prefer understanding over anger.

Mr. Cage: I accuse you for items #1 and #2, and hold you directly responsible for the situation described in item #3.

ITEM #1: You have systematically bastardized the art of music composition through the abuse of language. By redefinition of the word 'music', in a way which says, 'anything and everything is music' you have made the word 'music' meaningless. If everything is music, then *nothing* is music. And therefore, composers can no longer exist . . . there is simply nothing left for them to do.

ITEM #2: You have declared, 'My purpose is to eliminate purpose.' You would have all composers eliminate beauty, sincerity, joy, compassion, expression, and love from their music. You would have all composers ignore these basic qualities in music which humanity has enjoyed for several thousand years.

ITEM #3: As a result of your nihilistic philosophy of music, and your pointless musical-sociological experiments, most young composers have been completely alienated from other musicians and from concert audiences. Concert audiences (in the U.S.) are for the most part, completely disinterested in New Music, having been convinced there is no purpose or sincerity in the work of most 20th century composers. You have caused a near-total collapse of musical culture in this country, and left nothing for us (the young composers) to work with. We have no patrons, and our motives for composing music are constantly suspect.

I believe the Great John Cage, 'grand-father of modern music', is a nihilistic comedian playing to an audience of indoctrinated sheep. His art is not art at all: it is blasphemy.

Sincerely,

Charles Berry

JOHN CAGE

MESSAGE	REPLY

TO ⌜ Mr. Charles Berry ⌝

⌞ ⌟

DATE Nov. 21, 1982

It seems that what angers you are my writings, my ideas. I suggest you drop interest in them and focus on your own. Turn your attention to what you believe in. That is what I did. Thus I found alternative compositional means that would permit the introduction of noises and sounds available through new technology into musical works. I rediscovered the traditional purposes for making music

a) to imitate nature in her manner of operation, and b) to sober and quiet the mind thus making it susceptible to divine influences. Thus I was freed from self expression. Music became a discipline, a way of life. I have always noticed that very few people are interested in New Music. I was 50 years old before there was any supportive acceptance of my work. I am now much older but my work remains controversial as your feelings testify.

Sincerely,

John Cage

Detach and File for Follow-up

8 Dec 1982

Dear Mr. Cage,

Thank you for your letter. It has given me a much better understanding of the intent and substance of your ideas and your music. For the present I will take your advice and concentrate on my own creative instincts. However, I do feel compelled to study your work further.

At some future date I may, quite possibly, approach your work from a different perspective and find it refreshing and enjoyable.

Sincerely

Charles Berry

Charles Berry

1 The Challenge to Tonality

Prelude

Nineteenth century humankind, reasonably cloaked in the gifts of the industrial revolution, entered the final one hundred years of the millennium with optimistic and exploratory vision. H. G. Wells' prophetic "War of the Worlds" (1898) introduced millions to the planet earth, viewed finally as a sum of its parts, and to an electrical and even atomic future. It was an era of incredible change and challenge to established traditions. The very essence of its spirit rode tether with Orville and Wilbur Wright on a North Carolina beach in 1903.

The arts rarely detach themselves from social dynamics. The visual arts began (as early as the 1860s) to question the photographic realism of classicism with impressionistic and pointillistic explorations. Georges Seurat's 1886 oil painting *A Sunday Afternoon on the Grande Jatte,* for example, is composed of small dots of intense color systematically covering an enormous 6' 9" by 10' canvas. The docile and immobile figures are relaxed in a timelessness almost antithetical to the passionate points that bring it forth.

Poets Paul Verlaine (1844–1896) and Stéphane Mallarmé (1842–1898, whose poem *L'Après-midi d'un faune* was the source for Debussy's seminal Prélude) mirrored the sensuous and coloristic impressionist painters.

The Expressionists contrasted this exotic lyricism with intensely personal and emotive concepts. Vincent Van Gogh's (1853–1890) visionary early work produced violent and often tormented canvases. Georges Rouault's *Head of Christ* (see Figure 1.2) gives example of the Gothic brutality in Expressionism.

T. S. Eliot (1888–1965) and James Joyce (1882–1941) exemplified these qualities in their "stream of consciousness" novels and poetry.

Both Expressionism and impressionism, while in their own right significant schools of art, served as precursors for the abstractionists of the 20th century. Kandinsky's (1866–1944) *Sketch I for "Composition VII"* is a subtle impressionist "shaping" *and* an Expressionist "personal insight" while avoiding any covert realism or objectivism. Ambiguity of representation creates another level of viewing color and balance.

Figure 1.1. Georges Seurat (1859–1891): *A Sunday Afternoon on the Grande Jatte* (1886). Helen Birch Bartlett Memorial Collection. An example of impressionism.

Figure 1.2. Georges Rouault (1871–1958): *Head of Christ* (1905). Walter Chrysler Museum, Provincetown. An example of Expressionism.

Figure 1.3. Wassily Kandinsky: Sketch I for *"Composition VII"* (1913). Collection Felix Klee, Bern. An example of abstract art.

Concomitant to (even subscribed within) abstractive art is Cubism with its principal exponent Pablo Picasso (1881–1973). If abstract art "removes" image, then Cubism "abstracts" the removal. While *Three Musicians* is clearly that, the angular and often perspective-lacking juxtaposition of "cut-out"-like figures distorts the view, creating an amorphous catalog of queries into the underlying rationale. Picasso, like so many of the century's artists and authors, pursued active relationships with composers, playwrights and dancers.

By 1919 two endemically 20th century schools of art were born. The first, the Bauhaus, was a group of visual artists (both two- and three-dimensional) headed by Walter Gropius (a German-born architect) whose visionary work created a model for today's steel and glass skyscrapers. The second, the "Dadaists", was formed by poets André Breton and Tristan Tzara and spawned the talents of (among others) Marcel Duchamp (1887–1968), Man Ray (1890–1976) and Salvadore Dali (1904–). Dali also forged a third school called *surrealism*. His canvases often depicted plastic figures melted into impossible shapes similar to Picasso's Cubism but lacking its formal line, and creating power through supernatural images.

Figure 1.4. Pablo Picasso: *Three Musicians* (1921). The Museum of Modern Art, New York; Mrs. Simon Guggenheim Fund. An example of Cubism.

Figure 1.5. Left to right: Jean Cocteau, French surrealist author and filmmaker; Pablo Picasso; Igor Stravinsky, Russian composer; Olga Picasso; 1925.

Figure 1.6. Salvadore Dali: *The Persistence of Memory* (1931). Collection, The Museum of Modern Art, New York. An example of *surrealism.*

Each development and contrary turn in the road, whether it be style or content in art or literature, reflects the tenacity of the individual in times of great uncertainty. It is no accident that art parallels the tempo of world events. Contextualized by the "winds of change" in the visual and narrative arts, composers began similarly to divest themselves of the often unspoken presumptions of tradition and strike out for the edges of discovery.

Tonality: A Brief Overview

The "common-practice" period of music history (roughly 1600–1900) witnessed a flowering of musical resources into an enormously rich and complex language. Its basic force (tonality) still pervades much of today's popular and world musics. While a just summary of tonal vocabulary and techniques could take hundreds of pages, there are three primal forces that are important to note. The inexorable challenges to these central concepts spawned "new directions in music."

Figure 1.7. Wolfgang Amadeus Mozart (1756–1791): *Theme and Variations:*   *"Ah! Vous Dirai-Je, Maman"* and a derived C major scale.

First, concepts of "key" define the basic pitch material (the vocabulary) of tonality. Melodies reduced to source material become scales of ordered intervals. Figure 1.7 shows a melodic line and its theoretical scalular projection. Tonality defines these pitches as *diatonic* and those foreign to the "key" as *chromatic*.

Secondly, concepts of consonance (relaxation) versus dissonance (tension) permeate the relationships of tonal materials. The overtone series (pitches present in acoustic sound) is often argued as the rationale for vertical consonance. This series (infinite; shown here through 8 pitches) gives prominence in its lower (more audible) spectrum to three primary intervals: octaves, fifths and thirds—see figure 1.8. When projected as a simultaneity these create a triad (three note chord built in thirds). Pitches outside these basic sonorities are called "non-harmonic" and typically resolve (move towards) a chord member. Most tonal music consists of these harmonic triads contextualized by key (e.g. *diatonic* or *chromatic*).

Figure 1.8. The overtone series on C with primary lower intervals marked and a derived C major triad.

x = non-harmonic tones

Figure 1.9. (a) chords listed in tonal hierarchy; (b) Ludwig van Beethoven (1770–1827): *Sonata* Op. 2, No. 3.

Finally, subtle concepts of hierarchical relationships pervade most tonal music. Two primary pitches provide fulcrum and weight. The *dominant* note (or triad) is the fifth of the key. It acts principally as penultimate pitch to each gesture of the music (be it a single phrase or an entire piece). It begs resolution to the *tonic* note (or triad) which answers the dominant "question." The tonic is the first note of each key scale. Figure 1.9 shows the primary chords of tonic and dominant in tonal hierarchy with examples of other "secondary" chords. As well, the figure shows a fragment of a piece with the three tonal principles at work: key, consonance and hierarchy.

The interplay of these and other tonal principles provided a common language for thousands of composers. Their music, steeped in rich tonal traditions, parallels that of classic realism in the visual arts. So complex is the syntax of this language that relationships are often implied but not present.

As the century turned, tonal composers faced critical challenges with sophistication of syntax developing "slang" counterparts. The *chromatic* outweighed the *diatonic,* the non-harmonic overshadowed the harmonic, the heirarchy had become so implied as to become unreal.

Figure 1.10 demonstrates the complex tonal ambivalences of late 19th century (Romantic period) music.

Figure 1.10. Richard Wagner
(1813–1883): *Tristan und Isolde*
(Prelude)—1859.

Each of the three principal elements of tonality are barely perceivable. The very fabric of *diatonic* and *consonant* hierarchy is in crisis here. While many composers clung to tonal traditions (neo- Romanticists such as Elgar, Rachmaninoff, etc.) many felt need to strike out for new soil (though as with all historical models, based on older techniques).

Challenge to Key Structure

The major and minor scales, while not often used verbatim in composition, provide the basic source material of tonal music. Explorations of alternative patterns was one of the initial ways composers sought for a new order. Transitional and quasi-traditional modes, one of the direct antecedents of tonality (16th century) returned in new ways. Impressionism in music (*circa* 1894–1915), as in the visual arts, chose methods of alluding to yet blurring classic realism (in this case tonality).

Figure 1.11 shows six somewhat standard modes often used in impressionistic works, with their Renaissance (16th century) nomenclature.

Note that in each of the modes, the half-step patterns switch to different members of the series giving a significantly different sounding scale even though the pitch content of each is the same (piano white keys). Figure 1.12 shows a simple Aeolian mode on D as the basis for pitch materials.

Dorian.   Phrygian.   Lydian.

Mixolydian.   Aeolian.   Locrian.

Figure 1.11. The standard modes.

Figure 1.12. Claude Debussy (1862–1918): *Prélude, Des pas sur la neige* (Footsteps in the Snow) (1910).

A. Durand, Paris. An example of modal composition.

The first four measures state the mode through repeated tonic (D in bottom voice) and a scale-like melodic line. The B♭ creates a transposed mode with Aeolian half-steps between 2–3 and 5–6 (see figure 1.11). The C♯ which was often common as leading tone suggestion in the late Renaissance is conspicuously missing here. Debussy is obviously concerned about establishing modal integrity so that the variances with D minor can be emphasized. The B♮ beginning in measure 5 might briefly suggest D melodic minor, but the constant use of C♮ clearly identifies a modulation to D-Dorian (half-steps be-

Figure 1.13. *Claude Debussy.* A
caricature by Vera Jackovich (1908).
Trumbell Collection, New York City.

tween 2–3 and 6–7; see Figure 1.11). "Tonal" ears can often bend modal materials into tonal leanings. Debussy fights this tendency, avoiding leading tone
implications wherever possible.

Another popular resource in early music of this century was the whole-
tone scale. This scale divides the octave into six equal whole steps, creating
an interesting and definitely non-tonal mode. Figure 1.14 shows the basic
whole-tone scale beginning on C, and a second whole-tone scale beginning on
D♭. In actuality these are the only two different possibilities, since beginning
on D duplicates both the tones and intervals present in the C scale.

Figure 1.14. Two whole-tone scales.

Figure 1.15. Béla Bartók: (1881–1945):   136: "Whole-tone Scale." Boosey and
Mikrokosmos (1926–37) Volume 5, No.   Hawkes, New York City.

Figure 1.16. *Béla Bartók*. A caricature
by Vera Jackovich (1939). Trumbell
Collection, New York City.

Composers discovered that this limitation (lack of the real potential of modulating to different whole-tone "keys") is a severe drawback. As well, the characteristic sound of the scale soon wears thin. Figure 1.15 presents an example of the C whole-tone scale in use.

Composers of the early twentieth century adopted folk modes and materials as well as traditional modes and whole-tone scales. In Figure 1.17, Debussy employs a Spanish mode in *Habanēra* style.

Figure 1.17. Claude Debussy: *Soirée dans Grenade,* from *Estampes* (1903).   A. Durand, Paris. Use of folk modes in classical music.

Figure 1.18. Mode derived from Figure 1.17.

The melodic line (here on the bottom) convincingly states a D-based mode different from any yet mentioned.

The scale is clarified and established by repetition of the important intervals of difference between it and traditional tonality and modality. The augmented second suggests the harmonic minor on C♯, but the use of the D♮ (which would be a half-step above the tonic) negates that possibility.

Pentatonic (five note) scales derive in part from simplified versions of *oriental* and *Indonesian* folk music. These latter folk traditions encompass complicated and exotic tunings as well as subtle cultural connotations. Western tradition, however, extracted the simplified scale elements of five notes as shown in figure 1.19.

Figure 1.19. (a) Two pentatonic scales; (b) Claude Debussy: *Pagodes* from *Estampes* (1903). A. Durand, Paris.

The melody here is completely constructed of piano keyboard black-notes (as opposed to the white-key modal constructions of Figure 1.11). As with whole-tone scales, the lack of half-steps creates tonal ambiguity. As well, notice the reference to oriental temples in the title.

Synthetic scales involve the creation, usually by the composer, of unique scales for the purpose of composition. Figure 1.20 shows an example of a work (by an American impressionist, Charles Griffes; 1884–1920) based on a synthetic mode.

Figure 1.20. Charles Tomlinson Griffes:
Sonata (1918). G. Schirmer, New York.
Use of synthetic modes in twentieth-
century music.

Figure 1.21. Synthetic modes derived
from Figure 1.20.

Here the scale used does not conform to traditional tonal-modal shapes. In a), the scale based on F is clearly derived from these opening notes. In b), the scale of the entire movement is shown (space does not permit reproduction of the entire work). With synthetic scales composers are able to freely determine their own functional relationships. This is accomplished through the same resources available to the common-practice composer: repetition and cadence. Unfortunately, real definition of expectancy and fulfillment, so characteristic of tonal music, can only be suggested here since often only one piece (or at best a few) exists in any particularly synthetic scale design. Moreover, the composer using such scales must constantly be aware of the tonally-based experience of the listener. Synthetically derived materials can often be mistaken as tonal or modal in origin when this is not the case.

Any one of the scales mentioned herein, or an assemblage of two or more, might act as tonal substitute were it not for the lack of a consistent body of work utilizing the materials and techniques. More often than not, these new scales were devoured and then abandoned, victims of the lust for yet newer devices in hopes that a stable system might surface to replace tonality. At the same time the engaging qualities of works whose materials are unique cannot be overlooked.

The Challenge to Tertian Harmony

As melodic materials develop into more complex and subtle variants, so too do their harmonic counterparts. In early Western tonal traditions, one finds triads used without a great deal of non-triadic dissonances. As the common-practice developed, non-harmonic tones increased in number and, while still embellishing their harmonic function, began to pull gently at the triadic glue. As explorations continued, a hierarchy of dissonances surfaced. Some tones outside the triad itself seemed more consonant than others. Often these latter tones are extensions of building thirds upon thirds (the source of the triad itself). Figure 1.22 shows a series of triads with added thirds creating continuous 7th chords.

Figure 1.22. Eric Satie (1886–1925): *3 Gymnopédies* (No. 1)—1888. G. Schirmer, New York. An example of 7th chords.

I₇   III₉ VI   II₉ III
          (7)   (9)
          | |
      resolve   resolve

Figure 1.23. Maurice Ravel
(1875–1937): *Sonatine* (1903). An
example of 7th and 9th chords.

Note that where the non-harmonic tone "resolves" into the triadic structure, the 7th chord projections indicate no "resolution." Figure 1.23 shows a series of expanded harmonic structures (7th and 9th chords) with some tones resolving to chord tones and others not. This ambiguity is a trademark of the turn of the century impressionistic composer.

Further expansion of triads by thirds creates further complexity and depth of texture. Figure 1.24 shows a dominant 13th chord. Note how chord members remain fixed (do not resolve into a triadic structure).

Figure 1.24. Claude Debussy: *Prélude à*
"L'Après Midi d'un Faune" (1894). An
example of a dominant 13th chord.

Spacing is also a critical component. If the 13th chord of Figure 1.24 is collapsed within a single octave, a dissonant chord occurs where seconds rather than thirds seem to be the basic substructure. These tend to resemble "clusters" of sound (to be discussed in Chapter 3).

Figure 1.25. Collapsed 13th chord and
resultant dissonance.

Because 9th, 11th and 13th chords are often so vertically oriented (since non-harmonic movement is reduced with so many tones already present in the chord), constant contrary motion with chords of so many members can create contrapuntal chaos, with few of the voices distinguishable and often colliding with one another. Thus they are often used in parallel voice motion. This is called *planing* (creating "planes" or "levels" of register).

Planing basically involves "freezing" a chord structure and then moving it along as if it were a single melodic line. Harmonies become a by-product of melodic movement and are heard as moving groups of notes rather than separate entities. Figure 1.26 is an example of diatonic *planing*.

Figure 1.26. Claude Debussy: *Feuilles mortes* ("Dead Leaves," from the Preludes, Book II). (1913). A. Durand, Paris. An example of diatonic planing.

While the intervals change (e.g. major to minor) and the functions could be said to change on each chord, it is the horizontal movement that carries the vertical structure along. To evaluate "tonics", "dominants", and other functions within this is to simply ignore the real meaning of the music.

Figure 1.27 shows a more substantial use of *planing* from the same composer. Here the *freezing* of the basic pattern remains so fixed that the passage obtains a great variety of chromaticism. Again, it would be possible to carefully go through each and every harmonic structure and detail function. The vertical sonorities are, however, simply a by-product of the melodic line and the resulting chords and chromaticism formed by this *planing*.

The triads of Figure 1.28 create a full chromatic complement (all 12 tones) to the resolute "pedal point" G in the bass.

Composers also sought to create complex vertical structures (while hoping to retain some tonal identity) by combining two or more keys simultaneously. This "polytonality" creates a rich fabric of chromatic textures especially when the keys have few common tones. Figure 1.29 (reduced from orchestral score) shows an example of polytonality using the keys of C major and F♯ major simultaneously (note how the scales shown have only 2 notes in common: B and F [E♯]).

Figure 1.27. Claude Debussy: *Soirée dans Grenade* from *Estampes* (1903). A. Durand, Paris.

Figure 1.28. Maurice Ravel: *Le Tombeau de Couperin,* "Minuet" (1917). A. Durand, Paris. An example of triadic *planing.*

Figure 1.29. (a) Igor Stravinsky (1882–1971): *Petrushka* (1911). (b) Scales of C and F♯ major.

Figure 1.30. *Igor Stravinsky.* A caricature by Vera Jackovich (1953). Trumbell Collection, New York City.

The dissonance of the passage is greatly reduced by the simple use of triads in each key. The listener, though certainly pummeled with dissonance, can grasp the basic duality of the elements and perceive the contextualization. To effect this counterpoint of keys, composers often establish strong key centers rather than allowing the variants to intermingle and reduce the bi-tonal recognizeability. In Figure 1.31, Bartók uses different key signatures, different staves, and particularly different material for each key (B major melodic figuration versus C major harmonic *planing*).

Figure 1.31. Béla Bartók: *Out of Doors Suite* (1926). Universal Edition.

Some composers add the element of "collage" to polytonal techniques. This effect combines polytonality with quotation (usually popular or folk in origin). The result often creates polyrhythms, polymeters, polytextures and polyconcepts from the overlapping of widely diverse musical types. Figure 1.32 shows this process in use.

Figure 1.32. Charles Ives (1874–1954): "Putnam's Camp," from *Three Places in New England* (1914).

Here one idea is in Bb major (flutes, clarinets, trumpets, bass and lower violas), another in D minor (piano, violins, and horns), with a third suggesting F major (trombones). One line wavers slowly (top 'celli) around chromatic pitches Bb, A and Cb. The result might be chaos, but because each idea is uniquely orchestrated and identifiable as quotation, the "poly" concept works effectively. Collage techniques are therefore viable procedures to clarify and establish polytonality.

Composers also sought ways of constructing chords from intervals other than thirds. In Figure 1.33, the basic harmonic fabric is clearly 4th chords (four fourths creating five notes). Only the first chord of the second measure (with the word "wonder") defies this analysis.

Figure 1.33. Charles Ives: *The Cage* (from *114 Songs:* 1884–1921). Published by the composer and later by   New Music Edition. An example of chords built with fourths.

Note how the melodic line contrasts with the harmonic structure by moving almost exclusively in seconds. The "stacked" nature of the chords makes *planing* almost unavoidable. There is no doubt of the non-tertian nature of these chords since no tones resolve or even hint of a triadic base.

Figure 1.34 is a more complex interplay of non-tertian harmonies and develops a more contrapuntal basis of voice motion. The first chord is a "stacked" 4th chord (B—E—A) with a doubled B in the top voice. The third, fourth and sixth chords are similarly stacked in fourths. Chords five and seven are inversions of fourth chords and need only an octave displacement of one pitch (B below E for chord five, and F♯ between C♯ and B for chord seven) to be seen as similar projections of fourths. Chords two, eight and nine are ambiguous with either a note missing (e.g. chord two could be seen as stacked fourths if the B were in the bass and an E added just above it) or a triad with an added pitch.

Figure 1.34. Paul Hindemith (1895–1963): *Le Cygne* (from *Six Chansons*)—1939. B. Schott's Soehne, *Mainz*. Contrapuntal techniques in non-tertian harmony.

The final chord is a triad which by its simplicity seems almost dissonant (i.e. in its "contrary to context" meaning). Chromatic pitches here are not derived from tonal inflections but are the result of projections of "perfect" fourths.

Expanding triads into dense sonorities (9th, 11th and 13th chords), using more than one key simultaneously (polytonality) and exploring new interval foundations for harmonies all expand the composer's menu of available materials for vertical simultaneities. Each of these avenues, while initially focused on as elaborations of tonality, helps to defuse its very center—the triad—and in so doing provides exit routes into less widely interpretable vocabularies.

The Challenge to Tonal Hierarchy

As harmonic glue seeps from tonality, hierarchical structure slips away. Subtle chromatic embellishing chords with complex but expected resolutions seem to become so distant from basic key concepts that recognition of tonic and dominant becomes obscured. Simple rhyming phrases of tonality seem too obvious and phrases blur into a continuity which seems to lack clear hierarchical structure (i.e. primary structure: I, V; secondary: II, III, etc.; tertiary: chromatic chords, etc.). Busoni possibly says it more eloquently: "Let us take thought, how music may be restored to its primitive, natural essence; let us free it from architectonic, acoustic and esthetic dogmas; let it be pure invention and sentiment, in harmonies, in forms, in tone-colors (for invention and sentiment are not the prerogative of melody alone); let it follow the line of the rainbow and vie with the clouds in breaking sunbeams."[1]

With tonal superstructure gone, composers evolved uniquely "personal" languages that often did not last for more than a few works. As well, tonal emphasis on phrase structure and cadence implode into a preoccupation with single structures: "events." Scriabin's *mystic chord*, for example, is a kind of fourth chord (inclusive of both augmented and diminished forms).

1. Busoni, Ferruccio. *Sketch of a New Esthetic of Music.* New York City: G. Schirmer, Inc., 1911. Translated from German by Dr. Th. Baker.

Figure 1.35. Alexander Scriabin's *mystic chord.*

This becomes the organic source for melodic and harmonic development. Figure 1.36 shows a brief sample of how this structure permeates the fabric of Scriabin's work.

Figure 1.36. Alexander Scriabin (1872–1915): *Poème* Op. 69, no. 1 (1913).

The "event" concept, taken to the extreme, implies a momentary collapse of the lyric in music. The emphasis turns to the vertical subtleties of the event—its texture, timbre and duration—with a focus separate from cadence-directed motion. Figure 1.37 shows how groups of events can be organized into linear direction.

Figure 1.37. Anton Webern (1883–1945): *Six Bagatelles* for string quartet (1913). An example of musical pointillism.

The texture here is fluid yet shaped by a set of events or points of sound (pointillism—see Figure 1.1).

With music freed, as it were, from "architectonic" expectation, areas other than pitch also become available for experimentation. The rigor of the barline relaxes into what some have called "time-suspension." Figure 1.38 shows two of the many ways composers used to free music from the "tyranny" of the beat. First, on-beats are avoided (especially downbeats) to diminish their import. Secondly, irregular small subdivisions of the beat are created to blur suggested beat accent.

Figure 1.38. Arnold Schoenberg (1874–1951): *Sechs Kleine*   *Klavierstücke* Opus 19 (1911). Universal Edition.

The *atonal* (derogatory word often used to describe early works of this century) qualities of the pitch material are similar to that of Scriabin's *Poème* (Figure 1.36) and triadic references are rare. Public acceptance of these *atonal* works was quite mixed as the following (a review in the *Paris-Midi,* of May 29, 1913) indicates:

". . . musical cubism has made its appearance in the fair city of Paris. By singular irony of fate, it was in the venerable hall of the Conservatoire, the temple of all tradition, that this revelation took place . . . offering to its habitués the first performance of three piano pieces by Arnold Schoenberg. This composer hails from Vienna, preceded by an intriguing reputation. Every performance of one of his works in Austria and Germany has provoked disorders, police intervention, transportation of the wounded to the hospital and of dead bodies to the morgue. At the sound of the last chord the listeners would come to blows, and music lovers strewn on the floor would be picked up in bunches. So we waited with impatience the first contact of this explosive art with French sensibilities . . . But all expectations were deceived. True, there were some uncomfortable smiles, some anguished sighs, some stifled groans, but no scandal erupted. Arnold Schoenberg would not believe it.[2]

2. Slonimsky, Nicolas. *Lexicon of Musical Invective (Critical Assaults on Composers since Beethoven's Time).* Seattle, Washington: University of Washington Press. Second Edition: 1969. pp. 310–11.

Timbral explorations are likewise important and composers continued to expand the repertoire of acceptable musical sounds. Percussion sections of orchestras often "wagged the dog" as in works by Edgard Varèse. *Amériques* (1922) for orchestra, for example, requires ten percussionists utilizing 21 different instruments. This work also typically explores the resources of the traditional orchestra with normal complements of winds often doubled in size (e.g. six trumpets, five trombones, etc.). He also employs the Hecklephone, contrabass tuba and contrabass trombone. *Amériques* is a culmination of the post-Romantic tradition of gargantuan orchestras exemplified by Schoenberg's *Gurrelieder* (1911).

While some composers clung to tonal inheritance, content to articulate their musical thoughts through revisions of Western tradition, others saw this as a turning point for their musical style. The common language was gone for them and each was free to pursue an experimental direction. For some this meant the construction of new vocabularies and commonalities and for others it meant a complete reexamination of the very nature of sound and the complicated way in which the human animal acts and interacts in its presence.

Figure 1.39. *Arnold Schoenberg.* A caricature by Vera Jackovich (1948). Trumbell Collection, New York City.

Vectoral Analysis: Edgard Varèse: *Density 21.5*

Vectoral analysis (from *vector,* a quantity with both force and direction, here defined as a three-dimensional analytical technique rather than two-dimensional form analysis or one-dimensional harmonic analysis) will be used for all larger in-depth analysis throughout the text. Its seven-pronged view of each piece provides the perspective and thorough analysis necessary to understand contemporary music more fully, especially that of recent experimental vintage.

The following is a basic synopsis of the analytical process to be used.

1. Historical Background: This includes information of relevance to the piece under discussion relating to period of composition, school of composition (if any), inclusive dates of composition, country of origin, historical influences, and the composer's important teachers.

2. Overview, Structure and Texture: This includes general formal analysis and a careful look at composite structures (e.g., homophonic, monophonic, contrapuntal), general notational principles used, rhythmic ideas

Figure 1.40. Edgard Varèse. BMI Archives. Used by permission.

generated, compositional techniques influencing structure (e.g., mobile forms, graphic notation), and texts employed.

3. Orchestration Techniques: Basic timbre analysis, general instrumentation, unusual techniques (e.g., multiphonics, preparations), extreme ranges, unusual balance and/or inverted structures, relevant relation of timbre to form, and structure.

4. Basic Techniques: Includes pitch organization (e.g., tonal), motivic structures, and rhythmic detail.

5. Vertical Models: Presentation of significant samplings of vertical structures from the piece, including chord roots, centers, and voice leading between chord structures.

6. Horizontal Models: Presentation of significant samplings of horizontal melodic structures including cadence, balance, and motion.

7. Style: An integration of 1 through 6; a summary of the stylistic parameters employed by the composer; any relevant material not discussed above; general summation of harmonic, melodic, rhythmic, and formal techniques used; and their correlation.

Limitations of space do not allow for extensive dissertations for each of these categories (which indeed becomes a possibility when one begins to delve deeply into the bowels of most contemporary works), but rather a synoptical summary of the techniques and applications found under each reference.

1. Historical Background. Edgard Varèse (1883–1965) was born in Paris of Italian-French parents and studied principally mathematics and science at school until he was 18. He then entered the Schola Cantorum where he studied with Vincent d'Indy, Albert Roussel, and Charles Widor, becoming as well a very close friend and confidant of Ferruccio Busoni. He came to the United States in 1915, organizing both orchestras and concert societies for new music in New York City. A good portion of his early works were destroyed by fire. The greater part of the music we are now aware of was written during the twenties and thirties; for example, *Octandre* (1924), *Intégrales* (1925) and *Ionisation* (1931). From that time until the early fifties Varèse did not compose. The fifties brought *Déserts* (1954) and *Poème électronique* (1958) into existence, both works involving electronic forces. Varèse was clearly influenced by the French impressionists. More important, his style was affected by the iconoclastic Busoni and Carlos Salzedo (with whom he founded the International Composers' Guild in 1921). As well, his work shows marked influence of Stravinsky (particularly Stravinsky's early "primitive" period).

2. Overview: *Density 21.5* was completed in 1936 and written for Georges Barrere for the inauguration of his platinum flute (21.5 is the density of platinum). The work was revised in April of 1946 for a *New Music Quarterly* release in July of that year, and subsequent performances follow this latter form. The work is in three main continuous sections with the first and last having similar lyric qualities. The middle section is "event" oriented.

Figure 1.41. Opening materials of each
section for *Density 21.5*. (c) 1946 by
Colfranc Music Publishing Corp.

It is interesting that the first note of each of these sections, when taken out of context but grouped together, become the first three notes of the piece (F—E—F♯). This kind of "organic" writing (all materials flowing naturally from a single seed) replaces some of the tonal expectations of key, triad and hierarchy and provides a kind of consistency that gives a natural sense of flow to the work.

3. Orchestration: Most timbral features available on the flute are explored in this piece: range differences, dynamics within the various registers, articulations, etc. Figure 1.41 shows an excerpt employing "slapped" keys, a percussive effect produced by playing softly and hitting the key simultaneously (+).

4. The motive of the piece is clearly stated and separated from the body of the first phrase: F—E—F♯ (see Figure 1.41). Note that this motive also implies a concept of statement (F), new statement (E) and return to the first statement with variation (F♯) which characterizes the work's form. Within the first section, one finds constant references to the opening motive. Measure 2 continues the first phrase with basic expansion of intervals and extension (four notes instead of three). The second phrase begins exactly as the first, but continues with variations based on inversion (F♯—G—F♯) and repetition. The third phrase retrogrades the extension of the first phrase and intervallically expands the motive to G—B♭—G. Every note of the first section can realistically be evolved from the opening three-note motive. Some are extensive variations, while others are simple inversions. However, all reflect in some way the concept of statement—new statement—return with variation implicit in the motive of the piece. One can also note the synthetic scale use at the beginning and throughout the work (based on the 8-pitch base of the opening 8 bars).

Figure 1.42. The opening 8 bars of
Density 21.5 (c) 1946 by Colfranc
Music Publishing Corp.

Also noteworthy is the way in which Varèse "saves" important notes—notably D (which does not occur until bar 11) and B (which does not occur until bar 18).

The second section establishes a contrasting pointillistic theme (see Figure 1.41). However, note the "real" material here: E—C♯—E is clearly a variant of the opening motive. Even the highly contrasting and repetitive climax of the work is an extended inversion of the opening motive. The third section returns to the opening lyric style, but pitch content is varied (based on opening materials).

Varèse may have even attempted numerical relationships with the title of the piece. Interestingly, 70 out of the first 83 intervals of the piece are seconds, fifths or fourths (fifth inversion), or primes (1). Whether Varèse intended such relationships is really beside the point; such extreme consistency of intervallic structure contributes to the overall tightly integrated structure of the piece.

5. Vertical model: One does not expect to find vertical possibilities in a work for solo flute. However, it is interesting to note how figure repetition, after a period of time, blends and begins to suggest vertical simultaneities. In Figure 1.43 two of the prominent intervals (seconds and fourths) are underscored by notable repetition.

Figure 1.43. Repetition in *Density 21.5*.
(c) 1946 by Colfranc Publishing Corp.

The passage emphasizes tonal ambiguities (non-resolution of tritones) and contrasts these with highly directed dynamics. Note as well how the D♮ is "saved" and finally reached in an explosive triple *forte*.

6. Horizontal models: The expansion of the original motive is prevalent. Figure 1.44 shows how the second expands to the augmented 4th (as mentioned in vertical models).

Figure 1.44. Expansion techniques in *Density 21.5*. (c) 1946 by Colfranc Publishing Corp.

Note how the passage is a kind of "suspension" of musical time. Only the opening note is a downbeat with the remainder of the phrase freely sculpted from available duration rather than splintered from beats and sub-beats.

7. Style: Varèse's *Density 21.5* is a three-part work consistently hewn from an initial three note motive of major and minor seconds. The instrument's range and available effects are explored as are the concepts of expansion and diminution of intervals, saving pitches for intense climaxes. A "free" phrase structure dominates but without marked tonal references or resolutions. Lines are freely spun through time in a musical and balanced manner. The musical language used, however separate from a tonal sphere, is articulate and consistent. Varèse belongs to that group of composers intent on creating a new syntax from rich vocabularies of sound.

Bibliography

Further Readings*

Austin, William. *Music in the Twentieth Century.* New York: W. W. Norton, 1966. Good general coverage of mainstream developments of the post-Romantic tradition.

Backus, John. *The Acoustical Foundations of Music.* New York: W. W. Norton, 1969. This is the standard reference for acoustical information relating to music.

"The Composer Between Man and Music (Contemporary Music in the 1970s)" *Interface* Vol. 9, no. 3–4, 1980. Results of a widely broadcast questionnaire on contemporary music.

Forte, Allen. *Contemporary Tone Structures.* New York: Columbia University Press, 1955.

Griffiths, Paul. *A Concise History of Avant-Garde Music.* New York: Oxford University Press, 1978. An excellent overview of the origins of the *avant-garde,* though very biased towards European composers and works.

Machlis, Joseph. *Introduction to Contemporary Music* (2nd edition). New York: W. W. Norton and Company, 1979. The most complete work covering all aspects of twentieth-century music. Though the *avant-garde* is not its main thrust, it does give it more than "nodding" mention. The addition of short biographies of a wide diversity of younger composers is most useful.

Martin, W. R. and Drossin, J. *Music of the Twentieth-Century.* Englewood Cliffs: Prentice-Hall, 1980. This book provides good coverage of twentieth-century music of all types.

Mellers, Wilfred. *Romanticism and the Twentieth-Century.* New York: Schocken, 1969. Continues tonal idioms where this chapter leaves off.

Myers, Rollo W. *Modern French Music from Fauré to Boulez.* New York: Praeger Books, 1971. A very good study of French music from the impressionists to IRCAM (inclusive of the *avant-garde*).

Persichetti, Vincent. *20th Century Harmony.* New York: W. W. Norton, 1961. This is a good source book for those interested in continuing study of non-tertian chord structures and polytonality.

Salzman, Eric. *Twentieth-Century Music: An Introduction.* Englewood Cliffs: Prentice-Hall. Second Edition, 1974. A good general introduction to mainstream composers and works.

Slonimsky, Nicolas. *Music Since 1900.* New York: Charles Scribner's Sons. 4th Edition, 1971. A master-work of research and a most valuable tool for those interested in the details of a great number of events of this century.

Sternfeld, F. W., ed. *Music in the Modern Age.* Praeger History of Music, Vol. V. New York: Praeger Books, 1973. Interesting anthology of thoughts on twentieth-century music (what it lacks in continuity, it makes up for in insight).

*Addresses for record companies, periodicals, and music publishers mentioned in this Bibliography can be found in Appendix 4.

Stuckenschmidt, H. H. *Twentieth-Century Music.* New York: McGraw-Hill, 1969. An excellent general introduction but overly geared to the European scene.

Thompson, Oscar. *A Dictionary of Twentieth-Century Composers (1911–1971).* London: Faber and Faber, 1973. Good source for information on mainstream composers.

Yates, Peter. *Twentieth-Century Music.* New York: Pantheon, 1967. While in some ways outdated, this is a very important book dealing with issues as well as chronicling the "new music" scene at mid-century.

Recordings and Publishers*

Bartók, Béla. *Mikrokosmos,* Volume V (1935). Boosey and Hawkes. Recorded on DG 2740239.

———. *Out of Doors Suite* (1926). Universal Edition. Recorded on Nonesuch 71175.

Beethoven, Ludwig van. *Sonata* Op. 2, No. 3. C. F. Peters. Recorded on London 7028.

Busoni, Ferruccio. *Indianisches Tagebuch, for Piano* (1915). Recorded on Orion 74154.

Debussy, Claude. *Pelleas and Melisande* (1907). A. Durand. Angel Records SZX-3885.

———. *Préludes* Books I and II (1910–13). A. Durand. Recorded on Phillips 9500676 and 9500747.

———. *Prélude à "L'Après midi d'un faune."* (1894). A. Durand. Recorded on Columbia Records MS-7361. This seminal work made significant challenges to the common-practice and is *the* major example of musical impressionism.

———. *Soirée dans Grenade* (1903). International Music Corporation. Phillips 9500965.

Griffes, Charles Tomlinson. *Sonata.* G. Schirmer. Recorded on Orion 77270.

Hindemith, Paul. *Chansons* (6)—1939. B. Schott's Soehne, Mainz. Recorded on Nonesuch 71115.

Ives, Charles. *Concord Sonata* (1915). Associated Music Publishers. Columbia MS-7192. A masterwork of polytonality and collage.

———. *114 Songs* (1884–1921). Published by the composer and subsequently by New Music Edition. See the Schwann Record Catalog for currently available recordings of various songs.

———. *Three Places in New England* (1914). Mercury Music Corporation. Recorded on DG 2530048.

Mozart, Wolfgang Amadeus. *Theme and Variations: Ah! Vous Dirai-Je, Maman.* (K. 265) Kalmus Edition. Recorded on DG 2535115.

Ravel, Maurice. *Daphnis et Choloe Suite #2* (1913). A. Durand. Columbia M-31847.

———. *Le Tombeau de Couperin* (1977). A. Durand. Recorded on Quintessence 2712.

———. *Sonatine* (for piano). International Music Publishers. Recorded on DG 2530540.

Satie, Erik. *Trois Gymnopédies.* Kalmus Edition. Recorded on CBS M-36694.

Schoenberg, Arnold. *Pierrot Lunaire* (1912). Universal Edition. Recorded on Turnabout 34315.

———. *Sechs Kleine Klavier Stücke* Op. 19 (1911) International Editions. Nonesuch 71309.

Scriabin, Alexander. *Poème* Op. 69, No. 1 (1913). C. F. Peters. Recorded on VOX SVBX-5474.

---

*Addresses for record companies, periodicals, and music publishers mentioned in this Bibliography can be found in Appendix 4.

Stravinsky, Igor. *Petrushka* (1911). Edition Russe de Musique. Recorded on Columbia D3S-705.
Varèse, Edgard. *Amériques.* Colfranc Corporation. Recorded on Vanguard S–308.
———. *Density 21.5* (1936). Colfranc Corporation. Recorded on Nonesuch 73028.
Wagner, Richard. *Tristan und Isolde* (1859). Eulenberg Scores. Recorded on Angel S-3777.
Webern, Anton. *Six Bagatelles* (for string quartet)—1913. Universal Edition. Recorded on DG 2720029.

2 Premise and Analysis

As composers stretched ever outward to explore new visions, aural traditions continued to collapse. Audiences groped for tangible indications of commonality of style. Stravinsky remarks: "Is it any wonder, then, that the hypercritics of today should be dumbfounded by a language in which all of the characteristics of their aesthetic seem to be violated?"[1] Natural too is the composer's desire for new order to be able to spend more time "composing" and less "experimenting" with new materials and techniques.

Serialism and the Experimental Tradition

During the first two decades of the twentieth century, a number of mainstreams derived from Romantic traditions of the nineteenth century developed. The Germanic style (often presented as Beethoven-Wagner-Mahler-Schoenberg lineage) was steeped in motivic microdevelopment and supratonal (chromatic) concepts. The Franco-Russian composers (particularly Debussy, Ravel, and Stravinsky), the Primitivists (especially Béla Bartók), and the Iconoclastic composers (particularly Charles Ives in America) developed more fluid, less systematic techniques, often effecting fewer works in freer application.

One of the more important developments during this time was twelve-tone writing (often called *serialism*). It was clearly derived from a base of Germanic tradition, and presented composers with the prospect of a common language and context. The twelve-tone approach was developed primarily by Arnold Schoenberg during the years 1917–1923, during which time he wrote little music, devoting his energies to performance and development of the new techniques and applications he had discovered. Serialism seemed to him to be the natural conclusion of the extended complex chromaticism that had been developing in Western European music during the previous 120 years (since mid-Mozart).

1. Stravinsky, Igor. *An Autobiography*. New York: W. W. Norton, 1936, p. 176.

Figure 2.1. (a) Schoenberg *Variations for Orchestra*, op. 31; (b) Berg, *Violin Concerto;* (c) Webern, *Symphonie*, Op 21.

One of the basic properties of twelve-tone writing is the creation of a row. The only basic requirement of this line of twelve notes is that they all be different (i.e., the row must contain all twelve notes of the chromatic scale). Figure 2.1 shows how three different serial composers applied this principle. Note how Schoenberg's row (a) tends to void suggestions of tonal centers (i.e., successive notes tending not to exist in the previous note's key signature). On the other hand, Berg's row (b) holds strong tonal ties with continuous triadic reference (the first seven notes, moreover, existing in the G melodic minor scale). Webern (c) tends to develop certain integrated cross-referencing with the row itself (e.g., the second half of the row is a reverse of the first half).

Once a composer has created a row (called "prime"), certain variants are created based on the following: *retrograde* (the row played backwards), *inversion* (the row played upside down), and *inversion-retrograde* (the row played both upside down and backwards). Each of these is shown in figure 2.2 based on the Schoenberg row of figure 2.1. It is important to note from the outset that interval integrity must be maintained throughout (i.e., each interval is reproduced exactly with each variant).

The numbers above each note of the prime version (Figure 2.2) indicate the number of half steps separating each row member from the first note. In chromatic scale order, the initial pitch is labeled "O" and the last "11", accounting for the eleven half steps between the twelve different notes present. Composers find this approach more laden with information about rows than one which simply indicates row order (i.e. 1, 2, 3, etc. pitches of the series).

Figure 2.2. Prime, retrograde, inversion, and inversion-retrograde of row for Schoenberg's *Variations for Orchestra,* op. 31.

Each of these variants can now exist in twelve transpositions (each beginning on twelve different notes, again keeping their respective interval integrity intact). Figure 2.3 shows the original row beginning on B♭, then A, then A♭, etc., clearly demonstrating the different levels. Notice that the variations Schoenberg chose to develop his row properties are an extension of motivic development that German composers (particularly since Beethoven) used with extreme vitality.

Figure 2.3. Transpositions (beginning on successively lower notes) of row for Schoenberg's *Variations for Orchestra,* op. 31.

Note that the arabic numeral next to the "prime" indicates a new beginning pitch referenced to the ordinal numbering of the initial series.

One way composers chose to show all the versions of a row at once is called a *matrix*. This "box" of 144 squares is created by cross-thatching twelve vertical lines with twelve horizontal lines (actually thirteen in each case to provide the outer layers of the box itself). If the original row is placed across the top of the box (left to right) and the inversion placed down the left of the matrix (top to bottom), a frame can be created to define the interior rows. To complete the matrix, the composer fills in (left to right) the transpositions of the original, allowing the notes of the inversion to dictate the beginning notes. Figure 2.4 shows a completed matrix (again based on the Schoenberg row of fig. 2.1).

I →	0	6	8	5	7	11	4	3	9	10	1	2	
0	Bb	E	Gb	Eb	F	A	D	Db	G	Ab	B	C	2
6	E	Bb	C	A	B	Eb	Ab	G	Db	D	F	F#	8
4	D	Ab	Bb	G	A	Db	Gb	F	B	C	Eb	E	6
7	F	B	Db	Bb	C	E	A	Ab	D	Eb	Gb	G	9
5	Eb	A	B	Ab	Bb	D	G	Gb	C	Db	E	F	7
1	B	F	G	E	Gb	Bb	Eb	D	Ab	A	C	Db	3
8	F#	C	D	B	Db	F	Bb	A	Eb	E	G	Ab	10
9	G	Db	Eb	C	D	Gb	B	Bb	E	F	Ab	A	11
3	C#	G	A	F#	Ab	C	F	E	Bb	B	D	D#	5
2	C	F#	G#	F	G	B	E	Eb	A	Bb	C#	D	4
11	A	D#	F	D	E	G#	C#	C	F#	G	Bb	B	1
10	G#	D	E	C#	D#	G	C	B	F	F#	A	Bb	0
	10	4	6	3	5	9	2	1	7	8	11	0	

Figure 2.4. Matrix of row from Schoenberg's *Variations for Orchestra,* op. 31.

Note that one can now quickly read any version of the row from the completed matrix (originals, left to right; inversions, top to bottom; retrogrades, right to left; retrograde-inversions, bottom to top). The matrix can become an extremely important tool for use in analysis or composition of twelve-tone music.

A row seen in a matrix is void of absolute register. The B♭ (upper left corner) could appear in any octave. Each pitch becomes a distinct and related (by octave) "set" of pitches (all B♭'s in this instance). They belong to the same "pitch class." Composers are able to choose freely from any member of a certain pitch class and not be restricted to a given octave. Also noteworthy is the observation that the ordinal numbers of the inversion can be derived by subtracting the appropriately paired prime number from 12. For example, moving left to right and top to bottom, $12 - 0 = 12$ (or 0); $12 - 6 = 6$; $12 - 8 = 4$; etc. By using similar numerical relationships, composers have created a "set theory." While far too complex to discuss here, set theory provides an immense amount of information about intervallic sets of pitches for composition and analysis.

Composers typically utilize rows in two ways in serial composition. The first (here called category A) derives all successive notes from one version of the row at a time. Figure 2.5a shows a category A type of composition using

Figure 2.5. Category A (a) and category B (b) types of twelve-tone composition using Schoenberg row from *Variations for Orchestra*, op. 31.

the Schoenberg row. Notice that all notes of both melody and harmony are extracts from the single version of the original form of the row. In order to show this, numbers here refer to row ordering and not interval relationship to the initial pitch. The work could continue from this point with a repeat of this version or any other version used in a similar manner.

A second type of twelve-tone composition employs more than one version of the row at a time and is called category B. Figure 2.5b shows three versions of the Schoenberg row used simultaneously. Unlike the category A type of composition, it is difficult here to maintain a twelve-tone integrity (e.g., notes are frequently repeated immediately or simultaneously, often creating non-row-centered sonorities).

Early in the development of twelve-tone theory, Schoenberg and others adopted a variety of techniques which aid the composer in expanding the potential of the approach. These create interesting anomalies which can eventually lead to unique styles and works.

The most simple of these variations is *repetition*. Since most music includes repetition of individual notes as inherent to an important motive or line, this same attribute can be utilized in twelve-tone composition. Therefore, repeated notes and chords are acceptable, and not considered deviations from the basic structure of twelve-tone concepts. Patterns of notes (e.g., two-, three-, and four-note groupings) may also be repeated immediately after they have sounded, creating many possibilities for the composer to initiate individual stylistic motives.

Overlapping one version of the row with another is also fairly common in twelve-tone compositions. In this variant, the last note (usually) of one version becomes the first note of the next. Composers also use *anticipations* of coming material, creating interesting implosions of row contents. Figure 2.6 has the first eight notes of the row in the voice part:

Figure 2.6. Arnold Schoenberg: *Sommermud.* Example of note repetition and anticipation in twelve-tone composition.

The ninth through twelfth notes of the row are stated in the piano part even before the voice part begins (anticipation). These then are repeated with variation as accompaniment until they fall in their right place numerically.

Combinatoriality

Category B twelve-tone composition poses unresolved problems of harmonic continuity and homogeneity. While these problems do not exist in category A composition, composers seem more interested in the complexities available in the contrapuntal use of many variants of the row used simultaneously. Combinatoriality mechanics tend to absorb the discontinuities resulting from category B usage.

One of the first steps in understanding combinatoriality involves applying principles of subsetting. A *subset* is a group of notes, smaller than twelve, which is an evenly divisible integer of the whole (e.g., 2, 3, 4, and 6 are each evenly divisible into 12). Terminology includes: *hexachord,* a group of six notes (two in a twelve-tone row); *tetrachord,* a group of four notes (three in a twelve-tone row); *trichord,* a group of three notes (four in a twelve-tone row); and *dichord,* a group of two notes (six in a twelve-tone row).

Combinatoriality, the combining of versions of mutually exclusive note contents, is best understood when carefully observing the matrix. Looking back at figure 2.4, one notices that the second hexachord of the original row (i.e., D, Db, G, Ab, B, C of Pº in that order) equals the pitch content of the first hexachord of the inversion of the row beginning on G (I⁹ top to bottom beginning in the ninth square left to right). Important however, is that the order of the notes involved has changed remarkably (i.e., they now read G, Db, B, D, C, and Ab; 9, 3, 1, 4, 2, 10 instead of 4, 3, 9, 10, 1, 2). As would be expected, the second hexachord of this inversion has the same note content as the first hexachord of the original nontransposed version. This feature becomes important when one realizes that combining these two versions in a category B type composition provides a continuous twelve-tone (category A type) continuity and homogeneity, while at the same time providing the explorations possible in the contrapuntal environment of category B frameworks.

In figure 2.7 the top voice uses the twelve notes of the original form of the row, with the twelve notes of the inversion from G used in the bass voice. Note, however, that unlike figure 2.5b where the vertical chromaticism often produces irregularities such as octaves and repeated notes, this example does not. Clearly the first bar contains twelve different notes as does the second bar. This kind of hexachordal subsetting in the right combinations provides the basis for combinatorial composition.

hierarchical subsetting

each row (left → rig[ht])

Figure 2.7. Combinatoriality using the original (top voice) and the inversion (bottom voice) of the row from Schoenberg's *Variations for Orchestra,* op. 31.

Vertically all 12 tone are combined in each measure

Figure 2.8. J. S. Bach: *Well-Tempered Clavier,* Book 1, Fugue 24.

Total Control: The Parting of the Ways

Pantonality (this, not *atonality*, was the term used by Schoenberg), or "inclusive of all tonalities," is not important because of chromaticism (see fig. 2.8), but in its extreme control over compositional elements, a control that is predominantly inaudible and recognizable in general stylistic terms only. Total control or serialization of the other parameters of musical composition begins as it does in pitch organization, with the creation of a row and extended by the basic variant sets to create developmental techniques for variation.

Anton Webern's *Variations for Piano,* opus 27 (second movement) employs a dynamic row of nine values as shown in Figure 2.9.

f p f p f p f p ff → *prime order*

Figure 2.9. Anton Webern: *Variations for Piano,* opus 27, second movement. Dynamic row.

Webern follows this prime order with a variation of the retrograde (the third trichord—now the first—left in original order):

$f\ p\ f\!f\quad\quad p\ f\ p\quad\quad f\ p\ f$

Figure 2.10. Retrograde (variation) of the dynamic row of Figure 2.9.

Articulations are directly related to individual pitches of the row. Figure 2.11 shows how this is accomplished:

1.
2.
3.   − / · /
4.   / ·
5.   · / − / ·
6.   >
7.   >
8.   >
9.   \ / ·
10.
11.   ·
12.

Figure 2.11. Articulation row of Webern's *Variations for Piano,* opus 27.

For example, the second note of every version of the row used in the second variation is staccato, etc. Careful analysis of rhythm and form (a cyclic mirror canon) shows that these are also related serially to the basic structure of this piece. Whether any of these elements are audibly serialized is beside the point. Most tonal composers worked constantly with intricate motivic and chromatic techniques which become evident to the ear only after repeated listening and score study. Some critics of these techniques claim that their basic use is inherently 'non-musical.' Here again, the point relates to the particular composer using them; if used musically, they aid in the creation of good music. If used as a crutch to simply produce notations of mathematical import and interest without real aural meaning, then certainly they are 'non-musical.'

The following piano composition by Milton Babbitt demonstrates serialized control of dynamics, rhythm, and pitch:

Figure 2.12. Milton Babbitt: *Three Compositions for Piano,* 1947 (measures 1–8, Piece No. 1). Published by Boelke-Bonart, Inc., Hillsdale, N.Y.

Key: P = prime; R = retrograde (backwards); I = inversion; IR = inverted retrograde.

The pitch content of this piece is based on combinatorial principles. The basic row is shown in figure 2.13.

Figure 2.13. Row for Milton Babbitt's
Three Compositions for Piano.

Note that this form of the row appears in the lower voice of the first two bars. Babbitt carefully observed that the first hexachord of the orginal form of the row beginning on E contained notes that were mutually exclusive of those in the first hexachord of the original beginning on B♭. Therefore, by combining this version (as the upper voice) with the original nontransposed version, he was able to create combinatoriality. Note that the first bar contains twelve different notes as does the second bar, thus avoiding inconsistent repetitions or octave-unison doublings.

The rhythm of the piece equally involves serial principles. If one looks carefully at the hexachordal subgroupings within each bar of the composition, it becomes clear that a held note balances the other notes of equal duration. In the bass voice, for example, the held tone (fifth in the six-note sequence), suggests a five grouping followed by a single note. The same is true of the first hexachord of the row in the upper voice (i.e., 5/1). In the second bar, the grouping is distinctly different. Here the held note (fourth of the sequence), divides the hexachord into groups of four and two notes each (the same being true in the upper voice). The rhythm clearly follows a pattern based on the principle of 5/1/4/2; each voice holds that row intact. In the upper voice in bar 3 one encounters the order 2/4, with the next bar developing 1/5 (again, in the upper voice). This ordering (2/4/1/5) is the retrograde of the original rhythmic row.

To create an inversion of such rows becomes obviously different from similar groupings in tone rows. Babbitt creates such "inversions" here by inverting dichordal subsets (that is, reversing the order of the outer groups of two numbers each). Therefore, the inversion of 5/1/4/2 becomes 1/5/2/4 (and the inversion retrograde, 4/2/5/1).

Examining figure 2.12, bars 3 and 4 (bass voice), one can immediately recognize that the rhythm here is an inversion retrograde of the original row. Serialization of rhythmic principles continues in this manner for the remainder of the piece.

Dynamic serialization, while simpler in this piece, is still important to its basic structure. Here, each version of the row links with a dynamic (i.e., original, *mp;* retrograde, *mf;* inversion, *f;* and inversion retrograde, *p).*

P: 5 - 1 - 4 - 2
I: 1 - 5 - 2 - 4
R: 2 - 4 - 1 - 5
IR: 4 - 2 - 5 - 1

Figure 2.14. Rhythm rows for Babbitt's
Three Compositions for Piano.

In his now-famous article "Who Cares if You Listen," Milton Babbitt speaks of this "high degree of determinacy":

In the simplest terms, each such "atomic" event is located in a five-dimensional musical space determined by pitch-class, register, dynamic, duration, and timbre. These five components not only together define the single event, but, in the course of a work, the successive values of each component create an individually coherent structure, frequently in parallel with the corresponding structures created by each of the other components. Inability to perceive and remember precisely the values of any of these components results in a dislocation of the event in the work's musical space, an alteration of its relation to all other events in the work, and—thus—a falsification of the composition's total structure. For example, an incorrectly performed or perceived dynamic value results in destruction of the work's dynamic pattern, but also in false identification of other components of the event (of which this dynamic value is a part) with corresponding components of other events, so creating incorrect pitch, registral, timbral and durational associations.[2]

Oliver Messiaen (b. 1909 in France) was one of the first to use rigid rhythmic control (augmentation, diminution by one half, one third, one fourth, etc., of the original) over his materials. His *Quatre études de rythme* (especially number 2, *Mode de valeur et d'intensités),* published in 1949, was one of the first works to include integral organization of the "whole." Though based more on modal than twelve-tone principles, it did in fact serialize the basic musical components (36 sounds; 24 durations; 7 dynamics; 12 articulations).

Messiaen's influence over the younger composers of France, combined with twelve-tone theory, enabled Pierre Boulez to arrange twelve different durations, twelve articulations, and twelve dynamics in row forms, thus creating serialization possibilities over more compositional elements. This is particularly effective and noticeable in Boulez's *Structures* (1952) and *Second Piano Sonata* (1948). Figure 2.15 shows each of these series.

Bernd Alois Zimmermann's *Perspectives* for two pianos (1956) is row controlled from an aggregate of procedures pertaining to pitch, density, rhythm, dynamics, attacks and pedaling representing somewhat of a landmark in its degree of systematic composer control (see the article on the work in *die Reihe* #4 for complete analysis). Ruth Crawford's (1901–53) innovative String Quartet (1931) employs procedures of total organization. The third movement of this work includes an obvious systematic procedure of control in which

2 Milton Babbitt, "Who Cares if You Listen," *High Fidelity* 8, no. 2 (February 1958):38–40, 126–27.

Figure 2.15. Boulez: *Structures*
Serialization of parameters.

Figure 2.16. Pierre Boulez.

the compositional elements (pitch, duration, dynamics, and rhythm) are related and serialized. The foundation of the movement is a double canon in dynamics only (first canon in the viola and 'cello and the second in the two violins). The resulting dovetailing of dynamics (one voice in crescendo and the other in simultaneous diminuendo) foreshadows yet another technique of experimentation: timbre modulation (the opening intervals are major and minor seconds with the undulating dynamics creating timbre movements from one instrument to another).

These mathematical approaches are new only in their applications, for since Pythagoras and his followers, music theory has evolved through a process of scientific formulas applied during, though more often after, the compositional process. The increased requirements on both performer and audience must certainly have been in part responsible for the replacement of one by tape, and the diminishing size of the other (leaving even fellow professionals interested, but often confused, bystanders). Even without serialism, performance conflicts appeared to Charles Ives who, in the Postface to his *114 Songs* (1922) explained: "Some of the songs in this book, particularly among the later ones, cannot be sung, and if they could, perhaps might prefer, if they had a say, to remain as they are; that is, 'in the leaf'—and that they will remain in this peaceful state is more than presumable."[3]

In America the colleges and universities have replaced the courts, the church, and patrons of earlier times, offering the composer the only realistic terms for physical survival. The need in this academic environment to present composition as an ordered and intellectual pursuit, and the close physical proximity of so-called "disciplines" of scientific teachings, have contributed no small part to the large volume of systems and aesthetics in the past forty years. Pierre Boulez, in an interview with the author, referred to this environment:

Yes, academic, and in the strong sense of the word. It does not matter whether the academic is after Schumann, after Bach, after Wagner, or after a new serial type; the academic is something which I cannot accept at any time. The main problem, to my mind, is to find a purely musical way of thinking and not something which is parascientific.[4]

Clearly, then, composers began to define their actions and reactions in terms of highly intellectual processes. By the late forties, the lines between "more" control and "less" control had been clearly drawn and defined. The roots of this disagreement seem to lie, both nationalistically (Europe vs. America) and compositionally, in the concept that extremely highly organized music sounds very often like extremely unorganized music, with the row and total serialization representing the parting of the ways (see fig. 2.17).

This mobile shows the turn-of-the-century experimental tradition to the left of the *mainstream* composers (those bent on continuing tonal or quasi-tonal models of the nineteenth century). In the mid-thirties the experimental tradition branched and accelerated into a flurry of activity at the forefront of discovery and ever-reaching into the unknown: the *avant-garde*.

3 Charles Ives, "Postface to 114 Songs," in *Essays before a Sonata, and Other Writings*, ed. Howard Boatwright (New York: W. W. Norton & Co., 1961), p. 131.
4 Galen Wilson and David Cope, "An Interview with Pierre Boulez," *The Composer* 1, no. 2 (September 1969):79–80.

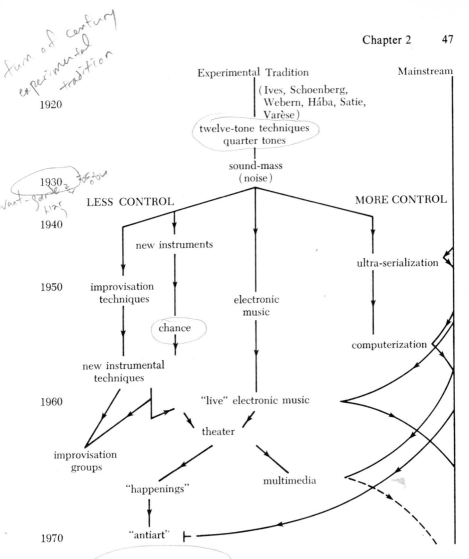

turn of century experimental tradition

1920

Experimental Tradition   Mainstream

(Ives, Schoenberg,
Webern, Hába, Satie,
Varèse)

twelve-tone techniques
quarter tones

sound-mass
(noise)

1930 *avant-garde*

1940   LESS CONTROL   MORE CONTROL

new instruments

ultra-serialization

1950   improvisation
        techniques

        chance   electronic
                                  music

                                            computerization

        new instrumental
        techniques

1960   "live" electronic music

                        theater

improvisation
groups   multimedia

        "happenings"

1970   "antiart"

Figure 2.17. An *avant-garde* mobile.

Vectoral Analysis: Webern: *Symphonie,* op. 21

(For information on vectoral analysis see Chapter 1).

1. Historical background: Webern was born in Vienna in 1883 and died in Mittersill (near Salzburg), where he had moved to avoid the Allied bombings. He studied with Guido Adler at the University of Vienna and received a doctorate in musicology in 1906. He conducted in the provincial theaters and the Vienna Workers Symphony Concerts (organized by the then socialist

Figure 2.18. Anton Webern (noted pointillistic composer and one of the originators of *Klangfarbenmelodien*).

city). He stayed in Germany during the Second World War, even though performances of his music were banned by the Third Reich (he worked as a proof-reader for a Viennese publisher). He died in 1945 of gunshot wounds delivered accidentally by an American occupation troop stationed in Mittersill, Germany.

2. Overview: This work is in two short movements (I, ♩ = 50; II, ♩ = 54). The first movement is a kind of two-part (each is repeated) 'binary' form with the second a large canonic development of the first. The second movement is a theme and seven variations.

3. Orchestration Techniques: The *Symphonie* is scored for nine solo instruments: clarinet, bass clarinet, two horns, harp, two violins, viola, and 'cello. The major difference between this and Webern's previous work (op. 20) is *klangfarbenmelodien* (defined as a kind of *pointillism*—see chapter 1's discussion of origins in the visual arts—that involves timbre). Note that in the opening of the work, Webern casts few notes without range and rest separation. There are often timbre separations (e.g., horn vs. harp vs. pizzicato cello, etc.).

Figure 2.19. First 14 bars of Anton Webern's *Symphonie,* op. 21, first movement. Beginning of double canon shown in first 7 bars.

4. Basic Techniques: The row of the piece is as follows.

Tritone

Figure 2.20. Row for Webern's
Symphonie, op. 21 showing palindrome
characteristic.

This palindrome row (one which reads with the same intervals in both directions) makes the initial series identical with its retrograde (transposed) and
the inversion identical with the retrograde-inversion (transposed). Therefore
only 24 forms of the row are actually possible (not the usual 48).

The work begins with a double canon in contrary (inverted) motion in
four parts. Horn #2 begins the original on A with imitation beginning in measure 4 (the original a major third higher) in the harp. The harp begins (in
measure 2) the inversion on F, which is imitated by the first horn (in inversion
beginning on A, measure 3).

Figure 2.21. Frozen notes and rotation
around "A" in opening section of
Webern, *Symphonie,* op. 21.

Note as well how the opening section "rotates" around A. These thirteen
notes (E♭ is doubled) are all that are sounded (register frozen). This is category B composition. All twelve notes do not appear until the twenty-third
pitch (E♭) is sounded in the harp.

5. Vertical Models: Harmonic identities do not play a major role in this
work. When more than one note sounds at a time, a consistent vocabulary
appears which is based on the minor second (and concomitant projections,
e.g., the ninth and seventh), augmented fourth, and the major sixth. These
are the intervals most commonly found and provide a perceptible model for
the category B compositional techniques.

6. Horizontal Models: The horizontal or melodic techniques are framed in the row itself reflected in the complex canonic treatment and the variants based on *klangfarbenmelodien*. The constant leaping of lines often voids a real linear function as do the rests that abound. Certainly the opening four bars in the second horn provide the frame or model for the entire work in terms of horizontal vocabulary.

7. Style: Webern's *Symphonie* (op. 21) is an enormously complex pantonal (twelve-tone) work whose pointillism, *klangfarbenmelodien,* and canonic interweaving of lines project a highly intellectual approach to the compositional process. The miniature ensemble (in contrast to the late Romantic orchestras of one hundred or more performers) as well as short duration create a crystalline edge to each note contributing critical material to the larger structure. The lack of doubling, the serial feel to articulations and dynamics, and the imitations of rhythmic developments all contribute to its synthesis of clarity and complexity.

Bibliography

*Further Readings**

American Society of University Composers. *Proceedings* I-VIII. A clear cross section of contemporary thought concerning the issues encountered in chapter 2.

Anderson, E. Ruth. *Contemporary American Composers: A Biographical Dictionary.* Boston: G. K. Hall, 1976.

Babbitt, Milton. "Set Structure as a Compositional Determinant." *Journal of Music Theory* 5 (April 1961):72–94. A good study in the thoughts and directions of the materials derived from this "determinate" composer.

Basart, Ann Phillips. *Serial Music: A Classified Bibliography of Writings on Twelve Tone and Electronic Music* (Berkeley: University of California Press, 1961). An excellent reference tool.

Beckwith, John, and Udo Kasemets. *The Modern Composer and His World.* Toronto: University of Toronto Press, 1961. A series of reports and discussions from the International Conference of Composers (1960) on the various aspects covered in this chapter.

Berg, Alban. "Why is Schoenberg's Music So Hard to Understand?" *The Music Review* (May 1952), pp. 187–96. The first printed translation—a fascinating early source for such information.

Boretz, Benjamin, and Edward T. Cone, eds. *Perspectives on American Composers.* New York: W. W. Norton and Co., 1971.

———. *Perspectives on Contemporary Music Theory.* New York: W. W. Norton and Co., 1972. Both of the above are useful books dealing with issues facing the contemporary composer in articles by contemporary composers.

Brindle, Reginald Smith. *The New Music: The Avant-Garde since 1945.* New York: Oxford University Press, 1975. A good source of information, particularly on European composers.

Chase, Gilbert. *The American Composer Speaks.* Baton Rouge: Louisiana State University Press, 1966. Very valuable, especially pp. 184–305. Consists of articles and statements by the composers themselves.

Composer Magazine, 1–20. A good source for a wide cross section of articles and interviews concerning subject matter in chapter 2.

Contemporary Music in Europe. Reprinted from *Musical Quarterly,* January 1965. Valuable but somewhat outdated view of the *avant-garde* on the continent.

Dallin, Leon. *Techniques of Twentieth Century Composition.* 3rd ed. Dubuque, Iowa: Wm. C. Brown Company Publishers, 1974. Includes a wide variety of new music in addition to excellent discussion of mainstream music, presenting a very sensible balance of musical styles.

---

*Addresses for record companies, periodicals, and music publishers mentioned in this Bibliography can be found in Appendix 4.

Hansen, Peter. *An Introduction to Twentieth Century Music.* Boston: Allyn & Bacon, 1967. Includes material to the point of this chapter, especially pp. 359–96.

Hitchcock, H. Wiley. *Music in the United States: An Historical Introduction.* Englewood Cliffs, N.J.: Prentice-Hall, 1969. Quite good as an introduction to new music in America, especially pp. 221–61.

"Hommage to Messiaen." *Melos,* 25: December 1958, entire issue. A good study of this man and his musical contributions.

Journal of Music Theory. Often contains articles pertaining to this subject matter.

Kolneder, Walter. *Anton Webern: An Introduction to His Works.* Berkeley: University of California Press, 1968.

Lang, Paul Henry, ed. *Problems of Modern Music.* New York: W. W. Norton and Co., 1960. A collection of chapters by various individuals involved deeply in the *avant-garde,* inclusive of Babbitt, Carter, Ussachevsky, and Krěnek, among others.

Machlis, Joseph. *Introduction to Contemporary Music,* 2nd ed. New York: W. W. Norton and Co., 1979. An extraordinary book covering a wide scope of new music since 1900.

Messiaen, Oliver. *The Technique of My Musical Language.* Paris: Alphonse Leduc & Cie., 1950. A complex theoretical and philosophical treatise of his highly specialized rhythmic control procedures.

The New Oxford History of Music (The Modern Age 1890–1960). London: Oxford University Press, 1974. Good introductory material on new music by country.

Numus West, 1–5. An excellent periodical devoted to the various aspects of *avant-garde* music.

Perle, George. *Serial Composition and Atonality.* Berkeley: University of California Press, 1962. Contains numerous analyses, especially of completely serialized compositions, and lists a large number of them as well for further study.

Perspectives of New Music. A periodical dedicated to new music idioms.

Rossi, Nick. *Music of Our Time.* Boston: Crescendo Publishing Co., 1969. Excellent source of examples, composers, and photos of new music (unfortunately segregated by country as in so many other books of this type).

Salzman, Eric. *Twentieth-Century Music: An Introduction.* Englewood Cliffs, N.J.: Prentice-Hall, 1967. Extremely good on new music, its only drawback being brevity. Pp. 155–86 especially good in treatment of "ultrarationality" vs. "antirationality."

Schwartz, Elliott, and Barney Childs, eds. *Contemporary Composers on Contemporary Music* (New York: Holt, Rinehart and Winston, 1967). Superb book and a continuation in spirit of Cowell's *American Composers on American Music.* It is a collection of articles by the composers themselves inclusive of a full range of topics relating to *avant-garde* musics (see especially Stefan Wolpe's "Thinking Twice," pp. 274–307, on complex serial and philosophical ideas; and "The Liberation of Sound" by Edgard Varèse, pp. 195–208, as well as a host of other very important articles which will be cited many times later in this book).

Sonorum Speculum. A valuable reference source for information on new music in the Netherlands.

Soundings 1–10. A very important periodical on new music. *Soundings* has likewise printed several extremely important books: *Soundings: Ives, Ruggles and Varèse, Music is Dangerous,* and a new series of books on Conlon Nancarrow. 948 Canyon Rd. Santa Fe, New Mexico 87501.

Spinner, Leopold. *A Short Introduction to the Technique of Twelve-Tone Composition.* (London: Boosey and Hawkes, 1960). Useful to the uninitiated.

Tremblay, George. *The Definitive Cycle of the Twelve Tone Row.* New York: Criterion Music Corp., 1974. An extremely complex text dealing in part with the 288 rows of any "cycle" from the 479,001,600 discrete twelve-tone rows possible: an eyeful of complex note control.

Vinton, John, ed. *Dictionary of Contemporary Music.* New York: E. P. Dutton & Co., 1974. An excellent source for subject headings listed in this chapter as well as biographical material on all the composers listed.

Yates, Peter. *Twentieth Century Music.* New York: Pantheon Books, 1967. A superb book dealing with the philosophies and backgrounds of the current *avant-garde.*

Recordings and Publishers*

Babbitt, Milton. *Quartet No. 2* (1954). Recorded on Nonesuch 71280.

———. *Quartet No. 3* (1969–70). Recorded on Turnabout 34515.

———. *Three Compositions for Piano* (1947). Boelke-Bonart. Recorded on CRI S–461.

———. *Vision and Prayer* (1961). AMP Publishers. Recorded on CRI–268.

Bartók, Béla. (Recordings too numerous to mention here may be found by consulting the Schwann Record Catalog.)

Berg, Alban. *Concerto for Violin and Orchestra.* Universal Edition. Recorded on Columbia MS 6373.

Boulez, Pierre. *Le Marteau Sans Maître* (1955). Universal Edition. Recorded on Columbia MQ 32160.

———. *Second Piano Sonata* (1948). Heugel Publishers. Recorded on FIN 9004.

———. *Structures* (1952). Universal Edition. Recorded on Vox 678.028.

Crawford, Ruth. *Quartet* (New Music Edition). Recorded on Nonesuch 71280 (along with quartets by Perle and Babbitt).

Dallapiccola, Luigi. *Sei cori di Michelangelo Buonarroti it Giovane* (for chorus and orchestra, 1933–36). Carisch Publishers. Recorded on Telefunken S–43095.

Křenek, Ernst. *Sestina* for voice and instrumental ensemble. Recorded on Orion 78295. An early example of total serialization.

Messiaen, Oliver. *Chronochromie* (1960). Leduc Publishers. Recorded on Angel S–36295.

Rudhyar, Dane. *Granites* (for piano, 1929). Published by Lengnick. Recorded on CRI S–247. Released in the July 1935 *New Music Quarterly.*

Satie, Erik. *La belle eccentrique* (1920). Sirene. Recorded (with a large group of Satie works) on Vanguard C–10037/8.

Schäffer, Boguslaw. *Introduction to Composition.* PWM, 1976. An excellent source for score excerpts and general overview of European developments to the mid-seventies.

Schoenberg, Arnold. *Variations for Orchestra,* op. 31 (1928). Universal Edition. Recorded on DG 2530627.

Webern, Anton. *Symphonie,* op. 21. Universal Edition. Recorded on DG 2711014.

———. *Variations,* op. 27. Universal Edition. Recorded on DG 2530803. N.B. The complete works of Webern (published primarily by Universal Edition), including his pointillistic orchestration of Bach's *Fuga* from *The Musical Offering,* are recorded on Columbia's four-record set, M4–35193 (supervised by Pierre Boulez).

---

*Addresses for record companies, periodicals, and music publishers mentioned in this Bibliography can be found in Appendix 4.

For further works one should consult the separate chapter bibliographies along with the following important sources: *Internationales Musikinstitut Darmstädt Informationszentrum für zeitgenössische Music: Katalog der Abteilung Noten* (Druckerei and Verlag Jacob Helene KG., Pfungstadt, Ostendstrasse 10), a very fine listing of works of new music by *avant-garde* composers, published yearly; *New Music Quarterly* (a publication of modern compositions which Henry Cowell edited from 1927–1945, followed by Lou Harrison and others; now out of print, it is still a fascinating source of music of twentieth-century American *avant-garde* composers); *Source Magazine* which, like *New Music,* published music, not articles, is an excellent source for new music.

3 Sound-Mass, Rhythm and Microtones

Sound-Mass Evolution

Sound-mass, in contrast to "total control," minimizes the importance of individual notes (and their order) while maximizing the texture, rhythm, dynamics, and/or timbre of a given passage. This refocusing of importance is of great significance in the development of the *avant-garde* movement. Sound-mass confronts one of the most profound technicalities of the music world—the fine differentiation between sound and noise (a derogatory term applied to sounds incapable of making music).

Mainstream composers utilized sound-mass (often called clusters) in a variety of ways, though rarely for any great length of time. Gustav Mahler, for example, uses two large panchromatic chords (inclusive of all twelve tones) in the first movement of his *Tenth Symphony* (1910). Béla Bartók employs defined cluster motions in his 1926 *Piano Sonata*. It is possibly most challengingly utilized, however, in Igor Stravinsky's *Le Sacre du Printemps* (1912), where a driving and repetitive string mass of sound is "charged" with unpredictable harsh accents. The rhythm of the accents becomes the thrust of the work at this point ("Danse des Adolescentes") reducing the importance of pitch. Figure 3.1 shows the "dance" and the resultant increased importance of rhythm (accents) and decreased importance of pitch as integral linear (melodic) or vertical (harmonic) contributors to the work. Clearly this chord is an F♭ (enharmonically E) ninth chord. However, the static use of this vertical sonority offers little pitch importance in the string orchestration of harsh replaced down-bows (frog: extremely close to the nut of the bow).

Henry Cowell's *The Tides of Manaunaun* (1911) and Charles Ives's *Majority* (piano and voice, 1921), present some of the first uses of traditional "noise" as an acceptable musical element. Cowell's *The Hero Sun* (1922) includes a right forearm cluster on the black keys (see fig. 3.2; note that the ♯ above indicates black keys while a ♮ would indicate white keys), a striking use of sound-mass as both a melodic and percussive device against the open consonances of the left-hand harmonies. Cowell's notations for clusters differ occasionally from piece to piece, but the basics are shown and explained in figure 3.3, taken from *What's This* (also 1922). These works, along with a large number of other innovative pieces (such as *The Banshee* discussed under *Instrument Exploration)* impressed a large number of composers (Béla Bartók

56

Figure 3.1. Igor Stravinsky: *Le Sacre Du Printemps:* "Danse des Adolescentes." Piano reduction of the string parts.

Figure 3.2. Henry Cowell: *The Hero Sun* (1922). Page 3. (c) Copyright Breitkopf and Härtel, Inc. Permission granted by the publisher. Associated Music Publishers, Agents in U.S.

The Symbol (♢, ♩, ♪, etc.) represents a silent pressing down and holding of the key in order that the open string may be subjected to sympathetic vibration.

It will be noticed that half and whole notes are written open, or white; while notes of other time values are written closed, or black. (Duration?)

When such tone clusters are small, the fist or open hand is to be used (The symbol x indicates the use of the fist).

In the larger tone clusters the forearm is to be employed. Care should be taken to play all the tones exactly together, and in legato passages to press the keys rather than strike them, thus obtaining a smoother tone quality.

Tone clusters to be played in the manner indicated by the symbol (♢) will be written as:

An arrowhead is used in connection with arpeggiation marks to indicate whether the arpeggiation is to be from the lowest tone upwards, as is customary, (⬆) or from the highest tone downwards (⬇)

R. F. Stands for right fist; L.F. for left fist.

R. A. Stands for right arm; L.A. for left arm.

Figure 3.3. Explanation of symbols from *What's This* (1922), by Henry Cowell. (c) Copyright Breitkopf and Härtel, Inc.   Permission granted by the publisher. Associated Music Publishers, agents in U.S.

in particular) and culminated in his writing of *New Musical Resources* (1930). Figure 3.4 reveals the depth to which Cowell studied both the musical properties and notation of sound-mass. About this example he has written: "Clusters that do in a certain sense move are, however, quite possible, and it is interesting to consider the various ways in which such movement can be introduced."[1] He notes both additive and subtractive clusters (subtractive in fig. 3.4), and thus predates a great deal of music (especially that of Penderecki) and articles (especially Kagel's "Tone-clusters, Attacks, Transitions" in *die Reihe* #5).

1. Henry Cowell, *New Musical Resources* (New York: Alfred A. Knopf, 1930), p. 126.

Figure 3.4. Henry Cowell: _New Musical Resources_ (1930), page 128. (c)

Figure 3.5. Henry Cowell. BMI Archives. Used by permission.

John Becker (1886–1961), regrettably a relatively unnoticed innovator of the twenties and thirties, includes large clusters in most of his works. His third symphony (1929) derives large sound-mass structures from long sustained chords built of seconds with instruments of similar color. In other sections the clusters twist sections of the orchestra into single percussion instrumental sounds by means of articulation (short, very loud, heavy accents).

Figure 3.6 shows the final five bars of the opening section from Becker's _Symphonia Brevis_ (Symphony No. 3, which first appeared in Cowell's _New_

Figure 3.6. John Becker: *Symphonia Brevis* (Symphony No. 3), page 3.

Copyright (c) 1972 by C. F. Peters Corporation. By permission.

Music Quarterly in January of 1930). As lines are overlaid in the rich contrapuntal fabric, the pitch content becomes pantonal (all twelve tones of the chromatic scale are presented) with the F♯ rooted chord spread over five octaves.

Edgard Varèse uses brass, organ, and Ondes Martenot in his *Equatorial* (1934) to achieve sound-mass. In reference to the work of Varèse, Robert Erickson writes: "These highly individual sound-blocks are images, ikons, in their own right. They exist as entities in the same way as a melody can be felt to be an entity."[2] Many consider Varèse's music the extension of Stravinsky's "primitive" period (e.g., *Le Sacre du Printemps;* period extending to the mid-twenties of this century when Stravinsky's so-called *neoclassic* period began). The massive dissonances of his *Hyperprism* (1923) and *Octandre* (1924) are strikingly percussive.

In *Octandre,* Varèse creates mirror-type sound-mass as shown in figure 3.7*a* and *b.* In *a,* Varèse balances the "stacked" chromatic pitches with a central B♮ (a minor third from each end of the cluster). In *b,* he separates two small groupings of chromatic half-steps by equal intervals (this time the major third). Each of these structures (bars 15 and 20 respectively) includes octave transpositions and interesting orchestration (inverted, with flute over an octave below the clarinet, for example) to create harsh dynamic thrusts of sound. The work abounds with similar vertical sonorities.

Figure 3.7. From Edgard Varèse, *Octandre.*

Wallingford Riegger's *Music for Brass Choir* (1949) is one of the first large ensemble works to use large "closed" clusters. The work opens with ten trombones, each with a different chromatic note, encompassing the range of a diminished seventh. The panchromatic final chord (ten trumpets, eight horns, ten trombones, two tubas, and percussion) expresses subtle dynamic shadings with the final four bars *lento e pianissimo.*

Twelve-note or panchromatic chords are logically derived from twelve-tone music. While wide spacing avoids "cluster chord" terminology, the effect is the same. *Sonate Harmonique* by Galen Wilson contains a near-panchromatic (nine-note) cluster effect (see fig. 3.8).

2. Robert Erickson, "Varèse: 1924–1937: Sound-Ikon," *The Composer* 1, no. 3 (December 1969):144.

Figure 3.8. Galen Wilson: *Sonate Harmonique*.

Current Examples

Luigi Nono's three choral works *Il canto sospeso* (1956), *La terra e la campagna* (1957), and *Cori di Didone* (1958) are based almost entirely on twelve-tone aggregate choral clusters creating masses of white sound within which the voices move as "fish through water."

Apart from the aforementioned Becker work, clusters (or sound-mass) occurred in orchestra works like *Metastasis* (1955) by Iannis Xenakis, and *Threnody for the Victims of Hiroshima* (1960) by Krzysztof Penderecki. Probably one of the best-known orchestral works of the past twenty years, *Threnody* employs a wide variety of string techniques (fifty-two string parts), surprisingly few of which are actually new. More immediately recognizable are the solid bands of sound which widen and contract by means of glissando. These clusters, involving quarter tones, create a "white sound" effect resolved by movement to a single pitch, and contain such heavy overtone influence that, even though only the area of a fifth may actually be covered, the aural impression is one of all audible sounds occurring simultaneously.

Figure 3.9 is the final 54 seconds of *Threnody*. Even though the notation is proportional (see Appendix 3), the visual cluster bands are similar to those that were suggested by Cowell in his *New Musical Resources* thirty years earlier (refer to fig. 3.4).

Iannis Xenakis utilizes sound-mass as a result of his stochastic procedures (see chapter 9 for more detailed discussion). Most of his works employ large "sonic-clouds" which sound incredibly dense as a result of large numbers of individual voices usually of like timbre (pizzicato or glissando clusters, for example). Indeed it is difficult to pick out a single one of his works which does not employ an elegant use of sound-mass (both in terms of rhythm and pitch). Xenakis has had considerable impact in Europe and many have attributed Penderecki's and the Polish School's use of sound-mass to his influence. In a 1955 article "The Crises of Serial Music," Xenakis remarks:

Linear polyphony destroys itself by its very complexity; what one hears is in reality nothing but a mass of notes in various registers. The enormous complexity prevents the audience from following the intertwining of the lines and has as its macrocosmic effect an irrational and fortuitous dispersion of sounds over the whole extent of the sonic spectrum. There is consequently a contradiction between the polyphonic linear system and the heard result, which is surface or mass.[3]

Henryk Górecki's (b. 1933 in Poland) *Scontri* for orchestra (1960), includes graphically notated blocks and bands of tones (large black boxes overlapping entire sections of the score).

3. Iannis Xenakis, "The Crisis of Serial Music," *Gravesaner Blätter*, no. 1 (1955).

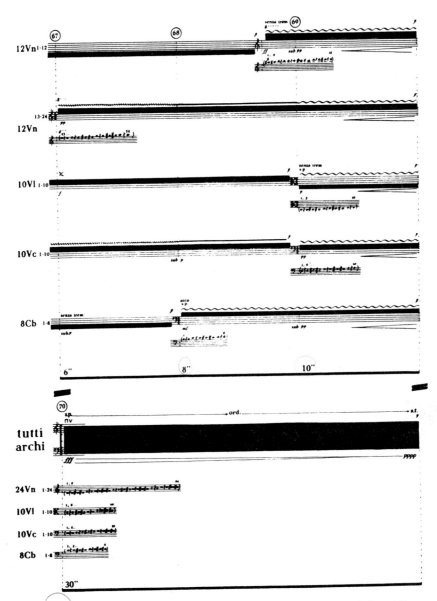

Figure 3.9. Krzysztof Penderecki: *Threnody for the Victims of Hiroshima* (final page of score). The notes for each cluster band are written out in traditional form beneath them, in this proportional notation. Copyright (c) 1961 Deshon Music, Inc., & PWM Editions. Used with permission. All rights reserved. The thick black lines here are explained by the parenthetical traditional pitch material below each representation. The two systems here are 24″ and 30″ in duration respectively.

In *Sonant* (1960), Mauricio Kagel calls for speaking and whispering from the ensemble at various pitch levels *ad libitum*, the result being a huge block or "cluster" sound-mass. The consequence of such experimentations is not only new notations, but direct applications of partially indeterminate procedures: though clusters are inevitable, exact duplication of numerous highly variable factors creates unpredictable results.

In the last few years, it has become increasingly difficult to ascertain whether the composer's motive for cluster effects has developed improvisational (partially aleatoric) procedures, or, whether these result from such procedures. *Improvisation ajoutee* (1962) by Mauricio Kagel, for four-manual organ and two or three adjunct performers, includes huge block clusters of sound, performed with hands, forearms, and feet, and rapid multichanges in registration with, as the composer states, "the improvisation arising through the statistical nature of timbre transformations."

The *Trois Poemes d'Henri Michaux* for mixed chorus and orchestra (1963) by Witold Lutoslawski includes cluster chords derived of approximate pitch notation. The rhythmic clusters in the second part ("Le grand combat") are created by extremely complex composite rhythms.

Stockhausen's *Mixtur* (1964) demonstrates huge cluster effects (spatially, as the five groups are placed around the audience) as a result of traditional notation approximated by lack of staves or other exact pitch identification. Obvious motivic structures occur, yet each performer's independent decision regarding pitch and rhythmic variety, results in extremely complex sound-mass structures.

Penderecki's *Passion According to St. Luke* (1965) compounds simple structures into dense bands of twelve-tone or panchromatic clusters. A continuous thread of contrapuntal material, even during these cluster effects, represents a unique approach to sound-mass construction. Half-sung, half-spoken backgrounds to crowd scenes create equally massive constructs of sound which owe their intensity to drama as well as to dissonance.

Pauline Oliveros's *Sound Patterns* (1961) creates cluster sound-mass effects with voices, employing whispers, tongue clicks, lip pops, and improvised pitches within areas of high, middle, and low registers. The results are often similar to choral effects in Penderecki's *Passion*, yet exist more as timbre clusters than as pitch clusters.

György Ligeti's *Atmospheres* (1961) involves the full complement of winds, strings, and percussion, orchestrated in such a manner as to create unique "clusters" of sound by overtones and resultant tones. In *Lux Aeterna*

(1966) and *Requiem* (1965) (for soprano, mezzo-soprano, two mixed choirs, and orchestra), Ligeti approaches effects in which instruments and individual voices are unrecognizable.

Ligeti's *Lontano* (1967) for orchestra often employs over fifty separate instrumental voices (Ligeti's music, unlike Penderecki's, is notated by traditional means) creating an ever-evolving and developing sonic texture. While seeming to lack recognizable melodic direction, this piece maintains an enormous musical impact in terms of the other available parameters (dynamics and timbre in particular).

"The important tones, the ones that are most plainly heard, are those of the outer edges of a given cluster."[4] Thus both composer and performer realized that order and exact notation of clusters could be described verbally or graphically. Theodore Lucas, in *Aberrations No. VII* for piano (fig. 3.10), evolves a system of cluster notation (white and black keys) denoting duration by horizontal length. Graphic structures show only approximate pitch and relative motion (notice here that the two sets of clusters remain static). Various cluster effects are dramatically notated by Stanley Lunetta in his *Piano Music*. Notice (especially with the indication "wiggle all fingers") the interpretative possibilities for the performer.

Figure 3.12, a dramatic portion of Karel Husa's *Apotheosis of This Earth* (1971) for concert band, demonstrates another means of achieving sound-mass: rhythmic densities so thick as to produce vibrating columns of sound. This approach allows for continuous development of motivic and melodic fragments.

North/White by R. Murray Schafer was, in the words of the composer, "inspired by the rape of the Canadian North . . . carried out by the nation's government in conspiracy with business and industry." The title derives from "white light" which contains all visual frequencies (the piece then contains all audible frequencies produceable by a symphony orchestra). The work begins and ends on a single note surrounding tapering clusters of sound. The form is a kind of "crab" structure with the first three main sections (1. slow cluster buildup; 2. repeated notes; 3. chromatic scales) presented in retrograde order in the second half of the piece. Schafer has created a dynamic and sometimes hostile work (from *Ear Cleaning:* ". . . take a sheet of paper and give it a sound. . . . By giving the paper a voice we have exposed its sound-soul. Every object on the earth has a sound soul").

4. Henry Cowell, *New Musical Resources* (New York: Alfred A. Knopf, 1930), p. 122.

Figure 3.10. Theodore Lucas:
Aberrations No. VII for piano.
Copyright 1969 by the composer.
(Published by Composers' Autograph
Publications.)

INSTRUCTIONS:

♪ ₒ   natural

♪   sharp

♪♪   short note

○━━━━━   long note
●━━━━━

♪ ▯   white key cluster

♪ ▮   black key cluster

♪ ▮▯   black and white key cluster

♪   written-out cluster

✺ cover the area indicated and rapidly wiggle all fingers—
   interpret the shape

◢ glissando

♫ spaced evenly

Great care has been taken to space all other notes to indicate
the rhythmical relationships. After each page-turn play each
system completely, following all instructions and playing all
visible notes.

Figure 3.11. Stanley Lunetta: *Piano
Music.* Performance instructions.
Permission granted by *Source: Music of
the Avant-Garde* Composer/Performer
Edition, Davis, California.

70   *Sound-Mass, Rhythm and Microtones*

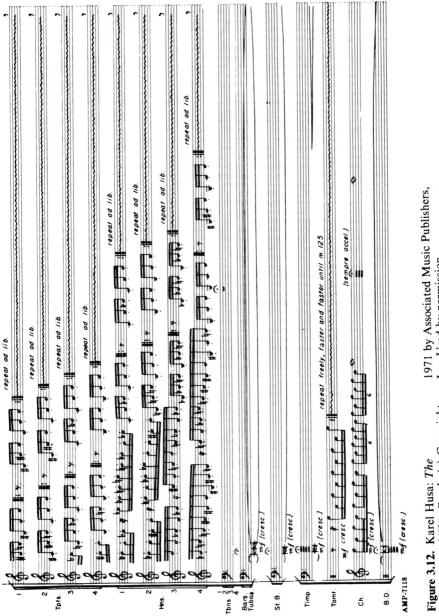

Figure 3.12. Karel Husa: *The Apotheosis of This Earth.* (c) Copyright 1971 by Associated Music Publishers, Inc. Used by permission.

AMP-7118

Rhythmic Developments and Control

Rhythmically motivated sound-mass structures, while not singularly identifiable as an organic evolution of new rhythms, have contributed greatly to the breakdown of vertical and horizontal traditions (one could most certainly devote a book and more to this one aspect of the twentieth-century *avant-garde* alone). Rhythm, viewed without the melodic or harmonic drive of most works prior to this century, becomes a rather simply used parameter of musical structure. It often seems strangled by the bar line or tied down to basic repetitions related to dance forms. Ligeti comments about this in notes for *Lontano* (1967): "The bar lines serve only as a means of synchronization; bar lines and beats never mean an accentuation, the music must flow smoothly. . . ."[5] The score is filled with double- and triple-dotted notes, entrances on inner positions of triplets, quintuplets, septuplets, etc., as shown in fig. 3.13, ever diffusing the bar line and beat and giving the rhythm a development and tangible diversity.

Figure 3.13. György Ligeti: *Lontano.*
Typical rhythmic entrances.

Boulez speaks to this point in his *Boulez on Music Today:*

The rational use of the opposition between multiplication and division of the [beat] unit will, moreover, give rise to striking contrasts due to the broader span of values brought into play . . . interaction of these various methods of organization can be extremely fertile, and will create an inexhaustible variety of objects—in the same way as in the field of pitch.[6]

Some composers turn to proportional notation to avoid the accent implications of bar lines and simplicity of beat structures. Thus a section is marked 30 seconds and the notations within performed as they reach the eye (as if the visual action of reading would take 30 seconds). No accents, other than those specifically marked, are implied by such notation, creating a great deal of rhythmic variety. By the same token, this inexactitude of notation disturbs some composers in that results often differ markedly from one performance to another.

5. György Ligeti, *Lontano* (New York: Schott Music Corp., 1969), from the performance notes in the score.
6. Pierre Boulez, *Boulez on Music Today* (Cambridge, Mass.: Harvard University Press, 1971), p. 58.

Elliott Carter attempts the same goal, but from quite a different perspective. In *Flawed Words and Stubborn Sounds* Carter speaks of his directions: "The result in my own music was, first of all, the way of evolving rhythms and continuities now called 'metric modulation,' which I worked out in the composition of my *Cello Sonata* of 1948." Later in the same book he speaks of new music in general: ". . . what is needed is never just a string of interesting passages, but works whose central interest is constituted by the way everything that happens in them happens *as* and *when* it does in relation to everything else."[7]

Metric modulation, though not an entirely new concept to Eastern music or music in the Western World prior to the advent of the so-called "common-practice period," is a highly complex procedure. In Carter's *Double Concerto* (1961) for harpsichord and piano with two chamber orchestras, there are many such modulations. As seen in Figure 3.14, the meter and the tempo very often change with the basic equalization across the bar lines. This, combined with a rich variety of complex rhythmic development within the bar, achieves a highly structured yet "bar-line" free momentum of sounds (though many of Carter's critics express grave doubt as to whether such "metric modulations" can actually be performed). Carter's earlier *Cello Sonata* has surprisingly few metric modulations compared with the highly technical complexities of the renowned *Double Concerto*.

Figure 3.14. Metric Modulations from Elliott Carter's *Double Concerto*.

Most composers take a middle road between the proportional and "modulation" principles examined here, utilizing both within a single work as does Ligeti in his *Aventures* (see in fig. 4.10 under Instrument Exploration).

7. Allen Edwards, *Flawed Words and Stubborn Sounds* (New York: W. W. Norton and Co., 1971), pp. 91–92.

Figure 3.15. Elliott Carter. BMI
Archives. Used by permission.

Electronic and computer music present an ever-growing potential source
for complex rhythmic structures and rhythm freed from bar lines. The author
discusses this in his own contribution to *Electronic Music: A Listener's Guide*
by Elliott Schwartz:

The major advantage to working with electronic equipment and sounds which seem
undiminished by overdone "exploration" is rhythmic freedom. No other ensemble of
instruments is equally capable of fractioning time into controllable particles as the
components of a well-equipped electronic music studio. While some listeners feel
that the opportunity to free rhythm from any immediately recognizable meters
removes some inalienable musical basic, it must be pointed out that to a large
degree meter was introduced only to keep performers together in ensembles; while
necessary, it was certainly not particularly musical in itself. The disposition of time
is much more controllable in the electronic studio.[8]

8. Elliott Schwartz, *Electronic Music: A Listener's Guide* (New York: Praeger Publishers, 1972);
from "Observations by Composers," p. 214.

Microtones

While notation and performance continue to confound composer's bent on freeing their music from the rigidity of the bar line, they also block microtonal possibilities (see Appendix 3). While twelve-note scales and the search for a single *stable* tuning system have existed for many centuries,[9] it seems to many contemporary composers that this search is a fruitless one, which results in a hybrid intonation (equal temperament) lacking the multifold potentials of flexible tunings. It is important to note here that while the piano may remain "fixed" in equal-tempered tuning, other instruments do not. Orchestral performers create a wide range and variety of tunings, usually a combination of *just* (based on the overtone series) and *equal* (each semitone equidistant from the next) temperaments (applied at the discretion of their "musical ears"). Similarly, tonal key regions with "leading tones," sevenths of dominant seventh chords and the like call for *adjusted* intonations. Mozart, for example, worked and *taught* with a 17-note scale, clearly identifying microtones through spelling (e.g., C♯ and D♭ were quite differently tuned, the first being higher).

Microtones do not correspond to pitches in equal temperament. Microtonal "systems" usually involve more than twelve tones per octave, thereby forcing one or more intervals to be less than an equal-tempered semitone apart. Quarter-tones (24 tones per octave) present a type of microtonal system with twelve pitches in equal temperament and twelve in the equidistant "cracks."

Non-Western music has used microtonal tunings for centuries. Western music, though couched in its secure twelve divisions of the octave, has (but to a much lesser extent) had its proposals, experiments, and protagonists for new intonations. Gerhardus Mercator's (sixteenth century) fifty-three tones per octave scale is a particularly notable example.

Many composers felt that the creation of equal temperament, and the resolution of the octave into twelve parts, creates arbitrary musical systems. Alois Hába (1893–1972) constructed a quarter-tone piano in the early twenties[10] and experimented with a sixth-tone system in the late thirties. Charles Ives (1874–1954) experimented with microtones in his *Three Quarter Tone Pieces* (1918?) for two pianos tuned a quarter tone apart. Harry Partch (1901–74)[11], in the process of working with microtones (an acoustical division of the octave into 43 tones), developed new instruments necessary for the realization of his experiments. He worked more in isolation than Hába, but has

9. cf. Zarlino (1558), Salinas (1577), Mattheson (1725), Jackson (1726), Liston (1812), Delezenne (1827), Poole (1850), Drobesch (1855), Bosanquet (1875) and Keonig (1876), to name but a few. See Fred Fisher, "The Yellow Bell of China and the Endless Search," *Music Educators Journal* (April 1973):30.
10. See Alois Hába, *The Theory of Quartertones* (out of print).
11. See Harry Partch, *Genesis of a Music* (Madison: University of Wisconsin Press, 1949).

received much attention in the past few years.[12] Composers such as Teo Macero, Calvin Hamilton and Donald Lybbert have recently continued similar experimentation.

Though quarter tones were used sparsely by Bartók (especially in his *Violin Concerto,* 1938) and Milhaud in the late thirties and forties, their true import had not fully been discovered. The use of twenty-four or more divisions of the octave requires abandonment or total revision of techniques of traditional instruments; creation of new or revised systems of notation; and increasingly complex harmonic and melodic vocabularies. New instruments (e.g., the tape recorder), notations (graphs, punch cards), and scientific vocabularies developed in the early fifties, often as a direct result of experiments with intonation.

Julian Carrillo in "The Thirteenth Sound" divides the octave into ninety-five different pitches and utilizes a fascinating system of numbering each pitch at the end of the stem where one would ordinarily find the note head.[13] Harry Partch's forty-three-note system (discussed as well under *Instrument Exploration*) is much freer. Through his creation of an entirely new set of instruments he has created a virtually "infinite" variety of both timbres and tunings. Most of these approaches, however, seemed doomed to either extremely limited usage or complete neglect. The main problem is that most theorists and composers continue to search for new *systems* not realizing that the devising of any such system is little better than the *system* in present use (a restricted set of pitches). It is indeed the flexibility or "nonsystematic" use of intonations which is most valuable. Composers such as Ben Johnston, Lou Harrison, James Tenney, Kenneth Gaburo, and many others are writing sections, movements, or works to multiple sets of intonations. Ben Johnston's *Fourth String Quartet* uses a varying number of proportional octave divisions from five to twenty-two, thus creating a flexible set of intonations based on the composer's ear and musical intuitions.

Johnston has written extensively on microtonal music and in writing about his *Fourth String Quartet* he sums up a great complexity in a few concise words:

> Over the whole of the historical period of instrumental music, Western music has based itself upon an acoustical lie. In our time this lie—that the normal musical ear hears twelve equal intervals within the span of an octave—has led to the impoverishment of pitch usage in our music. In our frustration at the complex

12. See also Elliott Friedman, "Tonality in the Music of Harry Partch," *The Composer* 2, no 1 (June 1970):16–24.

13. Julian Carrillo, "The Thirteenth Sound," trans. Patricia Ann Smith, *Soundings* 5, p. 64. This volume also contains a number of works by Carrillo using his number notations.

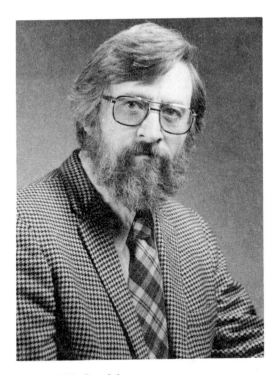

Figure 3.16. Ben Johnston.

means it takes to wrest yet a few more permutations from a closed system, we have attempted the abandonment of all systems, forgetting that we need never have closed our system.[14]

Johnston further describes the situation quite accurately in his "How to Cook an Albatross": "In our laziness, when we changed over to the twelve-tone system, we just took the pitches of the previous music as though we were moving into a furnished apartment and had no time to even take the pictures off the wall. What excuse?"[15]

Continued interest in intonation, microtones, and tuning systems abounds with notable recent activity, particularly on the American west coast. Periodicals such as *Interval* and *Xenharmonikon* (see particulars in the bibliography of this chapter) are indicators of increased interest. The potential of microtones is bounded only by the ability of the composer to hear ideas, the notation to express these ideas (see Appendix 3), and the performer to accurately perform the results.

14. From the April 28, 1974 program notes of a concert at the University of Wisconsin-Milwaukee by the Fine Arts Quartet.
15. Ben Johnston, "How to Cook an Albatross," *Source* no. 7:65.

Figure 3.17. Krzysztof Penderecki.

Vectoral Analysis: Penderecki: *Capriccio for Violin and Orchestra*

For information on vectoral analysis and procedures, see chapter 1.

1. Historical Background: Krzysztof Penderecki (*c* is pronounced as if it were an *s*) was born in Debica, Poland, in 1933. He studied music at the Music Academy in Cracow, where he eventually taught. Influences on his style include Iannis Xenakis (for sound-mass structures of thick multitimbred densities) and Luigi Nono:

In 1957, Luigi Nono came to Poland, to visit. He brought some scores with him, and he gave me some. I remember the *Five Pieces* of Webern. I was already writing my own music at that time (1957 or 1958). He gave me some of his music also. I think it was *Il Canto di Spezzo, Varianti* for violin and orchestra, *Cori di de Doni,* the piece for chorus, then *Improvisation sur Mallarmé,* by Boulez. All this was very new for me, and I tried to incorporate these techniques in a very short time. This was in 1958, till the middle of 1959. And then I decided to go my way.[16]

Nearly all his works require large forces for performance, and range from short experiments in sound (especially *Threnody,* 1960; *Polymorphia,* 1961; and *De Natura Sonoris,* 1967 for string orchestras) to large dramatic opera/ oratorios (notably *The Passion According to St. Luke,* 1965, and *The Devils of Loudon,* 1969). The thread of intense drama linked with subtle mystical religious overtones weaves through his mature musical style.

16. David Felder and Mark Schneider. "An Interview with Krzysztof Penderecki," *The Composer* 8, no. 1 (1977):12.

2. Overview: The *Capriccio for Violin and Orchestra* (completed in 1967) is a brief (ten minutes) concerto-type work in an abbreviated rondo-variations form (i.e., a set of variations with alternate variants referring noticeably to the opening material). After the brief opening timpani roll, a sound-mass occurs softly in the winds. Out of this texture grow individual crescendi contrapuntally strettoed (i.e., slowly increasing in number). This serves as a conceptual model for the remainder of the work, with variations deriving momentum due to a variety of parameters, such as timbre, dynamics, rhythm, and texture, rather than the more typical variants of pitch that one usually associates with this form.

3. Orchestration Techniques: The orchestra splits into sections (i.e., generally instruments of like timbre are employed in combination). Penderecki utilizes his large percussion battery (five players needed for performance) to create large slashes of sound (e.g., vibraphone, bells, triangles, chimes, harp, and piano used simultaneously on page 5 of the score for a bright attack of cluster material). Effects include playing on the other side of the bridge (strings) and bowing for noise (extra hard pressure on the string) with pizzicato (plucking) used on the piano. Double- and triple-tongued repeated notes in the winds give rhythmic drive to stacked clusters.

4. Basic Techniques: *Capriccio* is a free twelve-tone work (both free use of the twelve concept, i.e., eleven-note rows, as well as continual development of new rows rather than clinging to a single series). Interval content evolves from the minor second (chromatic clusters from the outset) and resulting octave displacements (major seventh, minor ninth). The major second and various thirds become important as the work progresses. Throughout the work there is the feeling of expansion, the result of intervals opening up, as well as general ideas becoming longer and more developed.

5. Vertical Models: Figure 3.18 demonstrates the kind of vertical clustering that is a mainstay of this work. Notation defines pitch content followed by duration in terms of thick black proportional lines.

I had to write in shorthand—something for me to remember, because my style of composing at that time was just to draw a piece first and then look for pitch. . . . I just wanted to write music that would have an impact, a density, powerful expression, a different expression. . . . I think this notation was for me, in the beginning, like shorthand, really, coming from drawing the piece. I used to see the whole piece in front of me—*Threnody* is very easy to draw. First you have just the high note, then you have this repeating section, then you have this cluster going, coming—different directions from the one note, twelve, and back—using different shapes. Then there is a louder section; then there's another section, then there is the section which is strictly written in 12-tone technique. Then it goes back to the same cluster technique again, and the end of the piece is a big cluster, which you can draw like a square and write behind it *fortissimo*. . . . I didn't want to write in bars, because this music doesn't work if you put it in bars.[17]

17. Ibid., p. 13.

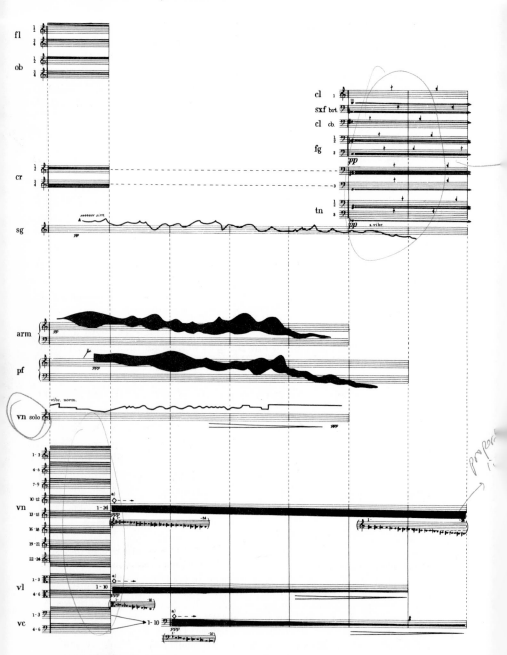

Figure 3.18. Krzysztof Penderecki: *Capriccio for Violin and Orchestra* (p. 29). Copyright (c) 1968 by Moeck Verlag. Used with permission. All rights reserved. See Figure 3.9 for explanation of these symbols.

In this example, the *arm (armonium* or "harmonium," a reed-type organ) and piano (using wire brushes on the inside) cover their approximate visual areas in the time allowed (2/4, with the quarter note approximately equal to M.M. 76, though no tempo is given in the score; the author determined such by carefully dividing the number of bars into the duration [ten minutes], including combinations of *ritardandi,* etc.). The resultant vertical textures vary, but nonetheless continue the chromatic clusters. A third type of vertical structure is shown in the upper right-hand corner of this score page. Here, a spread sound-mass moves by the use of microtonal (here, quarter tones) inflections in contrapuntal alternation.

Penderecki continually concentrates on the ever-widening possibilities of cluster techniques. In the opening sections, the work centers on minor second stacked clusters. Within the first minute he expands this to major second clusters (whole-tone). These eventually widen to octave-displaced minor second clusters.

6. Horizontal Models: As with the vertical concepts explored in this work, Penderecki concentrates on the use of the minor second. Over 80 percent of the intervals in the opening solo violin line are minor or major seconds. Often even thirds are augmentations of seconds. These lines become more angular by octave displacement of the seconds to include sevenths and ninths. The improvisatory solo violin line of figure 3.18 gives a strong impression of the "seconds" concept. Penderecki joins the vertical and horizontal developments so that one feels each proceeding at a similar rate of speed.

It is interesting to note Penderecki's own remarks concerning his linear writing for the violin in this piece.

Sometimes when writing a group of notes in a very fast tempo, like in *Capriccio* for example, I know it is impossible to play all of them. But I did it because then I had achieved a tension in the sound. If I would have written only four or five notes, he would just do it, you know, so you would lose all the tension I have in the piece. I know this exactly. Performers ask me all the time: "Please, this is impossible." I reply that it is absolutely possible— "You will do it." Maybe the player will miss two or three of them, but there is a tension there.[18]

7. Style: Penderecki's *Capriccio for Violin and Orchestra* is a tightly woven, freely chromatic work based on the exploration of the interval of a second (both melodically and harmonically). These explorations slowly expand through a variation form, over a rondo template. The dramatic context within which the work proceeds depends on large orchestral forces (especially large percussion), contrapuntal interweaving of nonpitch parameters (especially dynamics and rhythm), and various effects (including microtones). In contrast to the *Symphonie* of Webern (analyzed in chapter 2), Penderecki has produced an almost "stream-of-consciousness" dramatic style packed with sound-mass, rhythmic development, and microtonal inflections.

18. Ibid., p. 14.

Bibliography

*Further Readings**

Babbitt, Milton. "Twelve-Tone Rhythmic Structure and the Electronic Medium." *Perspectives of New Music* 1, no. 1 (1962):49–79.

Boatwright, Howard, ed. *Essays before a Sonata, The Majority, and Other Writings by Charles Ives.* New York: W. W. Norton & Co., 1962. A superb and fascinating study of the writings and thoughts of this man, many of which relate to sound-mass and rhythm.

Boatwright, Howard. "Ives' Quarter-Tone Impressions." *Perspectives of New Music* 3, no. 2 (1965):22–31. A good study of Ives's thoughts on the subject.

Boulez, Pierre. *Boulez on Music Today.* Cambridge, Mass.: Harvard University Press, 1971. Sheds a good deal of light on his own personal "controlled" approach to rhythmic structures.

Carter, Elliott. "The Rhythmic Basis of American Music." *Score* 12, no. 27, June, 1955.

Christiansen, Louis. "Introduction to the Music of György Ligeti," *Numus West* 2, Feb. 1972. Excellent overview of the works of this man and his contributions both in terms of sound-mass and rhythm.

Cowell, Henry, ed. *American Composers on American Music.* New York: Frederick Ungar Publishing Co., 1933. Gives excellent insight into two composers using sound-mass: John Becker on p. 82, and Wallingford Riegger on p. 70.

Cowell, Henry. *New Musical Resources.* New York: Alfred A. Knopf, 1930. Contains an entire chapter devoted to the structuring and techniques of clusters and sound-mass.

Creston, Paul. *Principles of Rhythm.* New York: Franco Columbo, 1964.

Dallin, Leon. *Techniques of Twentieth Century Composition.* 3rd ed. Dubuque, Iowa: Wm. C. Brown Company Publishers, 1974. Part of a chapter is devoted to "New Rhythmic Concepts" (p. 66).

Edwards, Allen. *Flawed Words and Stubborn Sounds.* New York: W. W. Norton & Co., 1971. Subtitled: *A Conversation With Elliott Carter,* this is an excellent source for thoughts on rhythmic complexities and development by this American composer.

Erickson, Robert. "Time Relations." *Journal of Music Theory* 7 (Spring, 1963): 174–92.

Felder, David, and Mark Schneider. "An Interview with Krzysztof Penderecki," *The Composer* 8, no. 1 (1977):8–20.

Forte, Allen. *Contemporary Tone-Structures.* New York: Columbia University Press, 1955. Has brief discussions of sound-mass.

Glasier, Jonathan, ed. *Interval (Exploring the Sonic Spectrum).* Published at Box 8027, San Diego, California 92102. Dedicated to microtonal exploration.

---

*Addresses for record companies, periodicals, and music publishers mentioned in this Bibliography can be found in Appendix 4.

Johnson, Tom. "Exotic Music: borrowing is not so bad." *Village Voice* 25:68 (April 14, 1980). This is an excellent article on world musics in the *avant-garde.*

Johnston, Ben. "Proportionality and Expanded Pitch Relations." *Perspectives of New Music* 5, no. 1:112–20.

Johnston, Ben and Edward Kobrin. "Phase 1-a." *Source* 7. As is his article in Vinton's *Dictionary of Contemporary Music* on microtones, this is an excellent exposition of Johnston's learned ideas on microtonality.

Kagel, Mauricio. "Tone Clusters, Attacks, Transitions." *Die Reihe* 5 (1959): 40–55. Interesting as a source of notations for opening and closing keyboard clusters and concepts.

Kirkpatrick, John. "The Evolution of Carl Ruggles: A Chronicle Largely in His Own Words." *Perspectives of New Music* 6, no. 2:146–66. An excellent study of this man of few works employing highly chromatic polyphonic sound-mass.

Makeig, Scott. "Expressive Tuning: The Theory of Interval Effect." Published in *Interval* (see above). A fascinating account of how tuning can affect emotions.

Marquis, G. Welton. *Twentieth Century Music Idioms.* New York: Prentice-Hall, 1964. Contains brief discussions of sound-mass.

Messiaen, Oliver. *The Technique of My Musical Language.* Paris: Alphonse Leduc & Cie., 1950. Excellent source for information on the extremely intricate and involved combination of proportional and metrical rhythmic language. Also a necessity for the understanding of much of Messiaen's rhythmically technical music.

"Microtonal Music in America." *Proceedings* 2, American Society of University Composers. Very good general discussion of the subject.

Nono, Luigi. "Geschichte und Gegenwart in der Musik von Huete." *Darmstädter Beiträge zur Neuen Musik* 3 (1960) pp. 41–47. Most interesting study of all the materials of this chapter as well as the remainder of the book.

Orga, Ates. "Alois Hába and Microtonality." *Musical Opinion,* July 1968. Reflects a distinctly Hába viewpoint but is excellent bibliographical material.

Partch, Harry. *Genesis of a Music.* New York: Da Capo Press, 1973. Second Edition.

Persichetti, Vincent. *Twentieth Century Harmony.* New York: W. W. Norton Co., 1961. Has brief discussions of sound-mass.

Pound, Ezra. *Antheil.* New York: Da Capo Press, 1968. Contains Antheil's "Treatise on Harmony" which might better be titled "Treatise on Rhythm," as the author-composer spends the majority of the article reflecting on the importance of *when* things happen rather than *what* happens in terms of harmony.

Riegger, Wallingford. "John J. Becker." *Bulletin of the ACA* 9, no. 1 (1959):2–7. Good study of this iconoclast and his rugged music.

Stockhausen, Karlheinz. ". . . How Time Passes. . . ." *Die Reihe* 3:10–40.

Varèse, Edgard. "New Instruments and New Music." In *Contemporary Composers on Contemporary Music.* Edited by Elliott Schwartz and Barney Childs, pp. 196–98. New York: Holt, Rinehart, and Winston, 1967.

Vinton, John, ed. *Dictionary of Contemporary Music.* New York: E. P. Dutton & Co., 1974. Includes a well-written analysis by Frederic Rzewski of contemporary ideas, pp. 618–25, along with an excellent bibliography.

Weisgall, Hugo. "The Music of Henry Cowell." *Musical Quarterly* 45 (1959). A good source of information on the works of this man contrasting the innovative with the conservative.

"Iannis Xenakis: The Man and his Music." Boosey & Hawkes, 1967. A good if brief look into the music of this composer who works almost exclusively with sound-mass.

Xenharmonikon. Published by Ivor Darreg, 349½ W. California Ave., Glendale, California 91203. Annual periodical devoted to microtones.

Yannay, Yehuda. "Toward an Open-ended Method of Analysis of Contemporary Music." Doctoral Dissertation, University Microfilms, Ann Arbor, Michigan. Includes a strong analysis of *Octandre* by Varèse.

Yasser, Joseph. *A Theory of Evolving Tonality*. American Library of Musicology, 1932. Quite extensive in its tracing of the history of microtones, but gets bogged down in the author's own equally "bogged" 19-note scale.

Recordings and Publishers*

Bartók, Béla. *Sonata* (1921). Universal Edition. Recorded on Capitol P8376.

————. *String Quartet No. 5* (1934). Boosey & Hawkes. Recorded on Columbia ML 4280.

Becker, John. *Symphony No. 3*. C. F. Peters. Recorded on Louisville S-721.

Bernstein, Leonard. *The Age of Anxiety*. G. Schirmer. See p. 59. Recorded on Columbia MS 6885.

Blackwood, Easley. *Symphony No. 1* (1958). Recorded on RCA LM–2352.

Blomdahl, Karl-Birger. *Aniara* (1959). Schott. See pp. 1–3.

Boulez, Pierre. *Le Marteau sans Maître* (1959). Universal Edition. Recorded on Odyssey 32–160154.

Britten, Benjamin. *The Turn of the Screw* (1954). Boosey & Hawkes. See p. 5.

Carrillo, Julian. *Mass for Pope John XXIII in Quarter-Tones* (1962). Recorded on CRI 246-SD.

Carter, Elliott. *Double Concerto*. Associated Music Publishers. Recorded on Columbia 7191.

————. *Cello Sonata*. G. Schirmer. Recorded on Nonesuch 71234.

————. *String Quartets* No. 1 (1951) and 2 (1959) AMP. Recorded on Nonesuch 71249.

Constant, Marius. *24 Préludes for Orchestra* (1958). Ricordi. Recorded on Heliodor HS-25058.

Cope, David. *Iceberg Meadow* (1969). Carl Fischer. Recorded on Capra 1201.

Cowell, Henry. *The Hero Sun*. Breitkopf & Härtel.

————. *The Tides of Manaunaun*. Breitkopf & Härtel, recorded on CRI 109.

————. *What's This*. Breitkopf & Härtel.(A number of Cowell's piano works are recorded on CRI S-281).

Crumb, George. *Black Angels* (1970). C. F. Peters. Recorded on CRI S-283.

Erickson, Robert. *Chamber Concerto* (1960). Theodore Presser, Recorded on CRI S-218.

Helm, Everett. *Concerto for Five Solo Instruments, Percussion and Strings* (1954). Schott. See p. 15.

Husa, Karel. *Apotheosis of this Earth* (1971). AMP. Recorded on Golden Crest 4134.

————. *Music for Prague* (1968). AMP. Recorded on Louisville S-722. Represents excellent use of sound-mass created both rhythmically in layers and by clusters.

Ives, Charles. *Majority*. AMP.

————. *Sonata #2* (1915). AMP. Columbia MS 7192, and CRI 150 SD.

————. *Songs*. New Music Edition. Recorded on Nonesuch 71209. (See Schwann Catalog for complete listing of recorded works.)

---

*Addresses for record companies, periodicals, and music publishers mentioned in this Bibliography can be found in Appendix 4.

————. *Chorale for Quarter-tone Piano.* Recorded on Avant 1008.

————. *Three Pieces for Two Pianos Tuned a Quarter-tone Apart* (1924). C. F. Peters.

Johnston, Ben. *String Quartet No. 2.* Recorded on Nonesuch 71224.

Kagel, Mauricio. *Improvisation ajoutée* (1962). C. F. Peters. Recorded on Odyssey 32-160158.

————. *Sonant.* C. F. Peters.

Liebermann, Rolf. *Concerto for Jazz Band and Symphony Orchestra* (1954). Universal Edition. See p. 1.

Ligeti, György. *Atmosphères* (1961). Universal Edition. Recorded on Columbia MS-6733.

————. *Aventures* (1962). C. F. Peters. Recorded on Candide 31009.

————. *Lontano* (1967). Schott. Recorded on Wergo 322.

————. *Lux Aeterna* (1966). C. F. Peters. Recorded on DG-137004.

————. *Nouvelles Aventures* (1965). Neues. Recorded on Candide 31009.

————. *Requiem* (1965). C. F. Peters. Recorded on Wergo 60045.

————. *Volumina* (1962). Recorded on Musical Heritage Society MHS 3482.

Lucas, Theodore. *Aberrations No. VII.*

Lutoslawski. Witold. *Trois Poèmes d'Henri Michaux.* PWM. Recorded on Wergo 60019.

Lybbert, Donald. *Lines for the Fallen* (1968). C. F. Peters. Recorded on Odyssey 32–160162. An excellent example of quarter-tone writing.

Macero, Teo. *One-Three Quarters.* Recorded on Odyssey 32–160162.

Messiaen, Oliver. *L'Ascension* (1934). Leduc. Recorded on Argo 5339.

————. *La Nativité du Seigneur.* Leduc. Recorded on Everest 3330. An excellent example of his rhythmic procedures.

Milhaud, Darius. *Piano Sonata* (1916). Salabert. See p. 10.

Moryl, Richard. *Chroma for Chamber Ensemble* (1972). Recorded on Desto 7143.

Nono, Luigi. *Il canto sospeso.* Schott.

————. *Cori di Didone.* Schott.

————. *La terra e la campagna.* Schott.

Oliveros, Pauline. *Sound Patterns.* Recorded on Odyssey 32–160156.

Penderecki, Krzysztof. *Capriccio for Violin and Orchestra.* Moeck. Recorded on Nonesuch 71201.

————. *Passion According to St. Luke.* Moeck. Recorded on Phillips 802771/2.

————. *Threnody for the Victims of Hiroshima.* Eulenberg. Recorded on RCA VICS-1239.

Persichetti, Vincent. *Symphony for Band* (1956). Elkan-Vogel. Recorded on Coronet S-1247.

Riegger, Wallingford. *Music for Brass Choir.* Mercury Music. Recorded on CRI S-229.

Ruggles, Carl. *Angels* (1921). Curwen. Recorded on Turnabout 34398. A good example of sound-mass.

————. *Lilacs and Portals* (1926). AME. Recorded on Columbia ML 4986.

————. *Sun Treader* (1932). Recorded on DG 2530048.

Schoenberg, Arnold. *Five Pieces for Orchestra* (1909). C. F. Peters. Recorded on Mercury and Columbia MG-50026.

Schuman, William. *Credendum* (1955). Merion Music. Recorded on CRI S-308. Uses sound-mass effectively.

————. *Symphony No. 8* (1962). Merion Music. Recorded on Columbia ML 5912.

Schwartz, Elliott. *Texture* (1966). A. Broude. Recorded on Ars Nova AN-1002.
Stockhausen, Karlheinz. *Mixtur* (1967). Universal Edition. Recorded on DG 137012.
Strandberg, Newton. *Xerxes*. Recorded on Opus One Records 16. Excellent for use of massive evolutionary sound mass as is his *Sea of Tranquility* (1969), Opus One 21.
Stravinsky, Igor. *Le Sacre du Printemps* (1913). Boosey & Hawkes. Recorded on Columbia M-31520.
Varèse, Edgard. *Equatorial*. G. Schirmer. Recorded on Nonesuch 71269.
————. *Hyperprism* (1933), and *Octandre*. G. Schirmer. Recorded on Columbia MG 31078.
————. *Octandre*. Ricordi. Recorded on Finnadar 9018 under the supervision of the composer with many other Varèse works.
Wilson, Galen. *Fantasy for Piano* (1968). Composers' Autograph Publications.
Wolpe, Stefan. *Chamber Piece No. 1* (1964). Recorded on Nonesuch H-71220.
Xenakis, Iannis. *Metastasis* (1954). Boosey & Hawkes. Recorded on Vanguard C-10030.

Instrument
Exploration

Evolution

Surprisingly, the desire for new and different sounds is probably the least significant of the driving forces behind the experimental or *avant-garde* composers in the past thirty years. Yet it is within this area that the contemporary composer has had the most serious division with audiences. John Cage referred to this in his 1937 lecture "The Future of Music: Credo": "Whereas, in the past, the point of disagreement has been between dissonance and consonance, it will be, in the immediate future, between noise and so-called musical sounds."[1] Philosophically, it is not "new" sounds that have disturbed the music world (since no significant new sounds have been developed that had not coexisted with music since the beginning), but the concept that these sounds are potentially valuable as a musical resource.

A group of Italian composers, called Futurists, wrote music for machine guns, steam whistles, sirens, and other "noisemakers" as early as 1912. Deriving their name from Marinetti's 1909 term *futurismo* (referring to extreme radicalism in all the arts), the Futurists were among the first composers to include noise as an inherent part of their music, not merely as a side effect. Francesco Pratella's theoretical "Musica Futurista" (reprinted in Nicolas Slonimsky's *Music Since 1900*) describes the "music" of steamboats, automobiles, battleships, railways, shipyards, and airplanes. Luigi Russolo (1885–1947), the most noted Futurist composer, constructed many of his own "noise instruments." Though his and most of the music of this movement was completely without popular success and approval, its significance lies in the fact that it proposed a concept and laid a foundation for other composers (though no *direct* relationship is implied). Varèse, for example, employed sirens and anvils. Mossolov, in his more imitative *Symphony of Machines—Steel Foundry* (1928), included the constant rattling of a metal sheet throughout the work. Equally unsuccessful, the Futurist movement in France *(bruitisme)* enlarged the concept of noise as a viable musical source. George

1. John Cage, *Silence* (Cambridge, Mass.: The M.I.T. Press, paperback edition, 1961), p. 4.

Figure 4.1. George Antheil arriving in
New York for the U.S. premiere
performance of his *Ballet mécanique*
(1927).

Antheil's *Ballet mécanique* (1924), probably the most "infamous" of noise
pieces, was largely influenced by the French movement. Its first Carnegie Hall
performance (April 10, 1927) brought about a violent audience reaction reminiscent of the first performance of Stravinsky's *Le Sacre du Printemps*. Antheil established the paradigm for the *avant-garde* to come, the "predictable"
unpredictability of which is expressed in "An Introduction to George Antheil"
by Charles Amirkhanian:

> Here is a man who once drew a pistol during a piano recital to silence a restive
> audience; a man who, in 1923, composed a piece of music calling for the sound of an
> airplane motor; a man who was mistakenly reported by the news media to have been
> eaten alive by lions in the Sahara Desert; and a man who collaborated with Hedy
> Lamarr in the invention and patenting of a World War II torpedo.[2]

Ezra Pound remarks that Antheil was possibly the first American-born musician to be taken seriously in Europe. This might explain John Cage's later

---

2. Charles Amirkhanian, "An Introduction to George Antheil," *Soundings* 7–8:176. Originally
printed in a KPFA Folio of November 1970.

successes there. The *Treatise on Harmony* by Antheil (a twenty-five-page book) repetitively dwells on the need for a reappraisal of rythmic ideas equal to those of melody and harmony: "A sound of any pitch, or combination of such sounds, may be followed by a sound of any other pitch or any combination of such sounds, providing the time interval between them is properly gauged; and this is true for any series of sounds, chords or arpeggios."[3]

Observations

In no other period of music history has the performer played such an important role in the development of new sound resources and instrumental techniques. Many instrumentalists have, during the past twenty years, created a significant impact in determining and exploring the sound capabilities of their respective instruments and have more than justified the claim that this immense potential can be applied as easily and as constructively as the use of electronic tape.

Bruno Bartolozzi, in his now famous book *New Sounds for Woodwind,* states the concept of the contemporary performer's role in new music as well as the role of instruments:

Their continued existence in the world of creative composition therefore depends to a very large extent on just what they have to offer the composer, just how much they can rouse his interest and provoke his fantasy. Some composers already show an obvious lack of interest in conventional instruments and have no hesitation in using the most unusual means in an effort to find new sonorities. . . .[4]

No traditional instrument has escaped the imagination of the composer's creative mind. Some performers have steadfastly maintained that any other than traditional "acts" upon their instrument violate inherent intention and should not be attempted. One must wonder if *plucking* and *muting* do not plunder the instrument's virginity. Certainly, short of physical damage to the instrument itself, even the most critical of traditionalists must admit the impossibility of being "just a little bit pregnant." Donald Erb sums it up well:

Music is made by a performer. It comes from him rather than from his instrument, the instrument being merely a vehicle. Therefore it seems logical that any sound a performer can make may be used in a musical composition.[5]

3. Ezra Pound, *Antheil* (New York: Da Capo Press, 1968), p. 10.
4. Bruno Bartolozzi, *New Sounds for Woodwind* (New York: Oxford University Press, 1967), p. 1.
5. Bertram Turetzky, "Vocal and Speech Sounds—A Technique of Contemporary writing for the Contrabass," *The Composer* 1, no. 3 (December 1969):169.

Traditional Instruments

Strings

Four major additions to string techniques have evolved:

1. percussive effects such as knocking, rapping, tapping, or slapping the strings or body of the instrument (especially in the works of Meyer Kupferman, Eugene Kurtz, and Sydney Hodkinson);
2. singing, speaking, or humming while playing (particularly apparent in the works of Russell Peck, Jacob Druckman, Charles Whittenberg, and Richard Felciano);
3. unusual bowings inclusive of circular bowing, bowing on or across the bridge, bowing between the bridge and tailpiece, bowing directly on the tailpiece, and *undertones* (subharmonics) created by bowing with great pressure on a harmonic node (actually creating notes well below the lowest open string of the instrument): these devices are used extensively in the works of Krzysztof Penderecki, Karlheinz Stockhausen, Mauricio Kagel, and George Crumb, among others.
4. combinations and extensions of traditional techniques (e.g., harmonics, glissandi, fingering without bowing, pizzicati, etc.) especially notable in the works of Krzysztof Penderecki, György Ligeti, Donald Erb, and Mauricio Kagel.

Figure 4.2 shows Krzysztof Penderecki's use of playing between the bridge and tailpiece (⊤ and �), highest note pizzicato (↑) and irregular tremolo (⟳) among others in his *Threnody for the Victims of Hiroshima* (for explanation of the proportional notation see Appendix 3).[6]

Notable performers of innovative works for strings are Paul Zukofsky and Max Pollikov (violin), Walter Trampler (viola), Siegfried Palm ('cello), and Bertram Turetzky and Alvin Brehm (contrabass). String groups particularly dedicated to new music and techniques include the Fine Arts Quartet and the Composers' Quartet, among others.[7] Kronos Quartet

6. For a more detailed discussion of new string techniques, see Bertram Turetzky's articles "The Bass as a Drum," *The Composer* 1, no. 2 (September 1969):92–107; and "Vocal and Speech Sounds: A Technique of Contemporary Writing for the Contrabass," *The Composer,* 1, no. 3 (December 1969):118–34; and his book: *The Contemporary Contrabass* (Berkeley: University of California Press, 1974).

7. It should be noted that throughout the course of this chapter the mentioning of performers' names is necessarily incomplete due to space limitations. Apologies to those many highly dedicated and talented performers who perform contemporary music, yet whose names are not included here.

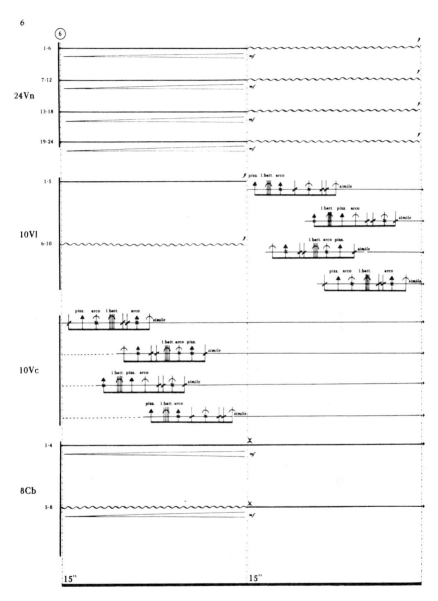

Figure 4.2. Krzysztof Penderecki:
Threnody for the Victims of Hiroshima.
Copyright (c) 1961 Deshon Music, Inc.,
& PWM Editions. Used with
permission. All rights reserved.

Figure 4.3. Bertram Turetzky, bassist.

Winds

Though there is a difference among the ways in which innovative techniques are applied to sections (brass and woodwind) and to individual instruments (particularly between the various single-reed, the double-reed, and non-reed instruments of the woodwind section), they are combined here for purposes of space and basic similarities. The author has grouped similar effects within six major categories:

1. multiphonics (or the creation of more than one pitch simultaneously on one instrument) created by either of two basic methods: singing along with playing and/or forcing the strong overtone content of a given fundamental to become audible (inclusive of altering embouchure, fingerings, overblowing, dynamics, and a combination of these). Figure 4.4 shows Toru Takamitsu's use and notation (in terms of open and closed holes for fingering) in his *Voice* (1971) for solo flute (also found in works of Donald Erb, Roger Reynolds, Russell Peck, and Jacob Druckman, among others);

Figure 4.4. Toru Takemitsu: *Voice.* Permission granted by Editions Salabert. All rights reserved. Each small vertical line equals 4.5″. Beamed notes indicate particular timbres or multiphonics (last 2 chords of first system).

2. color fingerings involving pitch and timbre fluctuations by changing the available fingerings on the instrument for the same note (particularly notable in the works of George Crumb);
3. jazz effects which include a large variety of hitherto avoided sounds such as *rips, fall offs, bends,* etc. (see particularly the brass works of William Sydeman, Phil Winsor, Donald Erb, and David Cope);
4. percussive effects such as rapping, tapping, fingering without blowing, fingernails on the bell tremolo, and hand-pops (the palm of the hand slapping the open bore of the mouthpiece) as noted in the works of Aurelio de la Vega, Iannis Xenakis, and many others;
5. use of mouthpiece alone or instrument without mouthpiece, both performable with actual or approximate pitch (see works by Donald Erb, Krzysztof Penderecki, and György Ligeti, among others);
6. extension of traditional techniques such as glissandi, harmonics, speed rates of vibrato, pedal tones, flutter tongue, circular breathing, and many others (see works by composers listed under 1–5 as well as works by Luciano Berio, Lukas Foss, and Gunther Schuller).

Donald Scavarda's *Matrix* for solo clarinet (1962), as shown in figure 4.5, contains a wide variety of new wind techniques including multiphonics (one of the very first such usages), smears, breath noise, overtone clusters, inverted mouthpiece, and undertones. Scavarda speaks to this point:

It was in trying to find sounds that were most natural to the clarinet that I discovered what are now called *multiphonics* in April 1962. Gradually I began to realize the exciting potential of the simultaneity of sounds that could be produced by the instrument. It was necessary first, however, to discard old habits and attitudes about what the clarinet should sound like. It required an open mind and much hard work and patience to explore and 'mine' these rich, natural complex sounds and eventually to bring them to the surface.[8]

Notable performers of woodwind and brass works of the *avant-garde* include: Aurèle Nicolet, Pierluigi Mencarelli, Savarino Gazzeloni, and Harvey Sollberger—flute; Joseph Celli, Lawrence Singer, and Heinz Holliger—oboe; Phillip Rehfeldt, Detalmo Corneti, and William O. Smith—clarinet; William Scribner and Sergio Penazzi—bassoon; Ken Dorn, and James Houlik—saxophone; Gerard Schwarz, Robert Levy, and Marice Stith—trumpet; James Fulkerson, Stuart Dempster, and Vinko Globokar—trombone; and Barton Cummings and Roger Bobo—tuba.

Percussion

It is in the percussion section that the maximum degree of enlargement and experimentation has taken place. The more traditional instruments (timpani, snare drum, xylophone, etc.) developed a wide variety of unusual techniques,

---

8. From notes to the score by the composer. *Matrix* (1962) published by Lingua Press (1980).

Figure 4.5. Donald Scavarda. *Matrix*

Figure 4.6. An example of traditional (left) *vis à vis* contemporary (right) percussion notation.

and especially experiments with various sizes and types of beaters (metal, wood, cloth, glass), to increase timbral resources. Exotic or foreign folk instruments were added mostly for particular effects, and used sparingly. Surprisingly, in considering the "noises" many percussion instruments (particularly the "whip") emit, many mainstream composers who use them nevertheless refuse to consider the musical potentiality of other less "noisy" instruments, including the oscillator. For a number of years, the most unusual and philosophically significant of these additions to the percussion section was the brake drum. The fact that a part of a car (or truck) had found its way into the standard percussion section of the symphony orchestra seemed to go unnoticed. Its use clearly implied that any object could act as a usable sound source.[9] Early experimenters in percussion music include John Cage, Edgard Varèse, Carlos Chavez, and especially John Becker, whose *Abongo* (1933) marks one of the first serious efforts in true percussion music. Percussion sections, since the late nineteenth century, have also required new notation systems, necessitated by the fact that performers must read as many as five or six instrumental parts simultaneously, and five-line staves are often impractical (see fig. 4.6).

The increasing need for explicit performance directions indicating type of mallet to be used, the action of the mallet, and its exact placement on the instrument, requires vastly new and different notations. Figure 4.7A shows the exact movement of the mallet across a timpani head within a certain period of time; figure 4.7B demonstrates the exact direction and striking surface

9. The brake drum is described and pictured in a number of contemporary orchestration books (e.g., Reed and Leach, *Scoring for Percussion* [New York: Prentice-Hall, Inc., 1969]).

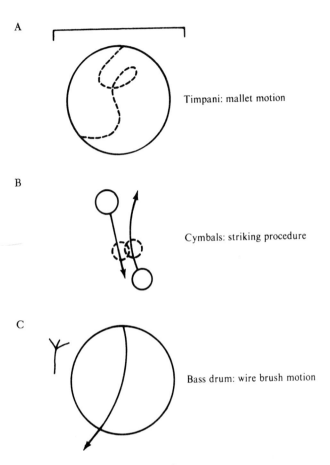

A

Timpani: mallet motion

B

Cymbals: striking procedure

C

Bass drum: wire brush motion

Figure 4.7. *Avant-garde* percussion notations.

of the crash cymbals; and figure 4.7C notates the sweep action of wire brushes on a bass drum. Since widely variable timbres can result from mallet direction and placement on each of these three percussion instruments, as well as from direction and amount of crash for cymbals, new notation becomes inevitable and increasingly more graphic.

An actual listing and numbering of percussion effects would create a book twice the size of this volume for just the unusual uses of the "standard" orchestral percussion instruments. The codification of the percussion section defines any instrument, no matter whether strings (e.g., piano), air columns (e.g., slide whistle) or others similar in kind to the orchestra "staples," as within "percussion" classification. This is particularly true when non-Western instruments are used with an orchestra: no matter what the context, the nature

Figure 4.8. William Kraft. Photo by
A. A. Friedman.

of the instrument, or the method of producing sound, it is included in the percussion section.

Notable *avant-garde* composers for percussion include Larry Austin, Karlheinz Stockhausen, Frederic Rzewski, Harry Partch, Edward Miller, Mario Bertoncini, Peter Garland, William Kraft, and many, many others. Performers include Max Neuhaus, Christoph Caskel, and William Kraft. Often, as here indicated (and more often than in any other section of the orchestra), percussionists tend to be composers as well. William Kraft is both a percussionist with the Los Angeles Philharmonic Orchestra, and a gifted and well-known composer for all instruments (which includes his extensive percussion solo and ensemble literature). The well-known Blackearth Percussion Group (see fig. 4.9) performed *avant-garde* music for percussion until recently disbanding.

Vocal

The voice, both in solo and choral situations, has in recent years become a focal point of innovative development, realized both in terms of dramatic emphasis of text and as an instrument separate from verbal associations. Its ability to be a "percussively stringed wind instrument" gives it nearly all of the

Figure 4.9. Blackearth Percussion
Group.

timbre potentials of all the aforementioned instruments. Only the physical
limitations of individual performers become obstacles to the composer's available resources (few can equal Roy Hart's eight-octave range and multiphonic
abilities).

Most vocal experimentation has taken place in three basic areas:

1. effects, such as panting, whistling, sucking, kissing, hissing, clucking,
laughing, talking, whispering, etc. (especially in the works of Hans Werner Henze, Krzysztof Penderecki, György Ligeti, Karlheinz Stockhausen,
Mauricio Kagel, Pauline Oliveros, Folke Rabe, Richard Felciano, Luciano Berio, and David Cope);
2. multiphonics (especially notable in the *Versuch über Schweine* by Hans
Werner Henze);
3. muting in the forms of humming, hands over mouth and slowly opening
and closing the mouth (employed well in works by Donald Erb and Robert
Morris).

Figure 4.10, the *Aventures* of György Ligeti, shows the breathing in and
out (measures 1–5 shown by symbols ▶ = inhale and ◀ = exhale) as well as
muting (closed mouth *m* in second brace). The work is notable for its many
other effects, its lack of text (replaced by a 112-letter alphabet for creating

Figure 4.10. *Aventures* by György Ligeti (page 1). Copyright (c) 1964 by Henry Litolff Verlag. Sole selling agents in the Western Hemisphere, C. F. Peters Corporation, 373 Park Avenue South, New York, N.Y. 10016. Reprint permission granted by publisher.

sounds), and the exchanging metric and proportional notations (shown clearly here between braces one and two). Hans Werner Henze's *Versuch über Schweine* (1969) for voice and orchestra is equally impressive in its incredible use of dramatic vocal gymnastics.

Singers who are known for their performance of new music include Roy Hart, Catherine Rowe, Jan DeGaetani, Bethany Beardslee, Elaine Bonazzi, Joan LaBarbara, Neva Pilgrim, Paul Sperry, and the late Cathy Berberian. The New Music Choral Ensemble (NMCE), founded by its director (Kenneth Gaburo) in 1966, stood as one of the world's foremost choral ensembles dedicated to the performance of new music.

Keyboard Instruments

The early experiments and compositions for piano by Henry Cowell (e.g., 1925, *The Banshee*, which involved plucking and stroking the strings inside the instrument), John Cage (e.g., 1938, *Bacchanale*, and 1946–48, *Sonatas and Interludes* for prepared piano) and Christian Wolff (whose *For Prepared Piano* appeared in *New Music Quarterly* in April, 1951) aroused great interest. At least a few performers became aware of the fantastic array of new sound resources that was available, and that these resources, combined with variable performance techniques, were just as viable as more traditional ones.

The prepared piano (a technique first explored by John Cage in the mid-thirties) involves the placement of objects such as nuts, bolts, and nails on, around, and between the strings, thus converting the piano into an instrument with an almost limitless variety of new timbres. Figure 4.11 (from Richard

Figure 4.11. From Richard Bunger: *The Well Prepared Piano.* Examples of piano preparations. Used by permission of the author and illustrator, Richard Bunger. Second Edition. Litoral Arts Press, 350 Firefly Lane, Sebastopol, California 95472 (1981).

Figure 4.12. From Richard Bunger, *The Well Prepared Piano*. Proper use of screwdriver in inserting preparations. Used by permission of the author and illustrator, Richard Bunger. Second Edition. Litoral Arts Press, 350 Firefly Lane, Sebastopol, California 95472, 1981.

Bunger's *The Well Prepared Piano*) shows a number of typical preparations. Resulting timbres can be altered by (a) location of preparation in regard to string length (e.g., placing at harmonic nodes creates a very different sound from that resulting when one places the object between these nodes); (b) striking techniques (i.e., initiating the sound via the keyboard creates a sound distinctly different from that obtained if one strikes the preparation directly with a mallet or similar instrument); and (c) elasticity and density of material utilized. Such preparations should do no damage to the instrument whatsoever if proper precautions are used (see fig. 4.12, which shows the use of a screwdriver, especially one covered with masking tape, to insert preparations, thus avoiding any harm to the strings).

Aside from preparation, the following new techniques are currently being used and explored:

1. muting (usually done by placing the right hand on the string inside the piano between the pin and the dampers and playing the notes on the keyboard with the left hand) is notated with an + above the note (used particularly in the works of George Crumb and David Cope);

2. harmonics (produced by touching a node of the string inside the piano with one hand and striking the corresponding key with the other) are employed much like those of string instruments (used in works by George Crumb, Larry Barnes, and many others);

3. bowing the strings (produced by making bows of fishline, threading them around and between the strings, and then drawing back and forth as one would on a string instrument) found particularly in the works of Curtis Curtis-Smith;

4. stroking, rapping, tapping, striking, or plucking the strings directly for a variety of different timbres (used primarily in the works of Henry Cowell, George Crumb, David Cope, Donald Erb, and others);

5. using other parts of the instrument by knocking, tapping, rapping, etc., particularly on the wood of the lid and body, the metal of the internal crossbars and soundboard, etc., with mallets, hands, and various other objects (notable in works like *Knocking Piece* by Ben Johnston, and works by John Cage, George Crumb, Donald Erb, and many others).

Pianists who are actively involved in the performance of new *avant-garde* works include David Tudor, David Burge, Richard Bunger, and Aloys Kontarsky. David Tudor, William Albright, and Martha Folts have been active in the performance of new music for the organ, as has Antoinette Vischer with the harpsichord. At present these experiments have been more theatrical (organ) and formal (harpsichord) than real in terms of sonic exploration (note especially works by Mauricio Kagel, Gordon Mumma, Christian Wolff, and William Albright for organ and György Ligeti for harpsichord).

Unique work with the player piano has been accomplished by Conlon Nancarrow in Mexico City. His *Studies for Player Piano* (one of which was published in *New Music Quarterly* in October, 1951 with many now published by *Soundings;* see bibliography) is a series of works (now numbering more than forty) utilizing punched piano rolls inserted in upright player pianos (the composer uses two Marshall and Wendell pianos, both with modified hammers; one set covered with leather and the other with steel straps). His extremely complex and original works vary from jazz-influenced shorter movements (especially the early studies) to mathematically proportioned canons (in the later works).

Harp

Carlos Salzedo (1885–1961) developed an extremely wide range of possible effects on this versatile instrument, as well as highly original notations and names for these techniques ("gushing aeolian chords," etc.). Most of these have become standard for the harpist and need not be considered *avant-garde,*

Figure 4.13. Conlon Nancarrow. Photo
by Gordon Mumma.

though they may sound like it to the uninitiated. Composers utilizing these
numerous effects include Salzedo himself, Luciano Berio, and George Crumb,
in particular.

The harp is indeed unique in that Salzedo, a pioneering and innovative
genius, composed during its maturing period. He proved that (more than any
other single instrument) it is capable of sounds virtually unexplored by the
avant-garde composer. It is not much of a gamble to predict that the harp will
in future years become a foremost attraction for the contemporary composer.

Mixed Ensembles and Unique Works

George Crumb's *Songs, Drones, and Refrains of Death* (1969) for baritone, electric guitar, electric contrabass, electric piano, harpsichord, and two percussionists, contain a great many of the effects discussed above (see fig. 4.14). The duet here (for electric guitar and electric contrabass) is scored in seven events. Each performer is required to sing or whisper while playing his respective instrument in a variety of unusual ways (e.g., harmonics, glissandi, tremolo, use of metal rod, etc.). Crumb's *Black Angels* (1970) for string quartet employs amplification of the instruments both for balance and for the unique timbre alteration which electronics adds to the ensemble. This procedure, employing the use of both contact and acoustic microphones, has within the past

Figure 4.14. George Crumb: *Songs, Drones, and Refrains of Death.*

twenty years become increasingly popular (discussed at greater length under "electronic music," see chapter 5). However, even the instrumentalists often don't recognize sounds from fellow performers, posing a problem contributory to the extreme difficulty of ensemble rhythmic performance. That problem is here solved by a procedure of notating *events,* in which exact timing is not as important as exact performance of the event itself. A broad spectrum of tone colors and "noise" is thus made available to the composer as musical material.

Barney Childs' *Mr. T. His Fancy* (1967) for solo contrabass draws upon the extensive sound resources of the instrument. The work involves many aspects of the aforementioned new string techniques, creating a vast new reservoir of sonic material for the composer.

Iannis Xenakis, long interested in preserving live and traditional instruments of the orchestra through creation of new techniques, proves convincingly in *Metastasis* (1953–54) that sixty-one traditional instruments can compete successfully with electronic sound sources.

Roman Haubenstock-Ramati was one of the first, in his *Interpolation* (1958), to utilize an unmanipulated prerecorded tape made by the performer. This enables a single instrumentalist to create a large number of ensemble effects using only a single instrument as source. His 1961 *Liaisons* for vibraphone includes provisions for a previously prepared tape to be started six to ten seconds after the performer begins. In this instance the tape serves not as an electronic device, but as a tool which enables both composer and performer to elicit more combinations of tones and effects, without losing the instrumental timbre.

George Green's *Perihelion for Concert Band* (1974) employs an incredible array of new and effective timbres often similar in nature (becoming clusters of like textures), though at times contrasted for purposes of form and direction.

David Cope's *Margins* (1972) ('cello, trumpet, percussion, and two pianos) emphasizes the "marginal" aspects of each instrument in a single movement structure. "The composer equally explores the contrast and developmental possibilities of dynamics and contrapuntal articulations. The tempo remains very slow throughout and the beat divides into multifold groupings of often very quick and pointillistic integrations from instrument to instrument."[10]

The previously discussed effects have also been used in combination or in conjunction with extracurricular performer activity, from finger-snapping and music stand-tapping to such dramatic effects as costumes, theatrical staging, and substitution of the original with other instruments. Often composers use whispers, speaking, and shouting (as in the aforementioned Crumb example, figure 4.14) along with the performance of additional instruments such as triangles hung from music stands, maracas, and a large variety of other percussion instruments.

10. From liner notes on recording: ORION ORS 75169.

Heinz Holliger's *Atembogen* is filled with orchestral effects, most of which involve some machination of subtle nuance or shading of breath or bow technique (examples for winds include exhaling, inhaling, using voice, embouchure but no tone, whistle-tone; and for strings, bow with too much pressure, bow with too little pressure, bow on tailpiece, and *col legno*). Most of these are used musically and there are no hostile contraptions evident. The piece is shaped in a through-composed series of large dramatic gestures based on quasi-physical motives. For example, *Atembogen*'s opening is four seconds of bowing and blowing without allowing sound to occur, with strings on up-bow and winds inhaling. The work ends similarly with the conductor doing a solo while the orchestra slowly releases bow and breath from their instruments in exhale fashion. Throughout the work there are like passages lending the "feel" of numerous episodes into deep textures and timbre explorations within the boundaries of the physical motion of bowing/breathing.

Whether in solo or chamber ensembles, the complete realization of all possible sonic events creates an entirely new performance situation with virtually endless combinational possibilities. The audience can no longer attend a string quartet performance, expecting that a traditional string quartet will be heard. New orchestral and multiorchestral combinations create almost endless possibilities equal to that of tape. Indeed, recordings of these works, without visual confirmation, distort beyond recognition the imagination's comprehension of the sound source. Ensembles of mixed instrumentation have contributed greatly to the development of instrument exploration. Such active groups commission, perform, and record new music and include the Contemporary Chamber Ensemble, The Aeolian Chamber Players, Die Reihe Ensemble, The Philadelphia Composers Forum, Cologne New Music Ensemble, The MW 2 Ensemble, da capo Chamber Players, and the Melos Ensemble, to name but a few. There also exists a large number of school-affiliated new music ensembles made up of faculty and students possessing both a high degree of professional ability and large repertoires.

New Instruments

Enlargement and transformation of sounds on traditional instruments represents only a part of new, non-electronic sound sources for the composer. Harry Partch, unlike Cage and Cowell, created new instruments rather than transforming existing ones (though his first such instrument was an adapted viola). His division of the octave into forty-three tones instead of twelve brought the need to create instruments capable of realizing his theoretical concepts (see his *Genesis of A New Music*). Except for his use of voice, almost all of his works employ original instruments (primarily percussion and struck string). Partch's *U.S. Highball: Account of Hobo Trip* (1943) and *Account of the*

Figure 4.15. Harry Partch *circa* 1967.

Normandy Invasion by an American Glider Pilot (both early works) reflect his fascination with instruments; an attempt at non-imitative music. In *Revelation in the Courthouse Square* (1961), the visual (theatrical) elements—the performers and their instruments—become an integral (in his words: *corporeal*) part of the work. *And on the Seventh Day Petals Fell in Petaluma* (a 1964 work comprising studies in the form of twenty-three duets, for *Delusion of the Fury,* a larger 1967 work) explores the possibilities of harmonic and melodic uses of microtones based on his tonal and polytonal theories of intonation (his word for major is Otonality, for minor, Utonality). I. A. MacKenzie also created new instruments—instruments that played themselves (wind sound sculptures).

More recent compositions have extended instrumental possibilities to anything which can be beaten, blown, or bowed, with each work demanding a new instrument for realization—cars, brake drums, even a jet engine, for example. Few of these "instruments" enter any standardized orchestra, as their intrinsic theatrical value lies in their being recognized as having a direct relationship to one work or composer.

Yoshimasa Wada has created a number of successful new wind instruments (see figs. 4.18 and 4.19) which, due to size, produce low sounds of soft

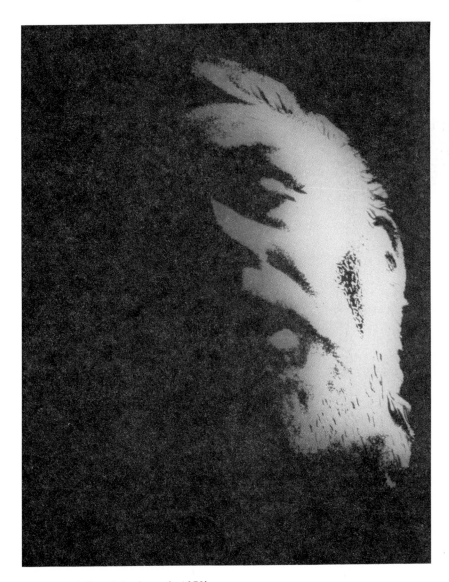

Figure 4.16. Partch in the early 1970's.
Photo by Jonathan Glasier.

A. Gourd Tree (1964)
   Cone Gong (1965)

B. Zymo-Xyl (1963)

C. Mazda Marimba (1963)

D. Chromelodeon 1 (1945–1949)

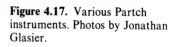

Figure 4.17. Various Partch
instruments. Photos by Jonathan
Glasier.

E. Bass Marimba (1951)

F. Diamond Marimba (1946)

G. Boo (1955–1957)

H. Surrogate Kithara (1953)

Figure 4.18. Instrument by Yoshimasa
Wada. Photo by Seiji Kakizaki.

dynamics often needing amplification for realistic acoustic projection. The
KIVA Ensemble of the University of California at San Diego continually explores new instrumental resources (see fig. 4.20) often coupled with electronic
amplification or modification. Arthur Frick has created a wide variety of new
instruments (see fig. 4.21), many of which are mobile and often have comic
overtones.

Figure 4.19. Instruments by Yoshimasa Wada. Photo by Seiji Kakizaki.

Figure 4.20. KIVA performance instruments. Photo by Solomon (UCSD).

Figure 4.21. Instrument by Arthur
Frick.

New instruments require "new" performers, with questioned virtuosity. One could hardly expect as practiced and polished a performance on an instrument created or adapted for one work alone as expected from a violinist after intense study of a Beethoven concerto. One of two alternatives is suggested: (1) a simple but fully notated score, or (2) a more free improvisational structure whereby the performer substitutes freedom and creativity for familiarity. Douglas Leedy chooses the latter in *Usable Music I* (1968), for very small instruments with holes. This work depends almost completely on graphic representation of activities (i.e., the use of symbols to indicate such general directions, as "blow" or "draw"), with less emphasis on exact rhythmic and pitch notation. Robert Moran, in *Titus* (1968), has the score projected on the stage upon an automobile, showing pictorially the performers' area and amount of activity (see fig. 4.22). Each of from five to fifteen performers, using contact microphones, files, hammers, and the like, move around and within the car, visually guided by the score.

In such works, there is an increasing necessity for performer creativity. Once the composer has admitted that the act of composition is a partially shared responsibility (for whatever reason), it is not difficult to understand the motivation inherent in graphic or less exact notational systems. New instruments and techniques have evolved from concepts of new sounds, creating new implications and philosophies of composer-performer relationships much more significant in their ramifications than the mere searching for different timbres.

Other composers and artists deeply involved in the creation of new musical instruments include Laurie Anderson (electronic tape-bow on violins); Christopher Charles Banta (large Marimbas); Bob Bates (mechanical instruments and music machines); Harry Bertoia (sound sculptures); Jim Burton (sound installations); Ivor Darreg (large numbers of microtonal string, wind, and electronic instruments similar in scope to those of Harry Partch); Paul De Marinis (electronic modules); Richard Dunlap (nonconventional instruments for improvisation and theater presentation); Stephen Scott (large sound sculptures); Bruce Fier (architectural sound designs); Cris Forster (notably *Chrysalis*); Ron George (original percussion instruments and ensembles); Jonathan Glasier (notably his *Harmonic Canon*); Stephen Goodman (automatic music instruments); Jim Gordon (percussion synthesizers); Jim Hobart (percussion and steel stringed instruments); Alzek Misheff (hot-air balloons containing portable electronic instruments); Max Neuhaus (sound installations); Jim Pomeroy (music boxes); Susan Rawcliffe (wind instruments); Tom

Figure 4.22. Robert Moran: Score of *Titus*. (Permission granted by *Source: Music of the Avant-Garde*, Composer/ Performer Edition, Davis, California.)

Recchion (folk instruments from found objects); Prent Rodgers (electro-acoustical instruments); Stephan von Huene (self-performing sound sculptures); Robert Wilhite (environments); and Richard Waters (notably the metal "waterphone"). More often than not, these composers/instrument builders are also the performers on their instruments, self-taught troubadours of the *avant-garde*.

Timbre and Spatial Modulation

The expansion of possibilities in the area of timbre modulation has proved to be a significant development resulting from instrument exploration. With the composer's increasing awareness of the subtle timbre alterations available in different registers of various instruments—muting, dynamics, attacks, and de-cays—comes the realization that a wealth of timbre overlap exists between instruments. Figure 4.23 shows three such overlaps with the evolving timbre changes inherent in the combinations. In the first example the piccolo is ini-tially masked by the triangle. Its slow crescendo gradually modulates the sound to solo piccolo through the decay of the triangle sound. In the second example the trumpet (with straight mute) slowly dies away as the like-timbred oboe crescendos, and so takes over. The effect is demonstrated by the intersecting vertical dotted line. At the beginning one hears only the trumpet. At the line one begins to hear a subtle combination of the two. Terms like "obet" or "trumboe" are often employed by composers to emphasize the significance of the truly "new" sound created by the modulation. Finally one hears the oboe alone. The third example demonstrates a direct approach to dynamics (the bass drum masking the piano attack completely) but a unique effect is achieved as the piano "rings" out of the bass drum (the piano chord slowly decaying beyond the hand-stopped percussion attack).

Works effectively employing timbre modulation include *Sinfonia* (1968) by Luciano Berio, *Lontano* (1967) by György Ligeti, *Ancient Voices of Children* (1970) by George Crumb, and *Apotheosis of This Earth* (1971) by Karel Husa.

Spacing and placement play an important role in the struggle for new directional sonorities from traditional instruments. A few historical examples are notable: Ives's *The Unanswered Question* (1908) for string orchestra, four flutes, and trumpet, isolated; Gabrieli's eight- and twelve-part canzonas; Mozart's *Don Giovanni;* Berlioz's *Requiem;* Berg's *Wozzeck;* Mahler's *Das Klagende Lied;* and Ives's *Symphony #4*. Henry Brant's experiments with the vast potential of vertical, horizontal, and circular arrangements have brought

Figure 4.23. Timbre-modulations.

meaningful solutions to acoustic problems. In his "Space as an Essential Aspect of Musical Composition," Brant describes many of his successful experiments in performer arrangement for optimum directional, acoustical, and balance effectiveness.[11] The spatial composing technique of one of his examples (*Voyage Four,* 1964) involves percussion and brass on stage, violins on one side balcony, violas and 'cellos on the other, basses on floor level at the rear of the auditorium, with various woodwind instruments and a few string instruments on the two rear balconies. Three conductors combine to direct the performers (including tuba, timpani, and chimes in the audience). Brant contends that, if the composer indeed intends to control his performance, each work should contain specific instructions for performer placement. Because every work is different in both structure and instrumentation, rehearsal experimentation is necessary for exact results, with no *right* schematic existing except in individual terms for each work or movement of a work.

Brant's *An American Requiem* utilizes spatial location of six different widely separated instrumental groups and four separated single players including an optional voice. The primary ensemble is a group of sixteen woodwinds sitting on the stage in a semicircle with their backs to the audience (the conductor faces the group and the audience is at centerstage). The horn, trumpet, and trombone sections contrast the individual parts of the woodwinds with unison rhythmic materials and are situated out in the hall. The fifth section is made of various bells (including "pipe-chimes," the construction of which are described by the composer loosely as three sets of seven pipes each set, a half inch or so different in diameter, with different pitches obtained by two or three inch length differential). Two tubas join the brass in homorhythmic unison with single parts for pipe organ, voice, church bells (recorded on tape if necessary) and timpani.

An American Requiem is a long (15′) three-section work. The first section opens with the formative material of the work: a nine-note horizontal motive of a half-step cluster bordered on each end by whole steps. Each note of this line is paralleled homorhythmically by eight other instruments forming a mirror of the horizontal material (i.e. a vertical cluster bordered on each end by whole steps). This kind of consistency of vocabulary between melodic and harmonic content continues throughout the work. Contrasting this dissonant idea in the winds is a static organ part of triadic content (C minor, B♭ minor, etc.) characteristic of both the first and third sections. The quasi-pitched pipe-chimes add a surrealistic touch to the multi-leveled music. The second main section

11. Elliott Schwartz and Barney Childs, eds., *Contemporary Composers on Contemporary Music* (New York: Holt, Rinehart,and Winston, 1967), pp. 223–42.

develops the polyphony of the first with contrasting sectional flutters in the brass, trills in the percussion and the carillon in hemiola with the rest of the ensemble. The third main section returns to the organ triads and variations of the initial expository material.

Spatial modulation, aided largely by developments in timbre modulation, involves the active motion of a sound from one point to another. An extreme example of this would be a large number of violins surrounding the audience, the sound beginning with one violin then slowly moving with the same pitch to each violin in turn until the first was encountered again. Works by Henry Brant, Donald Erb (*Fanfare for Brass Ensemble and Percussion,* 1971), Cliff Crego (*Implosions,* 1971), and many others employ this technique.

Elliott Schwartz's *Elevator Music* (1967) employs the vast acoustical, directional, and movement possibilities which a multi-story building provides. Twelve floors of a building become the performing areas for twenty-four performers (stationary) while the audience rides an elevator up and down through the constantly-changing environment of sound. The small spaces around the elevators make for a leakage of sound between the floors, thus providing an overlay of sounding materials. There is no distinct concept of twelve individual entities except when the conductor, who is also the elevator operator, stops at a certain floor and opens the elevator doors, while the performers on *all* floors are continuing to play regardless of elevator position. Dramatic change is available when the elevator stops at certain empty floors (empty in the sense of visual activity, but completely filled with sound due to the above-mentioned leakage from other floors), as explicitly outlined in the score.[12] Recording of this and many of Brant's works become virtually impossible, as the aspects of space, movement, direction, and theater are inherent in the structure of the works.

IRCAM (Institute for Research and Coordination of Acoustics/Music, a part of the Georges Pompidou Center in Paris) has developed a number of experiments to discover the variety of ways in which sound can be explored in physical spaces. Figure 4.24 is a diagrammatic exposition of the entire IRCAM installation, with figure 4.25 a closer view of the *Espace de Projection,* a performance hall with variable acoustic properties. Figure 4.26 shows Pierre Boulez (director of the Center) and Gerard Buquet (tubist) in the space with the variable shutters and "flats" (controllable by computers for variation during performance). The Center also includes computer and electronic music facilities.

12. For a complete description and score of this work, see *The Composer* 2, no. 2 (September 1970).

Figure .4.24. IRCAM installation.

Figure 4.25. IRCAM *Espace de Projection.*

Figure 4.26. Boulez with Gerard Buquet in *Espace de Projection.*

Non-Western Influences and Instruments

For centuries composers of the mainstream Western-European traditions have borrowed both stylistic flavors and actual folk materials from music of world cultures. The list of works and composers is too long to mention here, but includes Franz Liszt *(Hungarian Rhapsodies)*, Georges Bizet *(Carmen)*, Edward Lalo *(Symphonie Espagnole)*, Mikhail Glinka *(Spanish Overtures)* and Rimsky-Korsakov *(Capriccio on Spanish Themes)*. Notable mainstream composers of this century include Claude Debussy (see Chapter 1), Maurice Ravel *(Bolero)*, Stravinsky (use of Russian folk materials), Carlos Chavez (*Sinfonia India* using Indian and Mexican ideas), Heitor Villa-Lobos *(Bachianas Brasileiras)*, and Silvestre Revueltas (*Cuauhnahuac* for orchestra, utilizing large numbers of Mexican and Indian musical materials).

Colin McPhee (1901–64) spent a great deal of time in the early 1930s researching and studying the music and instruments of Bali, particularly the Balinese *gamelans.* His style changed considerably as a result, and such works as *Tabuh-Tabuhan* (1936) show considerable influence of the *gamelan gong kebyar* (a 20-25-player ensemble and development of the older *gamelan gong*).

McPhee translated the music of Bali into his own style and instrumentation (traditional Western orchestra). Alan Hovhaness (1911–   ) has been strongly influenced by the music of India and particularly Armenia (as exemplified by *Avak, The Healer,* 1946, and *Khaldis,* 1951). Again it is the basic style that has influenced Hovhaness's work, rather than direct materials (quotation) or instrument usage. The works of Chou Wen-Chung (Chefoo, China, 1923–   ), particularly *Soliloquy of a Bhiksuni,* and Oliver Messiaen (1908–   ), with the use of Indian *talas* (rhythmic patterns) in his musical ideas, have been clearly influenced by non-Western world music.

A few contemporary composers employ the use of non-Western instruments in the ensembles for performance of their music. Lou Harrison (1917–   ) has created a wide variety of works utilizing *gamelan*-type (Javanese) instruments (suggesting the *kempul, bonang, saron,* and *gender* of the Javanese *gamelan*) as well as American folklike homemade ensembles of *gamelan*-like instruments. His *Pacifika Rondo* (1963) is for a chamber orchestra of Western and Asian instruments and *Concerto in Slendro* (1961) for violin, celesta, and percussion orchestra shows strong *gamelan* influence.

Figure 4.27. Lou Harrison teaching at USC during 1978. Photo by Betty Freeman.

Figure 4.28. Lou Harrison and William Colvig. Photo shows a number of instruments built by either or both of these builder/composers. Photo by Betty Freeman.

Harry Partch's instruments (discussed earlier under "New Instruments") show strong influence of Hindu, African, and folk-American crossbreeding. John Cage's prepared piano works of the thirties and forties (particularly the *Sonatas and Interludes* of 1948) show strong influence of the *gamelan* orchestral style.

Quotation and stylistic embodiment of non-Western traditional music are evident in the works of David Cope (1941–   ). His work in the seventies includes a great deal of Navajo Indian quotation and influence, particularly *Arena,* 1974, *Rituals,* 1976, and *The Way* (1981), a part of the score to the former appearing later in this text. Ruth Lomon's *Five Ceremonial Masks* for piano (1980) also show Navajo influence. David Ward-Steinman's (1936) *Rituals for Dancers and Musicians* and *The Tale of Issoumbochi,* Ravi Shankar's (1920–   ) *Concerto for Sitar and Orchestra,* Roy Travis's (1922–   ), *Switched-On Ashanti for Flutes, African Instruments, and Tape,* 1933, and *African Sonata for Piano,* 1966, are true assimilations of this type. David Fanshawe's (1942–   ) *African Sanctus* is a hybrid of Western and non-Western music.

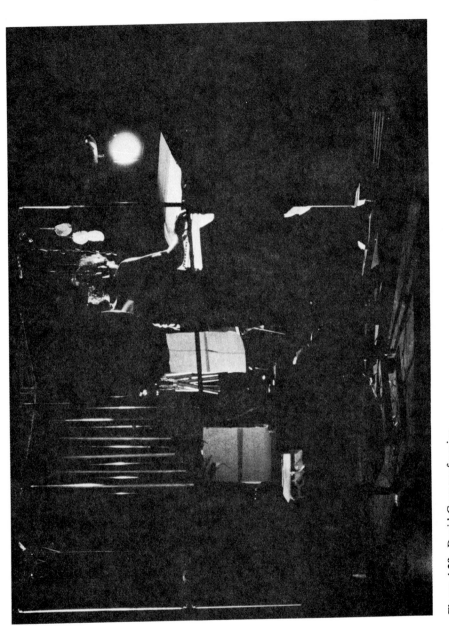

Figure 4.29. David Cope performing *The Way* for original instruments (1981). Photo by David Conway.

The styles of some composers fully depend on and develop from non-Western sources. Terry Riley's (1935–   ) *In C* (1964), for example, compares to the *jor* section of an Indian *raga* (term derived from the Sanskrit root *ranja,* "to color, to tinge"). One hears the slow process of variation by textural overlay. Similarly, the works of Steve Reich (1936–   ), especially *Drumming* (1971) and *Four Organs* (1970), show Eastern influence, as does *Einstein on the Beach* by Philip Glass (1937–   ).

The "ritual" elements of some non-Western musics have influenced a number of *avant-garde* composers, including Pauline Oliveros (1932–   ), Jon Gibson (1940–   ), and Alvin Lucier (1931–   ). Each has developed works built on ritual-like elements often taken from Indian, Zen, or Asian concepts. Lucier's *Queen of the South* (1972) takes its title from the mystical personality in alchemy known as *Sapientia Dei* (connected with the south wind, an allegory for the Holy Ghost). The relationship between this work and certain ritual Navajo sand painting techniques is clear in this description of the performance:

The performers sing into microphones or produce sound with oscillators. By means of electromagnetic transducers, large steel plates which are suspended horizontally near the floor are made to vibrate with these sounds. The vibrational patterns are made visible by sand and other granular materials which the performers sprinkle onto these plates. As they change the pitches of their sounds the granular images on the plates shift from one pattern to another. The performers, each with their own plate, are located throughout the performance space—ideally it is a gallery rather than a traditional proscenium theatre. The spectators move freely around these sonically and visually vibrating islands and choose their own degree of involvement with the ritual.[13]

Vectoral Analysis: Peter Maxwell Davies: *Eight Songs for a Mad King*

(For information on vectoral analysis and procedures see chapter 1.)

1. Historical Background: Peter Maxwell Davies was born in Manchester, England, in 1934, and studied in England at the Royal College of Music and in America at Princeton University with Roger Sessions. He was one of the founders of the Fires of London *(avant-garde* chamber ensemble; formerly the Pierrot Players), who are most noted for performing Davies' works. His music often includes quotations, new instruments, new techniques on traditional instruments, and a kind of stylistic heterophony. His better-known works include *Miss Donnithorne's Maggot* (1974), *Vesalii Icones* (1970), and *Dark Angels* (1974), all for chamber ensembles of various makeup.

13. Gordon Mumma, "Witchcraft, Cybersonics and Folkloric Virtuosity," *Darmstädter Beiträge zur Neue Musik,* 1974.

Figure 4.30. Peter Maxwell Davies.
Photo by Keith McMillan. Permission
by Boosey & Hawkes, Ltd., London.

2. Overview: *Eight Songs for a Mad King* was first performed on April 22, 1969, in London by Roy Hart (vocals) and the Pierrot Players conducted by the composer. The eight songs are based on texts created by Randolph Stow (suggested by a miniature mechanical organ playing eight tunes, once the property of King George III).

One imagined the King, in his purple flannel dressing-gown and ermine night-cap, struggling to teach birds to make the music which he could so rarely torture out of his flute and harpsichord. Or trying to sing with them, in that ravaged voice, made almost inhuman by day-long soliloquies, which once murdered Handel for Fanny Burney's entertainment. There were echoes of the story of the Emperor's nightingale. But this Emperor was mad; and at times he knew it, and wept.[14]

Each of the songs has a separate indicative title, and the texts resemble old English. Notation is metri-portional (that is, at times the composer writes clear indications of meter and at others the bar-line disappears and a free, time-proportionate-to-space notation takes over).

The forms of each of the movements are similar in that none take the usual part-form (simple AB or ABA), but rather develop intrinsically with the text in organic manner. Humorous colorations of the text and exaggerated gestures in the music of textual ideas are profuse throughout the set of songs (these at times become so obvious and blatant that they tend to create a kind of inverted meaning).

14. Randolph Stow, Program notes from Introduction to the score.

3. Orchestration Techniques: Instrumentation for *Eight Songs* includes flute (doubling piccolo), clarinet, piano (doubling harpsichord and dulcimer), violin, violoncello, and a single percussionist. This latter performer plays twenty-five different instruments, including crow call, steel bars, toy bird calls, foot cymbals, railway whistle, Christmas-type jingle bells, chains, small rachet, etc. As well, the voluminous number of instrumental effects throughout the score includes multiphonics (for voice, clarinet, and flute), tremolo (especially in the voice), use of inside-piano techniques, and vocal effects (breath only, glissandi, screams, harmonics, wide vibrato, etc.). Figure 4.31 shows a number of these effects and the notation used (in autograph score).

Here one can also see the proportional notation in use, notation for multiphonics (free), and the vertical lines that Davies uses to maintain simultaneous attacks.

Aside from unusual techniques and instruments, Davies also incorporates extreme ranges in all instruments, especially in the voice. In figure 4.31, for example, he uses 3½ octaves in the vocal part (eventually the range covers over five octaves).

The work also calls for four of the performers (on flute, clarinet, violin, and 'cello) to be placed in large cages on stage, adding an element of media presentation. Figure 4.32 shows a photograph of the author's own performance of this work (note the 'cellist in a large rope cage behind the "king").

Davies comments on the instrumental aspects of the piece:

The flute, clarinet, violin and cello, as well as having their usual accompanimental functions in this work, also represent on one level, the bullfinches the King was trying to teach to sing. . . .
In some ways, I regard the work as a collection of musical objects borrowed from many sources, functioning as musical "stage props" around which the reciter's part weaves, lighting them from extraordinary angles, and throwing grotesque and distorted shadows from them, giving the musical objects an unexpected and sometimes sinister significance. . . . The climax of the work is the end of No. 7, where the King snatches the violin through the bars of the player's cage and breaks it. This is not just the killing of a bullfinch—it is a giving-in to insanity, and a ritual murder by the King of a part of himself, after which, at the beginning of 8, he can announce his own death.[15]

4. Basic Techniques: Davies utilizes a hybridization of various techniques embodied in a dramatic and contrasting set of songs. Neotonal (almost impressionistic at times) chromatic techniques contrasts a fullbown tonality (created by association with one or more of the many quotes present in the work—particularly from Handel's *Messiah* and jazz inflections). Often the pitches chosen are so clouded by the harsh timbres as to be relatively meaningless. There is little doubt that Davies' consistent inconsistencies (i.e., constantly varying the basic techniques in use) are integral to his style.

15. Ibid.

Figure 4.31. Peter Maxwell Davies. *Eight Songs for a Mad King.* Bottom system of page 2. Examples of instrument exploration. Permission granted by Boosey and Hawkes. All rights reserved.

Figure 4.32. David Cope performing
Eight Songs for a Mad King by Peter
Maxwell Davies.

5. Vertical Models: Aside from the quoted tonal material and the various "noise" sections where pitch is of little consequence, the vertical sonorities seem based on a highly chromatic set of interval explorations (the fifth and the third) not unlike triadically based sonorities. Figure 4.33A shows a chord based primarily on different fifths (perfect, augmented, diminished), while figure 4.33B is triadically centered (G major) with an added minor ninth (G♯).

A   B

Figure 4.33. Two vertical models from
8 Songs.

6. Horizontal Models: As seen in figure 4.31, the vocal melody is characterized by wide leaps and elements of harsh dramatic multiphonics. Most of the nonquoted material irrevocably ties to the text and text meaning.

7. Style: In *Eight Songs for a Mad King*, Davies has created a dynamic and dramatic work fashioned around a mad king whose love/hate relationships with birds abounds. Characteristically, Davies creates a "mad" style replete with quotations, bird imitations, new instrumental techniques, flexible notations, extreme dynamic and timbral contrasts, chromatic yet somewhat triadically based harmonic systems, and word-painting (i.e., the music tends to imitate a word's sound or meaning). The results are a tight fabric of associative songs highly steeped in new instrumental techniques.

Bibliography

*Further Readings**

Backus, John. *The Acoustical Foundation of Music.* New York: W. W. Norton & Co., 1969. A must for those seeking expert knowledge in this area for spatial and timbre modulation.

Banek, Reinhold and Jon Scoville. *Sound Designs: A Handbook of Musical Instrument Building.* Berkeley: Ten Speed Press, 1980. An excellent resource for instrument design and specifications.

Bartolozzi, Bruno, *New Sounds for Woodwind.* London: Oxford University Press, 1967. Excellent source for new techniques on woodwind instruments.

Becker, John. "Finding a Personal Orchestral Idiom." *Musical America,* (February 1950). Much insight and subjective information from a man very much an innovator, especially in his use of percussion.

von Bekesy, Georg. "Musical Dynamics by Variation of Apparent Size of Sound Source." *Journal of Music Theory* 14, no. 1 (Winter, 1970):141. A fascinating study of traditional instruments and their acoustic variability in both psychological and spatial terms.

Brant, Henry. "Space as an Essential Aspect of Musical Composition." In *Contemporary Composers on Comtemporary Music.* Edited by Elliott Schwartz and Barney Childs. New York: Holt, Rinehart and Winston, 1967.

Brindle, Reginald Smith. *Contemporary Percussion.* London: Oxford University Press, 1970. A superb book devoted to the growing aspects of this section of instruments. It also includes a rather complete and detailed account of special effects, visual symbology of percussion instruments and mallets, and special performing techniques along with many examples from current literature.

Bunger, Richard. *The Well-Prepared Piano.* Second Edition, Sebastopol, Calif.: Litoral Arts Press, 1981. Superb book dealing with the essentials and potentials of this ever-increasingly-used "instrument."

Chou Wen-Chung. "Asian Music and Western Composers." In *Dictionary of Contemporary Music.* Edited by John Vinton. New York: E. P. Dutton & Co., 1974. An important source for information on ties between Eastern and Western music.

Cope, David. "Chronicles of a Cause." *The Composer* 1, no. 1 (June 1969). An interview with I. A. MacKenzie featuring his lucid though incredible accounts of his "sculptures."

———. "Modulations." *The Composer* 8, no. 1 (1977):25–30.

Cowell, Henry. *American Composers on Amercian Music.* New York: Frederick Unger Publishing Co., 1933. Contains a brief but interesting article on Carlos Salzedo (p. 101).

---

*Addresses for record companies, periodicals, and music publishers mentioned in this Bibliography can be found in Appendix 4.

√ Cummings, Barton. "A Brief Summary of New Techniques for Tuba." *Numus West* 5:62. A very good introduction to new sounds for this instrument in which interest is gaining rapidly among composers of new music.

Dempster, Stuart. *The Modern Trombone: A Definition of its Idiom.* Berkeley: University of California Press, 1980.

Erickson, Robert. *Sound Structure in Music.* Berkeley: University of California Press, 1975. A superb book whose title is a bit misleading in that it deals with timbre and texture primarily in new and *avant-garde* music. Highly recommended reading.

Goldstein, Malcolm. "Texture." In *Dictionary of Contemporary Music,* edited by John Vinton (New York: E. P. Dutton & Co., 1974.) A fine study of works in depth, often with concentration on both timbre and spatial modulation, though they are not so designated.

Heiss, John C. "For the Flute: A List of Double-stops, Triple-stops, Quadruple-stops and Shakes." *Perspectives of New Music* 5, no. 1:189.

————. "Some Multiple Sonorities for Flute, Oboe, Clarinet and Bassoon." *Perspectives of New Music* 7, no. 1 (Fall-Winter, 1968):136.

Howell, Thomas. *The Avant-Garde Flute.* Berkeley: The University of California Press, 1974. An excellent book containing the fingerings for an incredible number of multiphonics. Along with the Turetzky and Rehfeldt books mentioned later, it is the beginning of a most important series of books on new techniques for every orchestral instrument.

The Instrumentalist vol. 28, no. 10 (May 1974). Entire issue dedicated to new directions in instrumental music. Articles feature: strings, by Pat Strange; woodwinds, by Frank McCarty; percussion, by Dennis Kahle; band music, by Larry Livingston; and electronics, by Allen Strange.

Johnston, Ben. "Harry Partch." In *Dictionary of Contemporary Music.* Edited by John Vinton. New York: E. P. Dutton & Co., 1974. Exceptional article; a useful tool in understanding this man and his personal instruments.

Kaufman, Harald. "Ligeti's Zweites Streichquartet." *Melos* 37 (1970):391. A good study of Ligeti's techniques.

Kostelanetz, Richard. *John Cage.* New York: Praeger Publishers, 1968. An excellent source of information of all kinds about this revolutionary figure, especially on his piano preparation techniques and his ideas about new instrumental techniques in general.

Livingston, Larry, and Frank McCarty. "Expanding Woodwind Sound Potential." *The Composer* 3, no. 1 (1971):39. A good broad introduction to the area of using woodwind instruments for new sounds.

Musical America vol. 24, no. 4 (April 1974). Contains an interesting article on Jan De Gaetani, one of the most important of avant-garde singers (p. MA-6).

Palm, Siegfried. "Notation for String Instruments." *The Composer* 3, no. 2 (1972):63. A very good cross section of effects in current use for string instruments.

Partch, Harry. "And On the Seventh Day Petals Fell in Petaluma." *Source* 2, no. 1 (January 1968). Includes description of instruments and score.

————. *Genesis of a New Music.* New York: Da Capo Press, 1977. (Reprint of 1949 Edition).

Pooler, Frank, and Brent Pierce. *New Choral Notation.* New York: Walton Music, 1973. Fascinating source of various examples of new techniques for writing for the voice.

Read, Gardner. *Thesaurus of Orchestral Devices.* London: Sir Isaac Pitman & Sons, 1953. Huge and extremely useful volume.

————. *Contemporary Instrumental Techniques.* New York: Schirmer Books, 1976.

Reck, David. *Music of the Whole Earth.* New York: Charles Scribner's Sons, 1977. A great source for instruments and instrumental techniques of non-Western tradition music.

Reed, H. Owen, and Joel T. Leach. *Scoring for Percussion.* New York: Prentice-Hall, 1969.

Rehfeldt, Phillip. "Clarinet Resources and Performance." *Procedures* 7, no. 8 (1974). Fine article on multiphonics and other aspects of new clarinet performance.

———. *New Directions for Clarinet.* Berkeley: University of California Press, 1977. Another in the UC series of fine books on new instrumental techniques for the orchestral instruments written by a master performer of new music.

Rossi, Nick, and Robert Choate. *Music of Our Time.* Boston: Crescendo Publishing Co., 1969. Contains two excellent sections on personages involved with instrument exploration: Edgard Varèse (p. 220) and Henry Cowell (p. 339).

Salzedo, Carlos. "Considerations on the Piano and the Harp." *Harp News* vol. 3, no. 4 (Fall 1961). A fascinating article which originally appeared in 1923. The issue of *Harp News* cited here is dedicated to the memory of this innovative genius, and is well worth studying.

———. *Modern Study of the Harp.* New York: G. Schirmer, 1921.

———. *Method for the Harp.* New York: G. Schirmer, 1929. With the above, a classic in new techniques for this instrument which seem far in advance of their time.

Schuller, Gunther. "Conversation with Varèse." *Perspectives of New Music,* 3, no. 2:32 and idem, "American Performance and New Music," Ibid. 1, no. 2:1. Two general but very good articles.

Schwartz, Elliott. "Elevator Music." *The Composer* 2, no. 2 (1970):49.

Silber, John. "Writing." *Perspectives of New Music,* Spring-Summer, 1981, pp. 135–183. Excellent examples of new instruments at U.C.S.D. (photos, *et al.*)

Soundings 2 (April 1972). Half the issue is devoted to Harry Partch and his work, and includes a brief biographical sketch, the score to *Barstow,* and a short article by Partch, "A Somewhat Spoof."

Source: Music of the Avant Garde (Davis, California). Has included numerous articles and descriptions of new instruments. See especially Robert Erickson in vol. 3, no. 1 (January 1969), and Harry Partch in vol. 2, no. 1 January 1968).

Steinberg, Michael. "Some Observations on the Harpsichord in Twentieth Century Music." *Perspectives of New Music* 1, no. 2:189. A good introduction to this instrument's potential.

Turetzky, Bertram. "The Bass as a Drum," *The Composer* 1, no. 2 and "A Technique of Contemporary Writing for the Contrabass," ibid. 1, no. 3.

———. *The Contemporary Contrabass.* Berkeley: University of California Press, 1974. Superb book dealing with this man's original work on his instrument, as well as the many works written for him; contains chapters covering almost every conceivable aspect of the new techniques for this instrument.

Verkoeyen, Jos. "String Players and New Music," *Sonorum Speculum* 45 (Winter 1970). Short but interesting look into this subject.

Vinton, John, ed. *Dictionary of Contemporary Music.* New York: E. P. Dutton & Co., 1974. Contains numerous articles pertinent to the subject matter of this chapter, including contributions by William Brooks (s.v. "Instrumental and Vocal Resources"), and Henry Brant (s.v. "Orchestration").

Yates, Peter. "Lou Harrison." *ACA Bulletin* 9, no. 2:2. Provides a good bibliography of his works, especially those for percussion orchestra.

Recordings and Publishers*
Albright, William. *Organbook* (1967). Jobert. Recorded on CRI S-277.
Antheil, George. *Ballet mécanique* (1924).Templeton.
————. *Sonatas* (3). Weintraub. Recorded on Orion 73119.
————. *Symphony No.4* (1942). Recorded on Everest 3013.
————. *Transatlantic* (1929). Universal Edition. A most interesting and unusual Antheil opera.
Austin, Larry. *The Maze* (1965). CPE-*Source*. For three percussionists, tape, and projection; performers move from one group of instruments to another.
Bamert, Matthias. *Septuria Lunaris*. Recorded on London S-725. Very effective use of mass orchestral effects.
Becker, John. *Abongo* (1933). Autograph Editions. For percussion orchestra, two solo dancers, dance group.
Berio, Luciano. *Sinfonia*. Universal Edition. Recorded on Columbia MS-7268.
Blank, Allan. *Esther's Monologue*. Recorded on Orion ORS-75169.
Brant, Henry. *An American Requiem* (1973). Henmar Press (Peters).
————. *Fourth Millennium* (1963). MCA. Recorded on Nonesuch 71222. For brass quintet.
————. *Hieroglyphics* 3 (1957). MCA. Recorded on CRI S-260. For chamber group.
————. *Voyage Four* (1963). MCA. For three orchestral groups.
————. *Music 1970* (1970) MCA. Recorded on Desto 7108.
————. *Verticals Ascending*. MCA. Recorded on New World 211.
Cage, John. *Amores*. C. F. Peters. Recorded on Mainstream 5011.
————. *Bacchanale*. C. F. Peters. Recorded on Columbia M2S-819.
————. *Concerto for Prepared Piano and Chamber Orchestra* (1951). C. F. Peters. Recorded on Nonesuch 71202.
————. *Perilous Night, Suite for Prepared Piano*. C. F. Peters. Recorded on Avant 1008.
————. *Sonatas and Interludes* (1948). C. F. Peters. Recorded on Columbia M2S-819.
Celli, Joseph. *Organic Oboe*. Recorded on Organic Oboe records O. O. #1. A collection of performances by this master of new oboe techniques, including Stockhausen's *Spiral* and a spectacular performance of Malcolm Goldstein's *A Summoning of Focus*.
Chavez, Carlos. *Toccata for Percussion* (1942). Mills Music. Recorded on Columbia CMS-6447. A standard for the literature.
Chihara, Paul. *Logs* and other works. Recorded on CRI S-269. Use of subtle effects.
Childs, Barney. *Mr. T. His Fancy*. CPE-*Source*.
Chou Wen-Chung. *The Willows Are New* (1957). Published by C. F. Peters. Recorded on CRI 251SD.
Cope, David. *Iceberg Meadow* (1969). Carl Fischer. Recorded on Capra 1210. Use of partially prepared piano.
————. *Margins* (1972). Carl Fischer. Recorded on Orion ORS-75169.
————. *Rituals*. Recorded on Folkways 33869. (For 'cello, percussion, and voice, one performer). Score available from the composer.
————. *The Way* (1981). Recorded on Opus One Records 82. Score available from the composer.
Cowell, Henry. *The Banshee* (1925). AMP. Recorded on Folkways FX6160.

**Addresses for record companies, periodicals, and music publishers mentioned in this Bibliography can be found in Appendix 4.

Crumb, George. *Ancient Voices of Children.* C. F. Peters. Recorded on Nonesuch 71255.

————. *Songs, Drones, and Refrains of Death.* C. F. Peters. Recorded on Desto 7155.

————. *Black Angels* (1970). Peters. Recorded on CRI S-283. For amplified string quartet.

Crystal Rainbows: The Sounds of Harmonious Craft. Recorded on Sounds Reasonable SR 7801. Album produced by Jim Harman and William Penn, and includes a number of new and folk instruments (noteworthy: a steel 'cello).

Curtis-Smith, Curtis. *Rhapsodies.* Paris: Editions Salabert. Recorded on CRI S-345. A masterwork for "bowed piano."

Dahl, Ingolf. *Concerto for Saxophone* (1949). MCA. Recorded on Brewster 1203. Brilliant work by a master craftsman; a work for a much-maligned instrument.

Davies, Peter Maxwell. *Dark Angels.* Boosey and Hawkes. Recorded on Nonesuch 71342.

————. *Eight Songs for a Mad King.* Boosey and Hawkes. Recorded on Nonesuch 71285.

————. *Vesalii Icones.* Boosey and Hawkes. Recorded on Nonesuch 71295.

Dlugoszewski, Lucia. *Space is a Diamond* (1970). Recorded on Nonesuch 71275. For trumpet and piano.

Druckman, Jacob. *Incenters* (1968). MCA Music. Recorded on Nonesuch 71221.

Erb, Donald. *Fanfare for Brass and Percussion.* Merion Music. Instrumentalists scattered on stage, balcony, etc., for spatial effects.

————. *The Seventh Trumpet* (1969). Merion Music. Recorded on Turnabout 34433. Interesting use of rapping, tapping, etc., effects from orchestra.

Fanshawe, David. *African Sanctus.* Recorded on Philips 6558001.

Folkways Records. This company puts out many non-Western musics. Of special interest are:

    4273 Polynesian Songs
    4380 Songs of Assam, Uttan, Pradesh and the Andamans—India
    4401 Music of the Sioux and the Navajo
    4427 Folk music of the Congo
    4537AB-CD Music of Indonesia (2 vols.).

Foss, Lukas, *Elytres* (1964). Fischer and Schott. Recorded on Turnabout 34514. For flute, violin, piano, harp, and percussion.

Gaburo, Kenneth. *Lingua II: Maledetto.* Recorded on CRI 316-SD. Composition for 7 virtuoso speakers—important vocal effects.

Glass, Philip. *North Star.* Recorded on Virgin PZ-34669.

Globokar, Vinko. *Discours 11* for solo trombone. C. F. Peters. Recorded on DG137005.

Green, George. *Perihelion for Concert Band* (1974). Recorded by Cornell University Wind Ensemble, Record No. 15.

Harrison, Lou. *Canticle No. 1 for Percussion* (1940). Recorded by Mainstream 5011.

————. *Pacifika Rondo.* Recorded on Desto 6478.

————. *Concerto in Slendro.* C. F. Peters. Recorded on Desto 7144.

Haubenstock-Ramati, Roman. *Interpolations: a "Mobile" for Flute* (1, 2, 3), (1958). Universal Edition. Recorded on RCA VICS-1312.

————. *Tableau 1* (1967). Universal Edition. Recorded on Wergo 60049.

Henze, Hans Werner. *Versuch über Schweine.* Schott. Recorded on DG 139456.

Hodkinson, Sydney. *Imagined Quarter* (1967). BMIC.

Holliger, Heinz. *Atembogen* (1975). Mainz: B. Schott's Söhne.

Hovhaness, Alan. *Avak: The Healer.* C. F. Peters. Recorded on Louisville 735.

————. *Khaldis,* op. 91. C. F. Peters. Recorded on Poseidon 1011.

Husa, Karel. *Apotheosis of this Earth* (1971). AMP. Recorded on Golden Crest 4134.

Johnston, Ben. *Knocking Piece. CPE-Source.* Unconventional use of piano, with knocking on lid, sides, etc., and avoidance of keyboard.

Korte, Karl. *Matrix.* Recorded on CRI S-249. For woodwind quintet.

Kraft, William. *Triangles,* a concerto for percussion, ten instruments (1968). MCA. Recorded on Crystal S104. Very effective use of percussion by a professional percussionist/composer.

Kupferman, Meyer. *Infinities 22* for trumpet and piano. General Music. Recorded on Serenus 12000. Part of a cycle of infinities, all based on the same twelve-tone row.

Leedy, Douglas. *Usable Music I. CPE-Source.*

Ligeti, György. *Aventures* (1962). C. F. Peters. Recorded on Candide 31009.

———. *Atmosphères* (1961). Universal Edition. Recorded on Wergo 305.

———. *Lontano* (1967). Schott. Recorded on Wergo 322.

Lomon, Ruth. *Five Ceremonial Masks.* Published by Arsis Press. Recorded on Coronet LPS3121.

Mayuzumi, Toshiro. *Concerto for Percussion.* C. F. Peters. Recorded on Point 101.

McPhee, Colin. *Tabuh-Tabuhan* (1936). AMP. Recorded on Mercury MG 50103.

Messiaen, Oliver. *Oiseaux Exotiques* (1955). Universal Edition. Recorded on Candide 31002.

Meytuss, Julius. *Dnieper Dam.* Recorded on Folkways FX 6160.

Moran, Robert. *Titus. CPE-Source.*

Moryl, Richard. *Chroma for Chamber Ensemble* (1972). Recorded on Desto 7143.

Mossolov, Alexander. *Steel Foundry* (1928). Recorded on Folkways FX 6160.

Nancarrow, Conlon. *Studies for Player Piano.* (Published partially in traditional notation by *Soundings.* Book 4. 1977. #1, "Rhythm Study", was published in *New Music Quarterly,* in October, 1951). The complete studies are being released by 1750 Arch Street Records, with 2 volumes out to this date (S-1768 and S-1777).

Nørgård, Per. *Waves* for percussion. Wilhelm Hansen. Recorded on Cambridge 2824.

Partch, Harry. *Daphne of the Dunes* (1958). Recorded on Columbia MQ-31227, which includes other works as well, e.g., *Barstow,* which is published in *Soundings* 2. Features his own unique instruments.

———. *Delusion of the Fury.* Recorded on Columbia M2-30576. Album also contains a color booklet showing a large number of Partch's instruments.

———. *And on the Seventh Day Petals Fell in Petaluma. CPE-Source.* Recorded on CRI S-213.

Pellman, Samuel. *Silent Night.* Published by Alexander Broude Publishers. An amazing virtuoso work for fully prepared piano; a classic of the genre. Similarly the composer's *Dynamic Study* utilizes inner piano techniques in a fully *pianistic* manner.

Penderecki, Krzysztof. *De Natura Sonoris,* for orchestra (1966). Moeck. Recorded on Nonesuch 71201.

———. *Threnody for the Victims of Hiroshima.* PWM. Recorded on RCA VICS-1239. Extraordinary special effects.

Reich, Steve. *Drumming.* Recorded on DG 2740106.

———. *Four Organs.* Recorded on Angel S136059.

Reynolds, Roger. *Ping. CPE-Source.* Recorded on CRI S-285.

———. *Quick are the Mouths of the Earth.* C. F. Peters. Recorded on Nonesuch 71219.

Riley, Terry. *In C.* Published and recorded on Columbia MS-7178.

Salzedo, Carlos. *Chanson dans la Nuit.* Recorded on DG 139419. Not so much a composer as a master genius of invention.

Sampson, Peggy. *The Contemporary Viola da Gamba.* Music Gallery Editions. Canada. MGE 7. Fascinating new works for this Renaissance instrument.

Scavarda, Donald. *Matrix.* Published by Lingua Press. Recorded on Advance Records FGR-4.

Schoenberg, Arnold. *Five Pieces for Orchestra* (1909). C. F. Peters. Recorded on Columbia M2S-709 and Mercury. A masterpiece of orchestration.

Schubel, Max. *Insected Surfaces,* a concerto for five instruments (1966). Recorded on Opus One S-1.

Schuller, Gunther. *Seven Studies on Themes of Paul Klee.* Universal Edition. Recorded on RCA LSC-2879.

Shankar, Ravi. *Concerto for Sitar and Orchestra.* Recorded on Angel S-36806.

Smith, William O. *Five Pieces for Clarinet Alone* (1959). Recorded on Crystal Records 332.

Stockhausen, Karlheinz, *Zyklus* (1950). Universal Edition. Recorded on Mainstream 5003. For one percussionist.

———. *Gruppen.* Universal Edition. Recorded on DG-137002. For three orchestras which surround the audience.

Sydeman, William. *Texture Studies for Orchestra.* Okra Music.

Travis, Roy. *African Sonata* (for piano). Recorded on Orion 73121.

———. *Switched-on Ashanti* (1973). Orion 73121.

Varèse, Edgard. *Hyperprism.* G. Schirmer. Recorded on Candide 31028 and Columbia MS-31078.

———. *Ionisation* (1933). G. Schirmer. Recorded on Columbia MS-6146. One of the first full percussion orchestra works.

———. *Intégrales* (1925). G. Schirmer. Recorded on London 6752.

Villa-Lobos, Heitor, *Danses Africaines.* Recorded on Louisville LS-69 5.

Whittenberg, Charles. *Games of Five for Woodwind Quintet.* Joshua Publishers. Recorded on Advance 11 and Serenus 12028.

Xenakis, Iannis. *Metastasis* (1954). Boosey & Hawkes. Recorded on Vanguard C-10030.

5 Electronic Music

Brief Background

Electronic music,[1] or that music composed with or altered by electronic apparatus, has a long and involved history. Early experimental instruments include the "Clavecin Electrique" or "Electric Harpsichord" of Delaborde in Paris, 1761 and Elisha Gray's "Electroharmonic Piano" in Chicago, 1876.[2] Some composers typically utilized these instruments to imitate styles and materials of their times. Many composers, however, attempted to develop a unique aesthetic wherein *all* sounds could act as material for compositions. E.T.A. Hoffman's *The Automaton* in the early nineteenth century, and *The Art of Noises,* 1913, by the Italian futurist Luigi Russolo evidence these attempts. From 1920 to 1940, experiments with electronic instruments began to take place with composers such as Otto Luening, Norman McLaren, Pierre Schaeffer, Leon Theremin (who in 1923 invented the Theremin), Friederich Trautwein, Paul Hindemith, Ernst Toch, and many others contributing significantly to the new sound resources. In 1936, Edgard Varèse said: "I am sure that the time will come when the composer, after he has graphically realized his score, will see this score automatically put on a machine that will faithfully transmit the musical content to the listener. . . ."[3] A year later, John Cage remarked: "To make music . . . will continue to increase until we reach a music produced through the aid of electrical instruments."[4]

French composers Pierre Schaeffer and Pierre Henry developed the potentials of the first "electronic instruments": the tape recorder and the phonograph. By re-recording "natural" sounds at various speeds and splicing in

---

1. It must be made abundantly clear that the author does not seek to imply, by the use of the term *electronic music,* any stylistic or material similarity among composers who employ this medium. The term as used here does not connote an inherent style, something which is in fact nonexistent. In a lecture given in Los Angeles, Milton Babbitt argued that a recording of a Tschaikovsky Symphony is actually electronic music, in that all the sound actually heard is electronically produced. The term as used by the author here refers *only* to that music composed from or altered by electronic apparatus, and as such is as limitless stylistically as music for *string quartet* or *symphony* orchestra.

2. For more detailed history, see Otto Luening, "Some Random Remarks on Electronic Music," *Journal of Music Theory* 8, no. 1 (Spring 1964):89–98.

3. From a lecture given at Mary Austin House, Santa Fe, New Mexico, 1936.

4. John Cage, *Silence* (Cambridge, Mass.: The M.I.T. Press, 1961), p. 3.

Figure 5.1. Pierre Henry.

composer-controlled rhythms, this *musique concrète* became the first truly serious music of this genre. In Germany (until 1956) composers tended to shun *concrète,* using only electronic sources, often only sine waves. In America the pioneering work of composers like Percy Grainger (whose *Free Music* of 1935 used four Theremins) explored electronic resources. Along with Burnett Cross, Grainger later created a "free music" machine using various oscillators. The works of John Cage, Vladimir Ussachevsky, and Otto Luening brought attention to these new sound sources (all during the five-year period 1948–52—the years of real discovery and experimentation). The "Tapesichordists" (as Luening and Ussachevsky were termed in a *Time* magazine review of their renowned Museum of Modern Art concert of October 28, 1952), while not taken seriously until the early sixties, have steadfastly and consistently improved their working conditions, equipment, and technical knowledge. Very few observers now claim the creation of music by "electrical means" to be a passing fancy.

New sounds, however, become old quickly. New control (the composer becoming the performer capable of literally any microcosm of controllable elements in time) becomes equally available to those preferring lack of control. This latter point is strikingly evidenced by such contrasting works as Milton Babbitt's *Vision and Prayer* (1961) and Karlheinz Stockhausen's *Mikrophonie I* (1965). The former is composed of pure electronic sounds (with "live" voice) carefully notated by the composer, while the latter involves two performers acting on one six-foot gong with a score composed primarily of verbal descriptions of how the sounds should affect the listener ('grating,' 'scraping,' etc.). Two other performers control directional microphones, filters, and potentiometers (electronic timbre and volume control respectively).

Certainly the aforementioned creation of new, nonequal-tempered scales combined with nearly limitless rhythmic possibilities (no longer restricted to the ten fingers of the pianist or the thousand of an orchestra), present opportunities that many composers cannot resist. Few, however, would agree with "New Music for an Old World Dr. Thaddeus Cahill's Dynamophone An Extraordinary Electrical Invention for Producing Scientifically Perfect Music" titling a *McClures' Magazine* article of July 1906[5] or Casio's 1981 claim that one can ". . . become an instant musician . . . easily, without the long hours, years, of training necessary for mastering a regular instrument."

Nourished by the 1948 invention of the long-playing record, electronic music has become accessible to every listener's living room despite the singular neglect shown it by "serious music" radio stations. Moreover, electronic music's lack of visual interest in the concert hall has helped spawn a whole genre of interesting combinations of "live electronics"—tape with "live" performers—and has contributed greatly to the refinement and growth of media-forms.

Aesthetics

With the advent of tape and unlimited resources of sound and rhythm, such concepts as "noise," "consonance-dissonance," and "live performance" become increasingly difficult to define. Synthesizers enable composers to control all the elements of production (dynamics, envelope, duration, etc.), except performance acoustics and audience receptivity. This philosophy, if one is implied, has not gained a universal acceptance. Igor Stravinsky remarks:

What about the much publicized "infinity of possibilities" in connection with the new art material of electronically produced sound? With few exceptions "infinite possibilities" has meant collages of organ burbling, rubber suction (indecent, this), machine-gunning, and other—this is curious—representational and associative noises more appropriate to Mr. Disney's musical mimicries.[6]

Ernst Křenek seems almost to answer Stravinsky's objection in his article "A Glance over the Shoulders of the Young":

To the superficial observer, it appears that the phenomena demonstrated so far in electronic music: levels of colour, texture, density, consistency and mass of sound material, are of a considerably lower intellectual level of musical consciousness than the aspirations which were associated with the demanding music of the past.

5. Elliott Schwartz, *Electronic Music: A Listener's Guide* (New York: Praeger Publishers, 1973), p. 241 (from Otto Luening's remarks).
6. Igor Stravinsky and Robert Craft, *Dialogues and A Diary* (Garden City, New York: Doubleday & Co., Inc., 1963), p. 25.

Perhaps this only represents a beginning; history cites us many examples of the way in which creative energy has been expended on the achievement of progress of one dimension while temporarily impoverishing the other dimensions of the subject.[7]

Inexperienced electronic music composers can very often be "hypnotized" by complex patch-cord setups and the time required to make the exact sound needed. Visual studies of "spaghettied" patch cords often seem as necessary to the work as the sound itself. Other composers have noted that, up until the era of mechanical music, a composer/performer needed a certain physical energy to produce a *forte,* an energy corresponding in some ways, at least, to the energy of the sound itself. It is possible for one to lose that perspective when a small flick of the finger can create huge volumes of sound or the same flick can quiet the flow to nothing. Obviously a very different quality of action/ reaction is present in electronic music. *Psycho-acoustics,* the study of listener discrimination and receptivity of these complexities, has become a real and vital tool of the composer attempting to communicate.[8] Luciano Berio has commented:

When someone hears electronic music it doesn't reverberate to other levels of his experience, as instrumental music has and does. Up to now I feel electronic music has been developing, evolving as a bridge between what we know and what we don't know yet. It is not without reason that the best musical works that have been produced up until now (from the early 50s to the present) are those that try to make this connection.[9]

Fundamentals

Two basic sound sources exist: electronic, including the oscillators and generators; and nonelectronic, or *musique concrète* (e.g., instrumental sounds, sounds of nature). There seems to have been, at least in the early fifties, a definite desire by composers to make a choice between one or the other (with France dedicated to the *concrète* and Germany to the electronic). However, by 1960 (especially in Stockhausen's *Gesang der Jünglinge*), both sources were considered of equal potential. Certainly *musique concrète* involves less control and determinability. Experimentation with tape loops (continuous lengths of tape looped so as to pass and repass the playback head, creating rhythmic ostinati or continuous sound flow), and with gluing bits of recorded magnetic tape to white leader tape resulted in either a very controlled and measurable (in fractions of inches) rhythmic base or a random flux of sounds.

7. Ernst Křenek, "A Glance over the Shoulders of the Young," *Die Reihe I* (Bryn Mawr, Pennsylvania: Theodore Presser Co., in association with Universal Edition, c. 1958), p. 16.
8. See especially: Fritz Winckel," "The Psycho-Acoustical Analysis of Structure as Applied to Electronic Music," *Journal of Music Theory* 7, no. 2:194; and Milton Babbitt, "An Introduction to the R.C.A. Synthesizer," *Journal of Music Theory* 8, no. 2:251.
9. David Felder, "An Interview with Luciano Berio," *The Composer* 7, no. 1 (1976):11.

[handwritten annotation: → electronic or nonelectronic]

After choosing sound materials as shown in the following extremely simplified schematic (fig. 5.2), manipulation becomes important. At this point, material can be altered by combining sounds (with mixer, ring modulator), eliminating certain sounds (the use of various filters such as low-pass, high-pass, band-pass and band reject and filter banks—see Figure 5.3), or distorting sounds (by reverberation and/or various types of modulations: frequency, amplitude, and ring; along with speed changes of the tape recorder, etc.).

Amplitude modulation (AM), or continuously changing dynamics (also known as *tremolo*), and frequency modulation (FM), or continuously changing pitch (also known as *vibrato*) have brought about an important concept known as *voltage control*. When, for example, a composer wishes to "warm" a sound with vibrato, quick hand manipulation of the frequency control (repeatedly turning it back and forth) creates the desired effect. Assigning such repetitions to another module (i.e., the sine wave output of another oscillator at the proper frequency) however, is more efficient. The capacity of one oscillator (or for that matter any electronic instrument) to be controlled in one or more of its parameters by another oscillator is termed *voltage control*.

Synchronization, or the placing of all events into a composed order (by means of such devices as splicing, rerecording, mixing, speed alteration), readies the tape for playback. *Classic* studios utilize previously recorded sounds (or short groups of sounds), and splicing techniques. While most electronic music involves a certain amount of splicing, *classic* electronic music evolves *all* timing, order, etc., by splicing. This *classic* approach (used for example in the *Poème électronique,* 1958 by Edgard Varèse out of necessity, since synthesizers were not yet in use) is still employed by a number of composers, including Mario Davidovsky and Vladimir Ussachevsky. Prolongation of this tedious and time-consuming approach means one is constantly confronted by the splicing block for each new sound. The introduction of keyboards, sequencers, etc., and multitrack recorders, making "live" production on tape of as many consecutive sounds as the composer wishes without splicing, has eliminated many such *classical* approaches. While keyboards, sampleholds, sequencers, etc., make near "real-time" performance possible, some feel this leads to sonic masturbation rather than to great music. No doubt, *classic* and "live" electronic means can both serve the talented composer well, each having its share of advantages and drawbacks.

The playback stage cannot be underestimated in importance. The viability of a majority of compositions on tape require specific placement of loudspeakers. Some composers have even "composed" proper placement of the tape machine itself for theatrical or dramatic effect. In *Musik für ein Haus* (1968) by Karlheinz Stockhausen, exact locations of all electronic materials in a two-story house with patio are inherent to the "real" performance of the tape work.

Figure 5.2. Electronic music diagram: from source to playback.

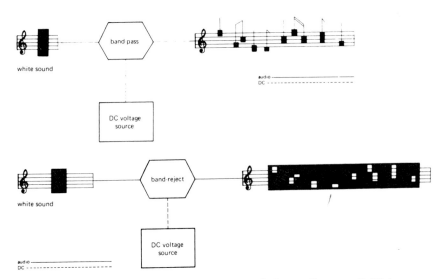

Figure 5.3. Band-pass and band-reject filtering. From *Electronic Music*, by Allen Strange. (c) Copyright 1972.

Wm. C. Brown Company Publishers, Dubuque, Iowa. Permission granted.

Acoustical considerations likewise become extremely important for the composer and/or performer in the placement of loudspeakers. Stockhausen discusses this:

. . . I should like to explain . . . just how loudspeakers are properly placed in an auditorium (a procedure which is becoming better and better known to me and which demands the greatest care in the particular place in question, as well as often up to four hours of time from me and several other collaborators sitting in various parts of the hall; in Madrid, for example, Kontarsky, Fritsch, Gehlhaar, Alings, Boje, and I took several hours to set the loudspeakers up; some of them were even lying on their backs up in the balcony, and others were on stands on the stage, and we had put pieces of wood under the front edge of each speaker so that they were pointed up at the ceiling and the sound was only reflected into the house at an angle at a greater distance; we set up two loudspeakers contrary to the usual way with their diaphragm sides at an acute angle directly toward the wooden walls in order to prevent hiss and to enable the people sitting right in front of these loudspeakers—at a distance of about 5–7 meters (16½ to 23 feet)—to hear the loudspeakers standing on the opposite side, as well as those which were diagonally opposite; in principle we try to send the sound of the loudspeakers, particularly when instrumentalists are playing at the same time, as *high* as possible into the house and to achieve a smooth acoustic match, especially in four-track reproduction).[10]

10. Karlheinz Stockhausen, "Not A Special Day," *The Composer* 1, no. 2 (September 1969):65–66.

Synthesizers

"Electronic studios" vary from a single tape recorder and splicing machine to
the R.C.A. Synthesizer valued at $250,000.[11] Unlike instrumental music, in
which the performance may vary with both the instrument and performer,
tape music generally has *one* performing version, that made by the composer
under studio conditions.

Synthesizers (synthesized sound producers) are a collection of devices
shown in figure 5.2, usually in module form (i.e., are independent and re-
movable instruments). More important, synthesizers contain many voltage
control devices so that parameters of one module may be automatically controllable by other modules (see fig. 5.4).

A standard unit might contain the following equipment: one or two voltage-controlled oscillators; three to five oscillators; one random signal generator (white and pink sound possibilities); one filter bank; one voltage-controlled
low-pass filter; one voltage-controlled high-pass filter; two envelope generators; two voltage-controlled amplifiers; one reverberation unit; one power sup-
ply; one keyboard controller; one ribbon controller. Such a unit would cost
from $1,000 to $4,000 depending on the numbers of each unit present as well
as the manufacturer involved. These synthesizers come in either portable or
console models. Larger models which include sample-hold units, sequencers,
ring modulators, digital controllers, and built-in linear mixers may cost upwards of $6,000, again depending on make and model.[12]

Studios

Pierre Boulez, in an interview with the author, offered the following observations:

> I think that you cannot do good work in this area until you have teams working
> together. You must have composer and technician alike. Four things, really:
> composer, technician, good equipment, and a company or factory with money to
> back the operation, as well as performers in some cases, and as long as these
> elements cannot work together you will have small laboratories without any
> outstanding results.[13]

---

11. *Music Educators Journal* 55, no. 3 (November 1968). A number of kits and guides to elec-
tronic music are currently available, including *Electronic Music* (with pictures and leaflets, from
Keyboard Jr. Publications); *Exploring Music: Grade Six* (Holt, Rinehart, and Winston); and
Nonesuch Guide to Electronic Music (Nonesuch HC-73018, a two-record set).

12. As of April, 1980. Prices subject to change; this sample from the Moog catalog gives the
reader an idea of price ranges. Up-to-date catalogs can be obtained by writing to the individual
companies (see figure 5.4 for addresses).

13. Galen Wilson and David Cope, "An Interview with Pierre Boulez," *The Composer* 1, no. 2
(September 1969):84–85.

(a)

(b)

Figure 5.4. (a) The Moog Synthesizer
(produced by R. A. Moog Co.,
Williamsville, N.Y. 14222); (b) The
Buchla Electronic Music System
(Buchla and Associates, Box 5051,
Berkeley, Calif. 94705); (c) The ARP
Synthesizer (Tonus Inc., 45 Kenneth
St., Newton Highlands, Mass. 02161):
(d) SYNTHI 100 (London).

(c)

(d)

Figure 5.4. *Continued.*

Figure 5.5. The SYNTHI 100 of
Electronic Music Studios (London)
Limited, 277 Putney Bridge Road,

London SW 15 2 pt, England. By
permission.

Highly sophisticated studios do exist, among them the Institute of Sonology at Utrecht State University in Holland (which contains four studios, six scientific staff members, four technical staff members, and two secretaries, with computer, *classic,* "live" and DC/AC patch panels and combination availabilities);[14] the EMS studio in Putney, England (see fig. 5.5) and a host of advanced studios based at American universities, including the aforementioned Columbia-Princeton Laboratory, studios at the University of Illinois, North Texas State University, University of California at San Diego, the Cleveland Institute of Music, and many others. The RCA Mark II Synthesizer, located at the Columbia-Princeton Center since 1959, has served as the source of a large number of important compositions by Babbitt, Ussachevsky, and Luening—especially the first totally synthesized extended work, *Composition for Synthesizer* (1961) by Milton Babbitt.[15]

14. For a more detailed and complete description of the Institute of Sonology with photos and block diagrams see *Sonorum Speculum #52* (Donemus, 51 Jacob Obrechstraat, Amsterdam, Netherlands).

15. Unlike the *analog* synthesizers previously mentioned, the RCA Mark II uses punched paper tape relatively the size of a player-piano roll instead of a keyboard. Though computer-like in appearance (with the *digital* input), the Mark II is not a computer: for computer information see the next chapter.

The last fifteen years or so have seen an increasing interest among educators in creating small electronic laboratories or "tape manipulation centers." Small studios, relatively inexpensive and designed primarily for classroom use, have been developed by Ionic Industries of Morristown, New Jersey (the Putney, VCS 3), and Electronic Music Laboratory, Inc. of Vernon, Connecticut (the "ElectroComp," EML-101) to help meet the increasing demand of music educators for equipment to implement their need to fulfill the blossoming student interest in experimental music. Each year new instruments in this category are put on the market: these include the Moog *Sonic VI* and *Mini-Moog*, the Buchla *Music Easel*, the ARP *2600*, and numerous others.

Other Developments

Experiments in 1940 by Norman McLaren with film sound tracks (especially dots and loops) have created a unique and less expensive approach to electronic "notation." By cutting notches in the film, and by scratching and painting on the sound track portion of the film, McLaren produced a wide variety of "electronic" sounds from the projector (the performer). Lejaren Hiller who with Leonard Isaacson wrote *Experimental Music* (McGraw-Hill, 1959), describes situations in which the composer, with a pen filled with magnetic dyes, could sit at his desk and compose on unmagnetized tape without the aid of any electronic equipment, excepting a tape recorder for experimentation and synchronization.

The major body of electronic music has come into existence within the past thirty years. Prior to 1954 composers were primarily interested in experimentation, personal technical understanding, research and upgrading of the physical conditions of their equipment and materials.

Notable Composers and Works

One of the most popular of early tape pieces, Stockhausen's *Gesang der Jünglinge* (1955–56), combines singing with electronically produced sounds. *Musique concrète* manipulation produces variable comprehensibility of the text (Daniel 3, "Song of the Men in the Fiery Furnace"). The score calls for five groups of loudspeakers to surround the audience. Stockhausen uses the spatial direction and movement of the sounds to create form, avoiding the traditional melodic or timbre repetitions.

Stockhausen's numerous other electronic works, especially *Kontakte* (1960), *Telemusik* (1966), and *Hymnen* (1969)—the latter a collage of electronically altered hymns and *concrète* sounds—has made him one of the most widely known of Europe's electronic composers.

Figure 5.6. Karlheinz Stockhausen. (Copyright: Werner Scholz.)

Luciano Berio's *Thema: Omaggio à Joyce* (1958) uses the human voice (completely *concrète*) first recognizably and then slowly transformed into a fantastic array of sounds (by means of splicing and tape speed variation) exploring an absolute minimum of materials. His *Visage* is a "classic" of electronic music (1961); an imaginative vocal-electronic treatment in a strikingly dramatic form (originally composed as a radio program). A voice (Cathy Berberian) speaks only one word (*parole:* Italian for "words"), but through intense crying, whispering, laughing, etc. evokes an emotional gamut virtually without peer in the history of music.

John Cage was among the first of the Americans to employ tape techniques. His *Imaginary Landscape No. 5* (1951–52) uses a prepared score for making a recording on tape. All of Cage's works must, however, be studied in the light of his *indeterminate concepts* of musical technique (see chap. 9) and as such must be considered for the most part a cooperative effort between himself and the performer. Therefore, the bulk of his electronic music is found scattered throughout this entire book, especially under the subject headings of chapters 9 and 10.

A large percentage of Vladimir Ussachevsky's early works (from 1951 to 1954), including *Sonic Contours, Transposition, Reverberation,* and *Composition* (all on Folkways FX 6160), were experiments only, principally based on sounds of piano and flute. His *A Piece for Tape Recorder* (1955) is less of an experiment, yet obvious enough in construction to serve well as a good educational or introductory tool in electronic music. His long-time associates Otto Luening and Milton Babbitt have produced, especially at the Columbia-Princeton Electronic Music Center, a large number of works, particularly tape in combination with live instruments. Ussachevsky's *Of Wood and Brass* (1965)

Figure 5.7. Vladimir Ussachevsky. BMI Archives. Used by permission.

is a unique work employing tape loops of varying lengths (on which are recorded *concrète* sounds "of wood and brass") fed through a ring modulator (which collects the sidebands and nullifies the original inputs, creating neo-electronic effects). This and others of Ussachevsky's later works are highly sophisticated examples of electronic music—quite individualistic and advanced in comparison with the early embryonic years.

Mario Davidovsky's *Study No. II* (1966) for tape is a truly incredible creation in that each of the extremely quick-moving electronic sounds were

Figure 5.8. Mario Davidovsky.

placed in order by splicing (*classic* electronic music). The straight-forward ABA form and the use of more or less "pure" electronic material (sine and square waves) marks another unusual feature of this work. The "limitless possibilities" are almost completely unexplored and, except for the obvious performance limitations, one could easily imagine the work as a string quartet.

More recently, Morton Subotnick (one of the founders of the San Francisco Tape Center) achieved much success with *Silver Apples of the Moon* (1967), commissioned to fit the two sides of an LP recording (Nonesuch H-71174), and *The Wild Bull* (1968; Nonesuch 71208). Both works employ contrasts in texture and timbre as organizational principles, and the composer has distinctly abandoned the "pure" electronic sounds (e.g., sine waves, traditionally the most "hostile" of the new materials) for more instrumental- and natural-like sounds. More recent works (in the '70s) in this genre by Subotnick include *Touch* (Columbia MS-7316), *Sidewinder* (Columbia M-30683), and *4 Butterflies* (Columbia M-32741).

Milton Babbitt's *Ensembles for Synthesizer* (1961–63) concentrates on compact rhythmic textures and formal aspects of the tape medium avoiding timbral displays. Charles Wuorinen's *Time's Encomium* (1968–69), also realized on the RCA Mark II Synthesizer at the Columbia-Princeton Center, evidences instrumental style in both its clear composer control (often twelvetone) and its extremely complicated rhythmic passages. The work contrasts what the composer calls "synthesized sound" (clarity of pitch) with "processed synthesized sound" (i.e., utilizing reverberation).

Figure 5.9. Milton Babbitt. By permission.

Figure 5.10. Charles Wuorinen.

A number of "rock" groups have employed electronic sound materials in their music. The Beatles (especially in *Sgt. Pepper's Lonely Hearts Club Band,* Capitol MAS-2653), Jimi Hendrix Experience (Reprise 6261), and The United States of America (Columbia CS-9614) used electronically produced or altered sound but, for the most part, these were only experiments, exploiting such sounds for shock or text emphasis rather than actual musical development. More recently, however, "rock" and "pop" groups have used portable synthesizers and various effects modules as standard instruments of their ensembles. Notable among these groups are The Grateful Dead ("Dark Star"), Soft Machine ("Joy of a Toy"), Mothers of Invention ("Penguin in Bondage"), Todd Rundgren ("Born to Synthesize"), King Crimson ("Pictures of a City"), Yes ("Close to the Edge"), Weather Report ("Nubian Sundance"), Tangerine Dream ("Rubycon"), and Frank Zappa ("Roxy and Elsewhere," "Lumpy Gravy," and "Uncle Meat"). The Who's Pete Townshend employs feedback effectively in "My Generation", a work which was quite influential in the creation of "punk rock." Devo (described by *Rolling Stone* as "a group of Captain Beefheart-influenced dadaists") includes massive electronic instrumentation. Even the singers' voices are continually modified by electronic devices. As rock enters the '80's it is difficult to find a group not "plugged-in" in some way. Most groups have an entourage of "roadies" who man mixer consoles that feed giant sets of speakers with electronically created, modified or amplified sound.

Walter Carlos (now known as Wendy Carlos), on the other hand, developed electronic "orchestrations" of works by Bach (e.g., *Switched-on Bach* and *"The Well-Tempered Synthesizer"*) which represent an interesting application of the Moog instrument. These works demonstrate levels of speed and accuracy far beyond human capability. Isao Tomita's realizations of Stravinsky's *Firebird,* Holst's *Planets* and Mussorgsky's *Pictures at an Exhibition* demonstrate the synthesizer's ability both to imitate acoustic timbres as well as to orchestrate quasi-real sounds in novel and striking ways. These records have provided the stimulus for some of the ever-increasing manifestations of the popularity of electronic sounds among the general public.[16]

Electronic music has also flourished in Latin America with composers working in a variety of private and institutional studios. Important composers represented on recording include Joaquin Orellana (b. Guatemala, 1939; particularly *Humanofonía I,* 1971); Oscar Bazán (b. Argentina, 1936; particularly *Parca,* 1974); Jacqueline Nova, (b., Belgium, 1936, d., Columbia, 1975; especially *Creación de la Tierra,* 1972); and Graciela Paraskevaidís (b. Buenos Aires, 1940; especially *Huauqui,* 1975); and Coriún Aharonián (b. Montevideo, 1940; particularly *Homenaje a la Flecha Clavada en el Pecho de Don Juan Díaz de Solís,* 1975).

Tape and . . .

The obvious loss (to the audience) of more or less theatrical or visual activity during performance of works on tape has inspired three alternatives: (1) combination of live performer with tape; (2) live electronic music: from the Syn-Ket (a complex, compact live electronic instrument invented and developed by Paul Ketoff in 1963) to extremely complex situations involving recording and playback in numerous arrangements in concert, and performers or audience intercepting light beams to set off oscillators; (3) tape used in conjunction with projections and/or theatrical events. In fact, as will be discussed in a later chapter, the need for auxiliary action in electronic music performance played a large part in the need for developing mixed-media presentations.

Works for live performer(s) and tape have been popular over the past few decades. Henri Pousseur (b. 1929), for example, in *Rimes pour Différentes Sources Sonores* (1959), treats orchestra and tape as antiphonal bodies, contrasting the available materials of each. The speakers are placed on stage, in "live" performance, in such a way as to visually accentuate the contrast. Otto Luening (b. 1900) and Vladimir Ussachevsky, who worked together on *Rhapsodic Variations for Tape Recorder and Orchestra* (1954), were among the

16. For a listing of these, see under "Electronic Music" in the Schwann Catalog.

Figure 5.11. John Eaton playing the Synket. Photo used by permission.

Figure 5.12. Otto Luening. By permission of the composer.

first to realize and experiment with live and prerecorded sound sources in America. Bruno Maderna (in *Musica su due Dimensioni*) began studies in this area in 1952 at the NW German Radio in Cologne. These early examples extended the contrast possibilities of live and recorded sources.

One of the most dynamic works written for tape and orchestra is *Collages* (Symphony No. 3) by Roberto Gerhard (1960). This large seven-section work employs a *concrète*/electronic tape (not unlike that used by Varèse in *Déserts*) contrasting a dramatically pointillistic orchestral score.

Mario Davidovsky has composed a number of *Synchronisms* for a variety of traditional instruments and tape. The first, third, and sixth of these are for solo instruments and tape (flute, 'cello, and piano respectively, the latter winning a Pulitzer Prize). These intense compositions require a great deal of "synchronized" rhythmic interchange from "live" to recorded source (all the *Synchronisms* are recorded; see chapter Bibliography for record numbers).

Kenneth Gaburo's 1962 work *Antiphony III (Pearl-white Moments)* combines sixteen soloists in four groups performing live with tape (through two speaker systems), incorporating antiphonal interplay between live and tape sounds (both acoustically and visually). *Antiphony III's* tape materials include both purely electronic sound sources and those more imitative of the live performers, expanding the echo and reiterative effects inherently restricted in totally live performances.

Donald Erb (b. 1927), in *In No Strange Land* (1968) for trombone, double bass, and tape, reflects more complementary possibilities of electronic and instrumental sounds. Imitative techniques involve instruments in neoelectronic sound effects, thus minimizing the musical and sonic disparities between electronic and instrumental materials. Composers like Robert Erickson have used prerecorded instrumental sounds with live performance. In *Ricercar à 3* (1967), Erickson (b. 1917) employs two prerecorded contrabasses with one live contrabass, allowing the performer to play with and against the tape (a source of unusual combinative effects).

David Cope's *Arena,* 1974 ('cello and tape), is a *classical* studio composition which reflects both a dialogue between live instrument and tape, and contrasting cohesion. Figure 5.13 shows a passage in which the tape "takes over" each pitch begun by the 'cello, in turn creating vertical sonorities from the horizontal line. The rhythm and pitch of the 'cello must be precisely in "sync" for the passage to work (including the quarter-tone inflection indicated by the arrows attached to the accidentals). The bottom staff reflects more interplay—the harmonics on the tape are only symbolically represented—answered by the artificial harmonics on the 'cello. This score reflects the often necessary, exact, and graphic notations used by composers for tape with "live" instruments.

Figure 5.13. David Cope: *Arena* ('cello and tape), page 7. (c) Copyright 1974 by David Cope. All rights reserved.

Figure 5.13. *Continued.*

Richard Felciano has written many works for a wide variety of combinations of traditional instruments and tape. *God of the Expanding Universe* and *Litany* are excellent examples of works for organ and tape. His *Crasis* and *Lamentations for Jani Christou* represent examples of chamber music with tape.

John Watts' *WARP* (1972) includes ARP-created electronic sounds on tape with brass quintet. The four-channel quadraphonic speaker setup heightens both the balance and the effective humor and drama of this work. Combinations of large ensembles with tape occupy an increasing bulk of current tape music composition. Works for tape and band include Donald Erb's *Reticulation* (1965), and Herbert Bielawa's *Spectrum*. Vladimir Ussachevsky's *Creation-Prologue* (1961) is for tape and choir.[17]

17. For a more complete listing, see *Music Educators Journal* 55, no. 3 (November 1968):73. Also consult publishers' listings.

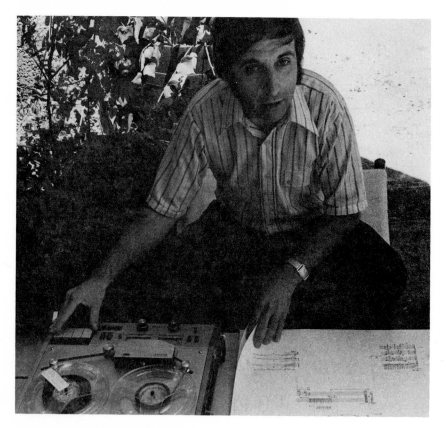

Figure 5.14. Richard Felciano. Photo
(c) Michelle Vignes. By permission.

John Eaton combines the compact "live performance" *Syn-Ket* and full orchestra in his *Concert Piece for Synket and Symphony Orchestra,* effectively utilizing visual "concerto" performance techniques with specially designed electronic equipment. Merrill Ellis includes soprano, live synthesizer, and orchestra in his *Kaleidoscope.* These last two works concentrate on the "live" performability of synthesizers or *live electronic music.*

Live Electronic Music

John Cage (b. 1912) was the first to employ entirely live electronic techniques in his *Imaginary Landscape No. 4* (c. 1949, first performed in 1951) in which twelve radios are performed by two performers each (twenty-four performers in all). His *Imaginary Landscape No. 1* (1939) uses recordings of constant and variable pitch frequencies in combination with more conventional percussion instruments.

In *Reconnaissance* (1967) Donald Erb employs a Moog synthesizer performed live with a group of other live instrumentalists (viola, piano, bass, percussion), achieving both the visual complement of "live" performance and the available sonic resources of electronic equipment. The work also utilizes a Moog polyphonic instrument (live, also): a keyboard instrument of four octaves (each divided into forty-three tones) capable of producing polyphony in a live performance situation (the synthesizer in use here can only produce chords of the same ratio in live performance).

A number of groups dedicated to the live performance of electronic music (most now disbanded) were formed in the '60's: The Sonic Arts Union (formed in 1966), with Gordon Mumma, Robert Ashley, Alvin Lucier, and David Behrman; *Musica Elettronica Viva* (1967, in Italy), with Frederic Rzewski, Allan Bryant, and Alvin Curran; the Once Group (Michigan), with Robert Ashley, Gordon Mumma, and others. Festivals of live electronic music at Davis, California (1967), Buffalo (1968), and Los Angeles (1968 and 1969), among others, have proved this concept of lasting significance. A live electronics group "It takes a year one earth to go around the sun," formed in 1970 by David Rosenboom (originator and director of New York's Electric Circus until 1969), with Jon Hassell, Gerald Shapiro, and Terry Riley, spent the summer of that year performing on electronic instruments designed by the members themselves, on "mesas in Wyoming, ghost towns in Death Valley, and lava caves in New Mexico." The works performed (by the composer/performers) are extremely loose in construction, serving as "launching pads" for the performers' rehearsed interplay.

Figure 5.15. Alvin Lucier. Photo by Mary Lucier.

Alvin Lucier's *North American Time Capsule 1967* involves a vocoder (Sylvania design), an instrument designed to encode speech sounds into digital information. The speech of the performers (coded material) acts as the electronic source material in "live" performance. Gordon Mumma's *Mesa* (1966) uses electronic sound modification as well. He uses a Bandoneon (an accordion-like instrument) instead of voices. Work with tape-delay techniques (in effect, echoes and canon) have been used in live performance by Pauline Oliveros (*I of IV*, 1966, and *Lightpiece for David Tudor*, 1965).[18] By separation of record and playback heads and cross-coupling, a large number of reiterative compositional techniques can be employed.

Several composers in the sixties explored the possibilities of interactive electro-acoustical, process-oriented composition. Representative works from the activity of this time include David Behrman's *Wavetrain* (1964), John Cage's *Variations V* (1965), Gordon Mumma's *Hornpipe* (1967), and Alvin Lucier's *Queen of the South* (1972). Behrman's *Wavetrain* involves the acoustical resonances of chordophones (typically grand pianos or zithers). Cage's *Variations V* uses the movements of dancers on the stage translated by photoelectric cells and capacitance sensors into electronic articulations for the accompanying sound. Lucier's *Queen of the South* (which is discussed in chapter 4), employs large plate surfaces, which are resonated with special loudspeakerlike transducers.

Mumma's *Hornpipe* is described in detail by the composer himself:

Hornpipe is an interactive live-electronic work for solo hornist, cybersonic[19] console, and a performance space. The hornist performs with various techniques on a valveless waldhorn and a standard "French horn." These techniques include a traditional embouchure, and the production of multiphonics with special double-reeds.

The cybersonic console, attached to the hornist's belt, has microphones with which it "hears" the sounds made by the hornist and the acoustical resonances of the space. The electronic circuitry of the console analyzes the acoustical resonances of the space, and responds interactively with the hornist. The console is connected by an umbilical cable to a stereophonic sound system, so that its responses are heard from loudspeakers. (See fig. 5.16.)

The cybersonic console has several functions. First, it makes an electronic map of the acoustical resonances of the space. This is achieved during the first few minutes of the performance by eight electronically resonant circuits that become automatically tuned to the acoustical resonances of the space. Second, each circuit has a memory that accumulates information about its resonant condition.

---

18. See Pauline Oliveros, "Tape Delay Techniques for Electronic Music Composition," *The Composer* 1, no. 3 (December 1969): 135–42.

19. A term coined by Mumma; refers to sound-control procedures in which the controls are automatically derived from the sounds being controlled.

Figure 5.16. Gordon Mumma
performing *Hornpipe* (1967). Photo by
Narrye Caldwell, 1974.

Technically, this condition is determined from the frequency (f) and the resonant efficiency (Q) of the circuit. (See fig. 5.17.) Third, when sufficient information is obtained, a VCA (voltage controlled amplifier) for each circuit is gated on, sending its electronically resonant response through the umbilical to the loudspeakers. Because each of the eight resonant circuits is somewhat independent, and has different memory and gating characteristics, these responses can occur in many different combinations.

A performance of *Hornpipe* begins as a solo, without electronic sound. When the responses of the cybersonic console are heard from the loudspeakers, the hornist can then interact with the electronic map of the cybersonic console. By playing sounds which reinforce the electronic map, the hornist can increase the responses of the

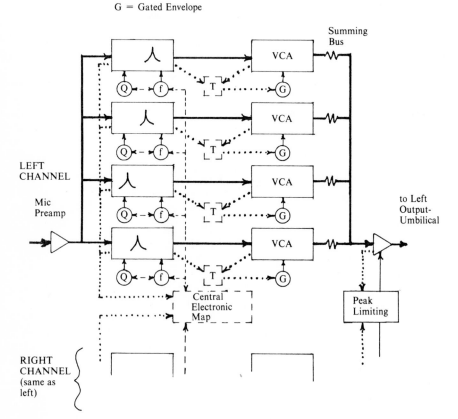

Figure 5.17. Functional diagram,
Gordon Mumma's *Hornpipe* (1967).

cybersonic console. By playing sounds which are anti-resonant (opposed) to the resonances of the electronic map, the hornist can decrease the responses of the cybersonic console.

The performer's choice of anti-resonant sounds strongly influences the continuity of a performance. Without the reinforcement of its original electronic map, the cybersonic console gradually makes a new map representing the hornist's anti-resonant sounds. In other words, having interacted with the responses of the cybersonic console, and learned the electronic map of the acoustical resonances of the space, the hornist can choose sounds which deceive the console into thinking it is in a different performance space. After the cybersonic console has developed a new map (of the hornist's anti-resonant sounds), it no longer responds to the natural acoustical resonances of the space. The performance of Hornpipe has evolved from an introductory solo, through an ensemble between hornist, cybersonic console and performance space, to a concluding solo section for horn.[20]

The score to Allen Strange's *Music of DOD* (1977), for virtuoso instrument and one player, lays out the design for an electronic instrument with a short performance note regarding dissonance and resolution (see fig. 5.18).

Notation

The notation of electronic music is complicated by U.S. Public Law 92–140 which makes it possible to copyright certain sound recordings if published with the notice after Feb. 15, 1972 (note that tapes, as of the late '70s, can now be copyrighted). At the same time this does not really solve the problem of unpublished tape compositions. Composers have reacted to these problems in a variety of ways.

Figure 5.19 is from Stockhausen's *Studie II* (1956, Universal Edition). The lower portion indicates dynamics (envelope). The upper portion denotes pitch (100 to 17,200 Hertz, or cycles per second) based on a scale of 81 steps "equal-tempered" at a constant interval ratio of $\sqrt[25]{5}$ (piano at $\sqrt[5]{2}$) and timbre. The middle portion indicates centimeters of tape at 76.2 centimeters per second. This score represents less than seven seconds of performing time.

Another reason for electronic notation is that of synchronization in tape and traditional instrument performances (see fig. 5.13, David Cope's *Arena*, for example).

Notation differs in exactness and form to the same degree composers and works differ. Standardization may come when exact methods for analog to digital processes are perfected with resultant computer printouts serving as notation (see chapter 6 for more details). Paul Beaver's *Nonesuch Guide to Electronic Music* booklet indicates only the bare essentials of necessities for re-creation of sound on tape. Unusual instruments such as the *Mellotron* (a keyboard instrument with prerecorded tape loops of traditional sounds enclosed, activated by depressing the keys and producing neotraditional sounds

20. Gordon Mumma, performance notes for *Hornpipe*.

Figure 5.18. *Music of Dod* by Allen Strange (1977).

Figure 5.19. Karlheinz Stockhausen: *Studie II.* (Reprinted by permission of Universal Edition; as it appeared in the English edition of *Die Reihe* No. 1, copyright 1958 by Theodore Presser Company, Bryn Mawr, Pa.)

of violins, etc.) create just that much more confusion in the dilemma of notation.

The close association of live electronic music performance and aleatoric procedures has caused most composers to rely on graphs and diagrams as "before the fact" scores (if indeed any score or directions are used at all). The extremely complex notation necessary for exact re-creation on electronic instruments complicates possibilities of live performance.

Vectoral Analysis: Edgard Varèse: *Poème électronique*

(For information on vectoral analysis and procedures, see chapter 1.)

For background information on Varèse, see Chapter 1.

Poème électronique (1956–58) was composed at the Philips Studio at Eindhaven, having been commissioned for performance in the Philips Pavilion at the 1958 Brussels Worlds Fair. The pavilion was designed by the French

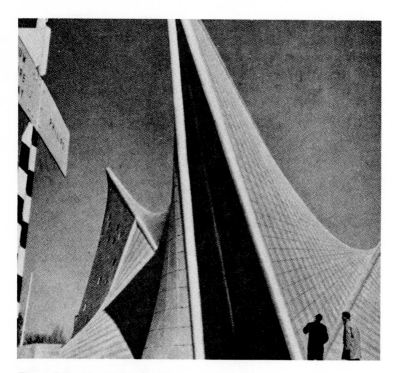

Figure 5.20. The Philips Pavilion at the Brussels Exposition (World's Fair) built by Le Corbusier where *Poème électronique* was first performed in 1958.

architect Le Corbusier (who was assisted, interestingly enough, by the then architect Iannis Xenakis, to be discussed in later chapters). The design of the pavilion included 400 or more loudspeakers, most of which were hidden in the walls or above the ceilings. David Ernst speaks of the elaborate setup:

> The taped sounds were distributed by telephone relays among various combinations of loudspeakers. These "sound paths" were determined by a fifteen channel control tape, each track of which contained twelve separate signals. Therefore, 180 (15 × 12) control signals were available to regulate the sound routes, lighting effects and a variety of light sources which consisted of film projectors and projection lanterns, spotlights, ultraviolet lamps, bulbs, and fluorescent lamps of various colors.[21]

Nearly 16,000 people per day for six months provided an audience for the performance of this work of purely taped sounds (both *musique concrète* and electronic sources). The projected images (various photographs of paintings, script, or other montages) were not synchronized with the sound in any particular manner (the projections were chosen by Le Corbusier to fit the elaborate and complex internal design of the pavilion).

2. Overview: Varèse often referred to his work as "organized sound" rather than traditional composition. Clearly *Poème électronique* is very highly organized sound. One method of analyzing electronic music visually "keys" certain sounds so that "paper" analysis becomes possible. Figure 5.21 shows one possible such "keying."

While there are obviously more than seven different sound sources and variants present in this piece, one can clearly identify the ones shown here as basic to its structure. The visual identities are drawn here to resemble in some way the aural image presented or in some cases the instruments suggested by the sounds.

Figure 5.22 shows how these symbols can be organized to represent a timeline of the piece (left-to-right, top-to-bottom). Occasional numbers within a diagram represent repetitions of a sound. Assorted "doodlings" between connections represent important but nonformal materials. When one symbol becomes an offshoot of another symbol, it represents a counterpoint, with the first stated material being more significant. Occasional reference to subjects represented by words (e.g., "low voice solo") clearly identify important characteristics that are varied in the context of the piece.

The form of the piece takes two distinct shapes. First one perceives a characteristic rondo (return) quality even on first hearing. One such interpretation is shown here above the symbols: the "inverted rondo" (here meaning that the main repeating sequence appears second rather than first). Note here that the "A" portion repeats twice (occurs three times) in the body of the work between sections of other materials (some of which, like "B," also repeat). At

21. David Ernst, *The Evolution of Electronic Music* (New York: Schirmer Books, 1977), p. 42.

= Gongs (large bells)

= Long, held tones

= Sawtooth-type noise elements

= Rising motive (2nds)

= Drums

– Rising glissandi

= Voice(s)

Figure 5.21. Key to diagrams used in figure 5.22.

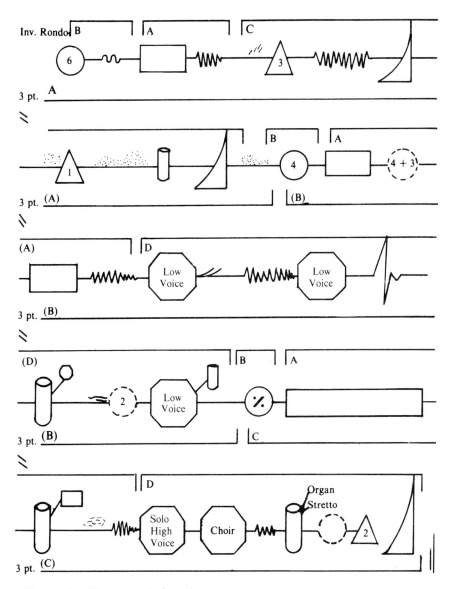

Figure 5.22. Diagrammatic formal
analysis of Varèse's *Poème électronique*.

least two other rondo possibilities exist here: one, with the opening gongs being "A" and occurring three main times with two "shadow" occurrences; and two, with the rising motive (the triangle) as the main idea (A) occurring on three different occasions.

A second possibility is shown (under the symbols) as "three-part." Here the form is defined as sectional (in three large parts), with each part beginning in nearly the same manner (i.e., gongs followed by long held notes). This separate and distinct formal possibility (from the rondo interpretation discussed above) should not be discarded even though it is less audible on first hearing.

3. Orchestration Techniques: Varèse uses two basic sound materials: *concrète* and electronic. Within each of those categories there are two main divisions: *concrète*, instrumental and vocal; electronic, sine-type tones (simple resonances) and complex (nearly noise) elements. His techniques of variation within these timbres are extremely subtle. A good example of this is the way in which he varies the initial six attacks of the gong-type motive at the beginning of the work. The sixth sound is filtered so that it sounds nearly an octave lower in pitch. The reverberation characteristic, as well as timbre of each of the bells is clearly different in the succeeding appearances of the motivic structure.

4. Basic Techniques: Most techniques presented here are a by-product of *classical* tape composition discussed earlier in this chapter. Most notable in *Poème électronique* are the tape speed changes (N. B. the solo female entrance where her range is extended beyond human potential), envelope control (cutoffs on the opening long note section, for example, show strong hints of editing executions), synchronization (e.g., the fast switching between drums and organ in the final stretto), and other techniques typical of this period of electronic composition.

5, 6. Vertical and Horizontal Models: Neither of these categories is particularly important in a work whose sonorities are determinates of chosen percussive materials. However, the final "long notes" section before the entrance of the low-voice solo clearly defines the harmonic context of the piece (near overtone intonation and of complex- upper partials-definition). The horizontal materials that most noticeably represent clear identities suggest either secondal (in seconds, minor or major) or widely leaping pointillistic diversity.

7. Style: *Poème électronique* represents an important work (along with Stockhausen's *Gesang der Jünglinge*, 1954) in the hybridization of electronic and *concrète* techniques. It is a classic studio work utilizing general rondo principles which are highly organized and defined. The recognizable sounds (jet airplane, drums, temple bells, human voices, for example) represent an interesting layer of separate identities, which, along with the often humorous "squeaks and squawks", present a dynamic and linear design not unlike the composer's instrumental works of earlier vintage.

Bibliography

*Further Readings**

Appleton, Jon, and Ronald Perera, eds. *The Development and Practice of Electronic Music.* Englewood Cliffs, N.J.: Prentice-Hall, 1974. Another in the growing list of excellent textbooks on electronic music.

Babbitt, Milton. "An Introduction to the RCA Synthesizer." *Journal of Music Theory* 8 (Winter-Spring 1964):251. Excellent survey and introduction to this instrument.

Beckwith, John, and Udo Kasemets, eds. *The Modern Composer and His World.* Toronto: University of Toronto Press, 1961. Has a group of articles and discussion (p. 109) by a number of active composers and physicists dealing with electronic music: Hugh LeCaine, Josef Tal, Vladimir Ussachevsky, among others.

Berio, Luciano. "The Studio di Fonologia Musicale of the Milan Radio." *Score* 15 (March 1956). Fascinating view of this, one of the early studios of electronic music in Europe.

Cage, John. *Silence.* Cambridge, Mass.: The M.I.T. Press, paperback edition, 1961. Provides many insights into the early experiments in electronics by this innovator in the field.

Ceely, Robert. "Thoughts about Electronic Music." *Composer* 5, no. 1 (1973): 11. A fascinating and direct view of this Boston composer.

Chavez, Carlos. *Toward a New Music: Music and Electricity.* New York: W. W. Norton, Inc., 1937. Outdated but visionary for its date (compare to Varèse and Cage predictions).

Christiansen, Louis. "A Visit to the Electronic Music Studios in Moscow." *Numus West* 5:34. Interesting look at this country's progress in the art form.

Coker, Cecil, Peter Denes, and Elliot Pinson. *Speech/Synthesis.* Farmingdale, N.Y.: Comspace Corp., 1963 (reprinted in 1970). Fascinating book on the physics of speech production and the mechanics of "reproductive" electronic instruments.

Cole, Hugo. *Sounds and Signs.* London: Oxford University Press, 1974. Has some interesting information on the notation of electronic music (p. 112).

Cope, David. "A View on Electronic Music." *db: The Sound Engineering Magazine* (August 1975). This is a broad article covering the problems currently encountered in the electronic music studio as relevant to the sound engineer.

———. "An Approach to Electronic Music Composition." *Composer* 6, no. 1 1975):14. One composer's view on the creation of electronic music.

Cott, Jonathan. *Stockhausen.* New York: Simon & Schuster, 1973. A fascinating view of the composer if one's tastes run to studies of the egocentric.

Cross, Lowell M., ed. *A Bibliography of Electronic Music.* Toronto: University of Toronto Press, 1967. A thorough source from one of the capitals of experimental music.

*Addresses for record companies, periodicals, and music publishers mentioned in this Bibliography can be found in Appendix 4.

Dallin, Leon. *Techniques of Twentieth Century Composition.* 3rd ed. Dubuque, Iowa: Wm. C. Brown Company Publishers, 1974. Has a very good section covering electronic music.

Davies, Hugh. "A Discography of Electronic Music and *Musique Concrete.*" *Recorded Sound* 14 (April 1964):205. An excellent source, though in need of updating.

Davies, Hugh, ed. *International Electronic Music Catalog.* Cambridge, Mass.: M.I.T. Press, 1968. Presents a wealth of material including an international list of electronic music studios, both public and private.

Dockstader, Tod. "Inside-Out: Electronic Rock." *Electronic Music Review* 5 (January 1968):15.

Douglas, Alan. *Electronic Music Production.* London: Pitman Publishing, 1973. An interesting book, though very much slanted towards British equipment and its usage.

———. *Electronic Music Instrument Manual.* 4th ed. London: Pitman, 1972.

Eimert, Herbert, and Karlheinz Stockhausen, eds. *Die Reihe* 1 (Theodore Presser Co., 1965; original German edition, 1955). Presents articles by the editors and Křenek, Klebe, Stuckenschmidt, Pousseur, Boulez, and Meyer-Eppler; a fascinating general text in the European middle-fifties concept of the development and structuring of electronic music.

Eimert, Herbert, F. Enkel, and Karlheinz Stockhhausen. *Problems of Electronic Music Notation.* Translated by D. A. Sinclair. Ottawa, Canada: 1956.

Electronotes (see Appendix 4). A veritable "tome" of information for the serious and knowledgeable electronic music buff.

Ellis, Merrill. "*Musique Concrète* at Home." *Music Educators Journal* 55, no. 3 (November 1968):94. Offers suggestions concerning small "tape manipulation centers."

Ernst, David. *The Evolution of Electronic Music.* New York: Schirmer Books, 1977.

Everett, Tom. "Five Questions: Forty Answers." *Composer* 3, no. 1 (1971):30. Questions dealing with electronic music with varied answers from N. K. Brown, Barney Childs, Sydney Hodkinson, Donald Martino, Richard Moryl, Pauline Oliveros, Elie Siegmeister, and John Watts.

"Four Views of the Music Department of the University of San Diego." *Synthesis* 1, no. 2 (July 1971). Diverse study of this school dedicated to new music, and of its electronic studios.

Fulkerson, James. "What Defines a Piece of Music." *Composer* 5, no. 1:15. An interview with Joel Chadabe, and good insight into new constructs and ideas for electronic music.

Griffiths, Paul. *A Concise History of Avant-Garde Music.* New York: Oxford University Press, 1978.

———. *A Guide to Electronic Music.* London: Thane & Hudson, 1979.

Judd, F. C. *Electronic Music and Musique Concrète.* London: Neville Spearman, 1961. Interesting but outdated.

———. *Electronics in Music.* London: Neville Spearman, 1972.

Kondracki, M., *et al. International Electronic Music Discography.* Mainz: B. Schott, 1979. The most current bibliography of recordings of electronic music.

Luening, Otto. "Some Random Remarks about Electronic Music." *Journal of Music Theory* 8 (Winter-Spring 1964).

———. "An Unfinished History of Electronic Music." *Music Educators Journal* 55 (November 1968):35. Superb study of the long history of electronic music.

———. *The Odyssey of An American Composer: The Autobiography of Otto Luening.* New York: C. F. Peters, 1981.

"The Many Worlds of Music." *BMI.* (Summer 1970). Entire issue devoted to electronic music, with an excellent discography by Peter Frank and articles by Carter Harman and Louis Chapin.

Mellotron: information available from Dallas Music Industries, 301 Island Rd., Mahwah, N.J. 07430.

Meyer, Robert G. "Technical Basis of Electronic Music." *Journal of Music Theory* 8. An interesting, mathematical and electronically oriented introduction (in four parts) to the basic mechanics of electronic sound production for those interested in their scientific foundation.

Nyman, Michael. *Experimental Music.* London: Studio Vista, 1974. Fascinating accounts of some provocative experiments with electronics as well as other avant-garde gadgetry.

Oliveros, Pauline. "Tape Delay Techniques for Electronic Music." *Composer* 1, no. 3 (1969), 135. Excellent source of information on "live" performance possibilities of electronic music.

Olsen, Harry F. *Music, Physics and Engineering.* New York: Dover, 1967. Short on electronic music but quite long on extremely important facts pertaining to acoustics, makeup, operation of instruments, etc.

Oram, Daphne. *An Individual Note.* London: Galliard Ltd., 1972. Most provocative, even bizarre book on "Oramics equipment" for electronic synthesis which, despite the "Cagean" writing, is far more significant than it at first appears.

Pousseur, Henri. "Calculation and Imagination in Electronic Music." *Electronic Music Review* 5 (January 1968):21.

Prieberg, F. K. *Musica ex Machina.* Berlin: Verlag Ullstein, 1960. Written in German; a truly classic history of electronic music.

Rossi, Nick, and Robert Choate, eds. *Music of Our Time.* Boston: Crescendo Publishing Co., 1969. Has a number of excellent studies of composers involved in the electronic medium (biographical as well as informative for study of works): Stockhausen, p. 181; Ussachevsky, p. 326; Babbitt, p. 348; Subotnick and Wuorinen, p. 380.

Russcol, Herbert. *The Liberation of Sound.* Englewood Cliffs, N.J.: Prentice-Hall, 1972. Good book on electronic music but suffers from erratic organization.

Schaeffer, Pierre. *A la Recherche d'une Musique Concrète.* Paris: Editions du Seuil, 1952. Valuable and incredibly fascinating study of Schaeffer's early work in *musique concrète.*

Schwartz, Elliott. *Electronic Music: A Listener's Guide.* New York: Praeger Publishers, 1972. Fine book on the subject with accurate materials on all aspects of the art from live electronic to computer sources.

"Setting Up Your Moog Synthesizer." Issued by Moog Music (P.O. Box 131, Academy St., Williamsville, N.Y. 14221) and valuable to those interested in this equipment.

Stockhausen, Karlheinz. "The Concept of Unity in Electronic Music." In *Perspectives on Contemporary Music Theory.* Edited by Benjamin Boretz and Edward T. Cone. New York: W. W. Norton & Co., 1972. Excellent article on this subject but a bit egocentric in relating to the author-composer's own works.

———. "Mikrophonie I and II." *Melos* 33:144. Fascinating and revealing study of these works by the composer himself.

Strange, Allen. *Electronic Music,* 2nd edition. Dubuque, Iowa: Wm. C. Brown Company Publishers, 1982. Fine textbook for use in electronic music classes. Introduction by Gordon Mumma.

———. "Tape Piece." *Composer* 2, no. 1 (1970):12. Explains correct care and use of the most important element of electronic music: the tape itself.

178   *Electronic Music*

Stroh, W. M. *Zur Soziologie der elektronischen Musik.* Zurich: Amadeus, 1980.
Trythall, Gilbert. *Electronic Music.* New York: Grosset & Dunlap, 1973. Brief but very good textbook on the subject.
Ussachevsky, Vladimir. "Notes on a Piece for Tape Recorder." In *Problems of Modern Music.* Edited by Paul Henry Lang. New York: W. W. Norton & Co., 1960. Excellent personal analysis of this historic work by its composer.
———. "Sound Materials in the Experimental Media of *Musique Concrète,* Tape Music and Electronic Music." *Journal of the Acoustical Society of America* 29:768. Quite interesting and informative.
de la Vega, Aurelio. "Electronic Music, Tool of Creativity." *Music Journal* 23 (September, October, November 1965). A defensive and more philosophical reflection on electronic music in general.
Vercoe, Barry. "Electronic Sounds and the Sensitive Performer." *Music Educators Journal* 55, no. 3 (November 1968).
Vinton, John, ed. *Dictionary of Contemporary Music.* New York: E. P. Dutton, & Co., 1974. See in particular the following, dealing with electronic music: "Apparatus and Technology," p. 205; "History and Development," p. 212; "Notation," p. 216. Volume also contains biographies of a great many of the composers listed in this chapter.
Weilland, Fritz. "The Institute of Sonology at Utrecht State University." *Sonorum Speculum.* A fascinating article on what is possibly one of the world's finest electronic laboratories.
Weinland, John David. "An Electronic Music Primer," *Journal of Music Theory* 13, no. 1 (1969).
Wells, Thomas, and Eric Vogel. *The Technique of Electronic Music.* Austin, Tex.: University Stores, 1974.
Wörner, Karl. *Stockhausen, Life and Work.* Translated by Bill Hopkins. Berkeley: University of California Press, 1973. A good view of this composer's work to date, but like Cott's book, a bit premature in its gamble on this composer's automatic "greatness."

Recordings and Publishers*

Albright, William. *Organbook II.* Jobert. Recorded on Nonesuch 71260. Uses organ and tape.
AMM "live electronic" improvisation group is featured on Mainstream's 5002, which also has the Musica Elettronica Viva.
Anderson, Ruth. *Points* (1973–4). Recorded on 1750 Arch Records S-1765. Realized at the Hunter College Electronic Studio.
Ashley, Robert. *Purposeful Lady, Slow Afternoon* (1968). Recorded on Mainstream 5010. This nearly pornographic "lady" highlights a collection of works performed by the Sonic Arts Union, including works by David Behrman, Alvin Lucier, and Gordon Mumma.
Babbitt, Milton. *Composition for Synthesizer* (1963). Columbia MS-6566.
———. *Ensemble for Synthesizer* (1967). Recorded on Columbia MS-7051.
Beerman, Burton. *Sensations for Clarinet and Tape.* ACA. Recorded on Advance Recordings FGR 15S.

*Addresses for record companies, periodicals, and music publishers mentioned in this Bibliography can be found in Appendix 4.

Berio, Luciano. *Thema: Omaggio à Joyce* (1959). Zerboni Editions. Recorded on Turnabout 34177.
———. *Visage* (1961). Turnabout 34046.
Beyer, Johanna. *Music of the Spheres* (1938). Recorded on 1750 Arch Records S-1765. Excellent example of early electronic music.
Bielawa, Herbert. *Spectrum.* Recorded by Cornell University Wind Ensemble, CUWE-1.
Blacher, Boris. *Electronic Impulses.* Recorded on Mace S-9097.
Bolcom, William. *Black Host* (1967). Recorded on Nonesuch 71260.
Borden, David. *Variations on America by Charles Ives* (1970). Recorded by Cornell Wind Ensemble, CUWE 7. For tape and wind ensemble.
Cage, John. *Aria with Fontana Mix* (1958). Recorded on Mainstream 5005.
———. *Imaginary Landscape No. 4.* C. F. Peters.
———. *Imaginary Landscape No. 5.* C. F. Peters.
———. *Variations IV* (continuation). Recorded on Everest 3230.
Ceely, Robert. *Elegia.* Recorded on CRI SD-328.
Chadabe, Joel. *Street Scene* (1967), and *Daisy.* Recorded on Opus One 16.
Cope, David. *Arena.* Carl Fischer. Recorded on Orion ORS-75169. For cello and tape.
———. *K.* and *Weeds* (1971). Recorded on Discant 1297.
Davidovsky, Mario. *Synchronisms 1, 2 and 3.* Edward B. Marks Corp. Recorded on CRI S-204.
———. *Synchronisms 4, 5, and 6.* Edward B. Marks Corp. Recorded on Turnabout 34487.
———. *Electronic Study No. 3.* Recorded on Finnadar 9010. This is an early masterwork by a *classic* electronic composer.
de la Vega, Aurelio. *Inflorescencia* (1976). This is a "lyric" work scored for soprano, bass clarinet and pre-recorded sounds. On Orion ORS 78302.
Dockstader, Tod. *Quartermass* (1964), and other works. Recorded on Owl Records 6, 7 and 8.
Druckman, Jacob. *Animus II* (1969). MCA Music. Recorded on CRI S-255. For mezzo soprano, two percussionists, and tape.
———. *Animus III* (1969). MCA Music. Recorded on Nonesuch 71253. For clarinet and tape.
Duckworth, William. *Gambit* (1967). Recorded on Capra 1210. For tape and percussion.
Eaton, John. *Concert Piece for Synket and Orchestra.* Recorded on Turnabout 34428.
Ellis, Merrill. *Kaleidoscope.* Recorded on Louisville S-711.
Erb, Donald. *In No Strange Land.* Merion Music. Recorded on Nonesuch 71223.
———. *Reconnaissance.* Recorded on Nonesuch 71223.
———. *Reticulation.* Merion Music.
Felciano, Richard. *God of the Expanding Universe.* E. C. Schirmer.
———. *Litany.* E. C. Schirmer.
———. *Crasis.* E. C. Schirmer.
———. *Lamentations for Jani Christou.* E. C. Schirmer.
Gaburo, Kenneth. *Antiphony III (Pearl White Moments).* Recorded on Nonesuch 71199.
Gerhard, Roberto. *Collages (Symphony #3).* Recorded on Angel S-36558.
Henry, Pierre. *Apocalypse de Jean.* Recorded on Philips 6521 002. By a master of *musique concrète.*
Henry, Pierre, and Pierre Schaeffer. *Symphonie pour un Homme. Seul.* Recorded on Philips 6510 012. Two giants of early electronic music presented at their best.

Hiller, Lejaren. *Machine Music* (1964). Presser. Recorded on Turnabout 34536. For piano, percussion, and tape.

———. *Malta* (for tuba and tape, 1975). Recorded on CAPRA Records 1206.

Ichiyanagi, Toshi. *Life Music* (for tape and orchestra, 1966). Varèse/Sarabande 81060.

Kagel, Mauricio. *Acoustica* (1970). Recorded on DG-2707059. For experimental sound generators and loudspeakers.

Korte, Karl. *Remembrances*. Recorded on Nonesuch 71289. For flute and tape.

Kupferman, Meyer. *Superflute*. Recorded on Nonesuch 71289.

Ligeti, György. *Articulation* (1958). Recorded on Wergo 60059.

Lockwood, Annea. *World Rhythms* (1975). Recorded on 1750 Arch Records S-1765. Realized at the Hunter College Electronic Music Studios.

Lucier, Alvin. *North American Time Capsule* (1967). Recorded on Odyssey 32-160156.

———. *Vespers* (1968). Recorded on Mainstream Records 5010.

Luening, Otto. *Synthesis* (1960). Peters. Recorded on CRI S-219. For orchestra and tape.

MacInnis, Donald. *Collide-a-Scope* (1968). Recorded on Golden Crest S-4085. For twelve brass instruments and tape.

Marshall, Ingram. *Fragility Cycle*. Recorded on IBU Records. Live electronic music with voice and other instruments.

McLean, Barton. *Genesis*. Recorded on Orion ORS 75192. This album also contains two other electronic works by this composer: *The Sorcerer Revisited* and *Dimensions II* (the latter for piano and tape).

———. *Song of the Nahuatl*. Recorded on Folkways FTS 33450. A graphic score was also made of this piece (part of which appears on the cover of *Composer Magazine* 10, no. 1, 1980).

McLean, Priscilla. *Dance of Dawn*. Recorded on CRI SD 335. This album also contains an electronic work by her composer husband Barton McLean: *Spirals*.

———. *Invisible Chariots*. Recorded on Folkways Records FTS 33450.

Miller, Edward. *Piece for Clarinet and Tape* (1967). Recorded on Advance FGR 17S.

Mimaroglu, Ilhan. WINGS *of the Delirious Demon*, and other works. Recorded on Finnadar 9001.

Mother Mallard's Portable Masterpiece Company. Music for 5 synthesizers with music by David Borden and Steve Drews. Recorded on Earthquack EQ 001 and 002.

Mumma, Gordon. *Mesa* (1966). Recorded on Odyssey 32-160158.

———. *Hornpipe*. Recorded on Mainstream 5010.

———. *Megaton for Wm. Burroughs*. Recorded on Lovely Music LML/VR-1091.

Nonesuch Guide to Electronic Music. Recorded on Nonesuch HC-73018.

Oliveros, Pauline. *I of IV* (1966). Recorded on Odyssey 32-160160.

———. *Bye Bye Butterfly*. Recorded on 1750 Arch Records S-1765. A classic tape composition made in 1965 at the San Francisco Tape Center.

Souster, Tim. *Spectral* (viola/tape delay/live electronics), (1972). Recorded on Transatlantic Records TRAG 343.

Stockhausen, Karlheinz. *Gesang der Jünglinge*. Recorded on DG-138811.

———. *Hymnen*. Universal Edition. Recorded on DG-2707039.

———. *Kontakte*. Universal Edition. Recorded on DG-138811.

———. *Telemusik*. Universal Edition. Recorded on DG-137012.

Strange, Allen. *Two x Two* (1968). Recorded on Capra 1210.

Subotnick, Morton. *4 Butterflies.* Recorded on Columbia M-32741. One of his major "music box" works written for a record.
————. *Sidewinder.* Recorded on Columbia M-30683.
————. *Silver Apples of the Moon.* Recorded on Nonesuch 71174.
————. *The Wild Bull.* Recorded on Nonesuch 71208.
Taylor, Dub. *Lumière.* Recorded on Varèse 81001. For synthesized and *concrète* sounds.
Thome, Diane. *Anäis* (for piano, 'cello and tape, 1976). CRI S-437.
Ussachevsky, Vladimir. *Creation-Prologue.* Recorded on Columbia MS-6566.
————. *A Piece for Tape Recorder.* Recorded on CRI-122.
————. *Of Wood and Brass.* Recorded on CRI S-227.
———— and Otto Luening. *Concerted Piece for Tape Recorder and Orchestra.* Recorded on CRI 227-SD. A masterwork of early work for tape and orchestra.
————. *A Poem in Cycles and Bells for Tape Recorder and Orchestra* (1954). One of the first (and most well known) works for this combination.
Varèse, Edgard. *Poème électronique.* Recorded on Columbia MS-6146.
————. *Déserts.* Published by G. Schirmer and recorded on Angel S-36786.
Wilson, Galen. *Applications.* Recorded on Capra 1201.
Wilson, George Blach. *Exigencies.* Recorded on CRI S-271.
Wuorinen, Charles. *Times Encomium* (1969). Recorded on Nonesuch 71225.
Xenakis, Iannis. His electronic music is featured on Nonesuch 71246.

Folkways 6301 and 33436 include collections of a variety of electronic music. Folkways FX 6160 contains some early electronic experiments including Ussachevsky's *Sonic Contours, Transposition, Reverberation,* and *Composition,* and Otto Luening's *Fantasy in Space.* Luening's and Ussachevsky's *Concerted Piece for Tape Recorder and Orchestra,* made at the Columbia-Princeton Music Center, is available on CRI S-227-SD, along with works by Mel Powell, and another Ussachevsky work.

Milton Babbitt's *Vision and Prayer* (1961) for soprano and tape (AMP) is part of CRI-268, a large two-disc collection, which includes also Varèse's *Déserts,* 1961 (AMP); Luening's *In the Beginning* (1956); Ussachevsky's *Computer Piece No. 1* (1968), and *Two Sketches* (1971); together with works by Smiley, Shields, and Davidovsky.

Orion 7021 features electronic works by Swickard and Heller. DG 137011 features four works composed at the Utrecht Institute of Sonology. Desto 6466 has works by Luening and Ussachevsky as well as *Incantation,* on which they collaborated.

The Schwann Record Catalog has a separate listing of electronic music records which is of value even though a number of European labels are not included (especially Wergo). A short list of works and records is listed in the *Music Educators Journal,* November 1968. The *Repertoire International des Musiques Electroacoustiques* (Electronic Music Catalog) which appeared as *Electronic Music Review* No. 2/3 (April/July 1967), compiled by Hugh Davies is, though out-of-date, still the best source for information on available nonrecorded electronic music.

6 Computer Music

Basic Concepts

Critically important to any full study of computer music is the differentiation between the terms *analog* and *digital.* The electronic music discussed in the previous chapter is *analog:* continuous, noninterrupted information. Sound (singing, breathing, etc.; most of the activities of life) is analog. *Digital,* on the other hand, refers to information stated in *digits* (commonly numbers); i.e., discrete, noncontinuous bits of information. Unlike analog synthesizers, computers are digital in nature, working only with numbers.

The *digits* that *digital* refers to in computers are binary (or containing two states). The binary system incorporates only the symbols "0" and "1." These occur in columns referencing the more traditional decimal (or base 10) system, and are listed right to left in exponential order:

etc.	32	16	8	4	2	1	decimal columns
	0	0	0	1	0	0	binary digits

A "1" in any column "trips" that full amount into existence, while a "0" signals that the column is not in operation. In the above example, the number presented is 4. Typically, the exponential listing is not shown, but rather taken for granted. These binary numbers can exist in traditional mathematical operations with one example shown below:

$$
\begin{array}{cccc}
0 & 0 & 0 & 1 \\
1 & 0 & 0 & 0 \\
\hline
1 & 0 & 0 & 1 \\
\end{array}
$$

Note here that addition exists in much the same way it does in decimal mathematics (i.e., $0 + 0 = 0$; $1 + 0 = 1$, etc.). Here the number 1 was added to the number 8, with the result (adding all "tripped" digits) equalling 9.

Understanding a "bit" of binary mathematics is important to one's understanding of computers (and consequently of computer music). The fact that numbers of any amount can be represented in two digits (0 and 1) makes computers possible. Any substance that can represent two states of existence can be used to represent and operate binary math. Doors (open/closed), mousetraps (set/unset), or even directions (up/down) all present real world binary equivalents. More important magnetic fields (positive/negative) or electric current (on/off) represent ways in which computers can operate using binary concepts. Since substances need merely show only two states of existence, the operations can be quick (often less than a trillionth of a second) and take little space (some designers are now talking in terms of "molecular" operations). It is this concept (that computers can operate with extreme speed and take little space) that makes the "digital" nature of computers important. In contrast, computers can lose a bit of their mystique; the complicated innards are often merely rows upon rows of millions of devices housing smaller devices whose only job is to be on/off, open/closed, or the equivalent.

Since sound is *analog* and computers *digital,* composers interested in the use of computers to create music found inherent contradictions in the compositional possibilities of the instrument. The speed at which computers operate, however, and the mass of material and control they possess were important attractions for composers exploring new compositional techniques. Composers (primarily in the early and mid sixties) such as Lejaren Hiller, Max Matthews (researcher more than composer), James Tenney, J. K. Randall, and Hubert Howe were among the first to become dedicated to the problems and advantages of computer music. Work at the Bell Laboratories (beginning in 1959) proved enlightening and led to the first MUSIC series of programs (discussed later in the chapter).

Significant to these early experiments was the exploration of an instrument called the *digital to analog converter* (often called the DAC). It is conceptually similar to that of film. If one looks at motion picture film it is quickly apparent that material present is "digital" (i.e., "fixed" images of discrete material); there is no analog motion. However, when these digital elements are shown through a projector at the typical speed of 24 per second, a "feel" of analog motion occurs. The same is possible with computers and sound. If one takes enough numbers representing waveforms and "projects" them through alternations in voltage, the analog impression of sound results. Though this concept is a simplified one, it does give the basic essence of the converter concept. Figure 6.1 demonstrates the ways in which computers are able to produce sound:

Figure 6.1. Stages of *computer generated sound.* J. Tenney. (Permission granted by the *Journal of Music Theory,* New Haven, Conn.)

In "stage one" the vast amount of numbers (termed *samples*) is produced (these are typically between 20,000 and 55,000 per second of sound). The second stage converts these numbers into voltages that are smoothed and filtered (in order to cancel the "rate" of numbers, which can sometimes be read as an extra frequency: called *aliasing*). The third stage produces the "electronic" sound through a standard "hi-fi" system. It should be noted that this early diagram contains a number of elements that today's computer composer finds unnecessary. The computer can now feed directly to the DAC and filter, and subsequently to playback facilities (note the five numbers over the appropriate equipment). This voids the need for so many stages and particularly for punched cards (replaced by video terminals) and digital/analog tapes. Figure 6.2 shows a series of functions and how they might be presented in terms of vibrato, envelope, and timbre.

Figure 6.2. Outline of a series of
functions. J. Tenney. (Permission
granted by the *Journal of Music
Theory*, New Haven, Conn.)

With the parameters of sound existing (in the initial state) in numbers, composers can control extremely small and often very precise data. Editing, for example, can be accomplished quickly by extracting "numbers," so much more exacting than the complicated physical necessity of splicing common to "classical" electronic music studios. Careful control of tuning (previously relegated to hand manipulation of knobs) and dynamics is possible and practical. In these ways, the computer offers the composer *more* control and precision in the compositional process.

Analog to digital (A/D) aspects of computer operation often prove as valuable as DAC. Here the composer or experimenter replaces speakers with microphones, and the computer acts as an analytical midwife. Instead of sound being initiated in terms of numbers, it is first analog and then translated into numbers for storage (digital recording), editing (manipulation), or composition (*musique concrète*). Live acoustical events can be recorded via digital mechanics and carefully categorized according to a wide variety of different available techniques for timbral data, spatial content, and reference to compositional potential.

The author has divided composer use of computers into three basic categories: (1) computer-generated sound, wherein the composer has precise control possibilities over musical materials and parameters; (2) computer-composed music, wherein the computer is used to compose or aid composition through various random selections within controlled parameters; and (3) hybrid operations, wherein the computer controls synthesizer functions. In addition to the discussion of these which follows, computer applications in notation and teaching will also be examined.

Computer-Generated Sound

Computer-generated sound (sometimes referred to as "computer sound synthesis") began at the Bell Telephone Laboratories in 1959 with Max Matthews and James Tenney. J. K. Randall and Hubert Howe, among others at Princeton, collaborated with the Bell Laboratories to produce the first effective computer program for sound generation: MUSIC IVB. This program, as well as the host of programs designed since, allows the composer extensive control over all the elements of composition (MUSIC IVB was a culmination of MUSIC IV designed by Matthews using the IBM 7090 computer; it eventually became MUSIC V for the GE 645 computer).

Other programs include the Music Simulator-Interpreter for Compositional Procedure (Musicomp) developed for the IBM 7090 by Hiller and Robert Baker, MUSIGOL developed by Donald MacInnis for the Burroughs 5500, and the Transformational Electronic Music Process Organizer (TEMPO) developed by John Clough at Oberlin College. All of these programs deal explicitly with composer control of all the available parameters of sound and use the computer (with digital input) as a high-speed "performer" to achieve a magnetic tape recording of their works as output (analog voltage on tape). It is important to note that, while control is a most important feature of *computer-generated sound,* this control need not in any sense be a "row"-controlled process as described in chapter 2. Indeed, any style can be served accurately by the computer and no dodecaphonic process is implied.

Research into computer-generated sound continues at many locations, most notably at the Center for Computer Research in Music and Acoustics (CCRMA) at Stanford University. There John Chowning, John Grey, James Moorer, Loren Rush, and Leland Smith continue to study digital recording techniques, digital signal processing, psychoacoustical information, advanced synthesis techniques, and the automatic production of musical manuscripts.

John Chowning's research and composition have received considerable acclaim. His early work centered on sound production techniques and basic modulation procedures. Early MUSIC V techniques called for instrument definition in terms of building complex tones from scratch (called Fourier or additive synthesis, it required that each overtone be added separately—a tedious and time-consuming process, though the results are often highly controllable). Chowning has worked primarily with concepts of frequency modulation, developing techniques using program and carrier waves. These produce highly complex tones including "inharmonic" materials and frequently sound like

Figure 6.3. John Chowning. Photo courtesy of the Stanford University News and Publications Service.

"bell tones." This procedure became so important to the development of certain computer programs for music that *Chowning FM* is the term often used to designate the technique. As well, his research of musical *space* using computer techniques and discoveries correlating reverberation (as well as dynamics, direction, and doppler) to spatial modulation have contributed greatly to the development of new programs and works. Both space and FM principles are apparent in his *Turenas* (1972) and *Stria* (1977), both computer-generated quadraphonic tape compositions. Chowning's *Phoné,* completed in 1981, forms elegant vocal effects derived from the use of vibrato (in quasi-random formant structure).

Figure 6.4 shows part of program input to the tape portion of David Cope's *Glassworks* for computer-generated tape and two pianos (1979) completed at CCRMA. P's stand for "parameter input data" with the format in SAIL (Stanford Artificial Intelligence Language).

Excellent examples of current computer uses with computer-generated sound are described in *Proceedings* 7/8, American Society of University Composers. A complete recording of the works referred to by their respective composers or programmers is included (Hubert S. Howe, Jr.: *Freeze;* David Cohen: seven examples including a Bach fugue, original studies, and computer-generated fragments; John Melby: *Forandrer;* and Donald MacInnis: *Quadrilith*). These, with their verbal annotations, prove invaluable to the uninitiated as well as to the experienced. Computer-generated sound has proven to be a most prolific and fertile resource for composers.

Computer Composition

Prior to these experiments, composers became interested in the computer's potential for generating information about style and context. Studies (primarily by Lejaren Hiller and Leonard Isaacson in 1955–56) began at the University of Illinois with the Illiac high-speed digital computer and involved programming of basic material and stylistic parameters. The computer was fed limits to choices it could make within number systems coded by composer input to basic musical note tables. In other words, the computer was "taught" certain conditional limits and fed the results (in terms of numbers) to researchers, who then translated such into traditional notes. The *Illiac Suite for String Quartet* (1957) resulted and was published in the April 1957 edition of *New Music Quarterly*. It was composed by the computer, but transposed to traditional musical notation by researchers for "live" nonelectronic performance.

```
21 JUL 1978    4:53      WHIPr222,BHCJ

RR MCVX/8 ,01,.1/7 .1,.3;
END;

TION 53,68;
P2 MCVE/8  .01,.03  .2,.4/7 .2,.4  1.5,2.9;
P3 SUBR MOVX/3 1260,1260 1239,1272/5 1239,1272 1074,1111/
7 1074,1111  1067,1080;
P4 .167;
P5 F1;
P6 .5 "F8" .5 "F6";
P7 0;
P8 0;
P9 0;
P10 0;
P11 MOVE/4 45,-345/11 -345,-340;
P12 1;
P13 .05;
P14 DF MOVE/8 1,1/7 1,3;
P15 "1";
RR MCVX/8 ,01,.1/7 .1,.2;
END;

PROG 0,99;
P2 -66;
P14 F2; P15 F5; P16 F4;
P17 "1";
END;

PROG 66;
P2 NUM/2/4//3/5/6/9;
P3 SUBR NUM/27,3/1,4/10.4/13.5/24,6/27.8/26.8/25.9/24.8;
P4 .14;
P5 MOVP/10 14,14.99  15,15.99/23 15,15.99  16,16.99;
P14 F2; P15 F5; P16 F4;
P6 F8;
P7 0;
P8 0;
P9 0;
P10 0;
P11 MOVE/33 150,200;
P12 1;
P13 .05;
P14 DF 1.5;
P17 "1";
END;

NOS 2,100;
P2 -66;
P14 F2; P15 F5; P16 F4;
P17 "1";
END;
```

Figure 6.4. From David Cope's *Glassworks* (1979); output from PDP 10 computer at Stanford showing controlled parameters (p numbers) in a basic spatial motion of computer-generated sound.

Figure 6.5. Lejaren Hiller. By permission.

The score of this work and research leading to its composition are described in *Experimental Music.*[1] Though these directions in "computer control" have not proven to be great artistic successes, the experiments were extraordinarily important, for they indeed opened the door to new vistas in the expansion of the computer's development as a unique instrument with significant potential. Research and composition involving the computer in this manner continue since (1) no special equipment (e.g., the DAC) is required (the computer does exactly what it was designed to do), and (2) extensive data concerning composition and music analysis, especially as it relates to "random" materials, can be important to a number of concepts.

Figure 6.6 shows a basic program for computer creation of twelve-tone rows and subsequent matrices. It is written in the "basic" computer language and can provide quick (usually less than a second, depending on computer use) generation of data. Extending this program could provide full compositions using the rows created and experimentation for the composer interested in the varieties of ways that random materials can interact.

Iannis Xenakis, using FORTRAN IV programming with the IBM-7090, has produced data for his free *stochastic music* (detailed in his *Formalized Music,* Indiana University Press, 1971, pp. 131–54). A number of his works (for traditional instruments) were composed with the aid of high-speed computations of probability theory made accessible by computer application. These works include *ST/10–1, 080262* (1962, with first performance on May 24 of that year at the headquarters of IBM in France), *ST/48–1, 240162* (for large

1. Lejaren Hiller and Leonard Isaacson, *Experimental Music* (New York: McGraw-Hill, 1959).

```
10 PRINT "THIS PROGRAM GENERATES RANDOM 12 TONE ROWS AS WELL AS  "
11 PRINT "THEIR INVERSIONS, RETROGRADES AND INVERSION RETRO-"
12 PRINT "GRADES."
13 RANDOMIZE
20 DIM N(12),M(12),N$(12)
21 DIM A(12,12)
30 N$(1)="C ":N$(2)="C#":N$(3)="D ":N$(4)="D#"
40 N$(5)="E ":N$(6)="F ":N$(7)="F#":N$(8)="G "
50 N$(9)="G#":N$(10)="A ":N$(11)="A#"
60 N$(12)="B "
80 FOR I= 1 TO 12
90 N(I)=INT(1+(12*RND))
100 IF I=1 THEN 140
110 I1=I-1
120 FOR J=1 TO I1
130 IF N(I)=N(J) THEN 90
140 NEXT J
145 NEXT I
150 REM INVERSION
160 FOR K=1 TO 12
164 IF  K=1 THEN M(1)=N(1)
165 IF  K=1 THEN 230
170 Q=K-1
180 P=N(K)-N(Q)
190 R=M(Q)-P
200 IF R<1 THEN R=R+12
210 IF R>12 THEN R=R-12
220 M(K)=R
230 NEXT K
240 &"ORIGINAL"
250 FOR A=1 TO 12
260 G=N(A)
270 &N$(G)"   ";
280 NEXT A
290 &""
300 &"INVERSION"
310 FOR B=1 TO 12
320 G=M(B)
330 &N$(G)"   ";
340 NEXT B
350 &"   "
360 &"RETROGRADE"
370 FOR C=1 TO 12
380 H=13-C
390 G=N(H)
400 &N$(G)"   ";
410 NEXT C
420 &"   "
430 &"RETROGRADE INVERSION"
440 FOR D=1 TO 12
450 H=13-D
460 G=M(H)
470 &N$(G)"   ";
480 NEXT D
482 &"  ":&"  ":&"  ";
485 &"DO YOU WISH TO SEE TRANSPOSITION MATRIX";:INPUT A$
490 IF A$="NO" THEN 999
500 REM THE TRANSPOSITION MATRIX MADE HERE
510 FOR E=1 TO 12
520  IF E=1 THEN R=0
```

Figure 6.6. 'Basic' language program
for the creation of 12-tone rows and
consequent matrices (Scott Lancaster).

```
530    IF E=1 THEN 570
540    R=M(E)-N(1)
550    IF R<1 THEN R=R+12
560    IF R>12 THEN R=R+12
570    FOR F=1 TO 12
580      G=N(F)+R
590      IF G<1 THEN G=G+12
600      IF G>12 THEN G=G-12
610      A(E,F)=G
620      NEXT F
630    NEXT E
632    FOR Q=1 TO 30
635    &" "
636    NEXT Q
640    &"MATRIX GENERATED BY ROW AND ITS INVERSION"
645    FCR G=1 TO 12
650      FOR H=1 TO 12
660      I=A(G,H)
670      &N$(I)" ";
680      NEXT H
690      &" "
700    NEXT G
999    END
```

Figure 6.6. Continued.

orchestra), *Atrées* (for ten soloists, 1962), and *Morsima-Amorsima* (for violin, 'cello, bass, and piano, 1962; the processes are described in the performance notes for this work). Notes were calculated by the electronic brain 7090 IBM in Paris in obedience to a special stochastic (probabilist) "programme" devised by Xenakis. This was derived from the thesis of "Minimum Rules of Composition," which he had already formulated in 1958 in *Achorripsis*. The "programme" is a complex of stochastic laws which the composer had been introducing into musical composition for a number of years. The computer defines all the sounds of a sequence, previously calculated, including the time of occurrence, kind of timbre (*arco, pizzicato, glissando,* etc.), instrument, pitch, the gradient of *glissando* (where it occurs), and the duration and dynamic of the emission of sound.[2]

In 1969, Lejaren Hiller and John Cage teamed to produce *HPSCHD.* Through the use of computer printout sheets of "highly sophisticated random numbers," they created the first recording with indeterminate performance possibilities. The listener performs on the record player knobs. Each printout sheet contains a different set of numbers for loudness and treble/bass control on each speaker. With both Xenakis and Cage, the computer serves (though to different ends) to achieve otherwise impossible results. In neither case has the computer actually produced the resultant sound; it has only aided the composer by virtue of its high-speed computations.

2. See Iannis Xenakis, *Morsima-Amorsima* (Boosey & Hawkes, 1967). From notes to the score.

Hybrid Composition

Research and composition in the area of direct computer control over synthesizer modules (oscillators, filters, etc.) has become very impressive in the past few years. In a sense, the sequencer referred to in the previous chapter is a mini-analog-computer. With various potentiometer settings (usually three to five per note) on a sequence of notes (variable number depending on the make and model of the sequencer) one can "program" a *series* of notes rather than one or two at a time.

New developments include the Synthi 100's Digital Sequencer 256 (E.M.S.), with solid-state storage capacity of 10,240 bits of information. It is capable of precisely controlling six different simultaneous parameters over a sequence of 256 successive events. Through several modes of operation, any or all of the 256 stored items and their time relationships can be retrieved and even varied without difficulty. This Sequencer 256 is indeed a small special-purpose digital computer, complete with analog-to-digital and digital-to-analog converters. Surprisingly compact (about the length of a five-octave piano keyboard, but one-third its depth and width), the 256 provides high-speed operation and full information retrieval. Buchla's (see the previous chapter for addresses of this and the E.M.S. studios) late '70's *Music Easel* has full analog retrieval and is especially designed for storage of traditional instrument sounds. More recently, Buchla's *300 Series Music Box* combines microprocessing units with an analog synthesizer. The two instruments function in a truly symbiotic relationship with "hands-on" capabilities in both analog and digital spheres.

Salvatore Martirano's *Sal-Mar Construction* (1973) is a semiportable "live-performance" computer with retrieval and storage capabilities. His performances and tours with this instrument have brought much attention to the "live" potential of the computer-synthesizer combination. MUSYS, developed by Peter Zinovieff, Peter Grogono, and David Cockerell, uses PDP8/L and PDP8/S computers to control special-purpose electronic equipment.

Many composers have begun to research and utilize the potential for microprocessors (small microcomputers) to be used in live performance situations. David Behrman has worked extensively in this area. His *On the Other Ocean* (1977), for example, involves flute, bassoon, and the Kim-1 micro-computer-controlled polyphonic analog synthesizer (hybrid microprocessor utilization). The live performers choose their pitches according to the synthesizer's accompaniment and the synthesizer chooses its accompaniment according to the live performer's pitches, producing a kind of 'live-looping' compositional process.

Figure 6.7. David Behrman. Photo by
Mary Lucier.

Notation and Future

New concepts and applications of the computer for the composer continue to
be explored. Visual input is an increasingly viable source for future experimentation. One method is to *draw* (using a special light pen) graph representations of wave forms directly on a cathode-ray tube (CRT-television-like
computer input). The computer then translates these to digital information,
processes and, through a D/A converter, produces an electromagnetic force
on tape (and/or "live" through studio speakers as the composer may wish).
Printed graphs can also be assimilated by computer functions through adap-
tion of *Graphos I.* Computer recognition of traditionally notated scores creates the potential for actual performances of incredibly difficult music without
the composer having any knowledge of computer languages. It presents composers with an incredible experimental laboratory: immediate performance of
works (with any degree of complexity included) for experimentation, revision,
and/or re-orchestration.

Leland Smith at Stanford's Artificial Intelligence Laboratory uses a large
PDP 10 computer to create exacting traditional music notation. The computer
(using light-sensitive paper similar to Xerox) is actually taught to "print" music
according to data fed into the terminal. Figure 6.8 is an example of this notation.

Advantages of this kind of notation/copying are:

1. Speed: the computer can produce copies rapidly once the information is
   stored internally;
2. Editing: since the storage is digital, simple computations can create quick
   transpositions (for transposing instruments) and corrections;
3. Flexibility: with data in numbers, it is easy to rearrange measure distri-
   bution for part-page turns as well as score layout;

Figure 6.8. Example of computer notation. System designed by Leland Smith at Stanford's CCRMA. Work is *Intermezzo and Capriccio for Piano* by Leland Smith. Computer Music Graphics, San Andreas Press, 3732 Laguna Ave., Palo Alto, CA 94306.

4. Extractions: once a score is in the computer, parts can be extracted in seconds (in transposition if necessary);
5. Versatility: pages can be rearranged quickly in a variety of ways for determination of best readability.

Clearly these procedures are significant tools for composers, even those who are not interested in computers for sonic applications and composition.

With the advent of inexpensive "home" minicomputers, classroom applications have increased (see fig. 6.9). Digital synthesizers of computers such as the APPLE II and *Syntauri* create inroads and potential in a wide variety

Figure 6.9. Mountain Hardware's *MusicSystem;* a digital synthesizer audio output (left) and light pen for notation on video (lower right).

of situations. ALF products and Mountain Hardware have developed both software (programs) and hardware (instruments) for less than $1,000. Theorists and teachers, such as Arthur Hunkins (University of North Carolina), Dorothy Gross (University of Minnesota), Fred Hofstetter (University of Delaware), Rosemary Killam (North Texas State University), Gary Wittlich (Indiana University), Wolfgang Kuhn (Stanford), Paul Lorton (University of San Francisco) and Herb Bielawa (San Francisco State), have all developed teaching programs (primarily sight-singing and ear-training) involving computers. The advantages that the computer offers include: (1) immediate feedback (visual); (2) storage and retrieval of scoring; (3) timbre versatility; (4) notation speed; and (5) long-term correlation of instructional viability of materials used.

New digital instruments such as the SYNCLAVIER II (see figure 6.10) promise to make computers as viable a resource for composers as the synthesizer became in the early sixties.

Figure 6.10. *Synclavier II*. New England Digital Corp.

A new digital guitar contains metal touch-plates and plucking bars instead of frets and strings. Built by Oncor Sound of Salt Lake City, it was adapted (by Cal Gold of New England Digital Corp.) for use with the Synclavier computerized synthesizer. Jazz artist Pat Methany was one of the first professionals to use the instrument.

Constant emphasis on miniaturization increases a system's accessibility. Casio, for example, has created a number of fairly inexpensive digital instruments capable of a wide range of functions. Figure 6.11 shows one of their larger models. Note the multitude of options, memory, and especially MS storage function (coiled wire and nozzle attached to the rear of the Casiotone 701). This equipment can "read" music from a coded sheet (see Figure 6.12) which can then be played back at various speeds and with different timbres.

Figure 6.11. The Casiotone 701 (Casio Inc., 15 Gardner Road, Fairfield, NJ 07006).

Figure 6.12. The Casiotone's MS
memory function "reading" an encoded
score.

This 5″ × 13″ × 37″ computer has more options than many electronic organs of a decade past, yet is but a fraction of their size. Yamaha's PS-20 exemplifies the competitive nature of the industry (see Figure 6.13).

Vectoral Analysis: Jean-Claude Risset: *Inharmonic Soundscapes*

(For information on vectoral analysis and procedures, see chapter 1).

1. Historical Background: Jean-Claude Risset (b. 1936, France) is currently the head of computer research at IRCAM (Institute de Recherche et Coordination Acoustique/Musique) in Paris. He studied piano with Robert Trimaille and composition with Suzanne Demarquez and André Jolivet. He earned the *Doctorates-Sciences Physiques* in 1967 at the *Ecole Normale Superieure.* He spent three years working with Max Matthews at the Bell Laboratories in the early sixties researching sound synthesis, imitation of real timbres, and pitch paradoxes. He published a catalog of computer-synthesized sounds in 1969 and set up a computer music installation in Orsay, France, in 1971.

Inharmonic Soundscapes is a reduction for tape of a larger work titled *Inharmonique* for soprano and tape (first performed in April, 1977, at IRCAM). All of the computer-synthesis for the work was done at IRCAM with a basic MUSIC V type program. Some sections were digitally mixed with the Stanford program titled MIXSND (mix-sounds).

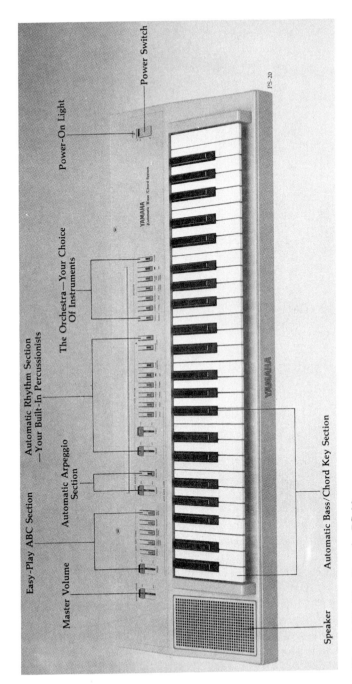

Figure 6.13. The Yamaha PS-20 (Yamaha; Nippon Gakki Co., Ltd., Hamamatsu, Japan).

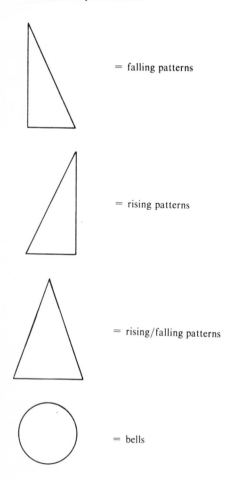

= falling patterns

= rising patterns

= rising/falling patterns

= bells

Figure 6.14. Symbology for analysis of Risset's *Inharmonic Soundscapes*.

2. Overview: *Inharmonic Soundscapes* falls cleanly into a cyclic arrangement of three main sections preceded by an introduction and followed by a brief coda (both of similar material). If one assigns basic block symbols to the sounds as in figure 6.14, then a formal layout would look like that shown in fig. 6.15.

The quote (three-fourths of the way through line one) indicates a timbral and pitch reference to the work analyzed in the previous chapter—*Poème électronique* by Edgard Varèse. Though possibly not intentional, it is certainly immediately observable when one is familiar with both works. The two transitions (overlapped symbols at the end of the first A and the end of the second A) integrate the basic sound materials.

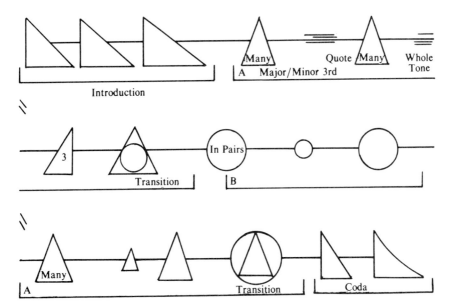

Figure 6.15. Symbolic analysis of
Risset's *Inharmonic Soundscapes.*

3. Orchestration: The bell-like sonorities of both basic materials (the bowed glass of "A" and the rung bells of "B") are the direct result of the "inharmonicity" described by the work's title. The spectrum of these types of sounds characteristically includes partials that do not conform exactly to the tuning specifications of the overtone series. This, combined with bell-like envelopes (dynamic characteristics), provides the basic consistency for the entire work. There is very little material present here, as well as only slight alterations and variants to that material. Yet the resulting diversity in terms of color is extraordinary.

4. Basic Techniques: The most notable technique, aside from the timbral resources, is rhythmic diversity. A random quality, edged with a directional (climax) touch, suggests computer control within parameters guided subtly by the composer.

5, 6. Vertical and Horizontal Models: For the most part, the harmonic sonorities of this piece results from the extended durations of the melodic attacks. Note that there are suggestions of pitch content, at two points in the top line in figure 6.15. In the first instance, a major/minor third is heard in varying guises (e.g., E♭, E♮, C) while in the second appearance, a whole-tone scale is implied (i.e., E, D, C, B♭, with a G below). Both of these are typical materials and suggest a relatively consonant vocabulary with tuning logically derived from the inharmonic materials.

7. Style: Risset has created a consistent vocabulary of inharmonic timbral material in *Inharmonic Soundscapes*. The form, while simple, supplies balance and direction to a work constructed from subtle variations of glass and bell-like timbres. The composer speaks of his use of the computer:

The computer, a powerful tool, makes new sound sources available. However, it is necessary to learn how to use these new possibilities to produce the desired results . . . in order to take full advantage of the vast potential of direct digital synthesis of sound, one needs a deep understanding of the nature of sounds and of the correlations between the physical parameters and the aural effects of sound: this psychoacoustic science is still in its infancy, but its present growth is promising.[3]

3. From IRCAM (31 Rue Saint-Merri F-75004, Paris); "document paru" or introductory booklet.

Bibliography

*Further Readings**

Abbott, Curtis. "Machine Tongues II." *Computer Music Journal* 2, no. 2 (1978):4. Good article on programming techniques.

Alles, H. G. "A Portable Digital Sound Synthesis System." *Computer Music Journal* 1, no. 4 (1977):5.

Baker, Robert A. "Music Composition—Music-Simulator for Compositional Procedures for the IBM 70/90 Electronic Digital Computer." *Technical Report No. 9*, University of Illinois Experimental Music Studio, 1962. Fascinating early account of techniques for computer-aid.

Bateman, Wayne. *Introduction to Computer Music.* N.Y.: John Wiley and Sons, 1980. A most practical (layman) guide to currently available resources.

Bayer, Douglas. "Real-Time Software for a Digital Music Synthesizer." *Computer Music Journal* 1, no. 4 (1977):22. Good article on creation of a language for interconnecting the synthesizer hardware and organizing software.

Chadabe, Joel, and Roger Meyers. "An Introduction to the Play Program." *Computer Music Journal* 2, no. 1 (1978):12.

Chamberlin, Hal. *Musical Applications of Microprocessors.* Rochelle Park, N.J.: Hayden, 1981.

Chowning, John. "The Simulation of Moving Sound Sources." *Journal of the Audio Engineering Society* 2–6 (1971). One of the first articles discussing computer control of spatial modulation.

———. "The Stanford Computer Music Project." *Numus West* 1:12. Throughly fascinating article on this developing project.

———. "The Synthesis of Complex Audio Spectra by Means of Frequency Modulation." *Journal of the Audio Engineering Society* no. 21 (1973):526. The *classic* article on this important technique in computer sound synthesis.

Cohen, David. "Computer Generated Music." *Southeastern Composers League Newsletter* 66. Fascinating early account of the origins and study of this growing area of music.

Divilbiss, J. L. "Real-time Generation of Music with a Digital Computer." *Journal of Music Theory* 8:99. Good treatment of its subject matter.

von Foerster, Heinz, and James W. Beauchamp, eds. *Music by Computers.* New York: John Wiley & Sons, 1969.

Gill, S. A. "A Technic for the Composition of Music in a Computer." *Computer Journal* 6, no. 2 (1963):129. Good account of early computer music techniques.

Gordon, John, and John Grey. "Perception of Spectral Modifications on Orchestral Instrument Tones." *Computer Music Journal* 2, no. 1 (1978):24. Interesting psychoacoustical phenomena.

*Addresses for record companies, periodicals, and music publishers mentioned in this Bibliography can be found in Appendix 4.

Grey, John. "An Exploration of Musical Timbre." *CCRMA Report No. STAN-M-2* (February 1975). Stanford University report; important for synthesis information on traditional timbres.

―――. "Multidimensional Perceptual Scaling of Musical Timbres." *Journal of the Acoustical Society of America* (May 1977). Good source for the computer composer interested in synthesis of unique timbres.

Hiller, Lejaren, and Leonard Isaacson. *Experimental Music.* New York: McGraw-Hill, 1959.

Holtzman, S. R. "Using Generative Grammars for Music Composition." *Computer Music Journal* 5:51–64, No. 1, 1981.

Howe, Hubert S., Jr. "Electronic Music and Microcomputers." *Perspectives of New Music* (Spring-Summer 1979):70. Good source of information concerning background, use, and futures of microcomputers in new music synthesis.

―――. *Electronic Music Synthesis.* New York: W. W. Norton & Co., 1975. Most informative.

Interface 2, no. 2 (December 1973). Contains a number of articles relating to computer music, including Steven Smoliar's "Basic Research in Computer-Music Studies"; "A Data Structure for an Interactive Music System"; and Barry Truax's "Some Programs for Real-Time Computer Synthesis and Composition."

Laske, Otto. "Toward a Theory of Interfaces for Computer Music Systems." *Computer Music Journal* 1, no. 4 (1977):53.

Lawson, James, and Max Mathews. "Computer Program to Control a Digital Real-Time Sound Synthesizer." *Computer Music Journal* 1, no. 4 (1977):16. Work at IRCAM in software involving a minicomputer.

Le Brun, Marc. "Digital Waveshaping Synthesis." *Journal of the Audio Engineering Society* 27, no. 4 (1979).

Lincoln, Harry. *The Computer and Music.* Ithaca, N.Y.: Cornell University Press, 1970. Directed more towards analysis and bibliographical techniques, but still an important source and tool for the composer.

Longton, M. "SAM: Priorities in the Design of a Microprocessor-based Music Program." *Interface* 10:83–95, No. 1, 1981.

Loy, Gareth. "The Composer Seduced into Programming." *Perspectives of New Music,* Spring-Summer, 1981.

Mathews, M. V., and Joan E. Miller. *Music IV Programmer's Manual.* Murray Hill, N.J.: Bell Telephone Laboratories. An important source for those interested in pursuing detailed information on computer programming.

Mathews, Max. *The Technology of Computer Music.* Cambridge, Mass.: M.I.T. Press, 1969. A superb book and the first major edition in its field; now suffers from outdatedness, but still a landmark on the subject.

Moore, F. R. "An Introduction to the Mathematics of Digital Signal Processing." *Computer Music Journal* 2, no. 1 (1978):38. First in a series of articles dealing with an important subject for the serious minded computer music composer.

―――. "The Futures of Music." *Perspectives of New Music,* Spring-Summer, 1981, pp. 212–226. Moore's law: our computer knowledge and capability doubles each year.

Moorer, James. "Music and Computer Composition." *Communications of the ACM* 15, no. 2 (1972).

―――. "Signal Processing Aspects of Computer Music—A Survey." *Proceedings of the IEEE* 65, no. 8 (1977):1108. An extremely good survey of basic computer techniques and developments through 1977.

Morgan, Christopher. *The BYTE Book of Computer Music*. New York: BYTE, 1980. Brief but interesting developments and experiments mostly for microcomputer technology.

Numus West 4. Entire issue devoted to computer music, with articles by Bruce Rogers, Otto Laske, Barry Truax, Leland Smith, Louis Christiansen, Herbert Brün, and Pauline Oliveros; a very good study in the variety of uses of the computer.

Proceedings (American Society of University Composers). Vol. 1 has a series of articles by J.K. Randall, Herbert Brün, Ercolino Ferretti, Godfrey Winham, Lejaren Hiller, David Lewin, and Harold Shapero, relating to computer music; also excellent reference material and diverse comments.

Roads, Curtis. "Artificial Intelligence and Music." *Computer Music Journal* 4:60–65 No. 2, 1980.

Slawson, Wayne. "A Speech-Oriented Synthesizer of Computer Music." *Journal of Music Theory* 13, no. 1 (1969):94. A most important article and, though a bit technical for the layman, highly original.

Smith, L. C. "Score, A Musician's Approach to Computer Music." *Journal of the Audio Engineering Society* (January 1972).

————. "Editing and Printing Music by Computers." *Journal of Music Theory* (Fall 1973).

Smith, Stuart. "Communications." *Perspectives of New Music*. (Spring-Summer, 1973). Fascinating but highly mathematical study of some of Xenakis's remarks in *Formalized Music*.

"Sound Generation by Means of a Digital Computer." *Journal of Music Theory* 7, no. 1 (Spring 1963):24. An excellent general source for coverage of printout cards, programming, digital tape, etc.

Tenney, James. "Computer Music Experiences 1961–64." *Electronic Music Reports* 1:23. Account of this composer's work in the studio at Utrecht State University.

————. "Musical Composition with the Computer." *Journal of the Acoustical Society of America* 34, no. 6 (1964):1245.

Truax, Barry. "Organizational Techniques for C:M Ratios in Frequency Modulation." *Computer Music Journal* 1, no. 4 (1977):39.

Vercoe, Barry. "The Music 360 Languages for Sound Synthesis." *Computer Music Newsletter* 2 (June 1971).

Zinovieff, Peter. "A Computerized Electronic Music Studio." *Electronic Music Reports* 1:5.

Recordings and Publishers*

Appleton, Jon. *In Deserto* (1977). Recorded on Folkways 33445. This record also contains *Synthrophia* (1977), *Zoetrope* (1974), and other works incorporating the Synclavier and other digital systems. As well, Folkways 3746 contains *Four Fantasies for Synclavier* (1979–81).

————. *Georganne's Farewell*. Recorded on Folkways 33442 along with works by Bodin, Pinkston and Brunson.

Behrman, David. *On the Other Ocean*. Lovely Music Records LWL-1041.

Cope, David. *Glassworks* (1979) for two pianos and computer-generated tape. Recorded on Folkways FTS-33452.

*Addresses for record companies, periodicals, and music publishers mentioned in this Bibliography can be found in Appendix 4.

Dartmouth Digital Synthesizer. Folkways FTS-33442. Record containing computer-synthesized works by Appleton (*Georganna's Farewell*), Pinkston (*Emergence*), Brunson (*Tapestry*), and Bodin (*Bilder*).

Dashow, James. *Effetti Collaterali* (1976). Published by Dawsonville. Recorded on Tulstar Productions, New Directions in Music, 1978.

Dodge, Charles. *Earth's Magnetic Field* (1970). Recorded on Nonesuch 71250. A computer-generated work.

————. *In Celebration: Speech Songs. The Story of Our Lives.* Recorded on CRI S-348. Examples of extraordinary speech synthesis techniques.

Ghent, Emmanuel. *Brazen.* Recorded on Tulstar Productions, New Directions in Music, 1978. Computer-synthesized sound using GROOVE at Bell Laboratories.

Gressel, Joel. *Crossings* (1976). Recorded on CRI 393-SD. Record also contains works by Hoffmann, Vercoe, Winham, and others for computer tape.

Hiller, Lejaren, and Robert Baker. *Computer Cantata.* Recorded on CRI 310-SD.

Hiller, L. and John Cage. *HPSCHD* (1968). Peters. Recorded on Nonesuch H-71224.

Hoffmann, Richard. *In Memoriam Patris* (1976). Recorded on CRI 393-SD.

McKee, William. *Episodes I and II.* Available on Tulstar Productions, New Directions in Music, 1978.

Melby, John. *91 Plus 5 for Brass Quintet and Computer.* Recorded on CRI SD-310.

Morrill, Dexter. *Studies for Trumpet and Computer.* Recorded on Golden Crest Records RE-7068. Interesting use of *Chowning FM* in combination with a live instrument.

————. *Six Dark Questions for Soprano and Computer* (1979). Available on Redwood ES-10 and includes works by Pennycook, Sullivan and Boyer, all completed at the Colgate Computer Music Studio.

Olive, Joseph. *Mar-ri-ia-a* (1973—an opera for soprano, chamber ensemble, and computer tape). Recorded on Tulstar Productions, New Directions in Music.

Peterson, Tracy. *Voices.* Tulstar Productions, New Directions in Music. Fascinating computer voice synthesis.

Randall, J. K. *Lyric Variations for Violin and Computer* (1967). Recorded on Vanguard C-10057.

————. *Quartets in Pairs* (1964). Recorded on Nonesuch 71245, which also includes works by Charles Dodge and Barry Vercoe. *Quartets in Pairs* is computer-generated.

Risset, Jean-Claude. *Inharmonic Soundscapes.* Published by Dawsonville. Recorded on Tulstar, New Directions in Music.

Thome, Diane. *Los Nombres.* Published by Paul Price. Recorded on Tulstar, New Directions in Music.

Truax, Barry. *Sonic Landscapes.* Melbourne SMLP 4033 (Vancouver Canada).

Wallraff, Dean. *Dance.* Published by Dawsonville. Recorded on Tulstar, New Directions in Music. Also contains the work of David Wessel (*Antony*).

Winham, Godfrey. *NP* (Two Pieces for Computer-Synthesized Sound). Recorded on CRI 39 3-SD.

Vercoe, Barry. *Synapse* for viola and computer. Recorded on CRI S-393.

Background and Aesthetics

Media forms are both the rational extension of composite forms such as ballet and opera, and the result of the need for visual activity in connection with tape music. Many multimedia forms grew from experiments with "chance" relationships between simultaneously produced art forms (e.g., *happenings*).

Alexander Scriabin's *Prometheus—The Poem of Fire* (1910) is one of the first examples of mixed-media compositions with origins not directly related to opera or ballet. The scoring calls for large orchestra, chorus, piano, organ, and *clavier à lumières,* an instrument with a keyboard-controlled lighting console. The part for the *clavier à lumières* employs traditional musical notation, and each key is associated with a color. Scriabin directly ascribed tonal regions with colors (e.g., *f* is blue, *the color of reason;* F, *the blood red of hell;* D, *the sunny key;* etc.). With *Prometheus* he envisioned far more than a superfluous "light-show." His concepts embodied a deeply philosophical and religious symbolism with beams and "clouds" of light moving throughout the hall. The chorus was to be draped in white robes and vocalize on ritualistic closed lips or vowel sounds. Unfortunately, *Prometheus* (which was completed in early 1910) was premiered in 1911 without the *clavier à lumières*—without any lighting, in fact. It waited until March 20, 1915 (just five weeks before the composer's death) to receive any mixed-media complement at all. Even then only weak color projections moved on a small screen, falling considerably short of the composer's intentions.

Schoenberg's *Die glückliche Hand* (opus 18, 1910–13) also required lighting effects, which proved technologically unfeasible. The resulting presentation was a poor realization of the composer's intent. *Prometheus,* at least, has had a media "revival" in the past few years, with numerous attempts made at fulfilling the composer's wishes. Unfortunately, most of the results seem diluted by the architecture of the concert hall's interior, or by the lack of real musical translation of sound into light.

The Dadaists and those who worked in the Bauhaus were among the first to openly confront media concepts (that is, try to *integrate* all the art forms available). While certainly one can trace other attempts through Wagner's *gesamtkunstwerk* back to Greek concepts, to do so would go beyond the scope

of this book and thereby neglect unique attributes of the "audience participation" aspects of today's media forms.[1] Aside from early commercial "shows"
which employed perfumes (*The Song of Solomon* was performed in Paris in
1891 with sound, light, and perfumes, for example) and Scriabin's aforementioned *Poem of Fire* which was not truly realized, Erik Satie's *Relâche* (1924)
was one of the first landmarks in media forms. René Clair's film (also a landmark in cinematography for 1924), the understated Satie music, the ballet,
the surrealistic scenery—all combined to create a vessel of often interplaying,
often contradicting images.

Theatrical elements in new music seem to have closer historical ties with
the ballet than with opera or oratorio. Though many mainstream composers
(notably William Schuman and Aaron Copland) have created ballets for dance
groups (especially for Martha Graham), it was John Cage and the Merce
Cunningham dance group that injected theater into the combination of art
forms, with each surviving by its dependence upon the other.

These directions, combined with the television-cinema age, and the need
in electronic music for auxiliary visual material, have contributed largely to
the contemporary revival of the *gesamtkunstwerk* concept in the form of
"happenings." Richard Maxfield writes: "I view as irrelevant the repetitious
sawing on strings and baton-wielding spectacle we focus our eyes upon during
a conventional concert. Much more sensible either no visual counterpart or
one more imaginatively selected such as lighting, cinema, choreography, fire-
works, trees. . . ."[2] The sophistication of equipment and techniques of lighting, still and moving projections have made many new multimedia possibilities
available to the twentieth-century artist-composer. Like all other facets of mid-
century life, the new forms of art must inevitably share responsibility with the
electromechanical environment in which they develop.

The aesthetics of media forms remain targets at which many an active as
well as passive participant or bystander seem to take special aim. Coming to
grips with the definitions and categorization of varieties of intentions involved
may help in the conciliation of some antagonists. Two composers, Robert Ceely
and Paul Goldstaub, tend to sum up the points of view quite succinctly:

Ceely: ". . . it [multimedia] is most interesting in that it usually fails."

Goldstaub: "The first time I conducted [Toshiro] Mayazumi's *Metamusic*
(certainly a multimedia work of classic stature) it brought home the simple truth
that people have overlooked for centuries: concert going is partially a visual and
social experience, as well as musical. If composers can *use* this to enrich the quality
of the experience of their music, everyone gains."[3]

---

1. The Bauhaus, founded by Walter Gropius in 1919, included very basic interdisciplinary media
such as art, architecture, and design. Though short-lived (until 1933) it served as an example in
the arts that has founded very solid ground for media studies in the American university.

2. As quoted in *An Anthology of Chance Operations*. La Monte Young and Jackson Mac Low,
eds. (New York: 1963). No page numbers.

3. Tom Everett, "Questions and Answers," *Composer Magazine* 4, no. 1 (Fall-Winter 1972):20–21.

Definitions

Multimedia is often used synonymously with a number of terms, most often *inter-media* and *mixed-media*. Adding to the confusion are the terms *theatre pieces, merged-medium, environmental works, happenings,* etc. To avoid continuing this terminology explosion, the author defines three major categories of *media forms*:

1. Multimedia: this form is a loose structure in which the various media do not depend on each other for meaning (*happenings* are excellent examples of *multimedia* events, in that each element is significant and structured in such a way that it could stand on its own merits);
2. Mixed-media: this form tends "toward equalization of elements," though "any hierarchial order is possible" (*environments* more often than not fit this media form in that, though the elements are dependent on each other, "they are mixed, but not truly integrated."[4]);
3. Inter-media: this form has all of its elements in equal balance and integrated to the fullest degree (*merged-medium* fits this category well in that ". . . all elements are equal and integrated"[5]).

A number of terms fall within these three main categories (some in more than one category as they may or may not attain balance or integration):

Multimedia	*Mixed-media*	*Inter-media*
(loosely knit composite forms)	(more integrated, with varying degrees of importance of elements)	(very integrated, each element depending on the others for the work to hold together)
happenings	environments	merged-medium
collage	opera	environments
theatre pieces	film and TV	films
opera	kinetic theatre	meditations
ballet		
light-show		
film and TV		

Two important factors must be considered carefully in observing the above listings:

1. Composers have been very flexible in their usage of the above terms. Indeed, their use of certain terminologies may not fit the above chart (the

4. Stanley Gibb, "Understanding Terminology and Concepts Related to Media Art Forms," *The American Music Teacher*, April-May, 1973, pp. 23–25. This is possibly the most well thought out and formulated writing on this subject and is highly recommended to those seeking real insight into media art forms. This author is highly indebted to Mr. Gibb.

5. Ibid.

author's own *Deadliest Angel Revision,* 1971, is a good example: it is billed as *multimedia* or a *theatre piece* when in fact it is *inter-media*). Therefore one cannot always accurately judge the composition by its "nomer."

2. None of the above classifications implies a quality judgment. Each is merely a starting point from which one can discuss the forms with some degree of consistency. Important works exist in each of the categories.

With this in mind it is necessary to note that the author has attempted to choose works which emphasize in particular each of the above categories.

Multimedia

April 17, 1958 saw the introduction of *Poème électronique* by Edgard Varèse at the Brussels World's Fair (see chap. 5). This multimedia presentation by Varèse, in collaboration with architect Le Corbusier, took place within a pavilion which was shaped externally like a three-peaked circus tent and internally like a cow's stomach. The composition, 480 seconds in length, was accompanied by projected images of paintings, written script, and montages. Neither of the artists made attempts at correlation between visual and aural images. The result produced occasional simultaneity of rhythm or spatial relationships, but more often separation of concepts. The intense organization of each artist's approach to his own material, however, was so apparent that correlation seemed almost inappropriate. The performance, attended by nearly three million people, remains as the most culturally significant representation of multimedia in history.

The summer of 1952 marked some of the first multimedia "happenings" when John Cage, David Tudor, Robert Rauschenberg, and Merce Cunningham teamed to play records, read lectures from stepladders, dance, use projections, and display "white paintings" at Black Mountain College. The concept was a random sequence of nonrandom materials. That is, the order and combinations were chance, but the lectures, projections, and paintings in themselves were not. The resultant "theater" of events allowed each art form to remain isolated, contributing to the whole only as each performer reacted to another's event or personality.

An important experimental media contribution developed during the late fifties and early sixties with the ONCE group in Ann Arbor, Michigan. Composers, artists, filmmakers, and architects focused their activities into the ONCE festival of contemporary music, the Space Theatre of Milton Cohen, the Cooperative Studio for Electronic Music of Robert Ashley and Gordon

Scott Wyatt's piece for Grad Chorale Krannert 25th anniversary

Mumma, and the Ann Arbor Film Festival of George Manupeli. Mumma's *Music from the Venezia Space Theatre* (1964), composed for Cohen's Space Theatre, was ". . . . an hour long program of light projection, film, sculpture, modern dance and electronic music, and (first) performed by an ensemble of the ONCE group. The projected images of the Space Theatre, which evolved continuously between the realistic and the abstract, were as diverse as the sound sources, and moved through the entire space surrounding the audience."[6]

Multimedia as an offshoot of the American experimental school has also developed along lines more indeterminate than structured. The thread of separation lies in the area of "theater": the necessity of partial indeterminacy for a play to "happen." Roger Reynolds's *Ping* (1968), based on a text by Samuel Beckett, is an excellent example of a somewhat improvisatory work which explores "theatrical" possibilities. Three performers (flute, piano, harmonium, bowed-cymbal, and bowed-tam-tam) create the "live" situation, augmented by a 25-minute tape. Their instruments are amplified using contact microphones. A 22-minute film and 160 slides (projected alternately to the left and right) of Beckett's story add visual material. Effects in and around the performance area are created by matrixed mirrors projecting secondary images, blurs, and colors: a cohesive factor enjoining sight and sound experience. The score[7], explicit as to materials, duration, pitches (for the most part), and dynamics, allows improvisation from *all* performers, including the projectionists. For example, the projectionists may, within certain limitations, alter images through the use of such devices as filters and prisms. Reynolds's *The Emperor of Ice Cream* (1962) includes the projection of the score (both graphic and traditional in notation) for the performers (eight singers, piano, percussion, and bass). Each projection, or score page, represents twenty seconds of time, and the position, movement, and "choreography" of each performer is indicated by dotted lines and the positioning of sound-symbols. Theatrical effects are written on the score in words, some as performance cues, others to be spoken, with performers becoming actors and dancers as well as sound producers.

Morton Subotnick's *Ritual Electronic Chamber Music* involves four performers at "game boards" (lighted buttons for channel or amplitude of the electronic tape or one of four projections). Each performer's choice of which button to press sets up choices for other "players." In the center, a "High Priestess" moves about, playing lights on her body and moving the sound throughout the room. The work may be performed without an audience or in a very small chamber group of interested persons.

6. Gordon Mumma, Program notes on Lovely Music, VR 1091.

7. Roger Reynolds, *Ping,* as published in *Source: Music of the Avant-Garde* (Composer/Performer Edition) 3, no. 2 (July 1969):70–86.

Figure 7.1. Morton Subotnick.

"Relevant action is theatrical (music [imaginary separation of hearing from the other senses] does not exist) . . ."[8] speaks John Cage of, among other things, the audience's ability to see and hear other sounds outside the performance area. Feelings, smells, and even tastes seem somehow neglected by most composers in the superficially imposed restriction of their creativity to sound alone. More often than not, Cage's approach to multimedia is philosophical: accept *all* sounds, sights, and other sensory experiences which occur in and around a performance situation, *equally,* regardless of their origin (this would include such things as car noises, coughs, the structure of the auditorium). Some of his works involve "stage" multimedia. *Water Walk,* for example (first performed over Milan television in 1958 by Cage, who was a quiz show contestant), includes banging a rubber fish inside a piano on the strings, Cage watering a vase of roses, and a pressure cooker spurting steam, among other "props."

Whether initiated by determinate or indeterminate procedures, multimedia is the result of a natural concern by the composer and artist alike to allow and/or control *all* the aspects of the human sensory system within the framework of the performance situation. Peter Maxwell Davies's *Eight Songs for a Mad King* (see analysis, chapter 4) requires that the flute, clarinet, violin, and 'cello players sit in cages "representing, on one level, the bullfinches

8. John Cage, *Silence* (Cambridge, Mass.: The M.I.T. Press, paperback edition, 1961), p. 15.

the King (George III) was trying to teach to sing . . . the percussion player
. . . the King's brutal keeper, who plays him off stage at the end, beating a
bass drum with a cat-o'-nine-tails."[9] While the visual forms of drama and
setting contribute to live performance intensity, the significance of this highly
acclaimed work is caught aurally on the recording (the media form is born in
the listener's mind via program notes, while listening to the record).

   Boguslaw Schäffer is an active composer of theatre music and happenings. His *Audiences No. 1–5* (1964; see fig. 7.2) is "music for actors" with
the texts by the composer, and involves projections, drama, and musical events.
His happenings include *Non-stop* (1960) for piano (with a duration varying
from six to four hundred and eighty hours), and *Incident* (1966) for an "ensemble" of *audience* (lasting four hours).

Figure 7.2. Boguslaw Schäffer:
Audiences No. 4.

   George Crumb's *Voice of the Whale (Vox Balaenae)* (1971), like the
aforementioned Davies work, has multimedia aspects which are related to live
performance only, and which in no real way deter from the music by their
absence (i.e., when the music is on a record). The work requests that the performers wear black half masks (or visor masks) and the stage be bathed in
deep blue light. Clearly, the music can easily stand alone and the visual aspects, though interesting in performance, are by no means absolutely essential

9. Liner notes on the recording (Nonesuch H-71285) by Peter Maxwell Davies.

to the work (i.e., the music retains its artistic identity with or without the visual complement).

Multimedia techniques have invaded *rock* idioms, with extraordinary results. *The Velvet Underground*, for example, toured America as a part of Andy Warhol's mixed media show *The Exploding Plastic Inevitable* in the mid-sixties. *Pink Floyd*'s 1980 performance of *The Wall*, an extensive light show, proved influential in commercial circles. The group played in front of and behind a huge wall (70 feet high) which was both constructed and destroyed during performance. Multidirectional speaker setups, along with complicated lighting and projections, contributed to an ambitious multimedia event. *Led Zeppelin's* laser shows and *Funkadelic* have since developed extensive media programs. Visual theatrics seem almost a requisite for "rock" performances in the '80's, with *Devo* and other *new wave* groups equally preoccupied with visuals and sound effects. *Kiss, Ted Nugent, Black Sabbath, Alice Cooper* and *Ozzy Ozborne* (who eats chickens' heads!) all contribute to a diverse popular multimedia (and theatrical) culture.

Recent work by Nam June Paik and James Searight in the area of video feedback (camera focused directly into the screen to which it feeds; i.e., looping) create interesting potential for the multimedia composer.

Allan Kaprow catalogs some of his basic concepts for multimedia categories in the following ways:

a. The line between art and life should be kept as fluid, and perhaps indistinct, as possible. . . .
b. Therefore, the source of themes, materials, actions, and the relationships between them are to be derived from any place or period *except* from the arts, their derivatives and their milieu. . . .
c. The performance of a Happening should take place over several widely spaced, sometimes moving and changing locales. . . .
d. Time, which follows closely on space consideration, should be variable and discontinuous. . . .
e. Happenings should be performed once only. . . .
f. It follows that audiences should be eliminated entirely.[10]

Clearly these techniques revoke the basic tenets of Western World artistic heritage and begin important contributions to the New Experimentalism (see chapter 10). Composers and artists involved in these techniques include Jean-Jacques Lebel, Wolf Vostell, George Brecht, Kenneth Dewey, and Allan Kaprow.

10. Allan Kaprow, *Assemblage, Environments & Happenings* (New York: Abrams, 1966), unpaged.

Mixed-media

When superficially (man-made) imposed definitions of art (e.g., music, painting, sculpture) exist psychologically within audiences, domination of one art form over another can exist. Projected scores or performer-interpreted projections share equally the difficulty of misinterpretation; "music seen" or "paintings as sound" represent displacement of traditional dogmatic categorization of the arts. Daniel Lentz's *Sermon* (1970) for string quartet modified by electronic filters, reverberation, ring modulation, and gate device, involves score projection. Once a score is visible to the audience it becomes obvious that it must be made visually interesting and artistic. Lentz has solved this problem by creating an artistic score in color: red = played, blue = sung, green = hummed, yellow = whistled, violet = spoken, brown = whispered, with an orange line surrounding the score page referring to time (at ten-by-twelve-inch projection, each half-inch representing one second). The result is greater visual excitement *and* more meaningful notation for the performers.

Allen Strange's *No Dead Horses on the Moon* requires seven 16mm projectors placed so as to surround the audience with visual images (see fig. 7.3). The recorded sound, projected from the four corners of the room, creates an environment. Correlation between visual and aural materials is obtained by written instructions to the performers (in this case the projectionists). In No. 6, for example, the projectionist is instructed to move his projector. The films to be shown are created by scraping the emulsion from 16mm black leader film and then constructing loops, creating a seven-fold visual ostinato (see example). The resulting flashing dots, lines, and "strobe" effects, along with the sound, engulf the audience in an imaginative "light-show".

At the same time, these concepts alter a basic concert ritual of audience-performer separation. Robert Ashley's *Public Opinion Descends Upon the Demonstrators* (1961) embraces the ideal of "total theater." Specific prerecorded sounds are produced by a single performer on electronic playback equipment only when a member of the audience acts or reacts in a certain manner (e.g., by speaking, glancing, looking about, gesturing, looking toward a loudspeaker, or leaving). Whether or not performance precludes knowledge on the part of the audience of the compositional concept, it soon becomes obvious that all participants (composer, performer, audience) share equal responsibility in creating the work.

Barton McLean's *Identity* series of compositions deals directly with man's relationship with his surroundings, perception of a work in a complete environmental setting, and audience control over sounds. More complete and detailed than Stockhausen's *Musik für ein Haus* or Sigmund Krauze's experiments with environmental music in Poland and Germany, McLean's

Figure 7.3. Allen Strange: *No Dead Horses on the Moon.* (Copyright Media Press, Champaign, Ill., 1969. Used by permission. All rights reserved.)

Identity series includes works for specific buildings and situations. One of these (for the Cultural Center in South Bend, Indiana) is, in the composer's words:

. . . a true environmental experience in that the hearer who walks through it reacts to the sounds both passively and actively. This latter aspect, perhaps the most unique in its conception, although allowing for the overall direction and control of the work to remain in the hands of the composer, nevertheless provides to the listener the opportunity to participate in smaller, but highly meaningful choices. Thus, the hearer, in exercising creative choices of his own which shape the smaller details of the work, enters into the actual creative experience. Furthermore, no musical training is necessary for this interaction, since it is set up so that all choices made by the hearer on this smaller structural level are equally valid. On the other hand, for those who have more time and intuitive ability, it is possible to grow with the work and, upon repeated hearings, to exercise intelligent choices on gradually higher and higher planes.[11]

The work (building) is controlled in terms of lighting, speaker activity, etc., by the audience motion which triggers a wide variety of sounds. By movement and by the audience's discovery of the planned placement of photoelectric cells, microphones, various visual control devices, the building becomes a self-contained environment.

Figures 7.4 and 7.5 show the extent to which media techniques have become sophisticated during the past few years. These diagrams represent two of the media aspects of the recently completed (late 1974) Learning Resources Center at Middle Tennessee State University in Murfreesboro. The figures demonstrate the incredible future and potential of media in education, the sciences, and communications, as well as in the arts.[12]

Composers, often lacking legitimate theater background, have consequently improvised techniques beyond the "time-honored" Grecian concepts of dramatic ritual. The physical aspect of any sensual act no longer distinctly separates one artistic ideal from another. Paul Ignace's *Feast* (1964) culminates all possible environmental encounters within the framework of a mixed-media work. The performers (even the composer) no longer exist except in concept. The audience is fed all aspects of sensual experience, the menu requiring only individual choice within reason. Preferably for two people, *Feast* enacts the "last request" prerogative of the death victim, making choices available on most levels of immediate desire, including choices of sounds, smells, tastes, touches, and sights. The composer here does not evoke *certain* responses, but makes available as many responses as possible. In *Feast,* mixed-media achieves the ideal philosophically implied and inherent within its thesis: no action (relevant or not) can be considered unimportant to the totality of a

11. The quote from the composer is from materials about the work made available to the author. Other environmental works and studies are included in chapter 8.

12. More information on this most interesting media center is available from Dr. Marshall Gunselman, Director of Learning Resources Center at Middle Tennessee State University.

Figure 7.4. Permission granted by the Learning Resources Center, Dr. Marshall Gunselman, Director; Middle Tennessee State University.

composition. Total theater environments cannot avoid the direction toward complete involvement in what traditionally has been called life. All the categories between "theater" and "reality" eventually fall away as even the simplest of media concepts projects to its ultimate end.

Mauricio Kagel's *Match* (for two violoncellos and percussion) is a dramatic game which unfolded in full-blown detail to the composer in a dream. Characterized by visual humor (which met with immediate applause at its premiere in Berlin in October of 1965), it is strikingly serious music (leading to what the composer has called a "shaking concert of derision" at the end of the first live performance).[13] The intense and dramatic music, when fused with the visual wittiness, results in a complicated *collage* of constantly varying grades of emotional polarities. Regarding a portion of *Match* the composer has noted:

During the first rehearsal of these uncertain measures I was told by the interpreters that the passage in question reminded them of the most memorable of the *circene* scenes: the death leap. Such an appreciation was already known to me; the

13. Mauricio Kagel, "On Match for Three Performers," *Composer* 3, no. 2 (Spring 1972); translated from *Sonda #3* (Juventudes Musicales, Madrid) June 1968, pp. 70–78.

TEMP. WIND HUM EXHST. RAIN ODOR

LIGHTING   THREE COLORS.
CONTINUOUSLY VARIABLE INTENSITY

OUTPUT DEVICES

OUTPUT MODIFIERS

POWER LEVELS

LOGIC LEVELS

DIGITAL
CONTROL
CONSOLE

REMOTE DEVICES

(Diagram does not denote number of devices. See specs.)

Figure 7.5. Permission granted by the
Learning Resources Center, Dr.
Marshall Gunselman, Director; Middle
Tennessee State University.

Figure 7.6. Mauricio Kagel.

similarity between this situation with what was dreamed a few weeks previously left no room for doubt: both musicians were suspended in mid-air with their cellos on top of their heads and by means of slow pirouettes they produced very sharp, brilliant sounds. The roll of the drum, that from some point in space resounded over the entire environment, maintained the spectators in pure tension until leading to an aggressive attack on the cymbal. Thus was overcome the first of the mortal leap with good fortune.[14]

Possibly one of the most prolific and well-known mixed-media composers is Robert Moran. His *Hallelujah* (for twenty marching bands, forty church choirs and organs, carrillons, rock groups, a gospel group, and the entire city of Bethlehem, Pennsylvania) was first performed in 1971 and is truly a landmark in mixed-media performance. His earlier *39 Minutes for 39 Autos* (for thirty-nine amplified auto horns, auto lights, Moog Synthesizer, thirty skyscrapers, radio stations, a television station, dancers, etc.—first performed on August 29, 1969 in San Francisco) provides further example of equally staggering proportions. Of these the composer has remarked:

In my work, *39 Minutes for 39 Autos,* I attempted to make everyone a musician. One hundred thousand persons participated in the premiere. My *Hallelujah,* commissioned by Lehigh University, used hundreds of musicians . . . in this composition I tried to make every musician a human being.[15]

Moran's works embrace an incredible variety of mixed-media explorations. *Divertissement No. 1, 1967* (for popcorn, electric frying pan, and any instrumental soloist), for example, requires the performer to read popping corn as noteheads on five-lined white-staved dark sunglasses. *Bombardments No. 4, 1968* (for trombone and tape, commissioned by Stu Dempster) requests that the trombonist, wrapped in a sack, become a visual analog gargoyle (legs, slide, arms, and body movements all sharing in the vision of struggling shape, lit dimly from both sides), and its aural counterpart.

In general, film music does not qualify as a particularly significant exploration of media forms. There are, however, a number of exceptions which should be noted. Aside from the *Relâche* film of 1924 by René Clair mentioned previously, work by composer John Whitney and his painter brother James is particularly significant. Beginning in 1940 they began their experiments with abstract film and infrasonics (in this case, a series of pendulums mechanically connected to a wedge-shaped aperture and influencing an optical sound track producing sine wave oscillations with a frequency range of a little more than four octaves). Like the *Three Pieces for Sound Projector* (to be discussed under intermedia) and the sound track notations of Norman McLaren (discussed under *Electronic Music*), the Whitney experiments have

14. Ibid., p. 73.
15. Robert Moran in a letter to David Cope.

provided a vast new source of media materials. However, these have not as yet produced a significant body of artistic achievement.[16] John Whitney speaks to this point:

It is hoped that the partnership of sound and picture will attract the attention it deserves in artistic circles. The problem that confronts the individual consists of a number of difficulties whose acquaintance he may already have made in the course of his experiences in modern music or painting. Whether the necessary technical apparatus will always be placed at the disposal of the artist is a question that touches on an elementary problem, whose solution lies hidden in the darkness of the future.[17]

Salvatore Martirano's *L'sGA* (1968) is a massive and intense mixed-media work overloading the senses with dramatic, visual, and aural messages. *L'sGA,* in the composer's words, is:

Lincoln's *Gettysburg Address* for actor, tape, and film, using a helium "bomb" which the actor breathes from at the end of the piece so that his voice goes up a couple of octaves . . . all you need to do is catch a few words now and then to understand what the meaning is. You hear "government" and you hear "people." And thus I would hope that the person watching would create the framework of specific and exact meaning according to how he sees things. Because I'm not forcing him to catch on to a sequence of events in which each one has to be understood for the next one to make sense. It's almost kind of throwing it in all different places and gradually, I would hope, the conception is built up in the audience.[18]

Groups devoted to mixed-media performance include ZAJ (pronounced *thack;* a Mexican Theater of the Absurd); THE; Harkins and Larson (formed in 1975 at CME in San Diego); and individual performers such as Stuart Dempster (performance of Robert Erickson's *General Speech for Trombone,* 1969, being most notable).

Inter-media

It is possible, using parallel techniques, to approach media forms in a determinate fashion. Exploration of some of the creative and psychological relationships between aural and visual composition demonstrates the increased number of parameters available in simultaneous projections and sounds. New creative procedures resulting from the combining of art and music cannot rely implicitly on the unique approach of either discipline.

Important is the articulation of those areas in common and those in contrast between aural and visual forms. Both deal in *color,* the most completely

---

16. Recent "popular" *visual music* devices wherein strobes or 3-D "color-organs" translate bass, treble, and midrange sounds into visual abstractions, while interesting, prove to be little more than *light-shows* of the most simplistic order.

17. John Whitney, "Moving Pictures and Electronic Music," *Die Reihe* 7 (1960):71.

18. Panel Discussion: *ASUC Proceedings* 3 (1968):43.

overlapping quality. Both deal in *time* (even the smallest still projection requires it) and all that time perception implies: rhythm, meter (or organized
groups of events in time), and especially *form*. The difference is in control of
time: except for motion picture projections, visual direction in time is uniquely
within the perceiver. The manner in which the observer develops rhythm, meter,
and form within the time of perception is not controllable as in music, where
these elements remain under the almost complete direction of the creator and/
or performer.

Both deal in *space,* though somewhat differently. All the spatial characteristics of visual perception apply to aural perception. For example, direction of material to the audience by means of physical positioning of sound-
producing objects (e.g., instruments and loudspeakers) can effectively par-
rallel visual directions. The recognition of space in inter-media is the easiest
and most controllable aspect of the overlapping elements. When directions are
the same (e.g., sound behind or coming from the visual object) and then are
suddenly changed radically (to, for instance, the opposite direction), the perceiver can lose the continuity of both.

It is much more difficult to recognize relationships of direction *within* the
material. Though "up" and "down" in music traditionally implies higher or
lower frequency, studies have shown that this aspect is learned but rationally
not real; that is, it stems from notation, not sound itself. Experiments quickly
show that when dots are placed on a screen in such an order as to imply "notes"
and corresponding sounds, the effect of up and down is apparent. When dots
are placed in unorganized structure with sounds, they do not appear wrong,
but just not spatially related in any way to the sounds. With any increased
complexity of aural and visual materials, these relationships are lost; however,
the relationships of simplicity and complexity remain. Experiments show immediate recognition (see fig. 7.7).

Experiments in *time* relationships have evolved a number of separate but
related rhythmic concepts:

1. Sound imitation of action ("Mickey-Mousing It," in movie jargon) is
possibly the simplest and least significant application.

Two screens were set up about ten feet apart and ten feet from the audience, the
speakers for the electronic sound track behind the screens. Duplicate projections
were run about two seconds apart, utilizing duplicate line and dot motion, while an
electronic sound track produced low and high sine waves, the first being continuous
(or line imitation), the latter a pointillistic and variable pattern run one second
behind the first projection or midway between the two projections. The canon effect
between aural and visual perception was immediately recognizable.[19]

Contrapuntal effects such as the one described above prove more observable than when using one or the other art forms separately. Recognition of

---

19. Experiment carried out by the author.

Figure 7.7.

imitative elements in rhythm between aural and visual elements seems heightened immeasurably by the combination of the two materials.

2. As in *space* study, rhythmic complexity vs. simplicity provides material for formal considerations.

3. Ostinato and similar rhythmic concepts between aural and visual materials work easily and effectively even when highly complex:

A "light-show" was constructed around flashing projections of green, blue, and red in repetitive pattern ♩. ♩. ♩ $\left(\flat = 92 \right)$ with sound ostinato ♩. ♩. ♩ $\left(\flat = 92 \right)$. When played beginning at the same time, recognition was immediate (by third repetition). When played at complex lag intervals, the effect was less immediately recognizable but nonetheless perceived. Even when the tempo of each was changed $\left(\text{visual } \flat = 120, \text{ audio } \flat = 76 \right)$, the counterpoint and effect was observable.[20]

Experiments in *color* relationships prove least effective. Obviously, no standard relationships of color frequency exist; therefore, each work must depend upon explanation of color relationships if one expects recognition.

20. Experiment by the author.

These experiments, though rudimentary in nature, indicate a vast range of communicable material relationships available to the artist for assimilation into form and style. The following is a short description of the compositional process of *Three Pieces for Sound Projector*:[21]

Piece I (fast) involves three visual and three aural elements. The visual elements (dot, line, and moving blob of rainbow colors) are exposed individually, simultaneously with aural counterparts (high-pitched staccato sounds, low continuous pitch, and blocks of white sound), though no rhythmic relationship is structured (the aural and visual materials appear at approximately the same time, but duration and rhythm of appearance is nonstructured):

Figure 7.8.

Section B of this piece involves use of two and three elements in combination again, with sight and sound approximating appearance at the beginning; however, as the section progresses (speed of appearance increasing), rhythmic simultaneity increases until, at the end of B, all elements of visual and aural activity are simultaneous:

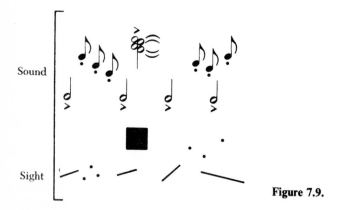

Figure 7.9.

21. The composer believes that his works should "stand alone" and therefore does not sign his name or the date of his works, and does not allow this information to appear on programs. In keeping with his belief, no such information appears here. The analytical information here was derived from conversations with the composer.

The third and final section incorporates overlapping ostinati on established patterns of the previous sections in two ways. First, it is with simultaneous visual/aural materials:

.Figure 7.10.

Secondly, it is with an ostinato canon between sight and sound in pairs, using different pairs in different ostinati.

Figure 7.11.

Piece II (slow) employs speakers, one in front of and one behind the audience. No correlation between object shown and sound is consciously established except in time. The still projectors are turned on and off, with different material chosen at random from a prepared selection. The first section sets up exact imitation: the sounds come on and off with the projections and from behind the screen. The first variation (aside from the variation in sound and slides in the projectors) involves a slow breakdown and return to order of the rhythmic simultaneity of aural and visual events.

Figure 7.12.

The second variation first substitutes speakers at the rear with those in front; when this substitution becomes haphazard, a rhythmic section based on direction is created:

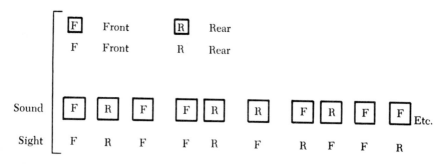

Figure 7.13.

After returning briefly to the original pattern, the final section accelerates a return to each of the previous variations, culminating in a rapid sum, utilizing all variations at once. Finally the original concept is stated again.

The final piece explores spatial relationships *within* the visual structure in both space and color. Three timbres were chosen at random and attached to three colors in the motion projections, so that whenever a visual color appeared, its appropriate timbre sounded. Even if a continuous pitch was involved, it changed to match the color. Pitches were randomly selected and attached to particular areas of the screen (four in all). Rhythm and dynamics were controlled by the rhythm and size of the color grains appearing on the screen. A continuously variable counterpoint exists throughout between color and direction, changing at highly variable rates of speed:

Figure 7.14.

The resultant serialization (and combination of sizes, directions, and colors) achieves the desired highly structured effect, with a high degree of variation available (the increased parameters using a minimal amount of material).

While at times *Three Pieces* takes on attributes of all three types of media forms, there is no doubt that the visual and aural elements as a whole are so closely integrated that one without the other would be only half a work and not viable as a complete artistic whole.

Figure 7.15 is *Metabiosis V: 'A Light, Sound and Audience Environment'* (1972) by Ronald Pellegrino. The total environmental system is explored in

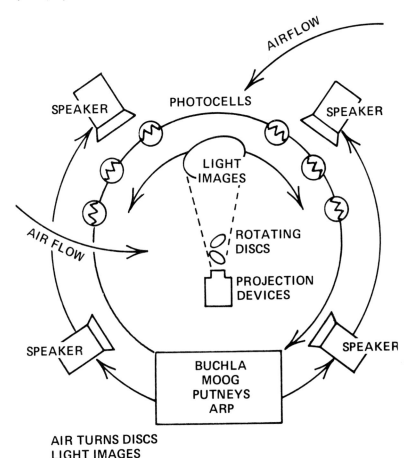

Figure 7.15. Metabiosis V: A light, sound, and audience environment by Ronald Pellegrino. Used by permission of *Proceedings* of the American Society of University Composers 7/8 (72–73) (c) ASUC, Inc., c/o American Music Center, 210 Broadway, Suite 15–79, New York, N.Y. 10023.

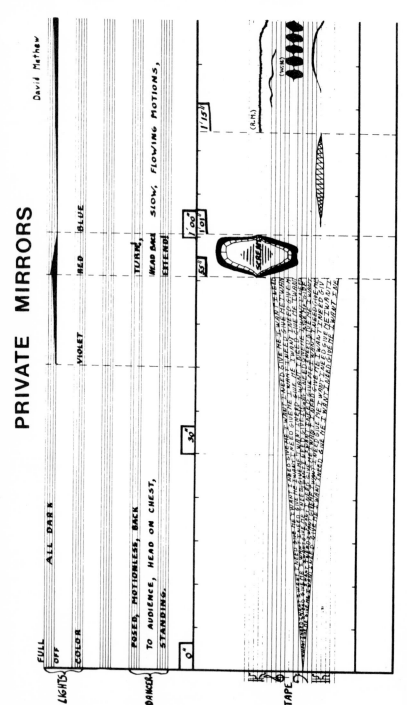

Figure 7.16. David Mathew: *Private Mirrors*. (c) David Mathew 1973. All rights reserved. Used by permission.

this work[22] with the incorporation of the given space and natural variables an intrinsic part of the design.

Private Mirrors by David Mathew (see fig. 7.16) uses an integrated approach to lighting, dancing and tape. The score itself (particularly the tape part notation) indicates the composition's aural and visual simultaneity with both elements intimately related to one another.[23]

Figure 7.17. Merrill Ellis (photo by Ron Bray: North Texas State University, Electronic Music Center, Denton, Texas).

Merrill Ellis's _Mutations_ for brass choir, electronic tape, and light projections is a dramatic and integrated approach to intermedia. The work begins with a standard concert setting. Suddenly the hall is plunged into darkness, the players leave the stage (making vocal and other unusual sounds) and, with the electronic tape becoming the main aural source, projections (in the form of films, lights, etc.) flash on the ceiling and walls, engulfing the audience in a "sea" of visual activity. _Mutating_ the ABA form (not as simplistic as it may appear here), the players return to the hall (rear this time) and perform again under a dim flashing light. The work concludes in total darkness and silence.

Landscape Journey (1963) by Donald Scavarda, for clarinet, piano and film projection, reflects the contrasting elements of aural and visual materials.

22. To be published as part of a book, _Thinking for the Electronic Music Synthesizer_ (chapter 6) as outlined in _ASUC Proceedings,_ 7/8.

23. This six-minute cyclic work involves as well the use of strobe and black lights—the dancer painted with red fluorescent body paint.

Sections of sound alone interplay with soundless projections to create an obvious alternating formal structure. The abstract fast-moving shapes and colors on *two* screens balance the contrast and dependence of the two *instruments* in use.

Scavarda speaks of inter-media implications in his work:

. . . these sounds (are synthesized) with abstract color film to create a filmic extension of the instrumental timbres. The plasticity of the slowly shifting instrumental timbre is further "pushed" by the use of dramatic silences and contrasts with the rapidly moving film which is gradually introduced as the work evolves. . . . Here the film does not have a notational function but rather is an intrinsic part of the structure of the piece. Thus, timbre is perceived visually as well as aurally. The two projectors, placed immediately in back of the piano bench, are "performed" by the pianist, who also operates a rheostat controlling a single lamp (which lights the scores) in an otherwise darkened hall.[24]

Quotation

Quoting a fragment from another composer or style within the framework of one's own work is a growing dramatic media form. While it is hardly new (almost every composer has at one time or another quoted other music, from Bach's borrowed chants to Mahler's quotations of his own music), the use of strikingly different styles in the twentieth-century *avant-garde* has taken a decisively novel direction. The hymn quotes of Charles Ives as well as his free borrowings of any material to suit his message (evident in such works as *Central Park in the Dark* and *Symphony No. 4*) are often starkly presented against highly dissonant textures highlighting the cognizant drama present. While one might contest the placement of this singularly aural activity in a *media-forms* chapter, it is argued that quite unlike the "theme and variations" quoting of previous centuries, this new actively polarized presentation of borrowed material results in a "psycho-dramatic" message.

Reasons for such quoting vary from composer to composer and often from work to work by the same composer. George Rochberg speaks of his usage:

The centerpiece of my *Music for the Magic Theatre* is a transcription, that is, a completely new version, of a Mozart adagio. I decided to repeat it in my own way because I loved it. People who understand, love it because they know it began with Mozart and ended with me. People who don't understand think it's by Mozart.[25]

Peter Maxwell Davies's use of Handel quotes in the aforementioned *Eight Songs for a Mad King* (1969) results in a strange periodization (George III period) as well as superimposed *collage* effect (especially in "Comfort Ye, Comfort Ye My People," of Song #7). Michael Colgrass achieves an Ivesian

24. From a letter to the author.
25. George Rochberg, "No Center," *Composer* 2, no. 1 (September 1969):89.

montage in *As Quiet As* (1966) for orchestra by using a multitude of effectively varied quotes framed by a background of subtle clouds of modulating chords.

Mauricio Kagel superimposes quote upon quote from Beethoven in his *Ludwig Van* (1970) creating, like Lukas Foss in his *Baroque Variations* (1967) and Stockhausen in his *Opus 1970,* a surrealistic intertwining of raw material stylistically consistent but rhythmically and texturally deranged. Each is contextually dramatic as additive overlays contribute to the increasing cognizant tension of "composer" intention.

The third movement of Luciano Berio's *Sinfonia* (1968) for eight soloists and orchestra, quoting extensively from Mahler and Debussy among others, possesses dramatic power through its use of striking text (likewise quoting from a number of sources including Samuel Beckett) and driving musical force (see analysis in chapter 11). Certainly more innocent, at least in its length and continuity, is George Crumb's use of a short Bach fragment in his *Ancient Voices of Children,* 1970 (this quote is shown in chapter 11). The performance (on a toy piano) complete with Baroque ornaments is possibly one of the most powerful quotes in recent music, though the dynamics of the movement barely rise above *mezzoforte.*

Phil Winsor's *Orgel I* (for pipe organ and prerecorded tape) includes some performer choice (e.g., *which* Bach fugue, prelude, etc.) yet the incredible diversity creates a constant rationale of forged opposites. Figure 7.19 shows

Figure 7.18. Phil Winsor. Photo by Julia Winsor.

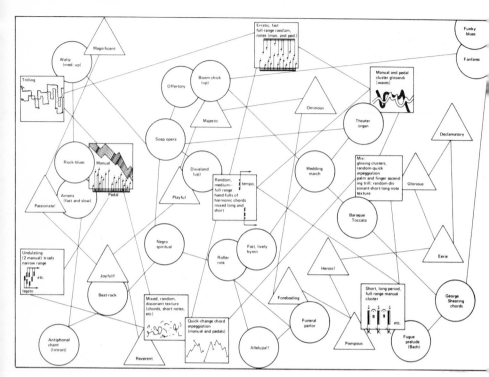

Figure 7.19. Phil Winsor's *ORGEL I* (page X). Copyright (c) 1975 by Pembroke Music Co., Inc. New York. International Copyright Secured. 62 Cooper Square, New York, N.Y. 10003.

page X, a page of directed choices from which at points in the score (not shown) the performer may choose items within a prescribed time limit. The tape, made by the performer, contributes further overlays of the given material resulting in massive densities of crowded triadic clashes. Each listener will, of course, recognize from experience only a percentage of the quotes. However, their often simultaneously polarized styles, and indeed the listener's inherent quest for message, creates intense drama.

Vectoral Analysis: Donald Erb: *Souvenir* (1970)

(For information on vectoral analysis and procedures, see chapter 1).

1. Historical Background: Donald Erb was born in Youngstown, Ohio, in 1927. After early years as a jazz trumpeter, he studied composition formally with, among others, Bernard Heiden (at Indiana University) and Nadia Boulanger. He is currently Composer-in-Residence at Southern Methodist

Figure 7.20. Donald Erb.

University in Dallas, Texas. His major works include *Symphony of Overtures* (1964) and *The Seventh Trumpet* (1969) for orchestra, *Harold's Trip to the Sky* (1972) for chamber ensemble, and *Concerto for Percussion and Orchestra* (1966).

Souvenir, for dancers, instrumental ensemble, electronic tape, projections, and props, was completed early in 1970 and first performed in February of that year at Oberlin College. Laurence Berger (dance) and Royce Dendler (sculpture) premiered the work and created subsequent performances in northern Ohio.

2. Overview: *Souvenir* is a brief (8½ minutes in duration) work of driving intensity. The sonic form of the work derives from the skeletal scoring for the 12–20 wind and percussion players (who surround the audience in the dark) and the electronic tape (created from electronic sources in the Cleveland Institute of Music electronic laboratory). The tape portion exists throughout the work and consists of a slighly out-of-tune "perfect" fifth interval (B—F♯), which acts as a continual drone. The live performers begin during the second minute (signaled by the conductor, whose primary job is to flash a light cue at the end of each minute during the performance). All play *pianissimo* using either long tones within a minor second of either of the tape pitches or short pointillistic effects on their respective instruments. These slowly and consistently grow throughout the piece until the *crescendo* reaches *fortissimo* (at around 7½ minutes). The parts are written in English and are easy to memorize (almost a necessity, since the piece is performed in the dark).

Elements are added according to the following schematic:

minutes: 0—1   action: nothing; just tape
        1—2   players quietly begin to play
        2—3   slide projections begin
        3—4   dancers enter
        4—5   weather balloons are added
        5—6   silly string is sprayed
        6—7½   continue
        7—8½ (or end)   conductor strikes gong, signaling
                         ping-pong balls to be "dumped."

The hall is filled with "black light" (nonvisible light that excites certain luminescent paints). The dancers, covered with Da-Glo (luminescent) tape, bring small props (i.e., sponge rubber balls of various sizes) also covered with Da-Glo paints of various colors (all of these glow in the dark). The projections (optional) are of the performers' choice, but in fitting with the joyous, positive nature of the work, and not so bright as to nullify the effect of the black lights. The weather balloons (8- to 12-feet war surplus balloons) are also covered with Da-Glo paints and bounced into the hall (whereupon the audience usually begins to participate). Da-Glo "silly string" is sprayed into the whole auditorium, inundating the performers and audience. The ping-pong balls (about 5,000) have been painted with Da-Glo and fall into the audience (becoming "souvenirs" of the performance). The activity clearly accelerates in correspondence with the sounds: a singular and direct *crescendo* from beginning to end.

3. Orchestration: The taped "perfect" fifth drone is created by sawtooth waves drawn through low pass filters. These in turn are slowly adjusted so that the timbre is continually altering during performance. The slight "beating" of the inharmonic fifth also contributes to the perception of change.

The live performance ensemble is free enough so that exact sounds are unpredictable. It is interesting to note, however, that the long tones, in the interval of seconds with the tape, create subtle shifts in motion and dissonant threads against which the pointillistic events are superimposed. All these occur spatially within the concert space.

4. Basic Techniques: Erb has employed a quasi-improvisatory verbal score that clearly defines limits in performance. The sensual overload that slowly occurs with aural, visual, and tactile elements gradually develops a counterpoint inherent in the "play-by-play" scoring.

5, 6. Vertical and Horizontal Models: Pitch content is limited (in the non-effect material) to seconds surrounding the taped fifth (i.e., B♭—C and F—G). These contribute to a dissonant yet static quality lacking the tension suggested by their "cluster" content. The stretto of effects (both aural and visual) contribute to the momentum of intensity that ensues during the performance.

7. Style: The style of *Souvenir* is possibly best summed up in the composer's own words: "One reason that it works (is that) it is an outgoing and happy work; non-neurotic."[26] The style is inter-media. Audiences (at least those observed by this author) become first mesmerized by the visual material and then, with growing anticipation, actively involved with pushing balloons in the air, dodging silly string and throwing ping pong balls during the near cataclysm of sound and energy surrounding them.

---

26. In a telephone interview with the author.

Bibliography

Further Readings*

Ashley, Robert, "Notes for *Public Opinion Descends Upon the Demonstrators." Asterisk* 1, no. 1 (1961):49. Presents score and information about performance of this work.

Austin, Larry. "SYCOM—Systems Complex for the Studio and Performing Arts." *Numus West* 5:57. A most interesting article pertaining to the potentials of media research and study of new combinational art forms.

Becker, Jurgen, and Wolf Vostell, eds. *Happenings.* Hamburg: Rowohlt, 1965. A good source of information on this topic from a European viewpoint.

Beckwith, John, and Udo Kasemets, eds. *The Modern Composer and His World.* Toronto: University of Toronto Press, 1961.

Cage, John, *M. Writings '67–'72.* Middletown, Conn.: Wesleyan University Press, 1973.
———. *Silence.* Middletown, Conn.: Wesleyan University Press, 1961.
———. *A Year from Monday.* Middletown, Conn.: Wesleyan University Press, 1967. All very useful books and collections of articles, many of which are related to this man's constant efforts at media connections, be they relevant or not. A bibliography of Cage articles and interviews exists in Kostelanetz's book on Cage and need not be reprinted here.

Chase, Gilbert. "Toward a Total Musical Theatre." *Arts in Society,* (Spring 1969):25. Good primer in this concept.

Cross, Lowell. "David Tudor," In *Dictionary of Contemporary Music,* edited by John Vinton. New York: E. P. Dutton & Co., 1974. Article ends with a group of works by Tudor who is probably the most prolific, in media forms, of any living composer aside from Cage himself.

Cunningham, Merce. *Changes: Notes on Choreography.* Edited by Frances Starr. New York: Something Else Press, 1969. Fascinating source book not only for the dance contribution to media forms but also for the variety of ways in which it has been included in the past.

Dallin, Leon. *Techniques of Twentieth Century Composition.* 3rd ed. Dubuque: Wm. C. Brown Company Publishers, 1974. Contains a brief but interesting commentary on multimedia.

Doubravova, J. "Music and Visual Art: Their Relation as a Topical Problem of Contemporary Music in Czechoslovakia." *International Review of the Aesthetics and Sociology of Music,* 11:19–28, No. 2 1980.

Gibb, Stanley. "Understanding Terminology and Concepts Related to Media Art Forms." *The American Music Teacher* 22, no. 5:23. Superb article which brought many insights to this author's consideration of the various forms.

Hansen, Al. *A Primer of Happenings and Time-Space Art.* New York: Something Else Press, 1968. Fascinating contribution to the media-forms literature.

*Addresses for record companies, periodicals, and music publishers mentioned in this Bibliography can be found in Appendix 4.

Higgins, Dick. *Postface.* New York: Something Else Press, 1964.

————. *FOEW & OMBWHNW* New York: Something Else Press, 1969. Reprinted by Printed Editions. Both are interesting contributions to the literature, and overlap significantly with materials in chapter 10.

————. *A Dialectic of Centuries: Notes Towards a Theory of the New Arts,* 2nd ed. New York: Printed Editions, 1979. An important collection of essays on Higgins' work in Intermedia.

Hiller, Lejaren. "HPSCHD." *Source* 2, no. 2 (1968). Discusses the work of the same name by Hiller and Cage, with photographs of both composers at the computers.

Hoffman, Paul. "An Interview with Robert Moran." *Composer* 4, no. 2 (1973):46.

Kagel, Mauricio. "On *Match* for Three Performers," *Composer* 3, no. 2 (1972):70. Fascinating account of one very involved in "media" works from the most bizarre to the most conventional.

————. "Uber das instrumentale Theater." *Neue Musik* (Munich, 1961). Interesting study of this man's views on the subject.

Kaprow, Allan. *Assemblage, Environments and Happenings.* New York: Abrams, 1966. Good source, interesting photographs.

Kirby, E. T. *Total Theatre.* New York: E. P. Dutton & Co., 1969. Most fascinating and a very good contribution to the literature though it is slanted in the indeterminate direction: multimedia.

Kirby, Michael. *The Art of Time.* New York: E. P. Dutton & Co., 1969. Relevant and interesting "conceptual" study of media-related forms and structures.

————. *Happenings.* New York: E. P. Dutton & Co., 1965. Good insight into the structure and beginnings of this multimedia form.

Klüver, Billy, Julie Martin, and Barbara Rose. *Pavilion.* New York: Dutton, 1972. A close look into arts and technology; a wide variety of media techniques are explored.

Kostelanetz, Richard. *The Theatre of Mixed Means.* New York: Dial, 1968. Though out of print, one of the best sources and pieces of writing on the subject yet available.

————, ed. *John Cage.* New York: Praeger Publishers, 1970. Fine book containing photographs and documents of the tradition of experimentalism started by Cage. Also contains excellent bibliographies relating to media presentations.

MacLow, Jackson. *The Pronouns: A Collection of Forty Dances for the Dancer's Station.* Barrytown, N.Y.: Station Hill Press, 1980.

"Conversation with Robert Moran." *Numus West* 3:30. Fascinating account of this man's work in the area of media.

Mumma, Gordon. "Four Sound Environments for Modern Dance." *Impulse, the Annual of Contemporary Dance,* 1967. Writing particularly on Cage's work.

Nyman, Michael. *Experimental Music.* London: Macmillan Ltd., 1974. Interesting look into a number of experimental media works of the 1960s.

Pellegrino, Ronald. "Some Thoughts on Thinking for the Electronic Music Synthesizer." *Proceedings* (American Society of University Composers) 7, no. 8 (1972–73):52. Interesting approach to many problems facing the media composer today.

Penn, William. "The Celluloid Image and Mixed Media." *Composer* 1, no. 4 (1970):179. Discusses philosophical aspects of the form.

Proceedings 3. (American Society of University Composers [August 1968].) Includes two very interesting discussions: "Theatre Music" with Richard Browne as chairman and a panel of Barney Childs, Ben Johnston, Salvatore Martirano and Roy Travis; and "Mixed-Media Composition" with Ross Lee Finney as moderator and panelists George Cacioppo, Edwin London, and Salvatore Martirano. Both are of value and interest, and show a multiplicity of views toward both media composition and the personalities involved.

Reynolds, Roger. "Happenings in Japan and Elsewhere." *Arts in Society* 5, no. 1 (Spring-Summer, 1968). Short but quite good reference to some very significant activities in the sixties in Japan by a number of visiting American composers as well as by composers from Japan.

Rochberg, George. "No Center." *Composer* 1, no. 2. (1969):86. Most interesting "train of thought" article which includes fascinating material regarding his ideas of "quoting."

Rossi, Nick, and Robert Choate. *Music of Our Time*. Boston: Crescendo, 1969. A number of references to multimedia with coverage of Cage *(HPSCHD,* p. 337ff.) and Subotnick *(Play! No. 1,* p. 377).

Salzman, Eric. "Mixed Media." In *Dictionary of Contemporary Music,* edited by John Vinton. New York: E. P. Dutton & Co., 1974. Good introduction to the subject. The *Dictionary* also includes many biographies of composers mentioned in this chapter.

Sondheim, Alan, ed. *Individuals. (Post-movement Art in America)*. New York: Dutton, 1977. Interesting work on Acconci and Lucier.

Subotnick, Morton. "Extending the Stuff Music is Made of." *Music Educators Journal* 55, no. 3 (November 1968): 109. Short but good study in the problems and origins of multimedia.

Tomkins, Calvin. *The Bride and the Bachelors*. New York: Viking Press, 1965. A brilliant book looking into the lives of four extremely important contributors to the media concept: Marcel Duchamp, Jean Tinguely, Robert Rauschenberg, and John Cage.

Whitney, John. "Moving Pictures and Electronic Music." In *Die Reihe* 7. Bryn Mawr, Pa.: Theodore Presser, 1965. Superb study in inter-media and a most important contribution to the literature.

———. *Digital Harmony*. Peterborough, N.H.: Byte Books 1980. An extraordinarily encyclopedic text by a pioneer of multimedia techniques.

Yates, Peter. *Twentieth Century Music*. New York: Pantheon Books, 1967. Follows the history of the experimental "ideal" in America, including happenings and multimedia developments.

Young, La Monte, and Marian Zazeela. *Selected Writings*. Munich: Heiner Friedrich, 1969. Referred to in chapter 10; quite apropos here as well. Interesting but centered around the activities of the two authors.

Youngblood, Gene. *Expanded Cinema*. New York: Dutton, 1970. Important information regarding computer films and inter-media concepts.

Recordings and Publishers*

Ashley, Robert. *Public Opinion Descends Upon the Demonstrators* (1961). *Asterisk* (magazine) 1, no. 1.

Austin, Larry. *Bass* (1967). CPE-*Source*. For bass, tape, and film. Performed over N.E.T. by Bertram Turetzky. Involves exaggerated gestures and mime.

———. *The Maze* (1965). Audience involvement with lights and dramatic actions by the performers. Both these works show the theatrical possibilities of standard performing situations.

Beerman, Burton. *Mixtures*. Media Press. Ensemble, tape, and candlelight procession.

---

*Addresses for record companies, periodicals, and music publishers mentioned in this Bibliography can be found in Appendix 4.

Berio, Luciano. *Laborintus II* (1965). Universal Edition. Recorded on RCA LSC-3267. For voices, instruments, reciter, and tape.

————. *Sinfonia* (1968). Universal Edition. Recorded on Columbia MS-7268.

Cage, John. Media works include:

————. *Theatre Piece* (1960). Peters.

————. *Variations III.* Peters. Recorded on DG-139442.

————. *Water Music* (1952).

Cage, John and Lejaren Hiller. *HPSCHD.* Peters. Recorded on Nonesuch H-71224. A "happening."

Colgrass, Michael. *As Quiet As* (1966). MCA. Recorded on RCA LSC-3001.

Cope, David. *BTRB* (1970). Brass Press. For any brass player; theatre piece.

————. *Deadliest Angel Revision* (1971). Seesaw Music Corp.

Crumb, George. *Ancient Voices of Children.* Peters. Recorded on Nonesuch 71255.

————. *Voice of the Whale (Vox Balaenae).* Peters. Recorded on Columbia M-32739.

Davies, Peter Maxwell. *8 Songs for a Mad King.* Boosey & Hawkes. Recorded on Nonesuch H-71285.

Ellis, Merrill. *Mutations.* Shawnee Press (New York).

Erb, Donald. *Souvenir.* Merion Music.

Erickson, Robert. *General Speech, for Trombone* (1969). Recorded on New World 254. An amazing theatre piece composed for (and played here by) Stu Dempster.

Foss, Lukas. *Baroque Variations* (1967). Carl Fischer. Recorded on Nonesuch 71202.

Ives, Charles. *Central Park in the Dark* (1906). AMP. Recorded on Columbia MS-6843.

Kagel, Mauricio. *Die Himmelsmechanik* (1965). Composition using vivid images of suns, moons, clouds, etc.

————. *Kommentar und Extempore* (1967). For three actors, singer, seven brass instruments.

————. *Ludwig Van.* Recorded on DG-2530014.

————. *Match* (1966). Universal Edition. Recorded on DG-137006.

————. *Variaktionen* (1967). Universal Edition. For four actors, three singers, and tapes.

Kasemets, Udo. *"It: Tribute to Buckminster Fuller, Marshall McLuhan and John Cage.* A computer-controlled audio-visual audience participation work.

Knowles, Alison. *Natural Assemblages and the True Crow.* New York: Printed Editions, 1980. A sound-tape collage with visuals.

Kraft, William. *Contextures: Riots—Decade '60.* Recorded on London 6613. For orchestra and projections.

Lunetta, Stanley. Four excellent theater pieces complete with flashing lights, projections, and sets; all available from CPE-*Source: The Wringer, Mr. Machine, A Piece for Bandoneon and Strings, Spider Song.*

Martirano, Salvatore. *L'sGA* (1968). MCA. Recorded on Polidor 245001.

————. *Underworld.* MCA. For four actors, two basses, tenor saxophone, and tape.

Moran, Robert. The following are available only from the composer: *Bombardments No. 4; Divertissement No. 1; Hallelujah; 39 Minutes for 39 autos.*

de Oliveira, Jocy. *Probabilistic Theatre 1.* Uses a map projection as score for musicians, actors, dancers, and lights.

Reck, David. *Blues and Screamer.* CPE-*Source.* An excellent aural-visual composite including an antiwar film and dramatic performer remarks (near the end of the score).

Reynolds, Roger. *Emperor of Ice Cream.* Peters.

————. *Ping.* CPE-*Source.* Recorded on CRI-285.

Rochberg, George. *Music for the Magic Theatre.* Theodore Presser. For orchestra. Desto DC-6444.

Satie, Erik. *Relâche* (1924). Salabert. Recorded on Vanguard C-10037/8.

Schäffer, Boguslaw. *Audiences No. 1–5* (1964). PWM.

————. *Non-Stop* (1960). PWM.

————. *Incident* (1966). PWM.

Scriabin, Alexander. *Poem of Fire.* Balawe Publishers. Recorded on London 6732.

Somers, Harry. *Improvisation.* A theater piece for voices and instruments.

Stockhausen, Karlheinz. *Momente* (1963). Recorded on Nonesuch 71157. Begins with players applauding the audience, with rhythmic notations.

————. *Opus 1970.* Recorded on DG-139461.

Strange, Allen. *No Dead Horses on the Moon.* Media Press.

————. *Palace.* CAP. For violin, tape, projections, and staging.

————. *Vanity Fair.* Another dramatic multimedia work.

Subotnick, Morton. *Mandolin* (1960). MCA. For viola, tape, and film.

————. *Play* (1962). MCA. Woodwind quintet, piano, tape, film.

————. *A Ritual Game Room* (1970). MCA. Without audience.

Tudor, David. See p. 769 of John Vinton's *Dictionary of Contemporary Music* for a compilation by Lowell Cross of Tudor's work in media forms.

8 Improvisation

Aesthetics and Definition

The morphology of any system which segregates its participants as completely as music has done (composer, performer, audience) becomes suspect. It has taken centuries for the music world to develop a set of symbols that serve to separate the creative mind from the audience. The inadequacy of these symbols cannot begin to represent the significance of a Mozart, a Brahms, or a Beethoven. Improvisation, even in its most simple forms, results from that realization and immediacy. Improvisation is not irresponsibility. It may, in fact, produce a result more faithfully representative of the composer's intentions than that of standard symbols. The composer who wishes this, for example:

Figure 8.1.

will find realization impractical and the result studied and imperfect. The notation or the direction "five 32nd notes from B♭ to low C" results in easy

Figure 8.2.

realization and immediate and practical communication of the composer's intention. Even fig. 8.3, often mistaken as indeterminacy, results in more accurate performance than studied notation.

Figure 8.3.

Improvisation is more a notational than a philosophical challenge to tradition. It must inherently exist to some extent in all music in which exact notation of every detail is not possible: therefore in *all* music. *Even* Beethoven (*even* because, as Lukas Foss has quoted him: "Does he think I have his silly fiddle in mind when the spirit talks to me?"[1]) must, in the last analysis, relent to performer decision. The following passage is from his piano sonata, opus 106, measures 264–66:

Figure 8.4.

might be more accurately represented:

Figure 8.5.

Beethoven's choice of the loose and interpretative word *ritardando* here encourages the performer's creative approach. While certainly more interpretation than improvisation, it does show strong suggestions and inflections of improvisatory ideas.

1. See *Perspectives of New Music* 1, no. 2 (Spring 1963):46.

The Baroque figured bass and the classical concerto cadenzas are two predominant examples of improvisation in traditional music. The figured bass provides only the bass notes and the intervals above them in terms of shorthand numbers below the note, allowing the performer the creative possibility of improvising and developing rhythmic and melodic fragments and motives. Cadenzas, up to the late eighteenth century, were very rarely written out in detail, giving each performer chances to "show off" in the manner best suited to his/her own particular talents (merely suggesting motives and harmonic relevance to the movement or the work as a whole). Donald Erb refers to the latter use in remarks about his own *Concerto for Percussion and Orchestra* (1966):

The work is cast in the traditional concerto format of three movements. The solo part is in the eighteenth and nineteenth century virtuoso tradition. The cadenzas in the second and, especially, the third movements harken back to the eighteenth century tradition of having the performer improvise much or all of the cadenza. A variation on this idea was used in the first movement, where instead of having the soloist improvise a cadenza I had the entire orchestra, other than the soloist, improvise it.[2]

As with the Erb *Concerto* it would seem logical for the composer, rather than refusing to admit the existence of (or making as insignificant as possible) the necessary improvisational aspects of the music, to use it to both his/her own and the performer's advantage. If indeed the "silly fiddler" shapes the final meaning of the work, would it not be more intelligent to work with performers, in hopes of making them (and consequently the work) less "silly," or to resort to magnetic tape and work with the manifest problem of "silly" speakers and variable acoustics?

The emphasis in improvisation is, in fact, more *creative* than *re-creative*. Audiences are often content to quibble over inadequacies in performances of music its hundredth time around. With improvisation they can experience sounds for the first time, and possibly the last, without the heroic image of individual idols.

Allan Bryant states that improvisation is "Similar to free jazz, oriental and African music, things which are impossible to write out"[3] and "Free, wild music and ideas that wouldn't come about with single composers working alone."[4] Foss adds: "Cardew is right to worry about ethics of improvisation.

---

2. Liner notes of the recording: Turnabout TV-S 34433 by the composer. Taken from the program notes of the first performance in 1966.
3. As quoted in "Groups," *Source: Music of the Avant-Garde*, 2, no. 1 (January 1968).
4. Ibid., p. 24.

It needs it. *Improvisation:* one plays what one already knows. . . . Improvisation that works is improvisation made safe."[5] Whether one works individually or in a group, improvisation is a form of composition. Communication and exactness are as important and explicit as those of traditional rituals of performance.

Immediate Background

The circumstances under which improvisation developed are unclear. Interest in this century may be rooted in jazz with such artists as Miles Davis *(Bitch's Brew* and beyond), Modern Jazz Quartet, John Coltrane, Albert Ayler, Denny Zeitlin, Pharoah Sanders, Coleman Hawkins, Django Rheinhardt, and Lenny Tristano, to name just a few.

A major work in *avant-garde* improvisational jazz is "Free Jazz," a 36½-minute uninterrupted "anthem" with Ornette Coleman (plastic alto saxophone) and Don Cherry (pocket trumpet). Eric Dolphy (bass clarinet), Freddie Hubbard (trumpet), Scott LaFaro (bass), Charlie Haden (bass), Billy Higgins and Ed Blackwell (drummers) also contributed to this extraordinary landmark of the jazz avant-garde. Cecil Taylor (first with Steve Lacy and Buell Neidlinger, later with Bill Barron and Ted Curson) was also an important pioneer. His keyboard skills and intense energy created imaginative improvisations. More recently George Lewis, Anthony Braxton, Sun Ra and the Art Ensemble of Chicago all have contributed richly improvised performances and albums.

A number of contemporary composers associated with improvisation are or were actively involved in jazz (particularly third-stream composers such as Gunther Schuller). It is more plausible, however, that *contemporary* improvisation sprang from the performers' inability to realize accurately the complexities of recent music; the composer, perhaps out of frustration, perhaps because the result was the same (or better), chose to allow a certain freedom in performance. Luciano Berio, for example, in his *Tempi Concertati,* requires the percussionist to hit everything as fast as possible; exact notation would be impractical or even impossible. The effect is predictable and effective even without a note or rhythm being written.

Improvisation differs from indeterminacy, as its meaning in music refers to the aspect of performer interaction, an activity more often than not controllable in rough shape by the composer, and even predictable within limits. Speaking to this point William Hellermann clearly defines that distinction:

It seems to me that there is a fundamental difference between aleatoric and improvisational music. Improvisation is concerned with the realization in real time of defined artistic goals. Aleatory, by its very nature, does not recognize the

5. Ibid., p. 17.

existence of goals. Both differ from the traditional "classic music" by leaving open to the performer the choice of the specific materials to be used in the piece. They are often lumped together for this reason and, also, because they are both thought to be "free." Actually, freedom is not really the issue. Improvisation, at its highest, seeks meaning through spontaneity. Aleatory declares meaning to be spontaneity. Both of these are very restrictive states. I find that in my own works I am increasingly concerned with improvisation, and never with anything I would call aleatory.[6]

The basic factor to remember in improvisation is that the composer has relinquished some control over musical events to the performer. However, this is done with the full belief that the performer will play with learned skills and an integrity of context and style. In summary, the *reasons* that most composers employ improvisation are:

1. Many composers (as well as performers and listeners) suggest that simply realizing notes from the printed page results in generally strained and somewhat uncreative results. Each performance is predictable and thus not as interesting as a certain amount of flexibility might make them. The 'live' and fresh aspect of improvisation can provide a unique performance each time a work is played.

2. In contemporary music, improvisation often results in rhythms and patterns that would paralyze the performer if completely written out. One can note this particularly in certain jazz music, where the subtle and refined improvisatory character of syncopations before and after the beat make full and exact notation a near impossibility. Even if it were possible, would it be performable in that state and, most important, would it have the same kind of fresh musical quality that it does when improvised?

3. Many contemporary composers feel that since improvisation exists in all music to one degree or another, it is only a small step to allowing more freedom with rewards far exceeding risks.

Improvisation Groups

The 1960s brought about a number of groups dedicated to improvisation: the New Music Ensemble (Austin, Lunetta, Mizelle, Woodbury, Alexander, and Johnson); Sonic Arts Group (Mumma, Ashley, Behrman, and Lucier); the *Musica Elettronica Viva* (Allan Bryant, Alvin Curran, Jon Phetteplace, Carol Plantamura, Frederic Rzewski, Richard Teitelbaum, and Ivan Vandor); and the University of Illinois Chamber Players, directed by Jack McKenzie. Whatever the means of producing sound (electronic or instrumental), the immediate and temporary creations were based solely on the interaction of the

6. Tom Everett, "Questions and Answers," *Composer* 2, no. 4 (March 1971):82.

Figure 8.6. Lukas Foss, Music Director
and Conductor, The Brooklyn
Philharmonic Orchestra. Photo
permission by Carnegie Hall, 154 W.
57th St., New York, N.Y. 10019.

performers (most of whom were composers). The responsibility was with the
ensemble, not a single personality. Lukas Foss remarks: "I thought I had invented a new kind of improvisation. I now know that I was merely the first
not to sign my name."[7] The 1957 U.C.L.A.-based Improvisation Chamber
Ensemble under the direction of Foss consisted of piano, clarinet, 'cello, and
percussion (among the first of such groups). The ensemble worked primarily
from charts indicating only initial ideas (e.g., motive, rhythm, pattern) needed
to create a work. Many rehearsals yielded a polished result in performances
which varied somewhat, but were more crystalline than live improvisation.
The group also performed improvised interludes between the movements of
Foss's *Time Cycle* (1960) for soprano and orchestra (first version, 1960).

7. As quoted in "Groups," op. cit.

Cornelius Cardew (of AMM, which also included Lou Gare, Eddie Prevost, and Keith Rowe), in the same article referred to earlier, adds: "The past always seems intentional, but at the time it appears to be accidental."[8]

The MW 2 Ensemble of Poland uses instruments of more traditional origin, while at the same time employing two dancers and an actor, with tapes, projection, and scenery (see fig. 8.7). Performer interaction therefore takes the form of visual as well as musical improvisation.

Figure 8.7. MW 2 Ensemble of Poland.

Group improvisational situations challenge the aesthetic of a "leading personality." The structure and immediate creation resulting from such groups challenges the audience's categorization of individual idols more than they philosophically or aurally alter traditional methods of creative intention.

Works

Improvisation varies from inexact pitch identification to whole sections left to performer interaction bordering on indeterminacy. One or more elements (or limits) is usually provided to act as a vehicle to shape the material more effectively into the context of the work. Roger Harris, for example, in *Kroma II*, provides notes and some relative durational indications (the composer has

8. Ibid., p. 18.

Figure 8.8. *Realization from Wind Sound Sculpture #1 (Kroma II) by* Roger W. Harris. Published by Composers' Autograph Publications.

noted in the score: "fragments or motives may be repeated at any tempo or dynamic level"), while tempo, dynamics, and composite structure are left to the performer's "reaction" to the audience's "reaction" (see fig. 8.8).

The concept of *time* provides an essential ingredient in the contemporary composer's approach. Morton Feldman expresses his ideas as to how objects exist *as* time, not of, in, or about time:

. . . This was not how to make an object . . . but how this object exists *as* Time. Time regained, as Proust referred to his work. Time as an Image, as Aristotle suggested. This is the area which the visual arts later began to explore. This is the area which music, deluded that it was counting out the seconds, has neglected.

I once had a conversation with Karlheinz Stockhausen, where he . . . began beating on the table and said: "A sound exists either here—or here—or here." He was convinced that he was demonstrating reality to me. That the beat, and the possible placement of sounds in relation to it, was the only thing the composer could realistically hold on to. The fact that he had reduced it to so much a square foot made him think Time was something he could handle and even parcel out, pretty much as he pleased.

Frankly, this approach to Time bores me. I am not a clockmaker. I am interested in getting Time in its unstructured existence. That is, I am interested in how this wild beast lives in the jungle—not in the zoo. I am interested in how Time exists before we put our paws on it—our minds, our imaginations, into it.

One would think that music more than any other art would be exploratory about Time. But is it? Timing—not Time—has been passed off as the real thing in music. . . .[9]

9. Morton Feldman, "Between Categories," *The Composer* 1, no. 2 (September 1969):75.

Realization of the inadequacy of standard notation leads not only to new notation, but to the lack of notation entirely. This destroys the composer/performer relationship, a hierarchy required by most traditional audiences. Lukas Foss, in works like *Echoi* (1963), hints toward this by employing stems without noteheads (though exact indications of rhythm, dynamics, and order are given).

William Duckworth's *Pitch City* (see fig. 8.9) for wind instruments instructs four performers to trace pitches from the corners to the middle; each note's duration is equivalent to the individual performer's ability to sustain the note(s) as long as possible (breathing between notes). More notes remain unplayed (73) than played (71), while at the same time a twelve-tone row (top

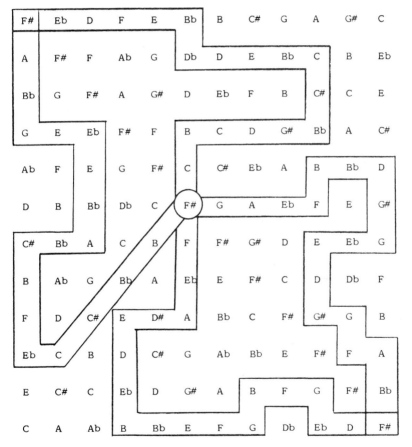

F#	Eb	D	F	E	Bb	B	C#	G	A	G#	C
A	F#	F	Ab	G	Db	D	E	Bb	C	B	Eb
Bb	G	F#	A	G#	D	Eb	F	B	C#	C	E
G	E	Eb	F#	F	B	C	D	G#	Bb	A	C#
Ab	F	E	G	F#	C	C#	Eb	A	B	Bb	D
D	B	Bb	Db	C	F#	G	A	Eb	F	E	G#
C#	Bb	A	C	B	F	F#	G#	D	E	Eb	G
B	Ab	G	Bb	A	Eb	E	F#	C	D	Db	F
F	D	C#	E	D#	A	Bb	C	F#	G#	G	B
Eb	C	B	D	C#	G	Ab	Bb	E	F#	F	A
E	C#	C	Eb	D	G#	A	B	F	G	F#	Bb
C	A	Ab	B	Bb	E	F	G	Db	Eb	D	F#

Figure 8.9. William Duckworth: *Pitch City.* (Copyright Media Press, Champaign, Ill., 1969.) Used by permission. All rights reserved.

line, left to right) is expressed in all versions—original, retrograde (right to left), inversion (top to bottom), and retrograde inversion (bottom to top)—and in every possible transposition. The composer's intention here is unmistakable: to prepare the complete logical and mathematical twelve-tone row structure, and then totally avoid any realization of this organization. This represents a philosophical blast at twelve-tone rationale that must play a distinct part in any educated performer's realization of the score (none of the outlined portions remotely follow twelve-tone direction). Improvisation occurs in rhythm, instrumentation, and resultant octave (depending on the instrument's range).

Duckworth's *Walden Variations* (see fig. 8.10) demonstrates improvisational graphic notation. The sheet shown here is the third and final score page which is a ". . . free improvisation sheet based on the design of the original sheet. The events and movements to and from events are ambiguous and can be freely interpreted. Dancers, readers, slides, movies, and/or lights may be employed as the performers feel it to be in keeping within the general spirit of the piece as they understand it."[10] Completed in 1971, *Walden Variations* is a nonstructured improvisation-based score with open instrumentation.

In *III for Double Ensemble,* Harold Budd employs boxes located in high, middle, and low approximate pitch areas around the staff, in which numbers appear indicating the number of notes to be played. Instructions such as pizzicato and staccato often accompany the boxed improvisation areas. In contrast to this (the jazz trio), the quartet (consisting of flute, clarinet, vibes and 'cello, and separated both spatially and visually from the trio) plays from exact pitch notation without rhythmic directions. Two improvisatory techniques thus enhance the stylistic distinction between the groups.

Etudes for Organ by Lukas Foss requires four different improvisational techniques, one for each movement. In the first, the performer varies an exactly-notated motor rhythm single-line melody by freely repeating note groups (no more than twelve score notes should be played without returning to some group of notes of the performer's choice). In the second, groups of notes (right hand) are scored for which the performer may choose order, rhythm, octave, and/or number of the notes desired. Forearm clusters dominate throughout the third movement, with spontaneous choice of rhythm, white or black key clusters. The form here is more articulate, being verbally presented in four sections: ABA-Coda. The fourth movement includes performer choice of a four-part "religious or patriotic" hymn around which two secondary performers playing four-note clusters at either end of the keyboard are asked (verbally, again) to interfere, *poco a poco,* with the hymn performance. Foss has

---

10. From notes to the score by the composer.

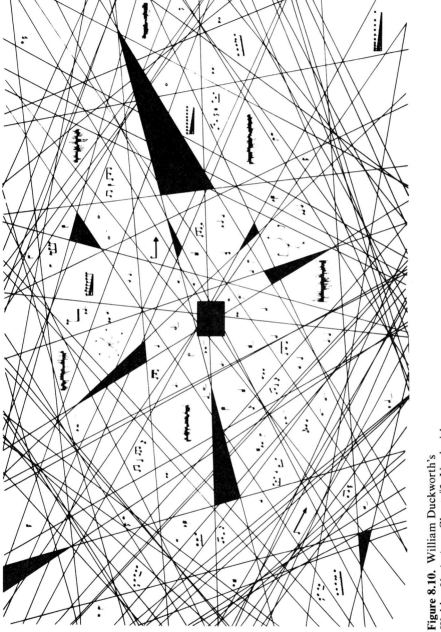

Figure 8.10. William Duckworth's *Walden Variations.* Sheet #3. Used with permission of the composer.

used notes (in I, II, and IV), rhythms (in I), timbre (in III), dynamics (in II, III, and IV), each in a somewhat traditional manner, at the same time freeing another aspect of composition and performance for improvisation.

In the above discussed works, the composer still claims one or more compositional aspects of his work. Giuseppi Chiari's *Quel Che Volette* is probably more apropos of Morton Feldman's statement: "Down with the Masterpiece; up with art. . . ."[11] The piece is entirely made up of verbal instructions ranging from indications suggesting materials not be played in a virtuosic manner, to exchanging instruments among performers. However vague the score may appear, close reading reveals a near determinacy, in "word painting" fashion, of composer intention, especially in regard to form (from "you must try and play in a traditional manner" and "play as if playing was a gift" to "We must never overdo"). Likewise, in *Sonant,* Mauricio Kagel employs verbal descriptions of the framework within which the performer may improvise. These often intricate instructions may be more accurate in terms of performance ease and understanding than traditional notation.

Alvin Curran's *Home-made* employs improvisational freedom effectively in contrast to exactly notated sections. Using boxes of composer instructions (e.g., *p* to *mf*), the performer reacts to the other performers and/or traditionally scored material. Curran alternates the effects of each approach successfully and maximizes the contrast: more-or-less random improvisation with precise *tutti* attacks in the notated material.

Luciano Berio's *Circles* (1960) for female voice, harp, and two percussion players includes a variety of "improvisation boxes." Figure 8.11 shows the two percussion parts (top and bottom groups of staves) with the voice in the middle (harp is not playing at this point). The "improvisation boxes" should not be confused with the small boxes in which the mallets are graphically shown: i.e., the first small box to appear in the two top lines from the left. The reasoning behind the "improvisation" is obvious: the percussion parts would become impossible if written out, or tight and "square." Pitches and instrumentation are usually indicated in specific detail. Rhythm is left to the performer. Often Berio stacks the notes vertically in such a way that the performer can proceed in any order he/she "feels". Occasionally the pitches are proportionally distributed within the box to indicate the approximate rhythmic placement or to introduce new "stacks" of notes. Dynamics, on the other hand, are often notated in terms of *limits* (i.e., *mf→pp*) with smooth *crescendi* and *diminuendi* indicated by dovetailing notation. The score contains no performance directions except those of placement of instruments; the composer, it seems, feels that these performance concepts are obvious. With the "boxes"

11. Morton Feldman, "Conversations without Stravinsky," *Source: Music of the Avant-Garde* 1, no. 2 (July 1967):43.

Figure 8.11. Luciano Berio: *Circles* (c)
Copyright 1961 by Universal Edition.
Used by permission.

occurring in only one or two parts at a time (there is little flexibility in the vocal line except its proportional non-metered notation), the composer maintains control over the direction and flow of the work, allowing the improvisation to give *life* to each successive performance.

Robert Erickson's *Ricercar à 5* (1966) for five trombones requires a number of improvisational techniques from the performers (the work may be performed with five trombonists or one trombonist and four prerecorded trombones on tape). The work varies from exact notation to control of only one or two elements (e.g., most often dynamics and pitch). The interplay between parts calls for sensitive and interpretative improvisatory techniques. The work was written for trombonist Stuart Dempster who, in a recent interview, speaks of these points:

Question (Frank McCarty): "So you began to compile a body of new sounds and techniques through research, practice, and mimicry. I assume you incorporated some of these in the improvisational music that was popular among the San Francisco composers of that era."

Answer (Stu Dempster): "Yes, those pieces gave me the first opportunity to couple my "funny sounds" with other "funny sounds" made by tapes and by other musical instruments such as Pauline's (Oliveros) accordion and Mort's (Subotnick) clarinet. I also became interested in working with composers, I did a demo for Berio in the early 1960's and asked him for a piece, never thinking he'd really do it. Later (1966), when I was working with Bob Erickson on a commission, I decided to resurrect the Berio idea. I wrote him a letter . . . and learned he was already right in the middle of the piece. The *Sequenza* (also involving improvisation techniques) was written in a way for two of us, myself and (Vinko) Globokar, who had played sketches of what became the B section. But as Berio and I worked together on the final version it became more and more my piece since he saw in me—in my performance—more and more the character of Grock, the famous European clown, about whom the piece is actually written. In the meantime, Erickson and I were spending many a Tuesday morning developing a vocabulary of sounds and sound-mixes which resulted in his composition of the *Ricercar à 5*. . . ."[12]

Figure 8.12 is from Witold Lutoslawski's *Livre Pour Orchestra* (1968) which contains a number of improvisational sections. These are marked "ad lib" and ". . . all the rhythmic values are approximate. In consequence, the placing of the notes one above the other in the score does not necessarily mean that they are played simultaneously."[13] These "ad libs" take place within each of the four movements and as "interludes" between movements.

The three initial movements of this work are rather intense. After each of them a moment of relaxation is required. The short interludes are to serve this purpose. . . . I imagine that the attitude of the conductor when he has given the

12. Frank McCarty, "An Interview with Stuart Dempster," *The Instrumentalist* 28, no. 10 (May 1974):36–37. Used by permission of The Instrumentalist Co.

13. From the composer's performance instructions in the score (PWM-Cracow 28.915. Edition Wilhelm Hansen, London).

Figure 8.12. Witold Lutoslawski: *Livre Pour Orchestra* (second "interlude"). Permission granted by J.&W. Chester Ltd. London, England. Polskie Wydawnictwo Muzyczne (PWM), Cracow, Poland.

single beat which begins each interlude would be exactly the same as during a pause between movements. An attitude which should suggest that this is the moment for the audience to relax, change position, cough, etc.[14]

Fig 8.12 shown is the second such "interlude": i.e., between the second and third movements. Pitch (and rest) materials are placed here in single bars with repeat signs. The material repeats for 20″ (upper left) with all resting subsequently for 5″ (far right fermata).

As with Lutoslawski's *Livre,* Ivana Loudova's *Chorale* for wind orchestra, percussion, and organ involves "ad lib" sections with notes (approximate rhythm) followed by unstaved dotted lines (continue in like manner). Often this results in extremely complex composite rhythms unattainable by any other method. While "theoretically" any rhythm is notationally possible, *possible* is not always *playable.*

Phil Winsor's *Orgel* (also discussed in the preceding chapter) includes a sheet of twelve basic improvisatory boxes for organ (and organ recorded on tape). The verbal stylistic indications above each box (see fig. 8.13) plus the timing and overlap directions of the score (not shown) make this "free" improvisation, and not graphic indeterminacy as a quick glance might suggest.

Improvisational techniques in the last few years have created a renaissance of live performance situations. Whether as a result of, or a reaction to, the composer isolation of electronic music, the newfound creative collaboration between composers and performers cannot help but enrich the continuum and significance of all music.

Vectoral Analysis: Witold Lutoslawski: *Les Espaces du Sommeil*

(For information on vectoral analysis and procedures, see chapter 1).

1. Historical Background: Witold Lutoslawski (b. Warsaw, Poland, 1913) composed first in a post-Bartók style (culminating in the *Concerto for Orchestra,* 1954), and then turned to serial techniques. He has recently (since the mid-sixties) developed a unique idiom combining techniques of indeterminacy, cluster textures, and improvisation fused with traditional lyric and motivic development. Notable works in this latter style include *Funeral Music* for orchestra (1958), *Trois Poèmes d'Henri Michaux* for chorus and orchestra (1963) and *Livre pour Orchestra* (1968), discussed earlier in this chapter. He composes very slowly, producing works for large forces every three or four years.

Les Espaces du Sommeil was completed in 1975 and first performed on April 12, 1978, with the composer conducting the Berlin Philharmonic Orchestra and Dietrich Fischer-Dieskau, baritone (to whom the piece is dedicated).

14. Ibid.

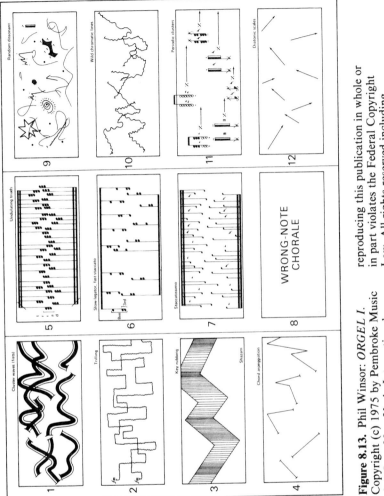

Figure 8.13. Phil Winsor: *ORGEL I.*
Copyright (c) 1975 by Pembroke Music
Co., Inc., New York. International
Copyright Secured. 62 Cooper Square,
New York, N.Y. 10003. Copying or
reproducing this publication in whole or
in part violates the Federal Copyright
Law. All rights reserved including
public performance for profit. Used by
permission.

2. Overview: The text for *Les Espaces du Sommeil* is a complete poem of the same title by Robert Desnos. The verse, in French, is lyrical, surrealistic, often allegorical, and contains subtle and effective onomatopoeia. A brief inner passage demonstrates:

In the night there pass trains
and boats and the mirage of lands where
it is day. The last breaths of the
twilight and the earliest tremors of dawn.[15]

The work, like the poem, is cast in three large sections preceded by a slow introduction and concluded with a brief coda. The introduction, scored for strings and percussion, is followed by a baritone solo (three repetitions of *dans la nuit*—"in the night"). At the outset of the work, Lutoslawski presents the basic contrast of the entire work: long slow-moving dissonant thick textures penetrated by isorhythmic modules of repeated figurelets. This contrast is highlighted (as through most of the rest of the work) by a separation of timbres (here the quick *ostinati* of the percussion contrast with the thick and slow-moving structures of the *divisi* strings).

The first main section comprises four interludes, each with alternating slow and fast material. Lutoslawski utilizes a metriportional approach, combining traditional metered sections with proportional materials (see Appendix III). The conductor activates the latter which, though notated with metric durational symbols, are then played freely (performers making no attempt to play together; note examples earlier in the chapter). The fourth interlude introduces for the first time a full panchromatic cluster and acts as a finale to the first section and a transition to the second.

The second section of the piece *(tranquillo)* continues the contrasts of the opening introduction in a subdued and lyric manner, developing the initial motivic tetrachord (see Basic Techniques, below) with a *recitativo* vocal style. The final large section builds rapidly ($\quad$ = 152) to a full orchestral climax (again a panchromatic cluster). Sections of the orchestra alternate in *stretto*, using extended chromatic (rising) linear writing. This is followed by a very slow *(lento)* coda reminiscent of the opening material, culminating in a brief splash of quick *tutti*. Surprisingly, this last flurry of proportional writing is not followed by a double bar (which enigmatically has been left out of the score).

3. Orchestration: This fifteen-minute work is scored for large orchestra: winds by threes, four horns, tuba, large percussion battery, harp, piano, full strings, and baritone solo. The voice, often lost in orchestral works, is carefully orchestrated and always clear and distinct. Lutoslawski adjusts dynamics and

---

15. Translation by Paul Griffith (Editions Gallimard).

ranges to separate the vocal timbre from the orchestral textures. Almost no effects are used except *glissandi* (an inherent part of Lutoslawski's style).

4. Basic Techniques: The many contrasts in this work are unified through a consistent use of an integrating motive: a tetrachord born of a three-note half-step cluster balanced by one pitch a perfect fifth (fourth) from its center note (i.e., B—C—C♯—F). This motive is used both horizontally and vertically.

Figure 8.14.

The rhythm of the work contrasts simple metric (almost plodding) designs and Lutoslawski's generic proportional improvisations. The latter are usually pitch secure (most notes given), but rhythmically at the discretion of the performer within given guidelines. Fragments are often followed by repeat signs and a long horizontal line indicating duration of the repetitions (see example earlier in the chapter).

5. Vertical Models: Harmonic vocabularies vary from full panchromatic chords to clusterlike tetrachords (see Basic Techniques, above). Intervallic separations seem centered on major thirds (resulting in augmented triads), minor seconds (resulting in clusters), and tritones (diminished fifths, used particularly in the lower voices).

6. Horizontal Models: Like the vertical materials, the melodic emphasis is based on the tetrachordal motive. Contrasting these are repeated note groupings and chromatic lines (motion by minor seconds).

Figure 8.15.

7. Style: Though not dependent on improvisatory techniques, Lutoslawski's *Les Espaces du Sommeil* creates a basic textural definition and motion from rhythmic improvisation. The composer derives both harmonic and melodic materials from the same sources and develops the form of the work through close text linkage and a three-part structure. Contrast (in timbre and texture) is an important dramatic factor as are *glissandi* motions and ruptured metric divisions. Cadence and breath evolve from rhythmic pause and careful control of dynamic envelope.

Bibliography

*Further Readings**

Ashley, Robert. His interesting accounts of the ONCE group may be found in both *Arts in Society* (Spring 1968):86, and *Tulane Drama Review* 10:187.

Boulez, Pierre. "Aléa." *Nouvelle Revue Française* 59 (November 1, 1957). The tight comparisons between European concepts of improvisation and so-called "aleatoric" music are drawn herein by the author in regard to his own work *Improvisations sur Mallarmé.*

Brinkman, R., ed. *Improvisation Und Neue Musik.* Mainz: B. Schott, 1979.

Chase, Gilbert. "Improvisation and Open Style." In *America's Music.* New York: McGraw-Hill Book Co., 1966. Interesting account of the origins of "American" improvisational styles.

Dallin, Leon. *Techniques of Twentieth Century Composition.* 3rd ed. Dubuque, Iowa: Wm. C. Brown Company Publishers, 1974. See especially pp. 237–38.

Foss, Lukas. "The Changing Composer-Performer Relationship: a Monologue and a Dialogue." *Perspectives of New Music* 1, no. 2 (Spring 1963).

———. "Work-Notes for *Echoi.*" *Perspectives of New Music* 3, no. 1, (1964).

Hibbard, William. "Some Aspects of Serial Improvisation." *American Guild of Organists Quarterly.* (October 1966), and (January 1967). A fascinating study into this rarely explored area of improvisation.

Hitchcock, H. Wiley. *Music in the United States: A Historical Introduction.* Englewood Cliffs, N.J.: Prentice-Hall, 1969. Contains a number of interesting comments on improvisation (see the index), some relating to its early roots in nineteenth-century America.

Mumma, Gordon. "Creative Aspects of Live Electronic Music Technology." Audio Engineering Society Reprint No. 550. A brief but credible account of how improvisation has been introduced into electronic music.

———. "The ONCE Festival and How it Happened." *Arts in Society* 4, no. 2:381.

Schuller, Gunther. *Early Jazz: Its Roots and Development.* New York: Oxford University Press, 1968. Good source for this stylistic type of improvisation and its inherent roots in today's improvisational concept.

———. See his contribution to *The Modern Composer and His World* (edited by John Beckwith and Udo Kasemets. Toronto: University of Toronto Press, 1961) for an excellent and forthright argument favoring the use of improvisation, and his comments about Boulez (especially pp. 38 and 39).

Source 2, no. 1 (January 1968). Contains interviews, remarks, and thoughts of the New Music Ensemble, ONCE Group, Sonic Arts Group, and the *Musica Elettronica Viva* which provide an excellent study of the conflict and interrelation between improvisation and indeterminacy.

---

*Addresses for record companies, periodicals, and music publishers mentioned in this Bibliography can be found in Appendix 4.

Recordings and Publishers*

Andriessen, Louis. *Hoe het* (1969). For electronic improvisation group and 52 solo strings.

Ashley, Robert. *In Memoriam Esteban Gomez* (1963). CPE-*Source.*

Austin, Larry. *Improvisations for Orchestra and Jazz Soloists* (1961). Recorded on Columbia MS-6733.

Ayler, Albert. *Music is the Healing Force.* Recorded on Impulse 9191. Excellent *avant-garde* jazz improvisation.

Berio, Luciano. *Circles* (1962). Universal Edition. Recorded on Candide 31027.

Boucourechliev, Andre. *Archipel I.* Recorded on Angel S-36655. Two versions of this improvised work for two pianos and percussion.

————. *Archipel IV* (for solo piano). Recorded on Finnadar 9021.

Boulez, Pierre. *Improvisations sur Mallarmé* (see Further Readings). Universal Edition.

Chiari, Giuseppe. *Quel Che Volete* (1965). CPE-*Source.* Along with the Ashley work cited above, represents borderline improvisation with indeterminacy, depending upon performance circumstances.

Coltrane, John. *The Mastery of John Coltrane.* A four-volume recording set (Impulse IZ-9 345–46–60–61) showing the improvisatory techniques of this jazz master.

Curran, Alvin. *Home-Made.* CPE-Source.

Davis, Miles. *Bitch's Brew.* Columbia PG-26. Incredible demonstration of improvisatory techniques.

Dempster, Stuart. *Standing Waves* (1976). Recorded on 1750 Arch Records S-1775. Improvisations in the great Abbey of Clement VI.

Douglas, Bill. *Improvisations III* (1969). Recorded on Orion 73125.

Duckworth, William. *Pitch City.* CAP.

Erb, Donald. *Concerto for Percussion and Orchestra.* Merion Music. Recorded on Turnabout TV-S 34433.

Erickson, Robert. *Ricercar à 5* (1966). Okra Music. Recorded on DG-0654084.

Foss, Lukas. *Echoi.* Recorded on Helidon 2549001.

————. *Etudes for Organ.* CPE-*Source.*

————. *Fragments of Archilocos.* Recorded on Helidon 2549001.

————. *Music for Clarinet, Percussion and Piano,* 1961 (out of print). Recorded on RCA LSC-2558.

————. *Time Cycle.* Recorded on Columbia MS-6280.

Harris, Roger. *Kroma II.* CAP.

Loudova, Ivana. *Chorale* (1971). Peters. Recorded on AWS-102.

Lutoslawski, Witold. *Concerto for Orchestra.* PWM. Recorded on Angel S-36045. Utilizes overlapping improvisation for sound-mass constructs.

————. *Livre Pour Orchestra.* J. & W. Chester Ltd. Polskie Nagrania SX 1370.

————. *Les Espaces du Sommeil.* Published by Chester Music.

Oliveros, Pauline. *Outline for flute, percussion and string bass: an improvisation chart* (1963). Recording on Nonesuch 71237.

Penderecki, Krzysztof. *Capriccio for Violin and Orchestra* (1967). Moeck. Recorded on Nonesuch 71201.

Reynolds, Roger. *Ping.* Peters. Recorded on CRI S-285. Interesting use of improvisation within limits.

————

*Addresses for record companies, periodicals, and music publishers mentioned in this Bibliography can be found in Appendix 4.

Schafer, R. Murray. *Requiem for a Party Girl* (1966). BMI Canada. Recorded on CRI S-245.

Schuller, Gunther. *Concertino for Jazz Quartet and Orchestra* (1959). Recorded on Atlantic S-1359.

————. *Conversations*. Recorded by the Modern Jazz Quartet, Atlantic S-1345. These two works explicitly locate the influence of jazz on improvisation within traditional techniques, as the previously cited Austin work.

————. *Seven Studies on Themes of Paul Klee* (1959). Universal Edition. Recorded on RCA LSC-2879. Fully defined Third Stream.

————. *Transformation*. Recorded on Columbia WL-127.

Tristano, Lennie. *Descent into the Maelstrom*. Inner 6002.

Trythall, Gilbert. *Entropy* for Stereo Brass Improvisation Group and Stereo Tape (1967). Recorded on Golden Crest S-4085.

Winsor, Phil. *Orgel*. Carl Fischer.

Woodbury, Arthur. *Remembrances*. CPE-*Source*.

Zeitlin, Denny. *Expansions* (recorded in 1973). On 1750 Arch Records 1758.

Mainstream's 5002 includes the live electronic improvisations of the *Musica Elettronica Viva* (Rome) and the AMM (London). Music of the New Music Ensemble is available on two discs from Source Records, Sacramento, Calif. (NME 101 and 102).

9 Indeterminacy

Background

William Hayes's *The Art of Composing Music by a Method Entirely New, Suited to the Meanest Capacity* (1751) describes a technique of composition using notes spattered onto staff paper by running a finger over a stiff brush dipped in ink. Mozart used dice-throwing to create music (*Musical Dice Game,* K. 294d). Other such indeterminate techniques have been attempted, even as early as the eleventh and twelfth centuries, but none with the vigor and philosophical implications of the "discoveries" since the late 1940s.

Figure 9.1 is the full score to Paul Ignace's *It Is* (1946). There are no performance instructions for interpretation as a musical composition. Obviously two performances of *It Is* could vary to extreme degrees in instrumentation and harmonic simultaneity. However, without prior knowledge of the composer's procedure or visual access to the score, the audience can make no real decisions concerning determinacy or indeterminacy. Earle Brown's later *December 1952* is similar in nature, but more visually musical in that its short vertical and horizontal bursts of lines of varying thicknesses more easily ignite some form of rhythmic, dynamic, and pitch realization.

Beginning in the early fifties an affinity for chance techniques was developed with the *I Ching.* Christian Wolff had brought the English translation to John Cage's attention at that time (his father Kurt Wolff being founder of the publishing house, Pantheon Press, which printed it). The *I Ching,* the first written book of wisdom, philosophy, and oracle (attributed to Fu Hsi, 2953–2838 B.C.), expresses directions of action as a result of six tosses of three coins (originally, the tossing of yarrow sticks). The example in figure 9.2 shows all combinations of ——— and — — with six tosses (heads = 2, tails = 3, the addition of points, if even, giving ———, if uneven — —). Having asked the question, "Should I use an example of the *I Ching* in this book?" and performing the required tosses, the author received the following answer (Chun) as a result: "Kun (indicates that in the case which it presupposes) there will be great progress and success, and the advantage will come from being correct and firm. (But) any movement in advance should not be (lightly) undertaken."

Figure 9.1. Paul Ignace: *It Is* (full
score).

THE HEXAGRAMS, in the order in which they appear in the Yî,
and were arranged by king Wǎn.

Figure 9.2. The Hexagrams from *I Ching*. (Permission for reprint granted by University Books, Inc., New Hyde Park, New York 11040. Copyright 1964.)

Definition

Experimental music, that is, actions the outcome of which are not foreseen, is more a philosophical than an audible phenomenon. Form, intended or not, is inherent in all matter and energy, and therefore subject to analysis. It is impossible, without prior knowledge of the composer or work, to distinguish the intention or nonintention of the composer, unless the sounds or actions presented are obviously from another source (intentional or unintentional). For example, John Cage's *4'33"* (1952), wherein the sounds presented are obviously of another source (nature or the audience itself), appear realizably unintentional except in concept.

It is with this latter idea, this psychoconceptual aspect, that the greatest single musical antagonism has been born. Audiences can be presented with highly organized and experimental compositions of the same general genre, instrumentation, and techniques, without reacting adversely. However, when prior knowledge exists, or when a work such as *4'33"* is played and the audience *realizes* the unintention involved, reactions can be much more violent.

Figure 9.3. John Cage. Photo: Dorothy Norman.

One struggles with the *concept,* not the sounds. "Therefore my purpose is to remove purpose," spoke John Cage in a 1962 interview with Roger Reynolds.[1] The idea is to let sounds "happen," to free them from the composer's control. Can one learn to accept *all* sounds equally? This concept truly rejects the past twelve to fourteen centuries of Western thought; not the music itself, but the *concept of* that music.

Separating oneself so completely from one's acts, artistic or otherwise, through chance or "forced stupidity," frees sound rather than controlling it. If *total* chance, *total* indeterminacy, is not possible, is it pointless to attempt merely to approach it? This question poses possibly the most serious and philosophical antithesis to indeterminacy. Cage has referred to his disappointment and compromise arising from the knowledge that he hasn't really "done it," but merely has been ". . . going along in that general direction."[2]

Indeterminacy is not a game or a passing fancy. It presents *the* philosophical challenge to the aesthetics, art, and ego of history. Its antagonists are numerous (Hindemith refers to chance as "one of the ugliest modern musical diseases."[3]). However, what most antagonists (and some protagonists) fail to realize is that one must deal with the *concept* of indeterminacy, *not* the sounds, *not* the forms, *not* the individuals involved. If it cannot be reckoned with in philosophical terms, then it will destroy (or possibly already has destroyed) the structure, terms, and aesthetics of music and art as contemporary Western civilization has come to know them.

Indeterminacy implies art as process: no beginning, no middle, no end. Each new performance, each new circumstance creates a continually variable process of ideas. As Cage has said, "If one is making an object and then proceeds in an indeterminate fashion, to let happen what will, outside of one's control, then one is simply being careless about the making of that object."[4] If art be process, however, then indeterminacy is the only viable way to proceed.

In "indeterminacy," Cage describes Bach's *Art of the Fugue* as an example of composition which is indeterminate with respect to its performance, based on lack of directions in regard to timbre, dynamics, sequence of the "determinate" notes, and duration, making available a wide range of possible realizations.[5] This philosophy disassociates man's significance as a creator, emphasizing creative performing/listening; understanding being something pedagogical and within the realm of language, not aesthetics.

1. *Contemporary Composers on Contemporary Music,* Elliott Schwartz and Barney Childs, eds. (New York: Holt, Rinehart and Winston, 1967), p. 341.
2. Ibid.
3. Ibid., p. 89.
4. Ibid., p. 345.
5. John Cage, *Silence* (Cambridge, Mass.: The M.I.T. Press, paperback edition, 1961), p. 35.

Figure 9.4. Morton Feldman. BMI Archives. Used by permission.

The terminology surrounding chance operations involves certain basic American/European divisons. The term *aleatoric* (derived by Boulez from *aléa,* French for "chance," and originally from the Latin word meaning *dice*) seems to be primarily a European concept which employs chance techniques within a controlled framework, more related to improvisation than true indeterminacy. Morton Feldman has remarked: "This is true of Boulez. This is true of Stockhausen. You can see this in the way they have approached American 'chance' music. They began by finding rationalizations for how they could incorporate chance and still keep their precious integrity."[6] After reacting to the personality behind this statement, Boulez expanded on these basic differences between aleatoric and chance techniques:

G.W.: Feldman refers to "chance" here. Do you feel that you conceive of "chance" in the same way that, say, John Cage conceives of it?
P.B.: No, not at all. I find that so highly unproductive, because "chance" is not an aesthetic category. "Chance" can bring something interesting only one time in a million. . . . Most of the time you do not get that one time . . . and, if you do get it, you get it in the midst of a hundred thousand possibilities which are not interesting.

6. Schwartz and Childs, op. cit., p. 365.

G.W.: Going to a "chance" concert, then, you feel would be like going to a baseball game, gambling for excitement?

P.B.: Yes, but even a baseball game has rules. Card games, which have much more chance, I suppose, still have rules. Can you imagine a card game with absolutely no rules?

D.C.: Like Mallarmé saying, "A throw of the dice will not abolish chance," . . . you are saying that, while nothing can be totally chance, nothing can be totally without chance.

P.B.: Exactly. With the combination of the two, you must integrate, and it is much more difficult to compose in this way, integrating on a high level than in more traditional ways. Composing by chance is no composing at all. Composing . . . means to put things together. I am interested as to what chance sounds occur on the street, but I will never take them as a musical composition. There is a big difference between unorganized sounds and those placed within complete organization.[7]

The division between American and European concepts of chance has grown deeper in the last several years. Boulez remarks: "Do you see what we are getting back to? Constantly to a refusal of choice. The first conception was purely mechanistic, automatic, fetishistic; the second is still fetishistic but one is freed from choice not by numbers but by the interpreter."[8] England's David Bedford and Brian Tilbury, however, have recently championed the American cause of experimental work in indeterminacy, mirroring in the late sixties much the same discoveries and excitement engendered by Cage and Feldman in the early fifties. Surviving, even thriving upon, the attacks from both here and abroad, the cause for freeing sounds continues.

Indeterminacy, as a step-by-step (even pedagogical) approach to erase control over compositional elements which so many have fought to retain, must first transcend man's loss of individual and "racial" ego. As such, it is merely the first step to a far-reaching eventuality: rejection of *all* homocentered creativity, and acceptance of *all* of the life around us, with man no longer in control, no longer the creator or destroyer of images or ideals, real or imagined.

Composer Indeterminacy

Indeterminacy involves total lack of knowledge about the outcome of an action in respect to composition, performance, or both. A number of works are *indeterminate in respect to composition but determinate in respect to performance.* This is primarily music which is predictable before performance but was composed with the use of some type of chance operations. Often these works come to the performer in very traditional notation. They always imply *determinate* performance.

---

7. Galen Wilson and David Cope, "An Interview with Pierre Boulez," *The Composer* 1, no. 2 (September 1969):82–83.

8. Pierre Boulez, "Aléa," *Perspectives of New Music* 3, no. 1 (Winter 1964):42.

In his *Music of Changes (1951)*, John Cage used twenty-six large charts indicating aspects of composition (duration, tempo, dynamics), following the *I Ching* to "create" every aspect of the composition. Forty-three minutes (in music) and nine months later, *Music of Changes* (every aspect except conception of which was based on coin tosses; a huge number) was completed. This rigid composition technique (not unlike that of the twelve-tone school), and the dedication and care necessary for the creation of *Music of Changes,* cannot escape philosophical implications, regardless of intention. Possibly no other work in the history of music has been so exact in its creation, its composer having purposely attempted to destroy his own control over it. Yet it shows little trace of either the composer or the *I Ching:* it "merely" *sounds.*

The *stochastic* and mathematical approach to music as represented in the music of Iannis Xenakis is often deeply rooted in a chance framework. Arbitrary materials feed into an extremely determinate composition system. The

Figure 9.5. Iannis Xenakis. Photo
courtesy of Indiana University.

resultant structure is composer indeterminacy written out in traditional notation for predictable results. Xenakis describes his concepts and procedures in his book *Formalized Music:*

As a result of the impasse in serial music, as well as other causes, I originated in 1954 a music constructed from the principle of indeterminism; two years later I named it "Stochastic Music." The laws of the calculus of probabilities entered composition through musical necessity. But other paths also led to the same stochastic crossroads—first of all, natural events such as the collision of hail or rain with hard surfaces, or the song of cicadas in a summer field. These sonic events are made out of thousands of isolated sounds; this multitude of sounds, seen as a totality, is a new sonic event. This mass event is articulated and forms a plastic mold of time, which itself follows aleatory and stochastic laws. If one then wishes to form a large mass of point-notes, such as string pizzicati, one must know these mathematical laws, which, in any case, are no more than a tight and concise expression of chain of logical reasoning. Everyone has observed the sonic phenomena of a political crowd of dozens of hundreds of thousands of people. The human river shouts a slogan in a uniform rhythm. Then another slogan springs from the head of the demonstration; it spreads toward the tail, replacing the first. A wave of transition thus passes from the head to the tail. . . . The statistical laws of these events, separated from their political or moral context, are the same as those of the cicadas or the rain. They are the laws of the passage from complete order to total disorder in a continuous or explosive manner. They are stochastic laws.[9]

Some have argued that Xenakis's music is not indeterminate at all. Bernard Jacobson has written:

He uses chance, but his music leaves nothing to chance. This is not the paradox it might seem. To Xenakis—as indeed, to most philosophers—chance itself is a scientific concept. Central among the scientific laws he has applied to music is Bernoulli's Law of large numbers, which provides that as the number of repetitions of a given "chance" trial (such as flipping a coin) increases, so the probability that the results will tend to a determinate end approaches certainty.[10]

Some composers utilize more traditional number systems as source material for various parameters of compositions. The Fibonacci series, for example, has been used for pitch, rhythm and timbre control. The series (based on Leonardo Fibonacci's mathematical discoveries of the thirteenth century) creates each new number in its series by adding the previous two (e.g., 1, 2, 3, 5, 8, 13, 21, etc.). As one goes higher in the series a special numerical relationship is created between successive entries. This is known as the "golden mean" and, while impossible to express in a pure stable state (each new entry will vary the results), a traditional model averages to 6.17.[11] Obviously works whose structure and substance derive from Fibonacci series construction have significant "golden mean" import.

9. Iannis Xenakis, *Formalized Music* (Bloomington: Indiana University Press, 1971), p. 9.
10. From the liner notes to Nonesuch Records H-71201 *(Akrata, Pithoprakta).*
11. A number of aestheticians argue the validity of this mean as a conscious or unconscious source of inspiration for many great works of art.

Magic squares (and cubes) have also been used as raw material for "formal" compositional techniques. These squares are matrices of numbers which seem to "magically" add, subtract, divide and/or multiply to the same number regardless of the direction one might take. Figure 9.6 shows a simple magic square and one possible way it might be interpreted in music values:

1	4	2	3	5
2	3	5	1	4
5	1	4	2	3
4	2	3	5	1
3	5	1	4	2

Pitch: (Using 0–11 ordination—beginning on C)
    Line 1—Lines 2 and 1—Lines 2, 1, and 3—etc.
    (Reducing numbers over 11 by 12—e.g.
    C♯ E D D♯ F D♯ G G E A G♯ G♯ B etc.)
Rhythm: 1 = ♪   2 = ♩   3 = ♩.   4 = ♩   5 = 𝅝
Timbre: 1 = horn   2 = flute   3 = piano   4 = violin   5 = cello

Figure 9.6. A magic square and possible musical interpretation.

Note that the addition of every line (including the two diagonal lines) is 15, and no line contains more than one of each of the numbers in use. Interpretation of this data as musical sound is completely at the discretion of the composer and may vary significantly from one work to the next.

Many wonder why such "formalistic" ends could not be achieved in more musical and less mathematical approaches, and so the enigmas around these ideas continue. Writings by and about Xenakis often contribute, for example, to these conflicts. The following is from a discussion between John Cage, Lukas Foss, and Iannis Xenakis:

Cage: I asked a Spanish lady scientist what she thought about the human mind in a world of computers. She said, "computers are always right but life isn't about being right." What do you say to that?
Xenakis: The opposite—life has reason and computers are often wrong.
Cage: You have been an architect and now you are a musician. Are you going to go to some other activity?
Xenakis: I'd like to but it is difficult.
Foss: Iannis, all the music of yours that I know is built on mathematical premise, mostly probability. Is there any aspect to chance that is not mathematical, that is, not probability theory?
Xenakis: All my music is not based on mathematics—there are parts of it which use mathematics. As to chance, it is not like dice or tossing a coin, this is ignorance, as if there were impossibility of predicting. What does chance mean to you?
Foss: Anything I cannot control. You left architecture for music—why?
Xenakis: Mostly because architecture was a business and music is less business.
Foss: In order to compose you need time, solitude—what else?
Xenakis: To live in a big city.
Foss: If someone imitates you (I know of an instance) does it flatter you or make you angry or both?
Xenakis: I am angry . . . angry and depressed.
Foss: What did you want to be when you were a child?
Xenakis: An elephant.[12]

The creation of Dick Higgins's *Thousand Symphonies* involved the "machine-gunning" of one thousand pages of blank orchestra manuscript. The performance, though necessarily constituting some performer interpretation of the "holes," is basically determinate. "My machine-gunning of scores actually represents the concretization of a fantasy I had of setting the police (or armies) to composing music with their most familiar instruments—guns, machine guns. In fact . . . we actually organized an orchestral performance of the gunshot notations according to a system I worked out, and it sounded quite lovely."[13]

Mauricio Kagel's *1898* (completed in 1973 for Deutsche Grammophon's 75th anniversary) is for eleven to seventeen players with only piano and percussion as obligatory to the orchestration. Twenty to twenty-five children's voices also take part in the form of either taped versions or live performance. The percussion is freely orchestrated so that even "home grown" non-pitched instruments can substitute for the indicated suggestions. Only vague hints regarding orchestration appear in the score.

12. John Cage, Lukas Foss, and Iannis Xenakis, "Short Answers to Difficult Questions," *Composer* 2, no. 2 (September 1970):40.
13. From a letter to the author.

Further observation into the instructions of the work provide a greal deal of insight:

> The purpose of these tape recordings, among others, is to demonstrate that what is needed is not 'reliable' musical education but the very opposite: an unorthodox system of changeable, ambivalent invitations to express oneself acoustically—rather than 'musically'.[14]

This is later followed by:

> What is the difference between proper and artificial laughter? One can almost be certain that the responses to the ambiguities inherent in this unambiguous question will produce complex aural situations.[15]

Each of these statements, and the others, seems addressed to stochastic solutions (i.e., indeterminacy so complex that determinate results soon follow). Be this confusing, it is clearly more defined than the composer's own directive: "Variations of a Motive, sung increasingly wrongly."

Performer Indeterminacy

Music which is *determinate in respect to composition but indeterminate in respect to performance* owes much of its development to the idea of "event." These works are "composed" in terms of individual sections or fragments yet mobile in the order of appearance, creating unpredictability before and during performance.

When the timbre, structure, and dynamics of two sounds are so different as to avoid the traditional concept of melody, they become *events* (see chapter 1). Each is equal in importance and does not necessarily build to a climax or cadence. The introduction of silence [16] as an integral part of a composition, and treated equally with sound, helps in identifying these events in time. As sounds move further and further apart, their order becomes less and less important. This reflects much the same concept as a "mobile" in art: that is, the shape, color, and design of each part is fixed, with the order and angle constantly changing.

Karlheinz Stockhausen's *Klavierstück XI, No. 7* (1957), printed on a long roll (37 by 21 inches), opens on a special wooden stand (supplied with the score). It contains nineteen "events," which may be played in any order. Performer instructions require glancing at the score and performing whatever event may "catch the eye."

14. Mauricio Kagel, *1898*. London: Universal (European American), 1979, p. 89.
15. *Ibid.*
16. Cage has often pointed out that "real" silence does not exist (see his book *Silence)*. The author refers here to lack of intentional sound.

At the end of the first group, he reads the tempo, dynamic and attack indications that follow, and looks at random to any other group, which he then plays in accordance with the latter indications. "Looking at random to any other group" implies that the performer will never link up expressly-chosen groups or intentionally leave out others. Each group can be joined to any of the other 18: each can thus be played at any of the six tempi and dynamic levels and with any of the six types of attack.[17]

The composer requires that when a fragment is reached for the third time the piece is concluded. This creates anywhere from three fragments (the first one randomly observed three times in succession) to thirty-eight! (that is 38! — or 38 times 37 times 36 times 35 . . . etc. — a truly staggering number indeed: 10! is over 3.5 million).[18] This, along with the tempo, dynamic and attack variances, creates a work whose notes in terms of fragments are controlled by the composer, yet the resultant performance is totally unpredictable.

Figure 9.7 shows the score from measures 27 to 32 of Stockhausen's _Stop_ (1965). This "Pariser Version" (the one shown in fig. 9.7—there is another version for full orchestra) is for eighteen performers in six groups (cued with the ◇ sign) of like timbres. This _recipe_ work has determinate form (note the duration lengths at the top of each "measure") yet lacks "determinate" directions for performance ("noises" is hardly a predictable notation). The composer is obviously very much aware of the outcome in general terms of form, contrast, balance, and direction (note the occasional exact notation overlapping events) but willing to allow performance unpredictability in terms of rhythm, entrance order, and pitch. This type of work, though very different from the _mobile_ structures of his _Klavierstück XI, No. 7,_ is still primarily composer-determined performer unpredictability.

Henri Pousseur's piano solo _Caractères_ (1961) includes cutout windows and randomly placed score pages so that the order of the "events" is not composer-prescribed. Henry Cowell was among the first of composers to provide blocks of sound with which the performer constructed the performance "form," (_Mosaic Quartet_—1934).

Affected by the mobiles of Alex Calder, Earle Brown has developed concepts of form and order in his music derived primarily from this "event" rationale. Referring to his _Available Forms I_ and _II_ (1961–62), Brown writes: "The title of the work refers to the availability of many possible forms which these composed elements may assume, spontaneously directed by the conductors in the process of performing the work. The individual musical events are rehearsed, but the performances are not."[19]

17. From the composer's directions on the score. Universal Edition No. 12654 LW.
18. "!" here is not an exclamation point but rather a factorial sign in mathematics (the number preceding the sign multiplied by stepwise diminishing numbers in turn down to 1).
19. From the program notes of the New York Philharmonic Society, February 1964.

Figure 9.7. Karlheinz Stockhausen: *Stop* (c) Copyright Universal Edition.

In Brown's *Available Forms I* for orchestra, the score is projected on the back of the stage for the performers to read. The conductor then indicates a number which represents one of the large numerals indicated on the score. The performers read and improvise within the context of the information given in the indicated block. The risk parallels that of the Stockhausen example, though it is not so great as to imply complete lack of composer control.

The antilyrical aspects of event concepts represent one of the ideas most profoundly antagonistic to Romantic thought. Barney Childs's *Nonet* (*Source: Music of the Avant Garde* 3, no. 1 [January 1969]) includes an "event machine" (a numbered acetate overlay and two rotating color-coded discs) which provides the order, timing, and selection of events, (provided by the composer). In Feldman's *Intersection 3,* the duration, number, and timbre of sounds are determined by the composer while the dynamics and range *(high, middle, and low)* are indeterminate during performance.

John Cage's *Atlas Eclipticalis* (see fig. 9.8), first performed by the New York Philharmonic in 1962, includes the use of contact microphones placed in various locations on the instruments. Though somewhat graphic, this work provides pitch indications and directions of movement. As seen in figure 9.9, *34'46.776" for a Pianist* (1954) is also a graphic but explicit work.

Musical "games" (or "strategy") take a variety of forms (e.g., Subotnick's *Ritual;* see chap. 7). Xenakis has characterized music without in-performance "conflict" as *autonomous* (inclusive of most music to the present day) and the music of games (introducing a concept of external conflict between groups or individuals in the performance situation) as *heteronomous* music. Xenakis's *Duel* (1958–59) comprises materials like that of the mobile structure: a set of six events, each written in the score in precise manner. Unlike mobiles, however, these strategic games employ definitive *tactics* with the events of length sufficient to permit interruption, and the choice of event a direct result of an "on the spot" performer decision.

Strategie (1962), for two forty-four-member orchestras, employs Xenakis's *strategie musicale* (application to music of the mathematical *theory of games).* Seven basic sound structures have a *stochastic* basis, which was calculated with an IBM 70690 computer with 400 combinations possible between the two orchestras (seated on opposite sides of the stage). An electric scoreboard is set at the end of the stage with points gained and lost by rules set by composer calculations. "At the end of a certain number of exchanges or minutes, as agreed upon by the conductors, one of the two is declared a winner and is awarded a prize."[20]

Roman Haubenstock-Ramati's *Mobile for Shakespeare* (for voice, piano, celeste, vibraphone, and three percussionists) is a prime example of "mobile"

---

20. Xenakis, *Formalized Music,* p. 122.

278   *Indeterminacy*

Atlas Eclipticalis, French Horn 5, Percussion 4, Cello 7, pages 245, 309, and 157

Figure 9.8. John Cage: *Atlas Eclipticalis, French Horn 5, Percussion 4, Cello 7,* pages 245, 309, and 157. Copyright by Henmar Press, Inc., 373 Park Avenue South, New York, N.Y. 10016 International Copyright Secured. All rights reserved. Permission granted by the publisher.

Figure 9.9. John Cage: *34'46.776" for a Pianist,* page 50. Copyright by Henmar Press Inc., 373 Park Avenue South, New York, N.Y. 10016. International Copyright Secured. All rights reserved. Permission granted by the publisher.

Figure 9.10. Roman Haubenstock-Ramati's *Mobile for Shakespeare.* (c)   Copyright Universal Edition, 1968. All rights reserved. Used by permission.

type structure indeterminacy (see fig. 9.10). Each box gives a fairly straight-forward, mostly traditionally notated fragment (there are a few relatively explicit graphic symbols). The order of each box is not predetermined and therefore while the composer has indeed "composed" each note, the performances are quite different and unpredictable.[21]

21. See the score for fuller explanation of complete performance.

Composer and Performer Indeterminacy

Music can be *indeterminate in respect to both composition and performance.*
"Chance" means produce a "chance" score: at no time is there a predictable
outcome. Christian Wolff's *Duo II for Pianists* (1958), for example, involves
no score and all materials are indeterminate, the only indication being areas
of limitation provided by the composer (the use of pianos with no silences
between performer responses). The work has no designated beginning or ending, these being determined only by the situation under which performance
takes place. Nam June Paik's *In Homage to John Cage* (1959) is equally indeterminate and in "happening" form. In its first performance Paik leaped
offstage to Cage's seat, removed Cage's jacket and, as Tomkins has it: "slashed
his (Cage's) shirt with a wickedly long pair of scissors, cut off his necktie at
the knot, poured a bottle of shampoo over his head, and then rushed out of
the room."[22] Paik later telephoned the audience to let them know that the
work was finished.

Cage is currently exploring "contingency"-type indeterminacy:

I have been writing pieces that I call "music of contingency," in which there is a
rupture between cause and effect, so that the causes that are introduced don't
necessarily produce effects. That's what contingency is. One piece, *Inlets,* uses conch
shells, for example; if instead of blowing a conch shell, you fill it with water and tip
it, it will sometimes gurgle and sometimes not. You have no control over it. Even if
you try very hard to control it, it gurgles when it wishes to . . . when it's ready to.
Sometimes if you rehearse with it and think that you've got it down pat, you'll
discover as I do, I'm sure, that it foxes you and gurgles when it chooses.[23]

John Mizelle's *Radial Energy I* (see fig. 9.11) allows the greatest possible
freedom in choice of sound sources, number of participants, location of performance, and interpretation (if any). In the sine chart and explanation accompanying the score, the composer describes in detail the silence periods
between performances (six, seven, nine, twelve, fifteen, seventeen, eighteen,
seventeen, fifteen, twelve, nine, seven, and six *years* for the first phase of the
chart, and the first point at which the piece may be concluded: i.e., one hundred
fifty years). Other "complete" performances may last over 382 years, depending on initial performance time, with duration of the performances (between the periods of silence) computed by addition, squaring, cubing, etc., the
initial performance duration (actual sound-producing performances could last
over fifteen years). Likewise the area of performance could be expanded, as
the composer states, "to other planets, galaxies, etc. When all of time and
space are transformed into sound, the piece (and the Universe) ends."

22. Calvin Tomkins, *The Bride and the Bachelors* (New York: The Viking Press, 1965), p. 134.
23. David Cope, "An Interview with John Cage," *The Composer* 10, no. 1 (1980).

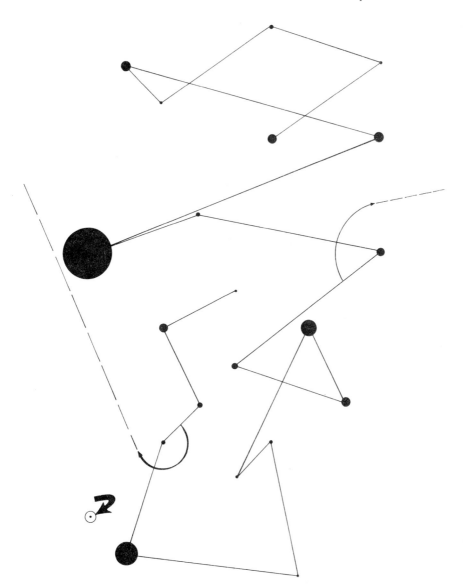

Figure 9.11. John Mizelle: *Radial Energy I*. Permission granted by *Source: Music of the Avante-Garde,* Composer/ Performer Edition, Davis, California.

Barney Childs's *The Roachville Project* (a sound sculpture for four to ten performers) verbally describes a situation in which performers *and* audience create an instrument out of available materials, improvising during and after construction. Emphasis is directed *away* from sound and toward situation, theater, and total participation (see fig. 9.12).

Sylvano Bussotti's *Five Piano Pieces for David Tudor* (1959), on the other hand, reflects a totally graphic concept in which interpretation or noninterpretation is fully within the performer's realm. The artistic drawings of Bussotti are more visual than aural; the composer becomes more an inciter than restrainer. Graphic scores such as this represent more than a breach with traditional symbols. Inherent in a nonsymbolic abstract representation is a concept of live creation. Bussotti's *Five Pieces* was performed in Los Angeles three times in one concert, by three different performers. More conservative members of the audience, obviously appalled by the lack of recognizable similarities among the performances in structure, length, instrumentation, or motive, reacted antagonistically to both performers and work. The problem seems to be rooted not in the sounds themselves, but in the categorization of who, in fact, is the creator of the sounds.

In reference to these performances Halsey Stevens has pointed out that:

. . . if Mr. Bussotti had wandered into the hall and didn't know what was going on, he would not have had the remotest idea that those three performances, or any one of them, might have been his own piece. They were so totally different in every respect that the only thing he could lay claim to was having designed the score, not to having composed the piece. Aleatoric music, it seems to me, as it is frequently pursued, is an amusing parlor game. . . .[24]

Had these performances been recorded and subsequently translated into traditional notation for performer "interpretation," they would have avoided the antagonism. Had the piece then been performed three times, repetition would replace the creative ideal of the indeterminate composer.

Figures 9.13 to 9.17 show the wide variety of notations John Cage has used, and a cross section of the types of his works. *Concert for Piano and Orchestra* (fig. 9.13, Solo for Piano) was written and first performed for the 1958 Cage Retrospective Concert in New York's Town Hall, with the composer conducting. The staging included a large battery of electronic equipment, with the conductor slowly bringing his hands together over his head, in clocklike fashion. This controlled the duration of the piece more than individual events (which are more or less indeterminate in sequence and number).

26'1.1499" for a String Player, 1955 (see fig. 9.14) is more graphic and has been "realized" by Harold Budd for Bertram Turetzky's Nonesuch recording of the work. Both *Variations I,* 1958 (see fig. 9.15) and *Fontana Mix,*

---

24. David Cope, "An Interview with Halsey Stevens," *Composer* 5, no. 1 (1973):30.

"The Roachville Project"

4 to 10 performers, minimum duration 30 minutes.

Provide a great deal of material, most of which should be capable of soundproduction, either immediately (wires, pipes, blocks, tubes, containers, bits and pieces of musical instruments, junk, &c.) or potentially (material which when assembled or altered or worked with can be made, maybe, to produce sound in some fashion).

The piece begins with the arrival of the performers at the material. They begin to assemble the material, as they please, any way they wish, into a "musical instrument" of sorts. The complete construction is to be a unit—that is, separate people may work for a while on separate sub-units, but these must eventually be built into the complete construction. All that is necessary for assembly, finally, is ingenuity: the means of assembly (nails, staples, glue, string, sticky tape, leather straps, baling wire, rivets, &c.) are up to the performers. Performers may converse together concerning problems of assembly and sound potential, but this must be done very quietly, and other conversation is to be avoided; performers may test parts they are working on for sound as they are assembling (i.e. test string tension by plucking, test resonances by tapping, &c.) but this must also be done very quietly. At a stipulated time, or when all agree that the instrument is completed, the performers improvise music on it, for any length of time. The composition is finished with the completion, at a pre-arranged time or by agreement among the performers, of this "piece-within-a-piece." All material provided need not, or perhaps will not, be used. If passing members of the audience with to become performers they may, as long as the total working number of participants never exceeds 10.

Deep Springs
April 1967

*Roachville and White Mountain City were "settlements just over the White Mountain summit from Owens Valley. . . . A writer visiting there in 1864 tells all that we know of those would-be mining centers. The 'city' from which he wrote was on Wyman Creek, on the Deep Spring slope; its rival, Roachville, was on Cottonwood Creek, and was named by its proprietor, William Roach. . . ."

W. A. Chalfant, *The Story of Inyo*

Figure 9.12. *The Roachville Project* by Barney Childs. (c) Copyright Universal Editions, 1968. All rights reserved. Used by permission.

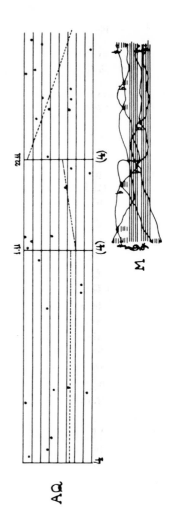

Figure 9.13. John Cage: *Solo for Piano* (*Concert for Piano and Orchestra*), page 30. Copyright by Henmar Press Inc., 373 Park Avenue South, New York, N.Y. 10016. International Copyright Secured. All rights reserved. Permission granted by the publisher.

26'1.1499" for a String Player, pages 59 and 84

Figure 9.14. John Cage: 26'1.1499" for
a String Player, pages 59 and 84.
Copyright by Henmar Press Inc., 373
Park Avenue South, New York, N.Y.
10016. International Copyright Secured.
All rights reserved. Permission granted
by the publisher.

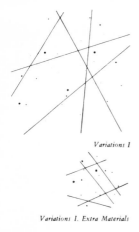

Variations I

Variations I. Extra Materials

Fontana Mix

Figure 9.16. John Cage: *Fontana Mix.*

1958 (see fig. 9.16) graphically plot areas and physical locations for performance. *Variations IV* (1963) involves laying score transparencies over a map
of the performance area, determining source and direction, of sounds. The
recording (made in a Los Angeles art gallery) includes the various sounds of
Cage at work with electronic equipment and the candid conversations of the
audience-performers. One microphone was placed outside the building to catch
street sounds. Cage created a final realization by splicing and selecting, eval-
uating and manipulating the resultant tapes.

The score to *Fontana Mix* represents the physical areas on the instruments used (indeterminate) and intersections (which could be striking areas).
Since the composer has not restricted instrumentation, it is not possible to
predict any real outcome of the score in performance. Moreover, since the
score is randomly made *by* the performer by overlaying various translucent

sheets, the score itself looks different in each performance. Once created, how-ever, and the score applied to the instruments used, performers should con-form to that score in some very 'determined' manner so that improvisation or reliance on past experience will not take place. The piece cannot be predicted or predetermined by either the composer or the performer; this implies full cooperation in indeterminacy by both parties.

Theatre Piece, 1960 (fig 9.17), in the Cage "happening" tradition, em-ploys number charts significant in their graphic representation of action. *Paintings* (1965) by Louis Andriessen (fig. 9.18), for recorder and piano, ex-emplifies a totally graphic indeterminate procedure. Even with the instruc-tions, the predictability of the performance is minimal. William Bland's *Speed* (1968) for organ (see fig. 9.19) uses traditional left-to-right reading, up/down pitch level interpretation, and block-cluster chord representation, at the same time graphically encouraging nonpredictable performance possibilities (e.g., center triangle with ink blur).

Figure 9.17. John Cage: *Theatre Piece Part VI.* (one of eighteen unnumbered pages). Copyright by Henmar Press Inc., 373 Park Avenue South, New York, N.Y. 10016. International Copyright Secured. All rights reserved. Permission granted by the publisher.

Figure 9.18. Louis Andriessen: *Paintings.* Flötenpart, Blatt 1. Copyright (c) 1965 by Herman Moeck Verlag. Used with permission. All rights reserved.

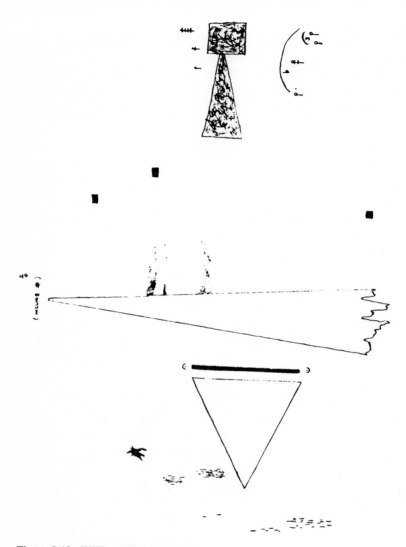

Figure 9.19. William Bland: *Speed* for organ solo. (Published by Composers' Autograph Publications.)

Other composers employ varied degrees of *graphic* notations to achieve equally varied ends. Anestis Logothetis's scores seem at first glance to be works of visual art. If one reads the instructions to his works carefully, clues appear that provide partial determinacy in terms of performer reaction and interpretation (e.g., *Clusters, Odyssee,* 1963, or *Ichnologia,* 1964). Robert Moran often utilizes *graphic* music, but unlike Logothetis, gives clear indication of instrumentation and "possible" interpretation of visual symbols (see *Four Visions,* 1963, in Karkoschka's *Notation in New Music,* or *Bombardments No. 2,* 1964, for one to five percussionists). Boguslaw Schäffer has pointed out a number of advantages of *graphic* music (at least for its usefulness to the mainstream of music). In his 1963 *Violin Concerto,* the cadenza (primarily thick black waves and twists of graphic art) is transcribed into one possible traditionally-notated version. The result, based on a rather exact or literal translation, derives time in terms of left to right proportionality, pitch in terms of "up and down" relativity, and flow in terms of visual motion. This revised version is an incredibly complex, nearly unplayable, concrete structure totally foreign to the direction of the work. The plasticity of the *graphic* notation allows for a free sound, every bit as complex as the traditionally notated one, yet without the studied end result (and, of course, without the "performance-to-performance" variability). In Schäffer's *Concerto* one hears the new elements, the surprises each performance offers. One does not judge a performer's mistakes or compare virtuosities in performance: it is indeed "composition in process."

Figure 9.20 is from Roman Haubenstock-Ramati's *Jeux 2,* 1968 (for two percussionists). Though mobile in structure, the graphic nature of the fragments themselves makes determinacy on the part of the composer or performer an impossibility. Note the difference here between *Jeux 2* and *Mobile for Shakespeare,* 1959 (fig. 9.10), the latter having composer control over the fragments, thus falling distinctly into a different category (that of *performer-indeterminacy*). Possibly Europe's most experimental protagonist of the varieties of indeterminacy, Haubenstock-Ramati continues to explore the areas founded by John Cage, Earle Brown, and Barney Childs (unlike Stockhausen, for example, who now works with *conceptual music, antimusic,* etc., each new area as it comes into view).

Figure 9.21 is Robert Moran's *Sketch for a Tragic One-Act Opera* (score is in colors which cannot be reproduced here). The graphic nature of the score (even though instrumentation is traditional in left margin) contributes to composer-performer indeterminacy. The indications here, since this is only a 'sketch', define texture and dynamics more than pitch or exact rhythms.

Other composers involved with indeterminate techniques include Folke Rabe, Bo Nilsson, Cornelius Cardew (though it should be noted that Cardew disowned his former style to compose "political-reformation" music), Roland Kayn, Allan Bryant, Joseph Byrd, Richard Maxfield, Philip Corner, Douglas Leedy, Robert Ashley, and James Fulkerson.

aus JEUX 2

Figure 9.20. Roman Haubenstock
Ramati: *Jeux 2* for two percussionists.
(c) Copyright Universal Edition, 1968.
All rights reserved. Used by permission.

Vectoral Analysis: John Cage: *Cartridge Music*

(For information on vectoral analysis and procedures, see chapter 1.)

Historical Background: John Cage (b. 1912, Los Angeles, California) began his studies with Henry Cowell and Arnold Schoenberg (with whom he studied counterpoint). Regarding the latter, Cage remarks:

My composition arises out of asking questions. I am reminded of an early story about a class with Schoenberg. He had us go to the blackboard to solve a particular problem in counterpoint (though it was a class in harmony). He said: "When you have a solution, turn around and let me see it." I did that. He then said: "Now another solution, please." I gave another and another until finally, having made seven or eight, I reflected a moment and then said with some certainty: "There aren't any more solutions." He said: "O.K. What is the principle underlying all of the solutions?" I couldn't answer his question; but I had always worshipped the man, and at that point I did even more. He ascended, so to speak. I spent the rest of

Figure 9.21. Robert Moran. *Sketch for a Tragic One Act Opera*. Used by permission of the composer.

Figure 9.22. John Cage (standing at left) conducting a recording session of a percussion work by Lou Harrison (white shirt, far right) about 1940. Accidental overlay of two photos (superimposition) created the music in upper center and bass drum.

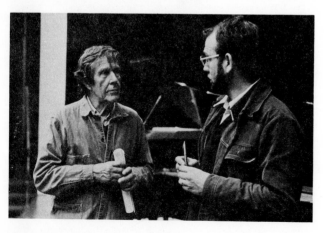

Figure 9.23. John Cage and David Cope. Photo by Carol Foote (1980). During preparation of a *Cartridge Music* performance.

my life, until recently, hearing him ask that question over and over. And then it occurred to me through the direction that my work has taken, which is renunciation of choices and the substitution of asking questions, that the principle underlying all of the solutions that I had given him was the question that he had asked, because they certainly didn't come from any other point. He would have accepted that answer, I think. The answers have the question in common. Therefore the question underlies the answers. I'm sure that he would have found my answer interesting; though he was very brilliant—he may have been thinking of something else.[25]

Cage's music through the mid-thirties developed chromatic concepts and used tone-row fragments, often with set rhythmic patterns. His *Sonata for Clarinet* (1933) is a good example of his work at this time. The work contains no effects whatsoever, but rather develops a kind of free twelve-tone procedure throughout (definite rows but little working out of systematic serial techniques).

A second period developed in the mid- to late-thirties concentrating on wide diversities of timbral resources and an aesthetic about "noise." The prepared piano (developed in 1938) increased his interest in percussion instruments. The *First Construction in Metal* (1939) and important contributions to electronic music, particularly the *Imaginary Landscape* series begun in 1939, are all characteristic of Cage's imaginative leap into new sonic and timbral realms.

A third period developed early in the fifties when Cage began to infuse indeterminacy into his works. The *Concerto for Prepared Piano and Orchestra* (1951), *4'33"* (blank score in which extraneous sounds to the performance become the work itself; 1952), and *Fontana Mix* (1958; for tape) represent his work at this time.

Throughout his career, Cage has actively referenced his work to the other arts (in collaboration with Merce Cunningham, dance; Robert Rauschenberg, art; and Jasper Johns, sculpture) as well as philosophy (e.g., Buckminster Fuller). His concept of and search for the "possibility of saying nothing" have influenced a wide breadth of composers, artists, and writers; few doubt that the present-day evolution of music would not exist without his vast input and contributions.

2. Overview: *Cartridge Music* was completed in 1960. The "score" consists of four transparent sheets described as follows: sheet one: nineteen ⅛-inch black dots arranged randomly; sheet two: ten ¼-inch circles arranged randomly; sheet 3: a single two-inch diameter circle numbered as a clock in five-second increments (0 to 60); sheet four: a very long curved dotted line with a circle (¼-inch at one end).

The score also contains twenty numbered nontransparent sheets having various shapes inscribed (the number of shapes corresponding to the number of the sheet). Each performer makes his or her own score from these materials.

25. David Cope, "An Interview with John Cage," *The Composer* 10, no. 1 (1980).

First, a nontransparent sheet is chosen with its number corresponding to the number of cartridges available to that performer (*cartridge* here referring to a contact mike or record player needle cartridge). The performer then places the transparent sheets randomly over the numbered nontransparent sheet with the last (curved dotted line) arranged so that the circle at the end of the dotted line contains a point outside a shape and so that the dotted line intersects at least one point within one of the shapes. Figure 9.24 shows how the score might look (only one of nearly limitless possibilities). Note that the dotted line (upper left) terminates in a "filled" circle and that it intersects a point *inside* one of the shapes (i.e., intersects a point inside the large shape, lower right-hand side of the score). One then "reads" the dotted line from one end to the other (either direction is acceptable), making note of intersections with lines, circles, and dots. Each of these intersections correlates with specific actions given in the performance notes (e.g., "intersection of the dotted line with a point within a shape indicates a sound produced in any manner on the object inserted in the cartridge corresponding to that shape.").

Timing of the work is gauged by the circle (stopwatch), here located in the upper center of the figure (9.24). First, this arrangement shown exists for only one moment of the work (any moment of the performer's choice, with total duration being fully at the will of the performers). Second, actions during that minute take place only over periods created by intersection of the dotted line with the time circle (in this case, since the circle has not been intersected, no specific times are given).

The performer should prepare such arrangements for each minute of the scheduled performance prior to the first rehearsal. Exact schedules of actions should be made with clear indications of what procedures are necessary in exact timing sequence. Each part should be prepared separately from any other performer's part. Instruments to be used in performance (i.e., on which the contact microphones are to be used) are at the performer's discretion. "All events, ordinarily thought to be undesirable, such as feed-back, humming, howling, etc. are to be accepted in this situation." Cage refers to a performance of the work in a recent interview with the author:

D.C. Did you in the process of recording the piece listen to what you were doing?

J.C. We did, so to speak, what we had to do. You are usually a bit too busy to listen. And the idea is that the players confound one another. That's one of the ideas of the piece. So that if you do listen to what you're doing, you're apt to get the wrong attitude toward the piece. What you have to develop is an indifference to whether your work is effective or ineffective; let happen what will. In my mind it arises from the experience that is so frequent in American life, of traffic congestion, and how to take it with what I call a sober and quiet mind, how to remain susceptible to divine influences.[26]

3. Orchestration: The choice of timbres involved is freely up to the performer (except that the sound will be initiated by the cartridge). In a recent performance, the author utilized the insides of a piano, connecting and performing with the contact mikes directly on the strings and the sounding board. Other performers chose percussion instruments (primarily bass drum and tam-tam respectively). Springs, wind-up toys, and a variety of other smaller 'instruments' were also employed with effective results. Cage remarks further:

I can't recognize *Cartridge Music* from one performance to the next. Somewhere I tell that story of going into a house . . . and the hostess to be nice had put *Cartridge Music* on in another room. . . . I turned to her and asked, "What is that music?" And she said, "You can't be serious." I said, "It's very interesting; what is it?" And then she told me. I was pleased that I couldn't recognize it. . . . I don't hear it, you see. I performed it . . . with David Tudor, and we made a recording when Earle Brown was in charge of Time Records. Earle asked David and me if . . . we wanted to hear the end result. Neither one of us wanted to hear it.[27]

4. Basic Techniques: Clearly the basic scoring of *Cartridge Music* is experimental in nature (actions for which the final result is not foreseen). Composer indeterminacy is nearly complete, with Cage having no predictable way to foresee the sounds in any given performance situation. The performer's making of the score is indeterminate in the first step (creation of the sequences of actions from the graphs), but rehearsed carefully in the second step (carrying out of those prescribed actions).

D.C. In a performance of *Cartridge Music,* does it cross your mind that this is a good performance, a bad performance, or enjoyable. . . ?

J.C. If I think that way then I won't hear very well. The only time that I think that things are good or bad is when some other intentions than are proper to the

26. Ibid.
27. Ibid.

piece take over. That happens so frequently with orchestral music, where the players don't do what they're supposed to do. Then I don't think that it's good or bad, but has moved out of the realm of music into the world of society and becomes a theatrical situation that was not intended at all.[28]

5, 6. Vertical and Horizontal Models: Since any and all possible timbres and textures can occur in this piece, no model can exist.

7. Style: *Cartridge Music* is representative of Cage's developed indeterminacy. He has carefully (through obviously involved processes) divorced himself from the process of creative control over the elements of this work. This separation is an intricate process (some say as intricate as that of trying to put one's personal creative process *into* a composition). *Cartridge Music* demonstrates mature Cage philosophies in full bloom. Relationships with Zen (a complex fusion of Western and Eastern ideas deserving far more space than is available here) are significant, with Cage standing as antithetical to the general flow of Western musical traditions.

28. Ibid.

Bibliography

*Further Readings**

Attneaw, Fred. "Stochastic Compositional Processes." *Journal of Aesthetics and Art Criticism* 17, no. 4 (1959):503.

Behrman, David. "What Indeterminate Notation Determines." *Perspectives of New Music* 3, no. 2 (Spring 1964).

Boulez, Pierre. "Aléa." *Perspectives of New Music* 3, no. 1 (Winter 1964). A vivid attack on indeterminacy.

Brown, Earle. "Form in New Music." *Source* 1, no. 1 (January 1967). Excellent discussion of the "event" concept, mobile structure, and open form in music.

Cage, John. "History of Experimental Music in the United States." In *Silence: Lectures & Writings* (see details of publication in listing below). Examines the composers and ideas of "events" and musical continuity (especially Cowell, Wolff, Brown, and Cage on p. 71) and "getting rid of glue."

———. *The John Cage Catalog.* New York: C. F. Peters Co., 1962.

A Book of Essays about John Cage and his Music, edited by Heinz-Klaus Metzger and Rainer Riehn. New York: C. F. Peters, 1981. Evaluates Cage's important "Address to an Orchestra."

———. *Empty Words: Writings '73–'78.* Middletown, Conn.: Wesleyan University Press, 1979.

———. *M: Writings '67–'72.* Middletown, Conn.: Wesleyan University Press, 1973. Continuation of the "collection" form of books that Cage has produced; begins to show a different side of Cage, especially in world and "semi-political" involvement.

———. *Notations.* New York: Something Else Press, 1969. A representation of 270 composers by single-page score reproductions.

———. *Pour les Oiseaux.* Paris: Pierre Belford, 1976.

———. *Silence: Lectures & Writings.* Cambridge, Mass.: The M.I.T. Press, 1966; first edition from Wesleyan University Press, 1961, paperback. See especially the article, "Indeterminacy."

———. *Writings Through Finnegans Wake.* N.Y.: Printed Editions, 1979.

———. *A Year from Monday.* Middletown, Conn.: Wesleyan University Press, 1967.

Cardew, Cornelius. "Notation-Interpretation, etc.," *Tempo* 58:24.

———, ed. *Scratch Music.* Cambridge, Massachusetts: The MIT Press; paperback edition, 1974. This is a book of scores and ideas by a great many composers involved with the *Scratch Orchestra* conducted by Cardew. Many of the works are indeterminate.

———. *Stockhausen Serves Imperialism.* London, England: Latimer New Dimensions Limited, 1974. Interesting account of this composer's about-face and repudiation of his own early works and those of other *avant-garde* composers.

*Addresses for record companies, periodicals, and music publishers mentioned in this Bibliography can be found in Appendix 4.

298   Indeterminacy

Charles, Daniel. "Entr'acte: 'Formal' or 'Informal' Music." *Musical Quarterly* (1965). A good analysis of European/American differences over indeterminacy.

Childs, Barney. "Indeterminacy and Theory: Some Notes," *Composer* 1, no. 1 (June 1969):15. An excellent "objective" approach to the subject. See also his contribution "Indeterminacy" in Vinton's *Dictionary of Contemporary Music*. New York: E. P. Dutton & Co., 1974. A superb presentation of the definition, history, and aesthetics of the subject (although the dictionary itself does not discriminate between improvisation and indeterminacy).

Cone, Edward T. "One Hundred Metronomes." *The American Scholar,* Vol. 46, No. 4 (Autumn, 1977). A fascinating article offering alternative viewpoints on new music techniques.

Copland, Aaron. "The Music of Chance," In *Our New Music.* New York: W. W. Norton & Co., 1968. Quite fascinating though not as penetrating as the rest of the book is toward other areas of new music.

Dallin, Leon. *Techniques of Twentieth Century Composition.* 3rd ed. Dubuque, Iowa: Wm. C. Brown Company Publishers, 1974. This third edition has a chapter devoted to indeterminate procedures (pp. 237–49) which is a good introduction.

Feldman, Morton. "Predetermined/Indetermined." *Composer* (England, Fall 1966).

———. "Between Categories." *Composer* 1, no. 2 (1969):73. Fine article on *time,* indirectly relating to a philosophical construct of indeterminacy.

Fuller, R. Buckminster. *Operating Manual for Spaceship Earth.* Carbondale: Southern Illinois University Press, 1969. Though not directly relating to indeterminacy, this book indeed relates to Cage and more relevantly to the possible implosion of indeterminate procedures in relation to all events, musical and otherwise; truly fascinating reading (as are all his books).

Hansen, Al. *A Primer of Happenings and Time-Space Art.* New York: Something Else Press, 1968.

Higgins, Dick. *Postface.* New York: Something Else Press, 1964. Gives some very interesting ideas and insights into indeterminate concepts from a neo-Cage point of view.

Kayn, Roland. "Random or not Random." *Horyzonty muzyki* (Cracow, 1966). Three lectures prepared for the Norddeutscher Rundfunk.

Kirby, Michael. *Happenings.* New York: E. P. Dutton & Co., 1965. Good historical survey of this indeterminate form.

Kostelanetz, Richard. *John Cage.* New York: Praeger, 1970. Superb in both text and pictures. A real must for any thorough study of Cage and indeterminacy.

———. *Master Minds.* New York: Macmillan, 1969. See especially "The American Avant-Garde," with part 2 relating particularly to John Cage and indeterminacy.

Layton, Billy Jim. "The New Liberalism." *Perspectives of New Music* 3, no. 2 (Spring 1964). Presents another attack on indeterminacy.

Logothetis, Anestis. "Gezeichnete Klänge." *(Neues Forum* 183, no. 1:177); "Kurze musikalische Spurenkunde." *Melos* 37:39.

MacKenzie, I.A. "The Critique." *Composer* 2, no. 4 (1971):92. Short but interesting letter to a critic with indeterminate procedures implied.

O'Grady, T.J. "Aesthetic Values in Indeterminate Music." *Musical Quarterly* 67:306–81, N. 3, 1981.

Olson, Harry F., and Herbert Belar. "Aid to Composition Employing a Random Probability System." *Journal of the Acoustical Society of America* 33, no. 9 (1961).

Reynolds, Roger. "It (')s Time." *Electronic Music Review* 7 (July 1968). "Indeterminacy: Some Considerations." *Perspectives of New Music* 4, no. 1 (Winter 1965). Both are exceedingly well written definitions of terms.

————. *Mind Models.* N.Y.: Praeger Books, 1976. Tough reading, but good discussion of the aesthetics of indeterminacy and other experimentalist techniques.

Tenney, James. *Meta (÷) Hodos: A Phenomenology of 20th-Century Music and an Approach to the Study of Form.* New Orleans, 1964. Related to a number of sections of this book in addition to indeterminacy.

Tomkins, Calvin. *The Bride and the Bachelors.* New York: Viking Press, 1965. Interesting biographical account of John Cage and related artists (Duchamp, Tinguely, and Rauschenberg).

Wolff, Christian. "On Form." *Die Reihe* 7:26. Relates to indeterminacy as does almost everything that Wolff writes, whether in words or music.

Xenakis, Iannis. *Formalized Music.* Bloomington: Indiana University Press, 1971. Quite interesting though mathematically complex even to those familiar with the subject.

Yates, Peter. *Twentieth Century Music.* New York: Pantheon Books, 1967. A bit outdated but does include some wonderful insights into Cage as well as into indeterminacy (see especially chaps. 30–32, pp. 303ff.).

Young, La Monte, and Jackson Mac Low, eds. *An Anthology of Chance Operations.* New York: La Monte Young & Jackson Mac Low, 1963. Excellent source for readings in chance philosophy and procedures, and includes articles by Young, Mac Low, and Maxfield in particular.

*Recordings and Publishers**

Andriessen, Louis. *Ittrospezione II* (1963). Donemus. For orchestra.

————. *Paintings.* Belwin-Mills.

Ashley, Robert. *in memoriam Crazy Horse* (1963). Recorded on Advance 5.

————. *Wolfman* (1964). CPE-*Source* IV.

Austin, Larry. *Accidents* (1967). CPE-*Source.*

————. *Piano Set* and *Piano Variations* (1964). Recorded by the Modern Jazz Quartet, Advance S-10.

Bedford, David. *Whitefield Music II.* For six to thirty-six players not trained in music.

Boulez, Pierre. *Structures I for Two Pianos* (1952). Universal Edition.

Brown, Earle. *Available Forms I* and *II.* AMP. The former recorded on RCA Vics-1239.

————. *Four Systems.* Recorded on Columbia MS-7139. For amplified cymbals.

————. *Hodograph I.* Recorded on Mainstream 5007.

————. *Music for Violoncello and Pianoforte* (1952). Recorded on Mainstream 5007.

————. *Quartet* (1965). Recorded on Mainstream 5009.

————. *December 1952.* (1952). C. F. Peters. Recorded on CRI S-330

Bussotti, Sylvano. *Coeur pour Batteur—Positively Yes.* Universal Edition. Recorded on Columbia MS-7139.

————. *Frammento.* Ricordi. Recorded on Mainstream 5005.

————. *Five Pieces for David Tudor.* Universal Edition.

Cage, John. *Amores for Prepared Piano and Percussion.* Peters. Recorded on Mainstream 5011.

————. *Aria with Fontana Mix* (1958). C. F. Peters. Recorded on Mainstream 5005 (also includes works of Berio and Bussotti).

---

*Addresses for record companies, periodicals, and music publishers mentioned in this Bibliography can be found in Appendix 4.

——. *Atlas Eclipticalis.* Peters. Recorded on DG-137009.

——. *Concert for Piano and Orchestra.* C. F. Peters.

——. *Cartridge Music* (1960). C. F. Peters. Recorded on Mainstream 5015.

——. *HPSCHD.* C. F. Peters. Recorded on Nonesuch 71224.

——. *Solo for Voice 2.* C. F. Peters. Recorded on Odyssey 32–160156.

——. *Fontana Mix.* C. F. Peters. Recorded on Columbia MS-7139.

——. *Indeterminacy.* (Cage, narrator; Tudor, piano). Recorded on Folkways 3704.

——. *Theatre Piece.* C. F. Peters.

——. *Variations I.* C. F. Peters. Recorded on Wergo 60033.

——. *Variations II.* C. F. Peters. Recorded on Columbia MS-7051.

——. *Variations III.* C. F. Peters. Recorded on DG-139442.

——. *Variations IV.* C. F. Peters. Recorded on Everest 3132.

——. *26'1.1499" for a String Player.* C. F. Peters. Recorded on Nonesuch 71237.

——. *34'46.776" for a Pianist.* C. F. Peters.

——. *4'33".* C. F. Peters.

Cardew, Cornelius. *Treatise* (1963–67). Buffalo: Gallery Upstairs Press. Graphic music for unspecified ensembles.

Feldman, Morton. *Chorus and Instruments.* C. F. Peters. Recorded on Odyssey 32–160156.

——. *Christian Wolff in Cambridge.* C. F. Peters. Recorded on Odyssey 32–160156.

——. *Durations.* C. F. Peters. Recorded on Mainstream 5007.

——. *False Relationships and the Extended Ending.* C. F. Peters. Recorded on CRI S-276.

——. *In Search of an Orchestration* (1967). C. F. Peters.

——. *Intersection 3.* C. F. Peters. Recorded on DG-139442.

——. *King of Denmark.* C. F. Peters. Recorded on Columbia MS-7139.

——. *Out of "Last Pieces."* C. F. Peters. Recorded on Columbia MS-6733.

——. *Viola in my Life.* C. F. Peters. Recorded on CRI S-276. In addition, Odyssey 32–160302 includes the following Feldman works: *Structures, Three Pieces, Extensions I, Projections 4, Intersection 3, Two Pieces, Extension 4,* and *Piece* (1957). All are published by Peters.

Foss, Lukas. *Geod.* Recorded on Candide 31042.

Haubenstock-Ramati, Roman. *Interpolation: a "Mobile" for Flute* (1,2,3), 1958. Universal Edition. Recorded on RCA Vics-1312.

——. *Jeux 2.* Universal Edition.

——. *Mobile for Shakespeare.* Universal Edition.

This composer's works are listed with examples in a brochure published by Universal Edition. Almost all deal in one way or another with indeterminate elements.

Higgins, Dick. *Thousand Symphonies* CPE-*Source.*

——. *Piano Album: Short Pieces* (1962–1982). New York: Printed Editions. Collection of graphic scores.

Kagel, Mauricio. *1898* (1973). London: Universal Edition.

Kayn, Roland. *Galaxis* (1962). Moeck. Uses variable instrumentation.

Logothetis, Anestis. *Ichnologia* (1964).

——. *Kulmination.* Edition Modern/Munich. Recorded on Wergo 60057.

——. *Labyrinthos* (1965). Universal Edition. For any soloists or any chamber orchestra.

——. *Odyssee* (1963). Universal Edition.

Maderna, Bruno. *Viola* (open and closed form versions). Recorded on Finnadar 9007.

Mizelle, John. *Radial Energy.* CPE-*Source.*

Moran, Robert. *Bombardments No. 2.* C. F. Peters.
———. *Four Visions.* Universal Edition.
Mumma, Gordon. *Mesa for Cybersonic Bandoneon.* Recorded on Odyssey 32–160158.
Nilsson, Bo. *Reaktionen* (1960). Universal Edition. For four percussionists; uses open form structures.
Pousseur. Henri. *Caractères* (1961). Universal Edition.
———. *Vôtre Faust.* Universal Edition. Variable operatic fantasy.
Rabe, Folke. *Pièce* (1961). W. Hansen. For speaking chorus, done in collaboration with Lasse O'Mansson.
Schäffer, Boguslaw. *S'alto* (1963). PWM. For alto saxophone and orchestra.
———. *Violin Concerto* (1963). PWM.
Stockhausen, Karlheinz. *Klavierstück XI.* Universal Edition. Recorded on Phillips 6500101.
———. *STOP.* Universal Edition.
Wolff, Christian. *Duo, Duet* and *Summer.* Recorded on Mainstream 5015.
———. *Duo II for Pianists.* C. F. Peters.
———. *Edges* (1968). CPE-*Source.*
———. *For 1, 2 or 3 People.* C. F. Peters. Recorded on Odyssey 32–160158.
———. *Trio 2* (1961). C. F. Peters. Piano, four hands.
Xenakis, Iannis. *Akrata.* Boosey and Hawkes. Recorded on Nonesuch 71201
———. *Duel.* Boosey and Hawkes.

10 The New Experimentalism

Fundamentals

The scope of this book does not permit fully detailed coverage of the cross-disciplinary aspects of the arts in general, and the added stimulus which the visual arts in particular have given to new music. The impetus generated by artists such as Marcel Duchamp, Man Ray, Robert Rauschenberg, Kandinsky, and many others has been profound. In the mainstream of music one finds composers like Schoenberg (who was himself an expressionist painter of repute) and Stravinsky influenced by Expressionism and painters like Picasso (see Chapter #1). In the *avant-garde* one encounters cross-relationships particularly between composers and artists such as Erik Satie (Man Ray), John Cage (Rauschenberg), and Earle Brown (Alexander Calder).

If one were to trace the roots of new experimentalism, the *Musical Sculpture* (undated) by Marcel Duchamp is noteworthy (showing a direct relationship with current concept music). His early work *The Bride Stripped Bare by Her Bachelors, Even* is especially provocative. Duchamp's *Erratum Musical* (1913) is a work of numbers substituting (in realization) a note for each number (Petr Kotik has made two current realizations, one for two pianos, the other for five instruments). The dada artists and later the antiart, concept art, and minimal art movements have all preceded parallel activities in music.

Paul Nougé (active in the surrealistic movement), in his *Music is Dangerous* (written in 1929), points out that the most known "uses" of music (relaxation, forgetting, and pleasure) are but subtle facades for its emotional dangers, drawing proofs from the ancient modal theories wherein each mode provoked distinct emotions (phrygian: excitement; lydian: calming; etc.).[1] His "iatric" music (medicinal music: noting that a great many medical terms end in "iatric" such as pediatric, etc.) further establishes music's profound remedial capabilities (possibly in the sense that a witch doctor has therapeutic powers, predating our current fascination with music therapy). Most importantly, however, Nougé proposes that the audience is not separate from or even "safe" from musical performance: "Our answer is that the concept of

---

1. Paul Nougé, *Music is Dangerous*, trans. Felix Giovanelli from *View* magazine. Reprinted in book form by *Soundings* (1973).

spectator, which seems to play so important a role in certain minds, is one of the grossest imaginable."[2] It is doubtful that Nougé's writings have had a direct influence over the new experimentalism of our present era; however, it is most noteworthy that such expressions as ". . . how we may defend ourselves against music. . . . Evidently, the easiest way is to refuse once and for all to have anything to do with it . . ." are not new or light divertissement as might be supposed.[3]

Questions regarding the most fundamental ideas, often more *about* than *with* sound, must inevitably arise from these concepts. The continual expansion of the definition of music to include *all* sound, regardless of origin or "beauty," and all concepts of sound, may eventually annul the new experimental designation used here. The primary motive behind this philosophy, however, remains: to destroy the concept of an "immaculate" art separate from life, with all its dangers and transiency. Indeed, the new experimentalist philosophy returns full circle to the primeval.

Robert Rauschenberg, possibly more than any other artist (aside from Jackson Pollock and Marcel Duchamp), has sustained a creative "antiart" movement which has substantially affected a number of composers. His *Erased de Kooning Drawing* is exactly that: a de Kooning drawing (one he obtained directly from the artist himself) erased as completely as possible using a special selection of erasers collected by Rauschenberg. The act of "decomposing" the work of art becomes in this instance the "act" of creation (of a white sheet of paper only barely showing hints of lines, or even less—slight depressions in the paper where the original drawing once existed). If one can deal with art as *change,* beauty as totally *relative,* any *act* as plausibly artistic, then Rauschenberg's erasure presents a work as significant as the original drawing. Whether one deals with it as such or not is of little consequence: it is antiart.

One composer has come close to this approach in music, but in an entirely different way. He has substituted an entire work of the past *verbatim* for his own. Paul Ignace indicates some of the rationale behind such actions in a letter to the author.

When I was first asked to compose a piece for orchestra I had no idea what they wanted, except an experience of some kind. I wrote and asked for a complete list of the other works included in concerts of the series, and when I discovered that the concert preceding the night of my premiere included Berlioz's *Symphonie Fantastique,* I made up my mind. I insisted that my work be unrehearsed (there wouldn't have been much anyway, as those things go) and that I would bring score and parts the night of the concert. Imagine the shock when the conductor and players opened their music to find the work that they had performed the night before . . . but they performed it, much to the anger and horror of the audience and

2. Ibid., p. 17.
3. Ibid., p. 24.

reviewers. They were angry, of course, not at the sounds but at my plagiarism (legal, according to copyright laws) but few realized they listened to the sounds in an entirely new way—something very good, very creative, in my way of thinking. No, I did not receive $$$ for my endeavor! (The work, by the way, was titled *Symphonie Fantastique No. 2.*)[4]

Yehuda Yannay's *Houdini's Ninth* (1970) is experimental theater quite apropos of this genre. Bernard Jacobson characterizes one performance in this excerpt from an article in *Stereo Review.*

A man cycled onto the stage, put a record of the (Beethoven) *Choral* Symphony finale on a phonograph, and proceeded to mix some kind of culinary concoction onto the surface of the actual disc, with bizarre effects on the sound. This was interwoven with an episode involving a double-bass player in a sort of straitjacket, and dominating the proceedings was a projection of an incredibly stupid poem published in *Dwight's Journal of Music,* Boston, on December 17, 1870. It was in honor of Beethoven's centenary, and took a very encouraging view of his affliction of deafness: "A price how small," it cheerily informed him, "for privilege how great, / When thy locked sense groped upward and there/ The shining ladder reaching through the air."[5]

Encouraged by the words of social philosophers Marshall McLuhan and R. Buckminster Fuller, and his own studies with Eastern philosopher Suzuki, John Cage has developed a personal philosophy expressed clearly in his sweeping statement: "Everything we do is music." His works encompass every aspect of the new concepts of the last twenty years: electronic, improvisatory, indeterminate, multimedia, exploration into new sounds, and the new experimentalism. From his work in the thirties, when he originated the "prepared piano," to his extension of multimedia "happenings," he has remained the remarkable enigma. His ideas and works amuse, startle, antagonize, and somehow also encourage the worlds of music, dance, and art. If *change,* not idolatry, be the mark of greatness, then John Cage has surely reached this pinnacle. Nothing can or will be the same after him.

Aside from Cage, no other composer has achieved the shock value of, and relevance to, antiart, except perhaps La Monte Young. In particular, his *Composition 1960 #3,* (the duration of the piece is announced and the audience told to do whatever they wished for the remainder of the composition) and *Composition 1960 #6,* (the performers stare and react exactly as if they were the audience) are excellent examples of the "anti" aspect at work.[6]

The new experimentalism is a returning to the soil. Works do not cease to exist, but a new awareness of *all* things, their disorder and order, their direction and nondirection in time, takes place. Man is no longer the center

4. From a letter to the author.

5. Available on film from the composer: 4044 N. Downer Ave., Milwaukee, Wis. 53211 (as of December 1974).

6. Barney Childs discusses these works and others in an excellent article, "Indeterminacy and Theory: Some Notes," *The Composer* 1, no. 1 (June 1969):15–34.

of the universe. As an artist, one no longer attempts gymnastic representations of life, but becomes a part of it. Like the antijoke, one relies on an audience expectancy of traditional forms; funny because it isn't funny, music because it isn't music: inherently temporary as awareness increases, constantly inevitable as all meaning requires opposites for significant identity.

Critics of these and other experimentalists address themselves to the "dead end" and "pointless" philosophies implied. To these, I.A. MacKenzie has replied:

Art is imitation, repetition, memory, or rejection of life. Nothing is created by man, just recreated: a storeroom to collect the bits and pieces of the whole he feels worthy of saving, to be brought to life again whenever the need occurs, but never as good as the original. Art exists only as a refuge against new experience, un-recreated experience with reality: second-hand living. The terms "musician," "painter," "writer," merely break these imitations down further for easier construction, assimilation and comfort. I am none of these. I am not an artist. I do not imitate, or need of developing [sic] a memory with art for a thousand million possibilities of the present confront me, and I don't want that number diminished by one.

I am a mapmaker, a suggester of possible routes for those interested in experiences with what has already been created—everything. I am similar to the "artist" in that I do not create, dissimilar with him in that I do not pretend to.

Untouched by style, convenience, or tradition, the elements I observe (not manipulate) I discovered, but only for myself and my discovery has style, convenience just as yours.

I do nothing that anyone else could not do easily and do not pretend to. I only give directions when someone wishes them and would be happy to stop anytime. . . .

Everything exists: why should I mechanically alter one thing into another, one thought into another? All exist—it is much more—to find the original.[7]

With these basic concepts and experiments, a transcendental form of expression emerges outside the realm of the arts. Communication rests more directly on the audience than on the creator, often philosophically—more often theatrically—antagonizing the experience of man. New experiments are *necessary, important,* and *contribute* to art without artificial values or misdirected definitions of terms.

Cage speaks of this in *A Year from Monday:* "Art's in process of coming into its own: life."[8] and "We used to have the artist up on a pedestal. Now he's no more extraordinary than we are."[9] Tzara states: "Art is not the most precious manifestation of life. Art has not the celestial and universal value that people like to attribute to it. Life is far more interesting."[10]

7. I.A. MacKenzie, as paraphrased by David Cope in *Notes in Discontinuum* (Los Angeles: Discant Music, 1970), p. 2.

8. John Cage, *A Year from Monday* (Middletown, Conn.: Wesleyan University Press, 1967), p. 6.

9. Ibid., p. 50.

10. Robert Motherwell, *The Dada Painters and Poets: An Anthology* (New York: Wittenborn, Schultz, Inc., 1951), p. 248.

These directions extend to include those sounds which destroy the mind *(danger music),* which don't exist *(minimal* and *concept music),* which come about without the hand of man *(biomusic* and *soundscapes),* or return to simple materials in unique ways (the new tonality).

Danger Music

The history of *danger music* is long indeed, and if one follows Paul Nougé's thinking in *Music is Dangerous,*[11] all music has such potential. While, as he points out, we may use it for "relaxation," "forgetting" or "pleasure" it . . . "probably entails serious consequences."[12] This fascinating book describes a number of accounts of man's unfortunate encounters with the dangers of music:

Sometimes we find peculiar stories in a newspaper. A few weeks ago, a young American went home after coming out of a performance of *Tannhäuser,* and killed himself; not without having first written a note in which he explained that where Tannhäuser had weakened, he, yes he, would set a better example of courage and grandeur.[13]

Most current *danger music* involves a more direct attack on the performer or spectator (e.g., Nam June Paik's *Danger Music for Dick Higgins* with the score reading: "Creep into the Vagina of a living Whale.").[14]

The visual arts have certainly had direct influence on *danger music.* Ay-o, for example, has created a number of finger boxes each containing a substance unknown to the "spectator." One experiences the art by placing fingers into these small creations some of which contain felt, fur, and similar "pleasantries." Some, however, contain razor blades, broken glass, and pocket knives. "Chance" has a new dimension here as one must weigh odds against the possible loss of small body members.

Though blood (and even death) are not unknown to *danger musics,* these seldom occur as a direct result of composer notation. "Accidents" are welcomed, however. Such was the case of two happenings in 1962: the first involved a somewhat "bloodied" Robert Whitman at Bennington College; the second involved a woman spectator/performer at an Al Hansen happening falling from a window down a number of stories and eventually through a glass roof.

The environment around us provides another source of danger: sound pollution. While discussed in more depth later in this chapter under *soundscapes,* the aural dangers of even the average household cannot escape the artist's cognizance. Robert Ashley's *Wolfman* (1964) exemplifies *danger music.*

11. Nougé, op. cit.
12. Ibid., p. 11.
13. Ibid., p. 11.
14. See John Cage's *Notations* (New York: Something Else Press, 1969), unpaged, for a copy of the score in full.

Figure 10.1. Robert Ashley.

Through use of a prerecorded tape and a voice "screaming" through a microphone involving electronic feedback, all turned to the highest possible level, the work easily reaches decibel counts above danger level. The recording of this work, with instructions "to be played at the highest possible volume level" indeed constitutes ear annihilation to the uninitiated in a small "live" room.[15] More recently, Ashley's *Private Parts* shifts toward a kind of 'rock' art form, achieving enormous success from a young audience often unaware of its origins in experimental tradition.

Phil Corner's adaptation of his own *prelude* from *4 Suits* creates interesting danger music:

I threw out a rifle and then slowly picked it up and pointed it at the audience (no one bolted for the doors, by the way) . . . counterpointed by a woman who slowly picked up a bouquet of roses—there was a countdown . . . at the end of which she threw the flowers into the audience, all over, with great love and joy, while I silently let fall the rifle and slunk offstage. Yet this was apparently not the right message for some, as I was accosted afterwards by one of the *Up Against The Wall Motherfucker* crowd, and yelled at "Next time a real rifle!"[16]

Corner's *"One antipersonnel-type CBU bomb will be thrown into the audience"* is another example of danger music used to express antiwar political views. Corner speaks of this work:

I tried to push the concert situation to a point where those present would *have* to feel the immediacy of the situation—*their* situation, since this had to be something in which those present shared a complicity. Failure! Could I have been that naive? For the audience reaction is *not* predictable. I discovered that right then and there.

15. *Wolfman* is published in *Source: Music of the Avant-Garde* 2, no. 2 (July 1968). Both the score and the recording are available.

16. From a letter to the author.

For that reason the thing was not even ever done. The defenses against identifying with the victims, with putting ourselves in their places, is too strong. Guilt is covered up by a selfish fear. A self-serving, even dishonest one, I might add. I felt it then and still do. The idea that that would really be acted on, that a real terrorist act would be announced so and carried out in this way seems to me incredible. Finally though, the "performance" would have been to announce the cancellation of the performance.[17]

Danger music is rarely sound; it is philosophy. Performances merge with reality. Danger music denotes war with music, war with the sanctity of sensual isolation. Daniel Lentz's comments in the Coda of his *Skeletons Don't Say Peek*[18] explicitly attack the hierarchy of traditional concert and instrumental performance routine:

I too am sad. In fact, I am very sad. Men are still fighting wars and playing music. Some are guerilla wars, and some are guerilla compositions. But they are, nevertheless, war and music. They are fought with weapons and instruments. There is so little difference. One type is used for the defense of an army or nation; the other, for the defense of a vestigial culture. Do we need the protection of generals and composers? Do we need their incredibly scary anti-ballistic-missile systems and synthesizers? Shouldn't we attempt their destruction, before they destroy us? From whom are they protecting us? From the Russians? The Princetonians? What, in the late-middle 20th century does weaponry have to do with music? Can we eliminate one without first eliminating the other? Won't the metaphor be too powerful until it is taken away? Has there ever been an instrument built which wasn't used? Couldn't the players you saw in action tonight just as well have been aggressive soldiers of war? Did you watch closely their gestures? Is there a real difference between them and the Special Forces? Are they not identical mentalities? They are out to kill us and you sit there waiting. Are you all crazy? Can't you see, nor hear? But wait . . . don't blame the players. We are only cogs in the great hierarchy. We follow directions. The artistic generals tell us what to do and when to do it and the manner in which it is to be done. They are not even specific. Aren't they kind, as they destroy us? We are like you: just poor citizens caught up in the immense musical-industrial complex. Sure, if you threaten us or our friends, we will play for you. We have no recourse but to protect our "raison d'être."

Prior to this final "performer" announcement, all the instruments have been taken from the performers, placed in front of the piano, and *saluted*. The act of not playing, the drama of attacking the performance situation, eliminate all vestige of traditional (and, for that matter, nontraditional) equipment, instruments, and concepts.

Daniel Lentz's works are often antiwar as well. *Anti Bass Music*, for example (see fig. 10.2), employs a number of notations relating concert situation and battlefield. The work, supplied with four optional endings (which may be

17. Ibid.

18. Part of Harold Budd's *California 99* (1969), the movements of which were composed by Turetzky, Oliveros, Austin, Childs, Lunetta, Mizelle, and Sherr.

Figure 10.2. Daniel Lentz: *Anti Bass Music,* page 11.

performed in multiples, that is, more than one ending may be employed), includes a reading of a list of American composers not killed in Viet Nam, and the use of twenty-five to one hundred laughing machines.

Minimal and Concept Music

Minimal and *concept music* are so closely related that separation becomes impossible (though both deserve distinct analysis). Minimal art is the closest "art" relative to *minimal music.* Works such as Robert Rauschenberg's *White Paintings* (canvases covered as evenly as possible with white paint) are parallel to such minimal works as John Cage's classic: *4'33".*

4'33" received its first performance in August, 1952, at Woodstock, New York by pianist David Tudor. Using a stopwatch, he covered the piano keyboard at the beginning of each movement, playing nothing, but timing the silences of each period marked by Cage in the otherwise blank score. Unfortunately, the brillance of Tudor had the adverse effect of limiting this work to piano, (the score mentions no instrumentation). The title ("for any instrument or combination of instruments") makes realization practical on almost any conceivable plane of sound or nonsound. Virtually anything with a total duration of four minutes and thirty-three seconds (and movements of one minute, forty seconds; two minutes, twenty-three seconds; and thirty seconds respectively) could successfully serve as a realization of the score, from thinking-in-a-bathtub to silence by a symphony orchestra.[19] Cage has clarified the concept behind such works:

. . . where it is realized that sounds occur whether intended or not, one turns in the direction of those he does not intend. The turning is psychological and seems at first

19. This work is published in *Source: Music of the Avant-Garde* 1, no. 2 (July 1967):46 ff.

to be a giving up of everything that belongs to humanity—for a musician, the giving up of music. This psychological turning leads to the world of nature, where, gradually or suddenly, one sees that humanity and nature, not separate, are in this world together; that nothing was lost when everything was given away. In fact, everything is gained.[20]

Rauschenberg's *White Paintings* link further with *4'33"* when one realizes that in the former the shadows of spectators, variance of lights, colored reflections, etc., turn the seemingly blank canvas into a veritable mass of visual activity. In the latter, the coughs, laughter, and other audible movements of the audience as well as the extraneous sounds from without the performance area become, in fact, the work. In both cases the act of the creator is minimal *and* conceptual.

Minimal music (most often minimal in materials and not duration, as will be seen) is also clearly defined in the works of La Monte Young. His *Composition 1960 #7* contains only the notes B and F♯ with the instructions: to be held for a "long time." *Composition 1960 #10* requests the performer to "draw a straight line and follow it."[21] In 1960, at Berkeley, he presented a composition which consisted of turning loose a jar full of butterflies (they made a sound however inaudible). . . .[22]

Others of that same year include his famous (infamous) "line piece":

My "Composition 1960 No. 9" consists of a straight line drawn on a piece of paper. It is to be performed and comes with no instructions. The night I met Jackson MacLow we went down to my apartment and he read some of his poems for us. Later when he was going home, he said he'd write out directions to get to his place so we could come and visit him sometime. He happened to pick up "Composition No. 9" and said, "Can I write it here?" I said, "No, wait, that's a piece. Don't write on that." He said, "Whadaya mean a piece? That's just a line."[23]

Minimal music is also apparent in the music of Harold Budd. His *Lovely Thing (Piano),* in which one chord is softly attempted many times over a period of fifteen to twenty minutes; *One Sound* for string quartet; and *The Candy Apple Revision* (1970), which states simply, "D-flat Major," all classify as minimal compositions. About his appoach, Budd remarks:

Ever since (a long time ago) I've pushed and pushed towards zero: Running it all down, a kind of on-going process of removal. There's an enormous difference, by the way, between Monotony and Boredom. Boredom, it seems to me, is trying to make something interesting. Monotony is making nothing interesting. And insofar as I feel

20. John Cage, *Silence* (Cambridge, Mass.: The M.I.T. Press, paperback edition, 1961), p. 8.
21. A great deal of material on and by LaMonte Young is found in *Selected Writings* by La Monte Young and Marian Zazeela (Munich: Heiner Friedrich, 1969).
22. Richard Kostelanetz, *The Theatre of Mixed Means* (New York: Dial Press, 1968), from the article (first page) on La Monte Young.
23. Young and Zazeela, *Selected Writings,* unpaged (from the Lecture 1960, copyright 1965 by the Tulane Drama Review).

Figure 10.3. Copyright (c) La Monte
Young & Marian Zazeela 1971.

Courtesy: Heiner Friedrich. (Photo
credit: Robert Adler.)

all art to be utterly worthless (no redeeming social values), I'm interested in that
what I do is pretty—("Terrifying," "Gripping," "Sensitive," "Relaxing,"
"Hypnotic," "Spiritual"—all to the side for a moment) an existential *prettiness;* a
kind of High-Art Uselessness. . . .[24]

Much of minimal music actually seems *maximal*[25] in nature (particularly
in duration). La Monte Young's more recent New York City-based (6 Harrison St.) *Dream Houses* (1968–funded by the Dia Art Foundation) are media
works of great duration (Alex Dea singing, Jon Hassell on horn, David Rosenboom, viola, and De Fracia Evans working slide projections). Like most
minimal works these contain drones and slowly overlapping (focusing in and
out) projections: a minimum of material. These works derive from earlier experiments such as "The Tortoise, His Dream and Journeys" (1964–), performed over extended periods of time by *The Theatre of Eternal Music* (John
Cale, a member of the *Velvet Underground* rock group, on viola and Tony
Conrad on violin).

24. From a letter to the author.

25. The term *process* is also used to describe music which unfolds slowly, one that carries the
thrust of invention by slowly processing one idea to another. Music in this genre, while appearing
minimal, achieves "mileage" through constantly generating variations of a single idea.

Many of these works find precedent in Erik Satie's *Vexations*. This 32-bar piece is to be played softly 840 times. His *musique d'ameublement* (1920) is also minimal music. This "furnishing music" co-composed by Satie and Darius Milhaud was played during intermissions and programs announced: "We urge you to take no notice of it and to behave during the intervals *as if it did not exist.*"[26]

Composers such as Charlemagne Palestine, Yoshima Wada (whose large horns are created from "plumbing pipes") build on drones and/or slowly overlapping motives creating an ever-changing but slowly evolving *somnambulistic* state. Max Neuhaus's underwater work, *Water Whistle*, utilizes 8–10 water driven whistles and can be heard only if you are submerged in the same water as the whistles (as well an overlap with *danger music*). Karlheinz Stockhausen's (*aus den Sieben Tagen*, 1968) is a verbal score containing only very brief performance directions such as "play single sounds with such dedication until you feel the warmth that radiates from you—play on and sustain it as long as you can." Frederic Rzewski (most notably *Coming Together*, 1972), and Philip Glass (*Music in Fifths* and *Music in Similar Motion*, both 1969) also compose using minimal materials.

Philip Corner is especially noted for his work with minimal concepts often lasting evenings, at other times lasting brief seconds (for example, his *One Note Once* which is just that; the instrumentation being flexible). His *Metal Meditations* are often collaborations with others involved in the *Sounds out of Silent Spaces* series in New York City: Carole Weber, Julie Winter, Elaine Summers, Annea Lockwood, Alison Knowles,[27] Daniel Goode, and Charles Morrow, among others. These are evening-long events featuring composer-constructed and traditional instruments struck softly but with intense aural experience. These meditations also involve "total experience" with "ritual food events," slide projections, and lights. Corner's *One Note Once, Cage's 4′33″* and Young's *Compositions of 1960* all approach the ultimate minimal structure: 0 duration, 0 instruments, 0 performers, 0 audience.

Many composers feel that the *avant-garde* as such is dead, and that the works in the 1960s point to a return of simplicity, a return to the foundations of sound itself: pitch, duration, and silence. These composers and their works no longer achieve the "shock" immediacy and notoriety that *avant-garde* works of the 1950s-60s characteristically received, nor the pretentious complexities of systems and scientific paraphernalia so in evidence with more mainstream academic-based composers. Steve Reich's *It's Gonna Rain* (1965), *Violin Phase*, and *Piano Phase* (both 1967), and *Pulse Music* for phase-shifting gate, an instrument invented by the composer (1968–69), are the most notable.

26. Pierre-Daniel Templier, *Erik Satie*, trans. Elena French and David French, 1932. (originally published by Presses Universitaires de France). Cambridge, Mass.: The MIT Press, 1969, p. 45.
27. Knowles (along with Jaran Downey and Gunther Maier) has recently been involved with *Other Media*'s production of *Music in the Key of J* in New York City. This was broadcast on Teleprompter's Channel J (produced by Charles Morrow).

Figure 10.4. Tom Johnson: Celestial Music for Imaginary Trumpets. (c) Copyright 1974 by Tom Johnson. All rights reserved. Used by permission. From *Imaginary Music* by Tom Johnson, Two Eighteen Press, N.Y.C.

Karlheinz Stockhausen's *Mikrophonie I* (1964) uses only one sound source, a large (about six feet) tam-tam upon which the performers manipulate the various verbal instructions of the score, "scraping, trumpeting," and so on.

Concept music, though often overlapping many of the aforementioned works, is also extremist (more powerful and often more interesting in premise than in the performance situation—if there is one). Eric Andersen's *Opus 48 ("Which turns anonymous when the instruction is carried out")* is sent through the mail on a piece of cardboard which states in total: "Place the chosen tautology." This is *concept art* (implication of music not being present). Tom Johnson, in his book *Imaginary Music,* includes a number of nonplayable concept pieces.[28] His *Celestial Music for Imaginary Trumpets* (see fig. 10.4) is clearly *concept music,* as performance is impossible; one is able to only "conceptualize" or imagine the work. Robert Moran's *Composition for Piano with Pianist* states: "A pianist comes onto the stage and goes directly to the concert grand piano. He climbs into the piano, and sits on the strings. The piano plays him."[29] This conceptual *message* is more important than any "real" act of sound production.

Concept philosophy is often implied only in the score and is not "real" to the audience. *Accidents* (1967) by Larry Austin, for example, contains instructions in which the pianist performs gestures while avoiding actual sounds. The speed of performance makes accidents unavoidable. As if repenting sins, the performer must return to each gesture in which an accident occurred (i.e., a sound made) and repeat it until error-free (i.e., no sound occurring).

---

28. Tom Johnson, *Imaginary Music.* New York: Two-Eighteen Press (P.O. Box 218, Village Station, New York, N.Y.10014), 1974.

29. Published in *Soundings* 1:44.

The New York-based movement *Fluxus* (which included Paik, Young, Dick Higgins, Eric Andersen, Thomas Schmidt, Jackson MacLow, and George Brecht) represented the basic directions in concept music for a number of years, finally becoming a publisher of art objects. Blank structures provide objectives in the experiments of these composers, poets, and artists. Often these works do not contain the slightest hint as to what action is intended or what materials are to be used.[30]

Text sound music involves minimal procedures and is based on the *text-ljud kompositioner* of two Swedish composers, Lars-Gunnar Bodin and Bengt-Emil Johnson in 1967. Termed sound poetry, speech music, and even lexical music, its origins extend back to the Futurists (in Italy) just after the turn of the century. Works in this genre expand reading and speaking concepts, utilizing onomatopoeia and other intricate textural mechanics to produce rhythmic and contrapuntal structures. Often these incorporate long repetitions of words in solo or ensemble situations, with changing and developing emphasis, accents, and meaning. Frequently these works are altered through electronic processes.

Composers aware of this form early in this century include Hugo Ball, Tristan Tzara, and Kurt Schwitters in the twenties; Marcel Duchamp in the thirties and forties; and John Cage in the fifties and sixties. Composers currently interested in the genre include John Giorno, Aram Saroyan, Brion Gysin, Beth Anderson, Robert Ashley, Anthony Gnazzo, Tim Bell, Stephen Ruppenthal, and Charles Amirkhanian. Amirkhanian has produced a large number of text sound works in recent years, including *Seatbelt Seatbelt* (1973), *Mugic* (1973), *Mahogany Ballpark* (1976), and *Dutiful Ducks* (1977).

Biomusic

Biomusic (music created by natural functions rather than by necessarily conscious attempts at composition) has taken some interesting turns in recent years. A number of composers have become interested in "brain-wave" music. Human (and, for that matter, other advanced animals') brains function with bits of electric currents. Amplifying such energy produces enough current to serve as control voltages on synthesizer functions (utilizing normal electronic music gear such as oscillators, filters, etc.). The brain directly controls sonic output.

"Brain-wave" experiments have created conflicting reports. Stockhausen notes:

. . . I attended a concert in which David Tudor, together with a composer at Davis, California, where I taught for six months, were performing a piece with "brain

---

30. *Fluxus* movements have also arisen in other countries, including Japan (Takehisa Kosugi, Chieko Shiomi) and Germany.

waves." The performance, in the beginning, seemed to be very magic-like, a table lifting society, and it seemed to promise quite a lot because of the way they were watching and looking at each other. The speakers' cardboard membranes were pushing the air, and these pulsations—a kind of colored low noise—were produced by the performer's brain waves. It's the same effect as if air were being pumped into a tire. So what? There's a certain periodicity which becomes more or less irregular, maybe interesting for doctors.[31]

Composer David Rosenboom has developed procedures far more sophisticated than those described by Stockhausen.[32] Success, of course, remains in the "heads" of the *performers* and their necessarily practiced art of controlling *alpha* waves.

Possibly one of the most fascinating areas of *biomusic* is the sounds of the humpback whale. Initial hearing proves this to be more than a preposterous joke. Indeed these advanced mammals are highly creative:

Quite apart from any esthetic judgment one might make about them, the sounds produced by Humpback whales can properly be called songs because they occur in complete sequences that are repeated. . . . Humpback whale songs are far longer than bird songs. The shortest Humpback song recorded lasts six minutes and the longest is more than thirty minutes.[33]

Not only have recordings and tapes of the "songs" of the humpback whale become popular in and of themselves, but they have equally impressed composers. George Crumb's *Voice of the Whale* (*Vox Balaenae,* 1971), ". . . was inspired by the singing of the humpback whale, a tape recording of which I had heard two or three years previously."[34] Likewise composers like Allen Strange and Priscilla McLean have completed works influenced by this most highly developed of water mammals.

Works involving a "rediscovery" of bioenvironmental sounds include Pauline Oliveros's *Sonic Meditation XIII:*

Energy Changes
(for Elaine Summers's movement meditation, Energy Changes)
© Copyright 1974 by Smith Publications. Used by permission.

Listen to the environment as a drone. Establish contact mentally with all of the continuous external sounds and include all of your own continuous internal sounds, such as blood pressure, heart beat and nervous system. When you feel prepared, or when you are triggered by a random or intermittent sound from the external or internal environment, make any sound you like in one breath, or a cycle of sounds. When a sound or a cycle of sounds, is completed re-establish mental connection with the drone, which you first established before making another sound or cycle of like sounds.

31. Jonathan Cott, *Stockhausen* (New York: Simon and Schuster, 1973), p. 43.

32. Prevalent in performances on such as the David Frost television show and others on NET (early 1970s).

33. Liner notes on Columbia ST-620, "Songs of the Humpback Whale."

34. Liner notes on Columbia M-32739.

Figure 10.5. "Training of musical
consciousness is a large order."
Composer Pauline Oliveros. Photo
credit: Becky Cohen, Del Mar, Calif.

Yehuda Yannay's *Bugpiece* involves yet another life form in a slightly
different manner, but is definitely *biomusic*. The work uses "live notation" in
the form of:

. . . one beetle, one centipede, and five or six ants. These insects were in a real sense
the "composers" and conductors, even if Yannay did set up the parameters as to
how the chance operations would work. All the lights in the auditorium were turned
off, the overhead projector was turned on so the audience and performers (with their
backs to the audience) could see the bugs running around in a plastic box set on the
projector. Different areas of the "playing field" represented varieties of loud and
soft. Green, yellow, and blue gels represented high and low pitches. The ants did
most of the running, even one was maimed. The beetle stayed around the sides, but
did make one mad dash across the field. To spark things up, the centipede was a late
entry, and he chased the beetle.[35]

An even later entry into the "bio" scene, *plant-created music,* is described
vividly in an article from the *Rolling Stone:*

It could be said they were singing, but that is too anthropomorphic a way to
describe the sounds the plants were emitting: strange electronic garglings, ethereal

---

35. Clifford Barnes, "Music: Melody sent into exile," *Cincinnati Post,* November 15, 1972.

chirpings and shriekings to a mysterious nonlinear rhythm that reveals the secret life-pulse of the vegetable kingdom. Then something very strange happened. A spectator gently held a knife to one of the stalks and addressed the plant. "Hey you! Perk up or you get it." The words plunged the room into sudden silence. The plants stopped singing. Coleuses may be pretty but they certainly aren't dumb. Somehow the threatened plant conveyed a warning of danger to its pot-mates, and they responded by entering a sort of suspended animation . . . discovery of an early-warning system among plants is just one of the revelations that have come to three electronic music specialists at Sounds Reasonable, Inc., a recording studio in Washington, D.C. There Ed Barnett, Norman Lederman and Gary Burge have been experimenting with ways to create music from the silent vibes of plants. So far their efforts have yielded a single, called *"Stereofernic Orchidstra"* . . . the record is a studio mix of four plants, an Indian azalea, a philodendron, a Boston fern and an amaryllis, recorded at the National Botanical Gardens. The first side features the raw plant "voices" tuned to different pitches on an oscillator. It sounds like a demonic, atonal violin section in electro-frenzy. On the second side the plants control the changes on an ARP music synthesizer. The result is more musical, but no less bizarre.[36]

John Cage speaks of his work in related areas:

I've had for a long time the desire to hear the mushroom itself, and that could be done with very fine technology, because they are dropping spores and those spores are hitting surfaces. There certainly is sound taking place. . . . It leads, of course, to the thought about hearing anything in the world since we know that everything is in a state of vibration, so that not only mushrooms, but also chairs and tables, for instance, could be heard . . . I have a project . . . to amplify a city park for children. It was to be done at Ivrea near Turino. . . . There is a marvelous hill in the center of the city that is high and has a beautiful view of the Alps and is isolated enough from the traffic sounds so that you hear the sounds of the plants. . . . I was spoiled by that marvelous situation in Ivrea where the silence—when you weren't playing the plants—was very audible and beautiful; you could hear it as if you were in a concert hall. In other words, I wanted the silence of the mountain to be heard by the children after they had heard the sounds that they themselves had made by playing the plants. . . . Every now and then the plants were going to become unplayable, and the children would be obliged to hear the silence.[37]

Biomusic, while in and of itself representing some of the oldest forms of organized sound on earth, is still, remarkably, engendering a wide variety of emotions from its spectators. Obviously this, as with most of the music described within this chapter, is primarily natural *artifact* becoming *art-in-fact.*

36. Jim Wiggins, "Lily Sings the Blues," *Rolling Stone,* September 12, 1975, p. 12. © 1975 by Straight Arrow Publishers Inc. All Rights Reserved. Reprinted by Permission.

37. David Cope, "An Interview with John Cage," *The Composer* 10, no. 1 (1980).

Soundscapes

Many composers articulate aural expression in terms of natural sound quite apart from *biomusic*. Among these are many of Pauline Oliveros's *Sonic Meditations*.[38]

V:
Take a walk at night. Walk so silently that the bottoms of your feet become ears.

and

XVII:
Ear Ly
(For Kenneth Gaburo's NMCE)
1. Enhance or paraphrase the auditory environment so perfectly that a listener cannot distinguish between the real sounds of the environment and the performed sounds.
2. Become performers by not performing.

The latter work combines all possible available sounds of the organic and inorganic environments.

Other composers, such as I.A. MacKenzie, verbally express actions, or concepts which often contain written directions toward action, but without any reference to sound other than that inherent in the environment of the situation (figs. 10.6, 10.7). His "wind sound sculptures" (1930s) involve the principle of instruments played by wind (later, he also produced water and fire sculptures) and need neither performer nor audience (see fig 10.8). The wish, before he died, of having these placed at some point where man would not be able to hear them, has been carried out, bearing close resemblance to the self-destructing sculptures of Jean Tinguely.

The following excerpts from an interview between the author and MacKenzie in 1968, just three months before his death, represent his direction towards anti-ego in art. He considered the concert stage the archvillain of true equality of sounds.

I.A.: Basically, I was curious about the fundamental concept of whether I, or mankind for that matter, was really important in the functioning of music. . . . I still followed traditional notation . . . but demanded less and less skill for the performer since it was not to be had anyway . . . my preoccupation seemed to be with creating instruments which played themselves. . . . Musicians and composers . . . seem to delight in creating codes and systems that will separate them more from the common man and, I'm afraid, their audiences. . . .
D.C.: Was publication possible?
I.A.: Out of the question. By 1927 my music had become so involved in new instruments of my own invention, the publisher would have had to publish the instrument with the music. By 1930, I abandoned the written music completely anyway, believing that I should be more interested in sound than codes. . . .

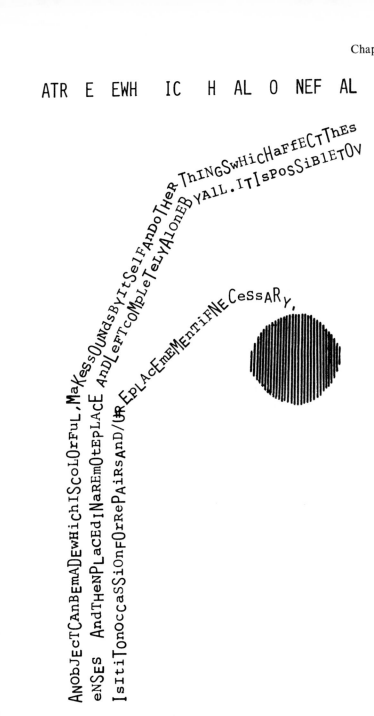

Figure 10.6. Copyright by Discant
Music, Los Angeles, California.

FEweR LoVEs THaN tImE ALLowS....

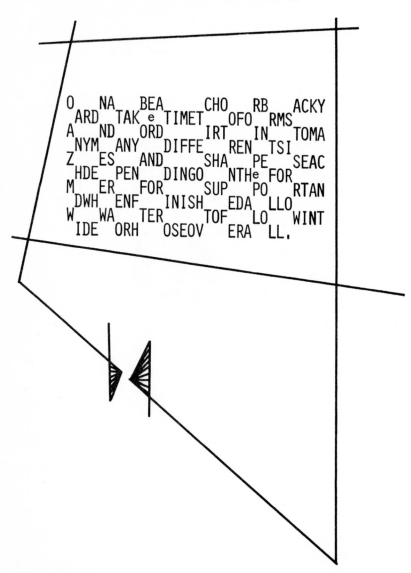

Figure 10.7. Copyright by Discant
Music, Los Angeles, California.

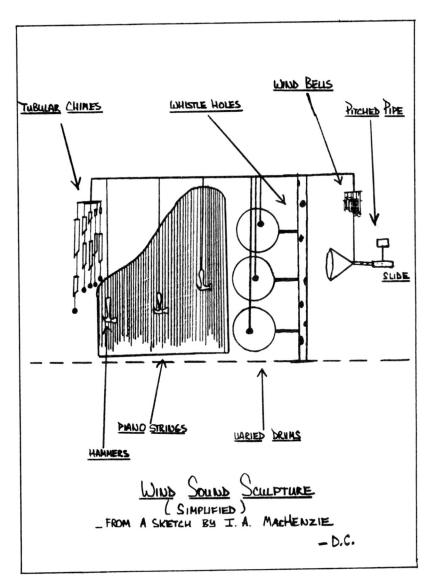

Figure 10.8. From *The Composer*, Vol. I, no. 1 (June 1969). Copyright by *Composer Magazine*, 1969.

D.C.: . . . What was your . . . reaction (to universities)?

I.A.: My reaction was harsh. . . . The teachers were very dull; more interested in talking *about* sound than *in* sound; mostly more interested in themselves. Many times I would hear visiting composers lecture on their works . . . only to find that the lecturer was just flesh and blood, not a god. . . . I found quickly that for me, at least, the university and its intellect and pomposity was creatively bankrupt: it offered nothing but security . . . and the same old traditional claptrap. . . . As long as people continue to raise gods, not people, the situation won't change. As long as so-called "great" performers are regarded as towering musical figures, instead of rather grotesque finger gymnasts, the situation won't change. The university has contributed to this as well, creating a caste system. . . .

D.C.: . . . you say that around 1930 you began just creating instruments.

I.A.: Yes. But, more important, instruments without human performers. By 1934, early spring, I had created my first wind-sound sculpture . . . an elaboration of the old Chinese wind chimes . . . in fact, that's where I got the idea. . . . I used to listen to storms approach through their sound and somehow felt I was "tuning in" on nature (nature being something I have always felt to be more impressive and profound than man or myself, to be exact). . . .

D.C.: What do you consider yourself?

I.A.: I don't. Categorizing, defining and such limit creativity. . . . Whether one thing is a work of art, and another not, is unimportant. This is cataloguing, not problem-solving. Problems are: God, beauty, nature; creating with or without them, or to them or from them. Creating is solving; cataloguing is avoiding. . . . I don't dislike systems or codes any more than money; but, as before, if these are used by someone to catalogue their own or someone else's work, they have become destructive rather than helpful. . . . I create what I like, in hopes that God, nature, and people (in that order) may like some or all of them. . . .

. . . My sketches are, I suppose, my musical notation. However . . . when I create the work, I let it go its own way, and I sort of follow along. Problems of balance and so forth are worked out as I go along; intonation is achieved through experimentation until I have what I want. . . . I am in complete control of pitch, timbre, and . . . length. . . . I hope the sculpture will last forever, though forever is a long time (I think).

D.C.: How do you regard the partially controlled aspects?

I.A.: With joy. Certainly rhythm is partially controlled . . . and the same with harmony and melody, which are the least controlled.

D.C.: Does it disturb you when, leaving the instrument alone, it is performing without human audience?

I.A.: Human audience? That's up to humans. It's never without an audience. . . . . . . I have been moving toward something, not away from something. I have never maintained that I am right or even important; I am just doing what I think I can do best. . . . I have learned two very important things about sound: (1) it exists, period. No more, no less. There is no good or bad except in individual terms . . . and (2) music (sound) communicates nothing. If I were to define (not categorize) Art, I would have to say it is that which communicates nothing. Rather, it incites or creates something new in each of us (I can say "Hello" and you can reply "Hello." This is communication, bad as it is, but it is not Art. Art's beauty and importance is that it does not communicate!) . . . *Sounds* hold an interest for me; I don't give a damn how one produces them. . . .

. . . One last thing: if one should consider the nightingale and its music and inspect closely the battery of technique in use, he might reconsider his own bloated self-view: certainly music is sound (the existence of the former term owes to social implications only) and man, or even his life, has contributed little enough to expand its vocabulary.[39]

Other sculptors and artists have begun work in similar areas. The German sculptor Hans Haacke, a member of *Atelier 17* in Paris and a founder (along with Pene, Mack, and Vecker) of *Group Zero* (a group dedicated to breaking ties with the past of nonobjective art), creates wind and water sculptures, as did Harry Bertoia. Japanese environmental artist Shinoda creates elaborate metal sculptures with sound as a by-product. Composer Jon Hassell has recently explored acoustical environments and objects, and large-scale outdoor sound-sculpture events (especially *Nadam,* a "sound-space" work). His *Landmusic Series* (1969–72) is a combination of minimal music and *soundscapes.* Some are like the Oliveros *Sonic Meditations,* being but brief suggestions: "Underground thunder spreading across an open field." Another in the series calls for compact battery-powered speaker, microphone, amplifier combinations to be planted in trees to produce subtle sound amplifications of "wind, leaves, birds, and squirrels who come near. . . ."[40]

The struggle, gaining intensity in the late sixties, for the safety and revitalization of the environment, holds close ties with the antiart movement. Besides the creation of works which incorporate the environment as is (without artistic distortion), the direction implies an immaculate concept of nature, with distrust of man's creations (and re-creations) in what appears to be their inherent destructiveness. Sound pollution, the technique of discounting the aural by-product of twentieth-century convenience living (e.g., the noise of freeways, airways, refrigeration), has exponentially compounded the situation. The need for *intensity* of sound to compensate for the increased level of accepted background noise, subsequently leads to a battle over dominance between organized and unorganized sound.

The *World Soundscape Project* was designed to explore and note trends in man's relation to his sonic environment. Based in Canada near Vancouver, and directed by R. Murray Schafer, the project attempts to bring together research on the scientific, sociological and aesthetic aspects of the environment and has five significant documents to date:

1. *The Book of Noise;*
2. *Okeanos* (a ninety-minute quadraphonic tape composition by Bruce Davis, Brian Fawcett, and R. Murray Schafer, dealing with the symbolism of the ocean);

39. David Cope, "Chronicles of a Cause: I.A. MacKenzie," *The Composer* 1, no. 1 (June 1969):35–42.
40. Tom Johnson, "New Music," *Musical America* 24, no. 11 (November 1974): MA-14.

3. *The Music of the Environment* (an article on the concept of the World Soundscape; the first treatment of the acoustic environment as a macro-cultural composition);
4. *A Survey of Community Noise By-Laws in Canada;*
5. *The Vancouver Soundscape* (a combination two-record set and booklet detailing a sonic study of the city of Vancouver and its environs, and concluding with two most significant chapters dealing in turn with "Noise Pollution Problems" and "Toward Acoustic Design").[41]

The records of this latter document include a variety of sounds, from surf to suburban baseball games. Most remarkable are the extremes of everyday sounds pinpointed in this collection; sounds which ". . . too often people ignore (or think they ignore). . . ."[42] The thrust of these concepts is focused in these comments taken from an open letter called "a brief introduction. . .":

Acoustics as a design study has been limited to closed environments: concert halls, sound-proof rooms and the like. It is time that acoustic design be applied to the environment as a great macro-cultural composition, of which man and nature are the composer/performers. To disguise an acoustic ambience with background music or masking noise, to block it out with ear muffs, cocoon-like sound-proof rooms or automobiles is not, in our view, a satisfactory solution to the problem of noise nor is it a creative approach to acoustic design.[43]

Within the framework of "Moozak at the Oakridge Shopping Mall," and "A Ventilator at Eaton's Department Store," one can hardly escape the immediate intimacy and beauty of "Full Surf . . . on a Gusty March Afternoon," or "Children's Voices, Recorded on the Playground of Seymour School. . . ."

Though quite a few years must pass before the trials of many of the experimental concepts and works included here expose their real contribution, their vitality and originality cannot be overlooked, regardless of their inherent threats to tradition.

The New Tonality

During the late 1960s, many composers began intense experimentation with tonal resources. This reacquaintance seems rooted in two traditions: minimalism and the basic pendulum that swings through music (and all other) history. In the first instance, composers discovered that utilizing basic tonal materials in a repeating minimal fabric allowed their music to have continuity

41. Available from Sonic Research Studio, Communication Studies, Simon Fraser University, Burnaby 2, British Columbia, Canada.
42. From "A Brief Introduction to the World Soundscape Project": open letter by R. Murray Schafer, Peter Huse, Bruce Davis, Howard Broomfield, Hildegarde Westerkamp, Barry Truax, and Adam Woog, Vancouver, 1973.
43. Ibid.

without the phrase/cadence structure of Classical tradition. In the second instance, the timing seemed right for the inevitable return to simplicity at a time when music was fragmented and without common threads.

LaMonte Young's work in the very early sixties (see section on Minimal Music) influenced a diversity of individuals on both coasts of the U.S. (notably New York City and Los Angeles). The simplicity of design and materials in Young's work, often based on justly tuned fifths, provided many composers with intriguing ideas suggesting further development: consonance and minimalism. James Fulkerson's *Triad,* for example, consists of a C major triad performed over a 12- to 20-hour period without variation. Robert Moran's *Illuminatio Nocturna* presents a C-rooted major thirteenth chord repeated slowly and softly for an extended period of time. This work and his subsequent "trance music" represent other manifestations of this drone-like approach to triadic materials.

Terry Riley's *In C* (1964) gave a needed impetus and visibility to this new school of composition. The work is constructed from repeated and overlapped motives in the "key" of C moving, over a period of 45 to 90 minutes, to E, back to C and then to G. This is not the tonality one finds in late Romanticism; rather, it is a minimal work (the complete score can be placed on a single sheet) structured around continuously repeating octave Cs. Two major works followed *In C: Poppy Nogood and the Phantom Band* (1968) and *A Rainbow in Curved Air* (1969). Both of these works continue the explorations begun with *In C.* Each develops richer and more complex interrelationships of tonal materials less associated with drones and rhythmic repetition.

Philip Glass began developing a similar kind of style in the late sixties with pieces like *Music in Fifths* (1969). This work evolves through expanding scalar cells in a kind of F-Dorian mode (three flats in the signature). He creates an "additive" structure common in his later works. For example, a three-note motive becomes four, then five, etc. with the initial motive repeated on each reoccurrence. His opera *Einstein on the Beach* (1976) is a massive tonal work which continues to receive wide acclaim. His audience is as eclectic as his music, with rock and pop followers as well as traditional and experimental "serious" admirers (a 1982 full page advertisement for Cutty Sark whiskey contains a painting of Glass and his written endorsement). His work with the Philip Glass Ensemble has contributed enormously to this success. Minimal tonal music is very difficult to perform due to both its maximal length and intonation requirements. Glass's ensemble epitomizes the precision necessary for proper performance.

John Adams' *Shaker Loops* for seven solo strings (1978) and *Phrygian Gates* for piano (1978) utilize triadic source materials. Both works create the atmosphere of self-regenerative energy and at the same time, lyric melodic curves traditionally associated with tonal music. Other composers committed to similar types of minimal/tonal composition include Beth Anderson, Gavin Bryers, Stuart Smith, William Duckworth and Phil Winsor (notably *Kyrie Eleison* for choir and tape drone, 1977).

In England, Cornelius Cardew's work with the *Scratch Orchestra* provided opportunity for both large scale improvisation (performers were largely unskilled) and performances of simple tonal works. His enormous work *The Great Learning* (1971, particularly *Paragraph 2*) provided precedence for renewed tonal activity. Cardew, however, motivated by political beliefs, moved towards a more traditional tonal style with works such as *Soon,* based on Maoist-like texts and ideals. The music consists of single lines with "chording" similar to popular music (C, F, etc. relating to triads) while at the same time containing an unmistakeable hint of Cardew's inimitable rhythmic subtleties and twists of phrase.

Lou Harrison has long persevered in this tonal realm. His *Mass to St. Anthony* (1962) is modal-tonal in key and sixteenth century in counterpoint. Even traditional cadences balance and direct the lines. Yet there is a subtle twentieth century inflection throughout. His work with the *American gamelan* is basis for a number of new works using rich tonal materials, though less traditionally Western in cadence and phrasing.

Robert Ashley's cryptic *Perfect Lives (Private Parts)*—"an opera in seven episodes"—is tonal (at least in basic pitch materials). Its composer-created text is "surrealistically" rooted in "sixties" nihilism as it comments on "Rodney's" life. Ashley's voice and the keyboard performance of "Blue" Gene Tyranny are so authentic in its recorded version (see bibliography) as to negate reproduction by any other performers. The cultural and anthropomorphic aspects of both the music and the poetry of this piece contextualize the tonal materials: the use of tonality provides a commentary on the soap opera nature of society.

Each of the tonal idioms mentioned above bodes a virulent future for tonality in the latter years of the twentieth century. The static and somnambulistic qualities of single resonant chords, though possibly less immediately conceivable as a style, could begin an entirely new language for tertian harmonies. Minimal tonal music, based on repetitions of ever varying melodic fragments, is reaching wider audiences than most recent *avant-garde* styles. More and more composers seem infatuated with its potential. Even works which imitate traditional models of tonality, either in admiration or parody, have gained significant following in recent years. If any aspect of twentieth century music seems providential, it is most surely this recent trend toward consonance.

Vectoral Analysis: Frederic Rzewski: *Coming Together (1972)*

(For information on vectoral analysis and procedures, see chapter 1).

1. Historical Background: Frederic Rzewski (b. Westfield, Massachusetts, 1938) has been strongly influenced by the work of Cage and to a degree by that of Stockhausen. He was a founder of the *Musica Elettronica Viva* in Rome during 1966 (a group that fused live electronics and improvisatory techniques). In the late sixties his work developed strong ties with the minimalist school influenced by the works of Riley and Reich. Regardless of influences, however, Rzewski (pronounced 'rChevsky) has retained a unique and eclectic (in the best sense of the word) style. *Attica,* for narrator and instruments (1972), *Variations on No Place to Go but Around* (1973) for piano, and *The People United Will Never Be Defeated* (a large work for solo piano, 1977) exemplify his mature style. Rzewski also attempts to infuse certain political views into his music. The text for *Coming Together,* for example, is taken from a letter written by Sam Melville from Attica Correctional Facility in the spring of 1971 (Melville was killed during a riot at Attica later that year).

Coming Together (it should be noted that only Part I will be analyzed herein) contains 394 measures of $\frac{4}{4}$ continuous running sixteenth notes in the bass clef (no other rhythm or duration occurs in the piece) followed by a single measure of rest (G.P. or "grand pause") of between thirty seconds and one minute in duration. A separate vocal line, written simply as words to be spoken, continues throughout the score (inclusive of intervals of silence) and is based on Melville's text. Tempo is defined as MM 80–84 and no *ritards* or *accelerandos* occur during the 6,304 repeated sixteenth notes.

2. Overview: *Coming Together* is structured in three massive and continuous (yet somewhat distinct) sections. The opening section is Dorian (i.e., G with one flat in the key signature). Throughout this first section, the note G repeats a varying number of times with the other notes (above) stated only once. Figure 10.9 shows the opening of the work and the importance of G as a center.

Figure 10.9. Frederic Rzewski: *Coming Together,* measure 1.

G continues as center throughout the first section, but with decreasing frequency. As well, the line maintains an upward flow, continuing until the G an octave higher is reached as a centerpost (see fig. 10.10) in measure 297. B♭ now becomes the note of repetition.

Figure 10.10. Frederic Rzewski:
Coming Together, measure 297.

This B section offers striking contrast as one realizes the dedication to the low G as center in the first part of the piece. This second section, however, is reached through subtle transition techniques.

The third section returns to the first material by measure 355 (see fig. 10.11), with the low G again the center through repetition and directed flow.

Figure 10.11. Frederic Rzewski:
Coming Together, measure 355.

There are no accidentals in *Coming Together*. The subtle shift upwards an octave as well as inversion to B♭ (B♭ Lydian in the middle section) become effective tools of variation in this minimal environment. It is clear at the end that the music has cyclically returned to the opening ideas.

3. Orchestration: The instrumentation for *Coming Together* is flexible. The minimum orchestration requires a bass instrument performing the entire score exactly and without variation and a voice to read the text. Rzewski has performed the work for solo piano (reciting the text himself). The composer refers, however, to more ideal situations:

One musician at least plays the melody straight through in very strict time on a bass instrument, preferably electric bass or bass guitar. The others do not play at all at first but enter gradually, playing long notes in the beginning with silences between them, then gradually shortening the durations of the long notes and the silences so that they become notes of medium duration, groups of notes, short melodies and fragments of melodies, etc. Most of these notes are octave doublings of notes in the bass line. . . .[44]

In duet versions the single line becomes manic in its obsession for onward mechanical flow. Larger instrumentations develop interesting contrasts between long held tones, then short melodic bursts. This alters the perception of the work immensely (both in form—more a continuous "variations"—and in

44. From notes by the composer accompanying the score, *Soundings* 3–4 (November, 1972), p. 44.

impact—less virtuoso and more dynamically forceful). In either form, the incessant repetitions of the motor rhythm (reminiscent in some ways of the Baroque era) is the focal point of the work. Orchestration (timbre), while important, is subservient to the rhythmic drive.

4. Basic Techniques: *Coming Together* links motivic development (particularly extension and diminution) directly to cross-accentual rhythmic pulsations. Motivic variants derive from extension of the opening third through the Dorian diatonic scale. The sixteenth note repetitions create a definite duple and quadruple feel of "beat." However, the motive lengths draped across these vary, often setting up cross rhythms to the basic pulse. Figure 10.12 is an example.

Figure 10.12. Frederic Rzewski:
Coming Together, measures 2 and 3.

The first two sixteenths frame the motive and the pulse in synchronization. The third, fourth, and fifth notes, however, extend the motive to three notes and cross the pulse at beat 2. The sixth and seventh notes are repetitions of the initial note (and center) with dual roles. For example, the first G can be considered the end of the extended motive or the beginning of the new version. While seemingly unimportant, these dual and even triple role inferences give the work its diversity. Notes 6 and 7 are linked to note 8 in such a way that the opening motive is repeated, but shifted in respect to the beat. Notes 9, 10, and 11 repeat the first variant of the motive, but metrically altered. Careful evaluation of the entire two bars (less than 1/100 of the piece) show a microcosm of action and reaction, of cross accents and cross rhythms, all of which contrast the lack of development in new pitch material or non-sixteenth note durations. The minimal material has not voided this composer's technical ability for development.

5. Vertical Models: The only potential here for vertical representation is by large performing forces using long notes in the opening part of the piece, or improvisations (permissible in some cases). Clearly instruments holding onto notes presented in the basic ostinato of the bass line create pandiatonicism (Dorian or Lydian).

6. Horizontal Models: The very first bar of the piece (see fig. 10.9) indicates the melodic thrust of the entire work. The variants discussed under basic techniques define the complex melodic development of a center pitch through repetition (a very traditional technique of "classical" composers). posers).

7. Style: The style of *Coming Together* can be defined only in performance. Significant, however, is the perception of levels or planes of experience. At one end, a macrolevel suggests a simple repetitive frame for the reading of a text. At the other end, one can perceive a microlevel of intricate cross-referenced rhythms. As well, there are a number of interactions between these two extremes.

The text involves interesting repetitions (e.g., the opening line: "I think the combination of age and a greater coming together is responsible for the speed of the passing time" is repeated over and over again with extensions). There is likewise a subtle shifting and overlap in the text that is similar to the processes at work in the melodic line development.

Finally, there are political (reform) overtones to the work which are welded into the music. *Coming Together* is a striking work from the minimalist school showing the diversity and potential of the new experimentalism.

Whether it be the awesome assault of danger music or the quiet and delicate exploration of triadic tonal sonorities, the experimental composer continues to develop iconoclastic methods and approaches to the act of making music. Clearly the evolution of future styles and approaches is dependent upon the intricate balance of definitions within the new experimentalism.

Bibliography

*Further Readings**

Ahlstrom, David. "Footnotes for Mr. T." *Composer* 2, no. 1 (1970):24. Annotated bibliography of writings about the *avant-garde.*

Austin, Larry. "Music is Dead, Long Live Music." *New York Times* (July 6, 1969).

Brindle, Reginald Smith. *The New Music: The Avant Garde since 1945.* New York: Oxford Press, 1975. This is an excellent overview of experimental tradition though very slanted toward European composers.

Brown, Anthony. "An Introduction to the Music of Morton Feldman."*asterisk* 1 (December 1974).

————. "An Interview with John Cage." * *asterisk* 1 (December 1974).

Byron, Michael, ed. *Pieces: An Anthology.* Vancouver. A.R.C., 1975.

Cage, John. *Notations.* New York: Something Else Press, 1969. Many of the selections contained herein fall into the categories covered in this chapter.

————. "To Describe the Process of Composition 'Music for Piano 21–52.' " *Die Reihe* 3:41. A most important example of the new experimentalism in process. Though "indeterminate" in initial look, this article leads one immediately to new concepts and analogies.

————. "Lecture on Nothing." In *Silence: Lectures & Writings.* Cambridge, Mass.: The M.I.T. Press, 1966, p. 109.

————. *Themes and Variations.* New York: Station Hill Press, 1982. A collection of mesostics on names who have most influenced his work.

———— and Geoffrey Bornard. *Conversations without Feldman.* New York: Printed Editions, 1982. First published by Black Ram Books in 1980. A long 1978 interview with Cage.

Cardew, Cornelius. ed. *Scratch Music.* Cambridge, Mass.: The M.I.T. Press; paperback edition, 1974. This is a book of scores and ideas by a great many composers involved with the *Scratch Orchestra* conducted by Cardew. Many of the works are indeterminate and quite a few belong to the new experimentalist category. Fascinating study for this area.

Cardew, Cornelius. *Stockhausen Serves Imperialism.* London, England: Latimer New Dimensions Limited, 1974. Interesting account of the author's about-face and repudiation of his own early works and those of other *avant-garde* composers.

Cope, David. *Notes in Discontinuum.* Originally published by Discant Music in 1970. Reprinted with biographical notes added in *Allos.* San Diego: Lingua Press, 1980.

————. "An Interview with John Cage." *The Composer* 10, no. 1. (1980).

Corner, Philip. *I can walk through the World as Music.* New York: Printed Editions, 1982. Verbal tales of a three-week private performance in 1966.

————

*Addresses for record companies, periodicals, and music publishers mentioned in this Bibliography can be found in Appendix 4.

Davis, Bob, and Rich Gold. *Break Glass in Case of Fire*. Oakland: Mills College (Center for Contemporary Music). An Anthology of experimental music from this West Coast source of new music.

Everett, Tom. "Five Questions: 35 Answers." *Composer* 2, no. 4 (1971):79. Quite contrasting views on a number of different subjects related to the new experimentalism by Earle Brown, Harold Budd, Philip Corner, Jim Fulkerson, William Hellermann, Karel Husa, and Elliott Schwartz.

The Experimental Music Catalogue. Published at 208 Ladbroke Crove, London, England.

Gaburo, Kenneth. *Collection of Works*. San Diego: Lingua Press, 1975. A very important collection of 32 compositions by this experimental composer.

Grayson, John. *Sound Sculpture*. Vancouver: A.R.C., 1977. A collection of essays by artists surveying the techniques, applications, and future directions of sound sculpture.

————. *Environments of Musical Sculpture You Can Build*. Vancouver: A.R.C. 1977.

Griffiths, Paul. *Modern Music: "The avant garde since 1945"* N.Y.: George Brazillen, 1981.

Henahan, Donal. "Music Draws Strains Direct from Brains." *New York Times* (November 25, 1970). Interesting account of David Rosenboom's work with brain-wave music.

Higgins, Dick. "Boredom and Danger." *Source* 3, no. 1 (January 1966). An excellent explanation of new experiments.

————. *A Dialectic of Centuries: Notes Towards a Theory of the New Arts*. 2d ed. West Glover, Vt.: Printed Editions, 1979. Many of the essays printed here are reprints from *foew & ombwhnw* brought out by Something Else Press in the 1960's. Important aesthetic inquiry concerning the *avant-garde*.

————. *Postface*. New York: Something Else Press, 1964. A detailed history of *Fluxus* and its concerns and experiments.

Huff, Jay. "An Interview with David Behrman." *Composer* 4, no. 1 (1972):29. Fascinating view of this man well-versed both as composer and "man of letters" in the *avant-garde*.

Johnson, Roger. *Scores: An Anthology of New Music*. New York: Schirmer Books, 1980. A good collection of experimental scores that can be performed with a modicum of resources.

Johnson, Tom. *Imaginary Music*. New York: Two-Eighteen Press, 1974. An exceptional contribution to the various aspects discussed in this chapter. See also his extremely informative columns on expressions of antimusic in *The Village Voice*.

Knowles, Alison. *More by Alison Knowles*. New York: Printed Editions, 1976. Performance pieces and environments.

Kostelanetz, Richard. *John Cage*. New York: Praeger, 1970.

————. *The Theatre of Mixed Means*. New York: Dial Press, 1968.

————. *Music of Today*. New York: Time-Life Books, 1967.

Kupbovic, L. "The Role of Tonality in Contemporary and 'Up-to-date' Composition." *Tempo* N. 135:16–19 (December 1980).

Lentz, Daniel. "Music Lib." *Composer* 4, no. 1 (1972):6. Interesting article on experimentalism as well as the activities of the California Time Machine's European Tour of 1970.

MacLow, Jackson. *An Anthology*. New York: Heiner Friedrich, 1970.

Maconie, Robin. "Stockhausen's *Mikrophonie 1*." *Perspectives of New Music* 10, no. 2:92. Interesting and sympathetic view of this piece.

Moore, Carmen. "The Sound of Mind." *Village Voice* (December 24, 1970). Another article about David Rosenboom's works with brain-wave music.

Motherwell, Robert. *The Dada Painters and Poets: An Anthology.* New York: Wittenborn, Schultz, 1951. Interesting as *art* background and insight into experimental concepts.

Nougé, Paul. Music is Dangerous." *Soundings* 1 (1973). See this same issue for Andre Breton's *Silence is Golden.* Both are truly unique and well worth reading.

Nyman, Michael. *Experimental Music.* New York: Schirmer Books, 1974. An excellent and well-balanced chronicle of 'the new experimentalism'.

Oliveros, Pauline. "Many Strands." *Numus West* 3 (1973):6. By an active contributor and innovator in new music.

————. *Software for People.* New York: Printed Editions, 1982. A collection of theoretical and historical writings and texts from 1962–1980.

Paik, Nam June. See this author's articles in each of the first five numbers of *Décollage* (Cologne).

Palmer, Robert. "A Father Figure for the Avant Garde." *Atlantic Monthly,* May 1981, pp. 48–56. Excellent article on La Monte Young and his recent works.

Partch, Harry. "Show Horses in the Concert Ring." *Soundings* 1:66. Good source for philosophical contributions to the subject area covered in this chapter.

Reich, Steve. "Music as a Gradual Process." In *Anti-Illusion Catalog of the Whitney Museum* (New York, 1969).

————. *Writings About Music.* New York: NYU Press, 1974.

Rosenboom, David, ed. *Biofeedback and the Arts: Results of Early Experimentation.* Vancouver: A.R.C., 1976. An important landmark in experimental works of biomusic; excellent resource.

Rzewski, Frederick. "Prose Music." In *Dictionary of Contemporary Music.* edited by John Vinton. (New York: E. P. Dutton & Co., 1974), p. 593.

Schafer, R. Murray. "Ezra Pound and Music." *Canadian Music Journal* 4:15. Interesting view of this poet's relation to music and the effects those relationships might have on experimental concepts.

————. *Ear Cleaning.* Vancouver: BMI Canada Ltd., 1974. This book, along with *The Composer in the Classroom,* is most helpful in acquainting the young (and young in experience) with experimental concepts through simple but effective performances.

Schwarz, K. Robert. "Steve Reich: Music as a Gradual Process." *Perspectives of New Music,* Spring-Summer 1981, pp. 373–394.

Soundings 7/8. Contains several works valuable to this chapter, including Harold Budd's *Madrigals of the Rose Angel* and Daniel Lentz's *You Can't See the Forest . . . Music (for three drinkers and eight echoes),* as well as a large number of other highly interesting works.

Stockhausen, Karlheinz. *"Mikrophonie I and II."* *Melos* 33:144.

Young, La Monte, and Jackson Mac Low, eds. *An Anthology of Chance Operations.* New York: La Monte Young and Jackson Mac Low, 1963.

Young, La Monte, and Marian Zazeela. *Selected Writings.* Munich: Heiner Friedrich, 1969. Excellent source for materials by this composer inclusive of interviews and the like. It also contains the concepts and drawings of *Dream House,* discussed in this chapter.

————. "Sound is God: The Singing of Pran Nath." *Village Voice* (April 30, 1970). More a study of the author than of the singer.

Zimmerman, Walter. *Desert Plants.* Vancouver. A.R.C., 1976. Conversations with 23 *avant-garde* composers.

Recordings and Publishers*

10 + 2: 12 American Text Sound Pieces. Recorded on 1750 Arch Records, 1752 and contains works by Cage, Giorno, Saroyan, Bysin, Dodge, Coolidge, Anderson, Amirkhanian, O'Gallagher, Gnazzo, and Ashley in text-sound composition.

Amirkhanian, Charles. *Lexical Music.* Recorded on 1750 Arch Street Records, S-1779. Album contains a number of Amirkhanian's text sound compositions including *Mahogany Ballpark, She She and She,* and *Muchrooms.*

Ashley, Robert. *Wolfman.* CPE-*Source* 2, no. 2 (July 1968); special record issue. Recorded on Source Records 4.

———. *Private Parts.* Recorded on Lovely Music LML-1001 and VR 4904.

Austin, Larry. *Accidents.* CPE-*Source* 2, no. 2 (July 1968). See Ashley, above.

Budd, Harold. *Coeur D'Orr* (1969). For tape, soprano saxophone, and/or voices. Recorded on Advance 16.

———. *Oak of Golden Dreams* (1970). Recorded on Advance 16.

Cage, John. *Variations IV.* Recorded on Everest 3132.

Corner, Philip. *Rounds. Soundings* 3, no. 4:92.

———. *Ear Journeys: Water* (1977). Printed Editions. Score includes a seaweed insert.

Crumb, George. *Voice of the Whale.* C. F. Peters. Recorded on Columbia M-32739.

Duchamp, Marcel. *The Bride Stripped Bare by Her Bachelors, Even, Erratum Musical* (1913). Recorded on Finnidar 9017.

Fulkerson, James. *Folio of Scores for the Composers Forum. Soundings* 3, no. 4:2.

Gibson, Jon. *Visitations.* Recorded on Chatham Square CS-LP-12. A 16-track multi-textured environmental soundscape.

Glass, Philip. *Music in Fifths.* Recorded on Chatham Square CS-LP-1003.

———. *Music in Similar Motion.* Recorded on Chatham Square CS-LP-1003.

———. *Music with Changing Parts.* Recorded on Chatham Square CS-LP-1001/2.

———. *Einstein on the Beach* (1976). Recorded on Tomato 4–2901.

Hassell, Jon. *Vernal Equinox.* Recorded on Lovely Music LML 1021.

Leedy, Douglas. *Entropical Paradise.* Recorded on Seraphim S-6060.

Monk, Meredith. *Key.* Lovely Music LML 1051. Expressive experimental music.

Moran, Robert. *Four Visions.* Universal Edition. Graphic score for flute, harp, string quartet.

Mother Mallard's Portable Masterpiece Company. Steve Drews, Linda Fisher, and David Borden. Recorded on Earthquack EQ-0001. Drones and steady pulses.

Oliveros, Pauline. *Sonic Meditations* (1974). Smith Publications.

Reich, Steve. *Four Organs* (1970). Recorded on Angel S-36059.

———. *It's gonna Rain; Violin Phase.* Recorded on Columbia MS-7265.

———. *Music for 18 Musicians* (1976). Recorded on ECM/Warners 1129.

Riley, Terry. *In C.* Recorded on Columbia MS-7178, and published with the recording.

———. *Poppy Nogood and the Phantom Band.* Recorded on Columbia MS-7315.

———. *A Rainbow in Curved Air.* Recorded on Columbia MS-7315.

Rosenboom, David. *Ecology of the Skin* (1970). Available from the composer, c/o Mills College, Oakland, California. Bio-feedback for performer and audience brainwave encounters.

———. *Portable Gold and Philosopher's Stones* (for brains in fours). Recorded on A.R.C. ST-1002 (Canada). Brainwave bio-music album also containing *Chilean Drought* and *Piano Etude #1.*

---

*Addresses for record companies, periodicals, and music publishers mentioned in this Bibliography can be found in Appendix 4.

Rzewski, Frederick. *Coming Together. Soundings* 3, no. 4, with composer commentary. Recorded on Opus One No. 20.

Satie, Erik. *Vexations* (1893). Salabert.

Songs of the Humpback Whale. Recorded on Columbia ST-620.

The Sounds of Sound Sculpture. A.R.C. ST-1001. Sounds from sound sculptures by Harry Bertoia, von Huene, Marxhausen, and David Jacobs. Excellent book is provided with the album.

Stockhausen, Karlheinz. *Aus den Sieben Tagen.* Universal Edition.

————. *Mikrophonie I.* Universal Edition. Recorded on Columbia MS-7355.

The Vancouver Soundscape (Sonic Research Studio, Simon Fraser University, Burnaby 2, B.C., Canada). Recorded on EPN 186.

Winsor, Phil. *Melted Ears* (1967). Carl Fischer. Recorded on Advance S-14.

11 The Post Avant-Garde

Evaluation

The term *avant-garde,* as applied to music over the past several decades, has become a designation for those composers or works displaying the newest technique (often anti-technique, i.e., chance music) or sound (often lack of sound, i.e., silence). The apparent dead-end features of this experimental school, as projected by its critics and enthusiasts alike, become obvious when, as one composer stated, "anything goes." It is difficult to create something *new* within the framework of that philosophy.

The decay of any movement or social direction begins when the thrust of its reason for existence is silenced. This "raison d'être" in the *avant-garde* movement centers around supposed shock value and "newness" of purpose and effect. Certainly the movement begins its death throes when an event in any of its art forms became so new, so shocking, as to virtually negate anything surpassing it.

Saying "anything goes" is still quite a far cry from *doing* "anything goes." Rudolf Schwarzkogler, a Viennese artist born in 1940, began his masterpiece in the late 1960s. It seems, as we pick up the story by Robert Hughes of *Time,* that Schwarzkogler, a prime mover of the *avant-garde* of his time, had decided that *his* art, at least, depended not on the application of paint, but on the removal of surplus flesh:

So he proceeded, inch by inch to amputate his own penis, while a photographer recorded the act as an art event. In 1972, the resulting prints were reverently exhibited in that biennial motor show of Western art, Documents 5 at Kassel. Successive acts of self-amputation finally did Schwarzkogler in. . . . No doubt it could be argued by the proponents of body art . . . that Schwarzkogler's self-editing was not indulgent but brave, taking the audience's castration fears and reducing them to their most threatening quiddity. That the man was clearly as mad as a hatter, sick beyond rebuke, is not thought important: wasn't Van Gogh crazy too? But Schwarzkogler's gesture has a certain emblematic value. Having nothing to say, and nowhere to go but further out, he lopped himself and called it art.[1]

1. Robert Hughes, "The Decline and Fall of the Avant-Garde," *Time,* December 18, 1972, pp. 111–12.

336

As the article states, Schwarzogler is indeed dead, a victim of his own art. This is more than one small step beyond Ay-o's little finger boxes. One is often reminded of the aforementioned work of Philip Corner entitled *"One anti-personnel type CBU bomb will be thrown into the audience"* (what kind of strange masochist would attend a program which had announced this work's performance?). While one finds the composer's suggestions asking the performers not to fulfill the probably small audience's desires, one wonders why some composer doesn't consider the Korean war as a next piece. The shock factor here is death, the "newness" that either of these be considered as art in the first place. Whether the act be real (as with Schwarzkogler) or imagined (as with Corner), it seems topped only by multi-deaths, war, and finally complete annihilation. Since none of these seems real (at least in the form of artistic development), one is led to believe that at least for those of us who are aware of what has been happening in the arts, "newness" and "shock" are over, and with them, the prime movers, the superstructure of the *avant-garde* movement.

Philosophically the *avant-garde* remains one of the most conservative areas of musical thought: a concept in which, indeed, anything does *not* go. The very nature of the *avant-garde* concept binds the composer to reject the past and work within a multitude of limitations often surpassing those of the strictest of traditional contrapuntalists.

Sensing the oblivion inherent in such rejection of the past, a number of composers have begun to accept the philosophy projected, but not carried out, by the *avant-garde;* that is, truly "anything goes." Not a statement of rejection, this, but of affirmation: the *post avant-garde.* While the phrase "anything goes" may immediately alienate those of us intent on saving the arts for (and in some cases from) people and significance, the words *with purpose* may be added. It is no longer the new sound, the new device, the new trick, that becomes important, but the new *work.*

Antagonists of this philosophy generally neglect the true depth of such a direction: once the composer has become unprejudiced toward sound, Bach is no longer an enemy; the major triad, tonality, need no longer be avoided; dissonance need not be a requirement to be contemporary. Redefined, the *post avant-garde* composer is *just* the composer: using anything that is necessary to fulfill the need to create music; accepting *all* sound and silence without being limited by current styles.

Likewise consistency, previously designated as the type of materials used (triads, noise, etc.) is implied and governed by the composer, not by period, audience, or fellow composers. The *post avant-garde* composer has also challenged the listener's prejudices: can one truly accept all sound, all styles, all meaning in music? In effect, can one listen to Bach, to Webern, to Cage, to rock; not rejecting any?

The struggle, however taut it may have once seemed, grows less and less tangible with each passing year. The *post avant-garde* works of this chapter, as different in sound and structure as they may seem, hold a fragile but distinctly recognizable common seed among them. Possibly Ben Johnston says it best in his article *On Context:* "Awareness makes free choice possible. Freedom requires responsiveness: responsibility."[2] Later in the same article his optimism is clearly focused:

It is as though we have to cross a chasm. If we are to build a bridge over it we will have to anchor its ends far in the past and far in the future. Tradition thoroughly assimilated will help us anchor in the past; only a sharp eye for where we are going can help us anchor in the future. Technology will help us build the bridge, which will not impose upon nature but will be possible because we understand how things happen and cooperate rather than interfering.[3]

Direction

There is no progress in music (or art). That is, while certainly an individual composer may get better and better with time, "newer" music (with its complex new instruments for creating much more diverse sounds) is no better than older music (or any worse for that matter). No invention, or creation, can "outdate" Machaut's *Mass* (c. 1360) as a newer car can, for instance, outdate the horse and buggy.

Notation, deeply rooted in battle during the prolific years of the *avant-garde,* seems best when it communicates the most of its designer's intention. The new techniques of notation engendered by many of the more profitable experiments of the *avant-garde,* are just now becoming standardized (see Appendix 3). These developments, however, cannot be construed to supersede or replace previous notational techniques as "better", but as different means of expression. The battles of improvisation and indeterminacy seem won, to the extent that we now agree—if a composer has no real intention, then unintentional notation certainly is the best vehicle. The return to faith in honest technique and musicality, whatever form it may take (as long as the ultimate purpose is to communicate composer intention), is now underway. Fortunately even the very patient have tired of the endless scribbles of masturbative visual art (as music notation) possessed of its own purposelessness.

2. Ben Johnston, "On Context," *ASUC Proceedings #3* (1968), p. 35.
3. Ibid.

Synthesis

There has existed, alongside the *avant-garde,* for the past twenty to forty years, a vast and somewhat sheltered mainstream of composers, often maddened, more often disgusted by what they saw and heard from the *avant-garde.* They have steadfastly held onto their historically justified techniques, and their ears. The *avant-garde* constantly shivered, however, above a pit of self-destruction. That difference, that canyon between the two divergent schools, is now the target of synthesis. The intelligent and talented composers on each side are beginning to realize that the radical claims of the initial proponents of both sides were not necessarily true.

One is reminded of the assertions set forth by two of the world's most renowned men of music: Igor Stravinsky, of *Le Sacre de Printemps* ("Very little tradition lies behind *Le Sacre* and no theory. I had only my ear to help me. . . . I am the vessel through which *Le Sacre* passed."[4]); and Pierre Boulez, the director of IRCAM in Paris ("Since the discovery by the Viennese, all composition other than twelve-tone is useless."[5]). Both men are, of course, incorrect; yet each viewpoint retains that grain of truth for which armies of artists and composers will clash for years. The last few years has witnessed the collapse of these armed camps surrounding the revisionist and the experimental.

We stand on the verge of one of the most creative and significant eras in the history of music. The prejudiced and insecure may still need shelter behind a mainstream door, yet those who now venture forth freely to take quiet advantage of the evident skills of both recent schools of thought (tradition and innovation, technique and intuition) are, will, and have been braving an exciting new credible sensitivity into new music.

Composers and Works

György Ligeti's *Requiem* is a four-movement work (around 26-minutes) for soprano and mezzo-soprano soloists, two choruses, and large orchestra. Composed during the years 1963–65, the *Requiem* fuses two basic concepts. *Klangflächenkomposition* creates sound-mass which ebbs and flows through constant overlapping of timbre and spatial modulations (evident in the extreme in his later *Lontano*). *Mikropolyphonie* creates highly complex densities of polyphonic motion in which no single voice dominates—only the overall fabric of resultant sound (notable in his *Aventures*). There is also a strong

---

4. Igor Stavinsky, "Apropos Le Sacre du Printemps," as printed on the cover of Columbia Records ML-5719.

5. David Cope and Galen Wilson, "An Interview with Pierre Boulez," *Composer* 1, no. 2 (September 1969):83.

Figure 11.1. György Ligeti. With
permission of Universal Edition.

synthesis of traditional and *avant-garde* techniques. Conservative procedures
are evidenced in the standard musical notation, text, extremely "determinate"
articulations, and rhythmic complexities. Special effects include muting bas-
soons with handkerchiefs and the "Langlois Effect" of squeezing the string
with thumb and forefinger rather than pressing it normally against the fin-
gerboard. The score is accompanied by a 23-page booklet of incredibly exacting performance directions. Like his earlier *Aventures,* the *Requiem*
occasionally moves from metered notation to "senza tempo" sections (especially in the third movement). Note that in figure 4.10 (in *Instrument Exploration*) his use of this effect is for *contrast.* In the *Requiem* the effect is
quite the opposite with even the bar lines being in the composer's words
". . . purely a means of synchronizing the individual parts."[6] Aside from its
obvious synthesis of new and old, *Requiem* creates a composer-controlled
"spatial movement." The composer has remarked about the work: "You have
a drawing in two dimensions and you give it perspective. . . . I was constantly thinking of achieving this illusion of a musical space, which has only
an acoustical existence in time."[7]

6. From the "Introductory Remarks" of the score: C. F. Peters: 30285.
7. Conversations with Ligeti at Stanford," *Numus West* 2 (1972):19.

Figure 11.2. George Crumb. With permission.

George Crumb's *Ancient Voices of Children* (1970) is a 27-minute work for soprano, boy soprano, oboe, mandolin, harp, electric piano, and three percussionists. The work consists of five basic vocal movements separated twice by purely instrumental dances. The texts are by Federico García Lorca and sung in Spanish. The synthesis present in this work is evidenced by the composer's own words about the piece:

In composing *Ancient Voices of Children* I was conscious of an urge to fuse various unrelated stylistic elements. I was intrigued by the idea of juxtaposing the seemingly incongruous: a suggestion of Flamenco with a Baroque quotation ("Bist du bei mir," from the Notebook of Anna Magdelena Bach), or a reminiscence of Mahler with a breath of the Orient. It later occurred to me that both Bach and Mahler drew upon many disparate sources in their own music without sacrificing "stylistic purity."[8]

Crumb's "stylistic purity" remains intact in this as well as his earlier works (beginning with his *Five Pieces for Piano,* 1962). It is characterized by three particularly distinct features: (1) extremely defined and thinly exposed textures often consisting of solo lines (almost one-third of this work is solo lines), dramatic silences (frequently expressed by square fermatas with duration in seconds: see fig. 11.3), and subtle motivic repetition and development; (2) the

8. From the score: No. 66303. C. F. Peters.

Figure 11.3. George Crumb: *Ancient Voices of Children.* Copyright (c) by C. F. Peters Corp., 373 Park Avenue South, New York, N.Y.. 10016. Reprint permission granted by the publisher.

Figure 11.3. Continued.

use of instruments and voice equally for their pitch and "special" timbral qualities:

> Certain special instrumental effects are used to heighten the "expressive intensity"
> e.g. "bending" the pitch of the piano by application of a chisel to the
> strings; . . . the mandolin has one set of strings tuned a quarter-tone low in order
> to give a special pungency to its tone.[9]

(3) the musical imagery: a reflection of the texts without programmatic connotations:

> I feel that the essential meaning of this poetry is concerned with the most primary
> things: life, death, love, the smell of the earth, the sounds of the wind and sea. These
> "*ur*-concepts" are embodied in language which is primitive and stark but which is
> capable of infinitely subtle nuance.[10]

Figure 11.3 shows the entirety of the fourth movement of *Ancient Voices* and exemplifies the synthesis referred to earlier. The simple use of the whole-tone scale (in the opening vocal part beginning on C♯), the triadic harmonies and the simple formal structure are all traditional. The marimba drones, the percussionists singing, and the Bach quote on the toy piano, are all *avant-garde* in nature. The movement, and indeed the work, holds together with a high degree of continuity despite the contrasting material and styles.

Apotheosis of This Earth (1970) by Karel Husa, for concert band, is a work "physically" impelled by dynamic and textural momentum. Its synthesis is not easily heard (it is truly a work fused in every sense). Its three-movement structure (Apotheosis, Tragedy of Destruction, Postscript) employs sound-mass resultant of repetitive composite motives (see fig. 3.12 in chapter 3) and cumulative sustained clusters (often panchromatic, e.g., measure 149, where the horns and trumpets attack and slowly "unvelope" a twelve-note cluster). The final movement employs whispering with both repetitive consonance attacks

9. Ibid.
10. Ibid.

Figure 11.4. Karel Husa.

and text ("this beautiful earth"). In *Apotheosis* one finds the fusion of *avant-garde* and traditional techniques so complete that neither is visible: a work of a unique and personal style.

Other works of varying degrees of synthesis include Donald Erb's *Symphony of Overtures* (1964) and Richard Toensing's *Doxologies I.* Both composers have evolved personal styles fused of elements equally *avant-garde* and traditional. The synthesis is complete: these works no longer "espouse" a single thought or gimmick nor express the fear of the use of any sonic material.

David Cope's *Threshold and Visions* (1979—a concerto for chamber orchestra) evolves a *post avant-garde* idiom through synthesis of a diverse number of *avant-garde* techniques (including sound-mass, instrument exploration, and a free serial technique). The thirty-five minute work is cast in five movements centered around a basic arch-type format.

Walter Mays's *Icarus* for large orchestra (1976) incorporates sound-mass, new instrumental techniques, electronic tape, improvisatory techniques, proportional notation, and indeterminate methods (stochastic). The effective large orchestration (calling for well over one hundred players) employs musical saw, bowed crotales, and electric organ to develop large volumes of complex sonic environments. David Felder's *Rondàge,* on the other hand, involves only five performers, fusing live electronics, sound-mass, structured improvisations and new instrumental techniques into a comprehensively consistent vocabulary.

Barbara Kolb's *Soundings* is a complex work performable in two versions (chamber orchestra and tape prepared by the ensemble, or full orchestra divided into three groups directed by two conductors). The extensive program notes discuss the central conception of the work: "*Soundings* is a technique which makes it possible to ascertain the depth of water by measuring the interval of time between the sending of a signal and the return echo" with the resultant sounds developing ". . . a sea-change into something rich and strange."[11] A montage of triply overlaid contrapuntal textures results (each mini-orchestra or tape channel, depending on version, being a separate but often simultaneous "sounding").

The piece clearly divides into three major sections. The first section is characterized by a straightforward ostinato in the strings (repeating beat by beat throughout the entire passage) with slowly evolving patterns in first the original "sounding" and then the reflections. Tension is created by thickening texture and increased chromaticism towards a fast rush of sound slowly relaxing in a high tremolo in harp and solo violin. The second section is soloistic, conversational, and full of tightly woven musical gestures interplaying in often very thin textures. The final section reverts to the thick textures of the first, contrasts it in content (often long held notes in rising chromatic lines) but parallels it in direction (again driving to a loud climax sliced by an immediate *pianissimo* passage marked "in the distance").

It is no longer possible to avoid the implications of the *post avant-garde*. Whether they be, in the final analysis, friend or enemy (or both), one must know and acknowledge them. Nothing is gained by ignorance. Varèse's comments are most apropos:

My fight for the liberation of sound and for my right to make music with any sound and all sounds has sometimes been construed as a desire to disparage and even to discard the great music of the past. But that is where my roots are. No matter how original, how different a composer may seem, he has only grafted a little bit of himself on the old plant. But this he should be allowed to do without being accused of wanting to kill the plant. He only wants to produce a new flower. . . .[12]

Vectoral Analysis: Luciano Berio: *Sinfonia*

(For information on vectoral analysis and procedures, see chapter 1.)

1. Historical Background: Luciano Berio (b. 1925, Oneglia, Italy) was a cofounder (with Bruno Maderna) of the electronic music studio in Milan (1955). He later taught at the Julliard School of Music (until 1973), Mills College in Oakland, California, and is currently director of the electronic music studio at IRCAM in Paris.

Berio's music separates into two major periods, though there is a defined continuity throughout his compositional career: (1) through the mid-fifties, a

11. Barbara Kolb, *Soundings*. New York: Boosey & Hawkes, 1981.

12. As quoted in *Contemporary Composers on Contemporary Music*, Elliott Schwartz and Barney Childs, eds. (New York: Holt, Rinehart, and Winston, 1967), p. 201.

Figure 11.5. Luciano Berio. BMI Archives. Used by permission.

post-Webern serialism prevails with *Chamber Music* (1952) as a good example; and (2) through the late seventies, an eclectic theater approach is expressed early on through electronic means (e.g., *Visage,* 1961) and more recently through large instrumental works (e.g., *Sinfonia,* 1968 and *Coro,* 1976 for voices and instruments). Other important works include *Circles* (for soprano, harp, and two percussion ensembles, 1962; see example in chapter 7), *Omaggio a Joyce* (1958), *Differences* (for five instruments and tape, 1959), and *Opera* (large "opera," 1972, with a revised version completed in 1977).

Berio is most known for his extraordinary music-theater works, many of which were greatly influenced by the abilities of Cathy Berberian (who for a number of years was married to Berio). Her gymnastic vocal talents fused with Berio's dramatic and lyric style to create *Visage* and particularly *Recital* (1971), a singular study of a singer's mental breakdown. Other works dedicated to Cathy Berberian include *Circles* and *Epifanie* (1960).

2. Overview: *Sinfonia* was originally composed in four movements and later (in 1968) altered to include a fifth (some maintain that the latter was added at a conductor's request for a "flashy" final movement). The work was commissioned by the New York Philharmonic Orchestra and dedicated to Leonard Bernstein (the conductor). It is scored for large orchestra (see orchestration) and eight voices (performed most notably since the premiere by the Swingle Singers).

The first movement is cast in two large sections melded together through a plastic transition. The opening of the work (ominously provoked by three tam-tams) sets repeated notes in motion. These vacillate through a variety of homorhythmic and heterophonic rhythmic variants utilizing timbral development (e.g., slow vowel changes in the voices, use of mutes in brass). This opening material is followed by similar groupings (i.e., initialization/pitch repetition development) of successively shorter and shorter duration. A second section emerges innocuously from this stretto by a short burst in the background from the piano. These outbursts increase in importance until finally (at J in the score) they take over completely, forming the nucleus of the second main section (characterized by loud quick blasts of sound followed by silences). These develop into an orchestral tutti. Occasionally one or more of the notes rings after being set in motion by the fast bursts. This allows Berio (in the final few measures) to recollect the opening or first section briefly in an illusion of a three-part form. Berio has cleverly allowed the second section to "grow" from the second part of the first section. The end of the movement resembles the first part of the first section (initialization of the repeated note structures).

The second movement (subtitled "O King") is a continuous organic form centered on the simple text: "Martin Luther King" (except for the vowel exchange carried over from the first movement, the only text for the movement). The idea from the first movement (excitation) continues in the piano, whose sudden single attacks on certain notes initiate the held soft pitches by the singers. The material centers on F, and a variety of chromatic scales emerge around this pivotal point (hybrid chromatic gestures, whole-tone scales, etc.). The end of the movement suggests a brief return to the blasts at the end of the first movement, implying (as the first does to itself) a cyclical use of materials. At the outset of the movement, all materials move upward from F, and at the end of the movement, all materials work down from the same F.

The third movement is an Ivesian barrage of quotations. Figure 11.6 shows a portion of the movement. The text here reads: "But now it's done, it's over, we've had our chance. There was even, for a second, hope of resurrection, or almost." It seems to encapsulate the almost narrative "stream-of-consciousness" flow of the work. Eclecticism abounds in both text and music. Text examples are drawn from such sources as Claude Levi-Strauss's book *Du Cru et du Cuit* (on Brazilian origin myths of water), Samuel Beckett, and Berio's own words (all set with performance directions in English, such as "impatient," "indignant," and "bewildered"—these taken, for example, from just four bars on page 12). Music quotes are prevalent throughout the third movement and include fragments from Debussy's *La Mer,* references to Berio's own music (primarily *Epifanie* and *Sequenza 4*), as well as quotations from "Bach, Schoenberg, Ravel, Strauss, Berlioz, Brahms, Berg, Hindemith, Beethoven, Wagner, Stravinsky, Boulez, Stockhausen, Globokar, Pousseur, Ives. . . ."[13]

13. From liner notes by the composer, Columbia MS 7268.

Figure 11.6. Luciano Berio: *Sinfonia*
Movement 3. (c) Copyright 1969

The major quote, however, is from Mahler's Second Symphony (Scherzo), which runs throughout the movement in one form or another. "As a structural point of reference, Mahler is to the totality of the music of this section what Beckett is to the text."[14] (The Beckett referred to is *The Unnameable*). Aside from the diverse juxtapositions of contrasting elements, the movement tends to shift around three centerpins: a short upbeat motion followed by a crashing cluster chord (at L, M, and Y in the score). Between these flow the overkill of musical information for which the work has become so noted.

The fourth movement returns to the reverie of the second and is a reaggregation of materials used in all three previous movements. The material grows upward (as in the second movement), particularly enveloping the major second/minor third intervallic set. Sudden bursts of sound suggest recapitulation of the second part of the first movement.

The treatments of the vocal part in the first, second and fourth sections of *Sinfonia* resemble each other in that the text is not immediately perceivable as such. The words and their components undergo a musical analysis that is integral to the total musical structure of voice and instrument together. It is precisely because the varying degree of perceptibility of the text at different moments is a part of the musical structure that the words and phrases are not printed here. The experience of 'not quite hearing' them is to be conceived as essential to the nature of the work itself.[15]

The fifth movement is set in a single variations type structure introduced by a piano/voice/flute trio soli section. The music, characterized by materials similar to those in the first movement, is more integrated and involves less contrast. The text continues to expose heterophonic multiple language collage, with clusters waxing and waning in an interlocking repeated pitch, or vacillating tremolo style.

In its five-movement form, *Sinfonia* resembles a Bartókian arch form:

I   II   III   IV   V

with the centerpiece (movement III) a striking compilation of diverse materials surrounded by two quiet, almost passive, sections and bounded externally by two agitated and dramatic movements.

3. Orchestration: *Sinfonia* employs an orchestra of eighty-one players and eight vocalists. The stage layout is given in the performance notes and includes a diagram of spatial locations for each of the sections. The violins divide into three (not the usual two) sections and are spaced diagonally from left to rear right, across the stage. The three percussionists are situated as far apart as possible, with percussion I in the center. The vocalists usually stand directly in front of the conductor and need amplification to be heard.

14. Ibid.
15. Ibid.

Berio gives the percussion (and particularly the piano) a very large role in the orchestra. Orchestration involves some doubling and incorporates a sectional approach (i.e., rare solos). Few effects are used (muting and harmonics are the exceptions) and balance is obtained by careful handling of dynamics.

4. Basic Techniques: While quotation and texts play an important role in *Sinfonia,* the underlying core of consistent materials and vocabulary ties the work together. These center rhythmically around expanding and contracting rhythmic units, metrically evolved through an interplay of duple and triple elements. Figure 11.7 is an example from the first few bars.

Figure 11.7. Luciano Berio: *Sinfonia,*
examples of rhythmic development.

These escalate to involved rhythmic schemes around repeated couplets (i.e., two-note groupings reoccurring in an environment of constantly shifting rhythmic design, reminiscent in some ways of Rzewski's *Coming Together*). Pitch seems generated by large structures of sound (discussed more fully under vertical and horizontal models) that are primarily based in seconds and thirds (with leaps developed out of their octave transpositions: sevenths, ninths, etc.).

5. Vertical Models: As mentioned earlier, harmonic structures in *Sinfonia* seem to be built primarily out of seconds and thirds. Figure 11.8 shows six of these in ascending order of complexity and dissonance.

Figure 11.8. Luciano Berio: *Sinfonia,*
examples of vertical sonorities.

The first is an often-repeated harmony found at the end of the first and fifth movement in the voices (again suggesting arch form) and in a number of other locations throughout the piece. It consists of a triadic-based minor triad with a major seventh. The second example, like the first, is generally consonant with suggestions of a whole-tone scale (extracted from the opening of the second movement). Example 3 (from the fourth movement) begins to show deepening complexity and illustrates the growth of dependency on the intervals of seconds and thirds (note as well the beginning of contradictory chromatism: D♭ and D♮). Example 4 (from the second movement) creates similar tension with slight variations, while Example 5 (from the beginning of the first movement) deepens the dissonance. The final example (from one of the large constructs of the third movement) is a near panchromatic (ten different notes) structure, again of stacked seconds and thirds. There is clearly no systematic application of specific rules, but rather an imaginative and intuitive approach to intervallic development.

6. Horizontal Models: Most of the vertical structures mentioned above arise out of slowly adding notes horizontally. All chord structures seen in figure 11.8, except 1 and 6, were created by adding notes from the bottom in orders that incorporate no leap larger than a third. These are typical of the melodic style that Berio incorporates throughout *Sinfonia*.

7. Style: *Sinfonia* is a prime example of the *post avant-garde* musical style. It is a contrapuntal work developing elements of quotation (media), clusters (sound-mass), improvisation (brief but important vocal ornamentations), and serial techniques (inherent in the post-Webern tradition). The culmination of these diverse elements in a *gestalt* represents the essence of the *post avant-garde*.

It would seem that such diverse elements as the work "talking about itself" ("Keep going, going on, call that going, call that on. But wait. He is barely moving, now almost still. Should I make my introductions?"—at which point the singers are introduced by name while the music continues), the extensive quotation, exploring nearly every conceivable sonority (from major thirds, triads and lush ninth chords to panchromatic clusters) and the use of massive dramatic bursts of sound within delicate frames of textures (the first movement primarily) could not possibly make sense. However, reflecting a society gone mad with self-preoccupation, *Sinfonia* forcefully drives its musical/dramatic point home, leaving few listeners with less than a profound disturbance borne of having indeed heard the through-composed expression of *self* without restraint. The work does indeed have continuity and a kind of frightening "madness," a macrocosm of dramatic fusion quite unlike the aforementioned Crumb and Ligeti works. While traditional in notation, material for quotes, form, and rhythmic flow, it is as well a highly *avant-garde* work in text, "act" of quoting, and eclectic, harmonic, and melodic idioms, and is a striking example of the *post avant-garde*.

Bibliography

Further Readings*

Burrows, David. "Music and the Biology of Time." *Perspectives of New Music.* (Fall-Winter 1972):241. A stimulating *post avant-garde* reference.

Cage, John. "The Future of Music." *Numus West* 5:6. An interesting article and, though garbed in the usual Cage linguistics, presents a different Cage than usual, and *his* future (". . . if there is one . . .") is one bred not so far from that described herein.

Cope, David. "Footnotes." *Composer* 4, no. 2 (1973):52. Relates directly to the *post avant-garde.*

————. *"A Post Avant-Garde." Composer* 3, no. 2 (1972):61.

Gilbert, Steven. "Carl Ruggles (1876–1971): An Appreciation." *Perspectives of New Music* (Fall-Winter 1972):224. A man of early synthesis.

Harbison, John. "Peter Maxwell Davies' *Taverner." Perspectives of New Music.* (Fall-Winter 1972):233. About a man active in the area of the *post avant-garde.*

"Musician of the Month: Karel Husa." *Musical America.* (August 1969):5. A good but short biographical sketch.

Ives, Charles. "Music and Its Future." In *American Composers on American Music.* edited by Henry Cowell. New York: Unger Publishing Co., 1962. Most prophetic.

Johnston, Ben. "On Context." *ASUC Proceedings* 3 (1968):32. Superbly optimistic article on this subject. See p. 35: "That's why I think it's spring." A most sincere and credible quote from this man of diverse musics.

Ligeti, György. "Metamorphosis of Musical Form." *Die Reihe* 7 (1960):5. An excellent article on this man's evolutionary and revolutionary process of thinking.

————, Witold Lutoslawski, and Ingvar Lidholm. *Three Aspects of New Music* (from the composition seminar in Stockholm). Stockholm: Nordiska Musikförlaget, 1968.

Petcock, Stuart. "Multiple Values in New Music." *ASUC Proceedings* 7/8; 75. A most interesting and relevant article on the relativity in criticism of new music.

Poissenot, Jacques M. "Luciano Berio." In *Dictionary of Contemporary Music,* edited by John Vinton (New York: E. P. Dutton & Co., 1974), p. 78. Excellent in its breakup of the composer's styles into four major periods to date: "serial, electronic, aleatory, and eclectic."

Rochberg, George. "The New Image of Music." *Perspectives of New Music* 2, no. 1:1. An interesting early approach to the concepts of unity in new music.

Salzman, Eric. *Twentieth-Century Music: An Introduction.* Englewood Cliffs: N.J.: Prentice-Hall, 1967. Has a fascinating *post avant-garde* ending (p. 186).

Santi, Piero. "Luciano Berio." *Die Reihe* 4:98. An interesting view of Luciano Berio at the time (1958).

————

*Addresses for record companies, periodicals, and music publishers mentioned in this Bibliography can be found in Appendix 4.

Varèse, Edgard. "The Liberation of Sound." Edited by Chou Wen-chung. In *Contemporary Composers on Contemporary Music,* edited by Barney Childs and Elliott Schwartz (New York: Holt, Rinehart and Winston, 1967). An incredibly well-edited and "composed" article on the futures of music as diverse as they may be. It prophesies the *post avant-garde* with great clarity (the article is based on lectures given by Varèse during the years 1936 to 1962).

Recordings and Publishers*

Berio, Luciano. *Sinfonia.* Universal Edition. Recorded on Columbia MS-7268.
———. *Epifanie.* Universal Edition. Recorded on RCA LSC-3189.
———. *Sequenza IV.* Universal Edition. Recorded on Candide 31015.
———. *Coro.* Universal Edition. Recorded on DG 2531 270.
Cope, David. *Concert for Piano and Orchestra* (1981). Recorded on Opus One No. 82.
———. *Re-birth.* Seesaw Music Corp. Recorded on Cornell CUWE-16A. For Concert Band.
———. *Threshold and Visions.* New York: Alexander Broude. Recorded on Folkways: FTS 33452.
Crumb, George. *Ancient Voices of Children.* Peters. Recorded on Nonesuch 71255.
Davies, Peter Maxwell. *Eight Songs for a Mad King.* Boosey and Hawkes. Recorded on Nonesuch H-71285.
del Tredici, David. *Final Alice* (1976). Recorded on London LDR-71018 (D).
Druckman, Jacob. *Windows* (1972). MCA Music. Recorded on CRI S-457. An extraordinary collage of different types of music.
Erb, Donald. *Symphony of Overtures.* Galaxy Music. Recorded on Turnabout 34433.
Felder, David. *Rondàge.* Published by Alexander Broude.
Husa, Karel. *Apotheosis of This Earth.* Associated Music Publishers. Recorded on Golden Crest 4134.
———. *Sonata for Violin and Piano.* Recorded on Grenadilla 1032. A superb example of the *post avant-garde.*
Ives, Charles. *Central Park in the Dark* (1906). AMP. Recorded on Columbia MS-6843. Interesting "pre-logue" of the *post avant-garde.*
Kolb, Barbara. *Soundings* (1981). Boosey & Hawkes.
Ligeti, György. *Requiem.* Peters. Recorded on Wergo 60045.
———. *Lontano.* Schott. Recorded on Wergo 322.
———. *Aventures.* Peters. Recorded on Wergo 60022.
———. *Melodien for Orchestra* (1971). Recorded on Decca Head 12 (England). Also contains versions of the *Double Concerto* (1972) and the *Chamber Concerto* (1970).
Rochberg, George. *Violin Concerto* (1974). Recorded on M-35149. Resurgence of post-Romantic tonality *vis à vis* "new tonality."
Schwantner, Joseph. *Aftertones of Infinity* (1978). Mercury 75141. An extraordinary work, shameless in its tonal references.
Stravinsky, Igor. *Variations (Aldos Huxley in Memoriam, 1964).* Boosey and Hawkes. Masterwork of a true man of synthesis. Recorded on Columbia MS-7386.
Takemitsu, Toru. *November Steps* (1967). Peters. Recorded on RCA LSC-7051. Interesting work of culminative opposites.
Toensing, Richard. *Doxologies I.* Recorded on Cornell University #9.

---

*Addresses for record companies, periodicals, and music publishers mentioned in this Bibliography can be found in Appendix 4.

I Glossary of Terms

This is an alphabetical listing of those terms used in the text which may need further clarification along with a brief definition. An asterisk (*) after a term within a definition signifies that the word so starred is itself defined within this glossary.

amplifier: an instrument used to expand or increase the power of a sound or signal.

amplitude: equivalent to the "loudness" of a pitch; the dynamics of sound.

amplitude modulation (AM): a periodic variation of amplitude* creating tremolo.

analog computer: a computer whose information is stored and processed using electromagnetic energy on wires or tapes, as opposed to a digital computer,* which employs numbers.

antimusic: a term denoting those works the concept or implication of which is "opposed to" the traditional meaning of music. In current terms, it refers to those compositions which either (1) include no reference to sound in their scores; (2) destroy one or more of the traditional composer/performer/audience relationships; or (3) are impossible to perform and exist only in concept.

atonality: literally, away from tonality, or no tonality. Atonality is truly impossible to obtain, as a group of sounds will by acoustical principles have one or more strongest tones (tone center = tonality), just as they will have form (intended or not). *Pantonality** (inclusive of all tonalities) has for the most part replaced the term *atonality* in reference to twelve-tone music (dodecaphony*).

augmentation: expanding the duration of a rhythmic set without disturbing the relationship of elements (e.g., doubling or tripling the value of each note).

autonomous music: Xenakis's term for music which does not employ "strategy" or "games" in its performance. This would include all of traditional music and all *indeterminate** music that does not result from group conflict (*heteronomous** music is the opposite term).

avant-garde: a French term literally meaning *advance guard* or *vanguard;* in the arts, applies to those who work in the newest areas of creativity. It may come to mean in music a certain period (such as "modern") roughly covering the years 1935–1975. Thus the term *post avant-garde* means after the earlier period: no longer can anything be really "new."

band-reject filter: an electronic filtering device that eliminates a particular band (group) of frequencies while allowing the remainder to pass.

band-pass filter: an electronic filtering device which allows a certain band to pass while rejecting all the remaining frequencies; often applied to white sound* in order to obtain a wide variety of timbres.

Bauhaus: an art school in Germany (founded in 1919 by Walter Gropius, and closed in 1933) in which the various art forms and crafts were taught as a combined unit. Faculty included Paul Klee, Vasily Kandinsky, and Mies van der Rohe (among others of like prominence), and was instrumental in encouraging the development of many of the media-forms extant today.

binary: a term used to denote a numbering system in "base 2." Only two numbers need be used (0,1), and can be represented by any system capable of two states. To create linear* numbers (1,2,3 . . . etc.), a code is created defined by columns proceeding to the left by increments following an exponential series (1,2,4,8,16 . . . etc.). In this way, any number can be represented and operated upon. 0 0 0 1 = 1; 0 0 1 0 = 2; 0 0 1 1 = 3; 0 1 0 0 = 4; etc. This concept is important to computers, since can be created to exist and move in two states.

black sound: used to denote silences as opposed to white sound* (inclusive of all frequencies).

brake drum: the housing of the braking mechanism of an automobile; also used as a percussion instrument.

chance music: often used synonymously with *indeterminate* music,* it means any music in which there is a "chance" result whether it be by composer, performer, or both.

circular bowing: on string instruments, a procedure whereby the bow is kept in motion (regardless of bow direction change) by a circular action of the bow across the string.

circular breathing: on wind instruments, the ability of the performer to breathe in through his nose while expelling air through his mouth, thereby needing no rests or "breaks" to regain breath. Performers well-versed in this procedure can play continuously for great lengths of time.

classic electronic music: electronic music created primarily by "splicing" one sound to the next rather than by using keyboards, sequencers, sample-holds, and the like.

cluster: a chord or sound which contains two or more intervals of a major second or less.

combinatoriality: a twelve-tone technique wherein hexachords* of different versions of the same row can be exchanged to create new rows (notes still add to twelve different pitches). Forms of newly created rows can be used simultaneously with the original to avoid unisons, octaves, etc., often characteristic of contrapuntal dodecaphonic* techniques.

computer-generated sound: music produced by "programming" a computer with digital information. Through high-speed operation and information retrieval, the computer "performs" under the composer's directions. A digital-to-analog converter interfaces* with an electromagnetic tape to produce one sound or an entire composition.

contact microphone: a certain type of microphone which requires physical contact for reproduction as sound.

cross-coupling: a tape-recorder technique of attaching the playback of one channel to the record of the other and vice versa to create a reiteration of attack with built-in decay,* usually employed in live-electronic music.*

DAC: Digital-to-analog-converter. An instrument designed to translate digital* information into analog* sound (primarily conversion of numbers into voltages and smoothing the result into continuous voltages for sound).

dada: international movement (beginning around 1916) which some feel originated with the poet Tristan Tzara. It included artists such as Man Ray and Marcel Duchamp among others, and attacked all conventional standards and aesthetics of "art." Exemplified by redefining machine-produced objects as works of art, by collages of newspaper, etc., it was (and some still feel it still is) one generating force behind the *avant-garde.*

decay: that aspect of a tone's envelope* in which the amplitude is decreasing.

digital computer: a computer whose information is stored and processed in binary* numbers; that is, two states of a switch [on or off], a hole or no hole in a punch card, etc.

dodecaphonic: a term commonly used to refer to twelve-tone music.

drift: in electronic music, any unintentional shift of frequency due to equipment failure or inaccuracy. All analog* oscillators* and generators* necessarily include a small amount of drift.

envelope: the amplitude* characteristics of a signal: attack, initial decay,* sustain, and final decay.* Envelope generators control both the amount and duration of each of these characteristics.

equal temperament: dividing the octave into twelve equal parts. Based on the twelfth root of two, this system represents to some composers an artificial solution to the problems encountered by just* intonation.

feedback: a result of cross-coupling.* Literally, any electronic device in which sound is fed back through the system one or more times to produce echoes or, depending on gain* adjustment, an increase of sound to limits of system tolerance.

filter: an electronic instrument designed to allow selection of frequencies from a signal: band-pass,* band-elimination.*

Fluxus: a group of *avant-garde* * composers beginning in the 1960s with intentional direction toward danger and boredom as viable concepts within art.

frequency modulation (FM): a periodic variation of frequency creating vibrato.

Futurists: Italian group of composers (1912–20) employing a wide variety of noise*-making instruments.

gain: amount of amplification. Variable gain would be the "loudness" knob on any sound-producing device (e.g., radio).

generator: sound source of all types of electronic signals except sine waves.*

gesamtkunstwerk: German term meaning literally "complete art work." Used to denote the nineteenth-century view of opera (particularly Wagner's), the composer creating and controlling all aspects of his work—staging, music, lyrics, dance, etc.—and all aspects contributing equally to the total effect.

graphic: in music, those scores which are more oriented toward visual incitement than communication of directions through symbols.

hardware: a computer term used to denote actual instrument technology as opposed to programmatic (software*) technology. Colloquially, hardware refers to "hard" physical instruments while software* refers to programs.

heteronomous music: music which utilizes "games" and "strategy" during performance, producing *conflict* and indeterminate* results. Term primarily used by Xenakis.

heterophony: "hetero" = several; phony = sounds. This term identifies music that contains many different lines occurring simultaneously. Unlike counterpoint, however, these do not relate in a systematic way harmonically or necessarily in terms of material.

hexachord: in its simplest form: a six-note chord. Commonly used in twelve-tone music to construct various further computations within the row.

improvisation: music which involves some performer freedom during performance within a certain set of parameters* created by the composer. As opposed to indeterminate* music, improvisation suggests (often demands) that the performer draw upon techniques and intuition (based on his previous experience) within a set stylistic framework. Nonscored cadenzas of the eighteenth-century concerto form are excellent examples of pre-twentieth-century improvisation.

indeterminacy: act of composer, performer, and/or both, in which the outcome is unpredictable. In general, unlike improvisation (where the performer is asked to draw upon previous experience and techniques), indeterminacy requires a *real* "letting of sounds be themselves" (as John Cage has put it) with performers and performing situations allowing any sound to exist within the framework set by the composer. The term *aleatoric* is sometimes used to denote indeterminacy.

interface: any instrument which allows two instruments of different operating procedures to function together. In computer music (especially computer-generated sound*) the digital-to-analog (D/A) interface allows the digital computer to produce analog sounds on tape. In the simplest of terms the digital computer "samples" a sine-wave (the sampling rate being variable; for our example, say 10,000 per second) creating a set of points on a graph looking in general like the original sinewave. These are, however, just points and it is through the D/A interface that these points are "smoothed" to create continuous electromagnetic force (sound when amplified and processed through amplifier and speakers).

inversion: stating something upside down. In twelve-tone music this refers to rearranging an entire row exactly by calculating intervals up for down and vice versa.

isorhythm: a compositional technique of Gothic music (c. twelfth- to fifteenth-century, primarily in Machaut) in which a set rhythm (usually very long) is repeatedly applied throughout the composition to iso-melodies of different duration and number of notes.

just intonation: tuning systems based on the overtone series.* The intervals of the fifth and the major third are calculated (ratios 3:2 and 5:4 respectively) from the series and projected into various systems.

klangfarbenmelodien: German term denoting color pointillism*: individual notes have distinctly different timbre, and are further separated by range.

klangflächenkomposition: sound-mass* which ebbs and flows through constant overlapping of timbre* and spatial* modulation.

laser: as used loosely in multimedia,* an intense beam of directed light usually connected to a receiving device which, in turn, usually leads to an oscillator.* When the beam is broken (by performer or object), the oscillator is triggered by the receiving device. It is also common to reverse the effect so that breaking the beam creates "no-sound." Other forms include voltage control* of "colored" beams such that the electrical current (often a music input) activates movement of the laser apparatus, creating complex projections.

linear: literal meaning: pertaining to line. In traditional music "linear" refers to melodic or contrapuntal flow. In electronic terminology "linear" refers to a "straight" line flow as opposed to exponential sharply accelerated flow.

live-electronic: sound created by a performer working "live" using electronic instruments in a concert situation. "Live" also refers to an approach opposite to that of composing electronic music on tape by splicing procedures (classical*).

matrix: a box of 144 squares that provides all versions of a twelve-tone row. The original is placed across the top with the inversion top to bottom; all notes are then filled in according to transpositions. This is an important device for analysis and composition of twelve-tone music.

microtone: an interval which is less than an equal-tempered half-step. Quarter-tones* are one example.

mikropolyphonie: highly complex densities of polyphonic motion in which no single voice dominates.

mixer: an electronic instrument designed to combine signals by algebraically summing their amplitudes.

modulation: a process in which any aspect of a sound or signal is varied (e.g., amplitude modulation* and frequency modulation*).

montage: a visual overlapping of images.

multimedia: a work which employs two or more traditionally separate art forms. "Happenings" are multimedia events which are more or less aleatorically conceived. Often called mixed-media.

multiphonics: the technique (particularly on wind instruments) of obtaining two or more sounds simultaneously. Obtained by control of the overtone* series so that one or more of the partials becomes prominent enough to be heard as a separate tone. Another voice can be added by humming.

musique concrète: music which employs nonelectronic sounds on tape. The tape recorder is most commonly the compositional tool, and sounds are manipulated after recording to achieve the desired effect.

noise: traditionally defined as undesirable sound. Today, however, as composers continually employ sounds which were in the past "disliked," or considered "nonmusical," it has come roughly to mean those sounds whose complexity is such that individual frequencies are no longer determinable and/or audible. White sound* is often called "white noise."

oscillator: an electronic instrument designed to create sine waves.*

oscilloscope: a device used to show (via cathode-ray tube screen) the characteristics of incoming signals (amplitude,* frequency, etc.).

ostinato: a rhythmic grouping which is repeated many times.

overtone: all sounds except sinusoidal forms contain small secondary pitches called overtones, the alteration or filtering* of which alters timbre.

panchromatic: inclusive of all chromatic tones. Usually used to refer to cluster* chords in which all or most of the twelve (traditional) pitches occur.

pandiatonicism: inclusive of all diatonic (or key-scale) notes. Pandiatonic clusters* include all seven scale notes (e.g., a white key forearm cluster on piano = key of C pandiatonic cluster).

pantonality: inclusive of all tonalities. Like atonality* it is impossible to achieve, and thus very loosely applied to twelve-tone music.

parameter: any characteristic element (of sound) or concept (of sound) which can be controlled.

pitch class: the set of pitches related to a given pitch by octave transposition (e.g., all B's are a part of the same pitch class).

pointillism: a term derived from the graphic arts; as applied to music, each sound becomes more an entity in itself, separated distinctly from those before and after by space (frequency), distance (silence) and/or timbre.

potentiometer (pot):   a variable resistor used to control the energy in a given system. Most usually found as a volume control.

prepared piano: a piano the timbre of which has been altered by the placing of various objects between, on, or around the strings inside the instrument.

program: computer software* designed by the programmer to initialize and control the computer in specific operations. In composition, programs are set up in advance to create the parameters* of the computer's "musical" language as well as interface* the "programmer" and the computer.

process music: music created by overlaying short motives of different lengths. The "process" is as important as the resultant variations.

psycho-acoustics: the study of sound and its complexity, and its realistic communication both physically and psychologically to man.

pulse wave: any form of wave that instantaneously moves from a negative to positive function. This includes all square and rectangular wave-forms.

quarter-tone: the distance between two tones which are one-half of a semitone (half step) apart. Those instruments capable of variable intonation (e.g., string instruments) approach quarter-tones in correct performance of traditional tonal music (a Db, for example, is differentiated from a C♯ according to context).

real-time: a term used to denote composition time equivalent to performance time (as opposed to abstract or nonreal time, in which, due to notation requirements, conception and composition requires much more time than performance). Electronic music events, and even complex series of events, can be composed on tape in exactly the same amount of time as a performance would require. This opens many new avenues of composer experimentation and variation of materials.

retrograde: literally meaning "backwards." In twelve-tone music, a row is permutated in twelve retrogrades (R) or readings of the original versions backwards. All intervals must be kept exact.

ring modulator: a signal multiplier circuit, combining signals to produce the sum and difference of their frequencies, with only the resultant sidebands exiting.

sampling: the ability of a computer to calculate as points the characteristics of a wave-form. The higher the sampling rate the better the resultant fidelity of sound in analog output through speakers.

sequencer: a device capable of storing programmed control voltages in order to "play" them at any given speed and rhythm. Sequencers vary from models with eight notes (three parameters per note) to huge quasi-computers capable of storing and retrieving thousands of notes and their stored parameters (articulations, dynamics, duration, etc.). The sample-hold is a sort of "random" sequencer capable of many "sequencer-like" sounds but without the determinate composer control.

serialization: the ordered and intellectual logic applied to any or all aspects of compositional technique. This term no longer applies only to twelve-tone mechanics.

sine-wave: a tone which contains no overtones.*

software: computer programs.* As opposed to hardware,* software refers to programs and data; i.e., "soft" as opposed to "hard" instruments (the computer itself).

sound-mass: a block of sound in which individual pitches are no longer important and/or perceptible. Used instead of *noise** to avoid negative connotations.

spatial modulation: the compositional technique of moving sound evenly and continuously from one physical location to another.

square wave: a pulse wave* with equal positive and negative functions.

splicer: an instrument to cut and place together segments of tape for synchronization. It is used extensively in classic* electronic music.

stochastic music: mathematician Jacques Bernoulli's term from the Greek meaning, literally, "target." Stochastic laws state that the more numerous indeterminate* activities become, the more determinate their outcome. Stochastic music suggests that if enough "random" but similar-in-timbre activities occur, the results will always be the same. While Xenakis was the first to apply the term to music, many composers utilize the basic concept of stochastic music, usually using huge "collages" of sounds which are often improvisatory or indeterminate in isolation, but in mass create the same construct of sound-mass*, mikropolyphonie* and/or klang-flächenkomposition.*

strategic music: heteronomous* music composed of "live-performance" games.

synthesizer: a loosely-applied term, literally meaning a device to build up or compose a larger idea or object from lesser ones, used in electronic music to refer to a more or less complete battery of smaller electronic units (such as oscillators*) placed together to form a larger or more complete unit. Voltage control* is also an important concept applicable to synthesizer definition.

tetrachord: a group of four notes. Often used to designate one of the three groups of four notes making up a twelve-tone row.

timbre modulation: the compositional technique of moving sound continuously and evenly from one timbre to another.

triangle wave: waveform that, when viewed on an oscilliscope,* takes the shape of a triangle. It contains every other overtone.*

trichord: any group of three notes. Often used to designate one of four groups of three notes making up a twelve-tone row.

vibrato: in electronic music terms: frequency modulation.* This is different from the tremolo created by amplitude modulation.*

vocoder: an instrument designed to code sounds (speech) into digital information for communication over cables or by radio (subsequently decoded upon reception). It is now used by some composers to create new sounds by modifying traditional ones.

voltage control: the ability of one module in a synthesizer to control another. A vital concept for electronic music allowing many techniques (AM,* FM,* etc.) to take place without manual control (impossible at high speeds).

white sound: sometimes referred to as white noise; sound which contains all possible frequencies (called white, from white—inclusive of all colors—light). Often used in conjunction with various filters* to create a wide variety of timbres.

wind sound sculptures: sculptures designed to allow wind to create sound; similar to Oriental wind chimes.

II Biographical Data

A listing of many of the composers discussed in this book, with brief biographies and/or current information about each, appear here in alphabetical sequence. Omissions are due either to lack of definite information concerning the composer, and/or necessarily limited space.

ANDRIESSEN, Louis (b. 1939, Utrecht) is a leading composer of Holland where he currently serves as musical advisor to the Globe theater group of Amsterdam.

ANTHEIL, George (1900–59) was noted as America's *Bad Boy of Music* (book by Antheil published in 1945), and during the twenties and thirties one of the most confusing figures in the world of music. His *Ballet mécanique* (inclusive of airplane motors, doorbells, and the like) is considered by many to be a milestone in the origins of the *avant-garde*. His music is as stylistically diverse as his character. Charles Amirkhanian's *An Introduction to George Antheil* (*Soundings* 7–8:176) is an excellent beginning to the study of this man.

ASHLEY, Robert (b. 1930) was cofounder of ONCE (at one time an annual festival of new music in Ann Arbor, Michigan) and coordinator of the ONCE Group. He is active as both composer and performer of new music and holds degrees from the University of Michigan and the Manhattan School of Music.

AUSTIN, Larry (b. 1930) was the editor of *Source: Music of the Avant-Garde,* a biannual publication devoted to the music of the *avant-garde.* He is currently teaching in the music department at North Texas State University. His works have appeared as part of a number of important festivals, including the New York Philharmonic 1964 *Avant-Garde* Series and the 1965 Rome *Nuova Consonanza.* He cofounded the New Music Ensemble (NME) in which he also acted as a performer. His recent works include theatrical, multimedia, and live-electronic techniques.

BABBITT, Milton (b. 1916) is professor of music at Princeton University and a director of the Columbia-Princeton Electronic Music Center. Educated in mathematics as well as in music, he is particularly well suited for the complicated intricacies of programming and detailed acoustical knowledge necessary for composition using the Mark II Synthesizer. As one of the major representatives of American music, his work has received numerous performances throughout the world. He retains all possible control over compositional elements whether his materials be electronic or instrumental.

BEHRMAN, David (b. 1937) was cofounder of the Sonic Arts Group (performers of live-electronic music) and a producer of recordings of new music for CBS and Odyssey Records. As composer/performer, he has participated in many festivals of new music, including the Angry Arts Festival in New York, and the Lincoln Center

Library New Music Concerts. He continues to organize and support concerts and recordings of *avant-garde* music both here and abroad. He currently works with live computer music (via microprocessors).

BERIO, Luciano   (b. 1925, Italy) founded the electronic studio at the Italian Radio in Milan with Bruno Maderna in 1955. A prolific composer and conductor, he lived in the U.S. and taught at Juilliard School of Music until 1973. He now conducts and composes in Europe and his music continues to rely on an intuitive "dramatic" approach, an emphasis not unlike the operatic heritage of his native Italy.

BOULEZ, Pierre   (b. 1925, France) is founder (in 1953) of the new music series *Domaine Musicale,* and continues to be active in his support of new music. In 1970, he took up duties as head conductor of the New York Philharmonic, replacing Leonard Bernstein. A prolific composer and author, his music and approach continues to be a major influence in the European *avant-garde.* He is currently director of IRCAM in Paris.

BRANT, Henry   (b. 1913), whose first works appeared in the then *avant-garde* publication *New Music Quarterly* (early 1930s), continues to contribute as both theorist and composer to the spatial composing techniques now finding great popularity in the multimedia, electronic, and theatrical elements of the *avant-garde.*

BROWN, Earle   (b. 1926) has been composer-in-residence at several universities including University of California, Berkeley, the University of Southern California and the Peabody Conservatory of Music. During the 1950s his association with John Cage led to indeterminate techniques. This, together with influences derived from Alex Calder's mobiles, has led him further toward graphic and mobile-type structures, a composite of indeterminate and improvisatory techniques. His music is performed widely and he is acclaimed as one of the foremost exponents of the *avant-garde.* Notable among his writings about music is his "Form in New Music," *Source: Music of the Avant-Garde* 1, no. 1, (January 1967).

BUDD, Harold   (b. 1936) whose works have appeared at FFLEM (First Festival of Live Electronic Music) has enjoyed numerous performances by Bertram Turetzky among others. He has also composed for documentary and art films. His music and philosophies are inflenced in part by recent art, especially "minimal art."

BUSSOTTI, Sylvano   (b. 1931, Italy) is active as composer and promoter of *avant-garde* music, notably at the Cologne series *Music of our Time,* the Munich series *New Music,* and the Florence concerts *Vita Musicale Contemporanea.* His scores are primarily graphic with emphasis on live performing/composing situations.

CAGE, John   (b. 1912) is unquestionably the world's leading exponent of the *avant-garde.* His writings (*Silence, A Year from Monday* and *Notations,* among others) and music continue to explore and experiment with the basic concepts, techniques, and philosophy of all the *avant-garde* forms presented here. His percussion concerts in early 1936 (Seattle), experiments about the same time with prepared piano techniques, and his first compositions on tape (1951), along with the inclusion of chance operations involved in compositional process, culminated in a 25-year retrospective concert of his music in Town Hall (New York) in 1958. He continues to make extensive United States and European lecture tours. Very few concerts of new music have failed to include the name and music, or at least the influence of John Cage.

CARTER, Elliott   (b. 1908), under the encouragement of Charles Ives, studied at Harvard with Walter Piston and in Paris with Nadia Boulanger. He has taught at Juilliard, Columbia, Cornell, Yale, and other schools and is particularly noted for his rigid and iconoclastic views of rhythm (metric modulation) and harmonic space.

His works, like those of Carl Ruggles, come very slowly (usually at the rate of one every one or two years), and are regarded by their performers (he does not compose electronic music) as *extremely* difficult. His *Double Concerto*, and the *Concerto for Orchestra*, are considered by many to be the most difficult in orchestral literature.

CHIARI, Giuseppe   (b. 1926, Italy) is coorganizer (with Bussotti) of the *Musica e Segno* and a member of *Gruppo 70* in Florence. An active member of the European *avant-garde* movement, his works have been performed at the 1963 *Internazionale Nuova Musica* at Palermo, the Festival of the *Avant-Garde* in New York, and several *Fluxus* festivals. His concepts point towards a new theatrical form of music dependent on inclusion of all aural materials.

CHILDS, Barney   (b. 1926) is a graduate of Stanford University (Ph. D.) and studied at Oxford University as a Rhodes Scholar. His many awards include the Koussevitsky Memorial Award in 1954, and he was an associate editor of *Genesis West*. His book (coedited with Elliott Schwartz) *Contemporary Composers on Contemporary Music* is a most important contribution to contemporary music literature and, with his endeavors for Advance Records, he has achieved a foremost position among those furthering the cause and works of new music. His works involve improvisatory and some indeterminate methods, often including audience participation but avoiding the overly-theatrical. He currently teaches at the University of Redlands in California.

COWELL, Henry   (1897–1965) was editor of *New Music* from 1927 until the midforties (the periodical continued until the 1950s with Cowell on the executive board), a publication devoted to the innovative scores of that period. His 1930 book *New Musical Resources* is devoted to the new possibilities of harmony and rhythm which would later form a cornerstone for *avant-garde* experimentation. Until his death, he promoted new music with great vitality and composed prolifically in countless styles and with considerable diversity, freely open to new and creative ideas.

CRUMB, George   (b. 1929) studied at the University of Michigan with Ross Lee Finney and currently teaches at the University of Pennsylvania in Philadelphia. His *Echoes of Time and the River* for orchestra won the 1968 Pulitzer Prize. His scores are unique both musically and in notation (all of his published works are autograph scores, as his manuscript is both incredibly neat and his notations unique [see examples in the body of this book]).

CURRAN, Alvin   (b. 1938) has been a recipient of both the Bearns Prize and BMI Student Composers award. An active member of *Musica Elettronica Viva* in Italy (live electronic performance group), his recent music is theatrical and concerned with new sounds, both electronic and nonelectronic in origin.

DAVIDOVSKY, Mario   (b. 1934, Argentina) currently composes and teaches in New York City. His *Synchronisms No. 6* for piano and tape won the 1971 Pulitzer Prize. Like Carter and Ruggles, he composes very slowly and his electronic works are *classical* in construction. He has been active for many years in the Columbia-Princeton Electronic Music Center.

DAVIES, Peter Maxwell   (b. 1934, England) resides in England and has been active with *The Fires of London* and the *Pierrot Players*. His music, like that of Berio, is highly eclectic and dramatic.

DRUCKMAN, Jacob   (b. 1928) teaches at the Yale School of Music and has been active in the Columbia-Princeton Electronic Music Center. His *Windows* for orchestra received a Pulitzer Prize. A great deal of his music, especially the *Animus* series, is for traditional instruments and tape. He has also been involved in the creation of new sounds for traditional instruments, and their resultant notations.

DUCKWORTH, William   (b. 1943) founded and was president of the Association of Independent Composers and Performers, dedicated to the performance of new music. He currently teaches at Bucknell University. His music often employs process techniques.

ERB, Donald   (b. 1927) has received grants from the Ford and Guggenheim Foundations and from the National Council on the Arts. He is currently Composer-in-Residence at Southern Methodist University in Dallas. His music often employs both live and taped electronic sounds in combination with performers on traditional instruments. His works are performed widely both here and abroad and are recorded on Nonesuch and Ars Nova discs.

FELCIANO, Richard   (b. 1930) currently teaches at the University of California at Berkeley, and has received grants from the Ford Foundation (two), Fulbright Foundation, and Guggenheim Foundation. His works are primarily for traditional instruments and tape and are published by E. C. Schirmer in Boston.

FELDMAN, Morton   (b. 1926) is one of the major influences on young composers today, through both his music and his writings about music. His works generally require very soft dynamics and are published by C. F. Peters and recorded on Columbia, Odyssey, and Time Records. His work, though influenced by painting (especially the works of Pollock and Kline) and dance (Merce Cunningham), constantly underplays the theatrical.

FOSS, Lukas   (b. 1922) is currently conductor of the Brooklyn Philharmonic orchestra. His music revolves around a controlled concept of improvisation based on historical concepts of live performance-creation combined with intentionally used "non-musical" sounds for drama and expression.

HAUBENSTOCK-RAMATI, Roman   (b. 1919, Poland) studied at the University of Cracow and is presently living as a free-lance composer in Vienna. His music is predominatly indeterminate.

HILLER, Lejaren   (b. 1924) studied with Milton Babbitt and Roger Sessions at Princeton while achieving his Ph.D. in chemistry. After 1955 he turned toward composition and with Leonard Isaacson he began experiments in computer music (first at the University of Illinois and later at the State University of New York at Buffalo). A great deal of his most recent composition is intermedia.

HUSA, Karel   (b. 1921, Prague) studied at the Prague Conservatory as well as at the Ecole Normale de Musique in Paris (composition with Arthur Honegger). Since 1954 he has taught at Cornell University. His music is a strong fusion of the traditional and *avant-garde,* and his *Music for Prague* and *Apotheosis of this Earth* have made the concert band a more viable ensemble for contemporary composers.

ICHIYANAGI, Toshi   (b. 1933, Japan) formed a new music performing group called *New Direction* in 1963. His works have been performed both here and abroad, notably by David Tudor. His music often is graphic and live-electronic. In the last few years, his concepts have turned to mixed-media in the form of environmental works.

IVES, Charles   (1974–1954) was (and still is) a major influence on almost every facet of *avant-garde* tradition. Almost everything done in the *avant-garde* (whether directly traceable to him or not in terms of lineage) seems predated by Ives many years before their so-called discovery. He is without question the most remarkable innovator in music history. Laurence Wallach's article on Ives in *The Dictionary of Contemporary Music* is excellent and useful.

JOHNSTON, Ben   (b. 1926) teaches at the University of Illinois and has received a Guggenheim Fellowship and grants from the University of Illinois and the National Council on the Arts and Humanities. His writings have appeared in *Perspectives of New Music* and *The Composer*. His music is highly structured and often utilizes unique sound sources and microtones.

KAGEL, Mauricio   (b. 1931, Argentina) currently resides in Cologne, where he serves as composer/conductor for the *Ensemble for New Music*. Many of his recent works involve written directions rather than notes, employ some improvisatory and aleatoric elements, and are based primarily on theatrical concepts.

KNOWLES, Alison   (b. 1933) is a visual/performance/graphic artist. Her work has been influential in environmental media (e.g., *The Hour of Dust,* 1968–71). She currently works in New York City.

KRAFT, William   (b. 1923) is currently percussionist with the Los Angeles Philharmonic Orchestra. He has studied with Otto Luening, Vladimir Ussachevsky and Henry Cowell, among others, and has written extensively not only for percussion, but for full orchestra as well. His *Contextures: Riots-Decade '60* is a classic intermedia orchestral composition.

KRÉNEK, Ernst   (b. 1900, Germany) began his composing career as a twelve-tone composer. He has never ceased to explore all available materials and concepts of his craft. His music is intellectual and complex with an approach directed towards individualizing each work both in concept and sound.

LENTZ, Daniel   (b. 1942) has had numerous performances of his works both here and abroad. His music, generally graphic and dramatic (multimedia), often expresses political messages, and his unusual use of colors to represent instruments and/or effects gives both the visual and aural image of his works a marked individuality.

LIGETI, György   (b. 1923, Transylvania) worked from 1957 to 1958 in the Studio for Electronic Music of WDR in Cologne. Since 1961 he has been professor of Composition at the Hochschule für Musik in Stockholm. Though largely nonelectronic, his music has explored the vast sonic possibilities of traditional orchestral and choral instruments. Despite the fact that his ideas are extremely complex, he continues to employ traditional notation and exact composer control. He has attained wide acclaim as a leader of the *avant-garde* both through his recordings on DG and exposure in the sound track of the motion picture *2001:A Space Odyssey.*

LUENING, Otto   (b. 1900) is a foremost representative of electronic music in America. His models and ideas of the early 1950s continue to represent effective techniques and procedures for contemporary composers. His historical surveys of electronic music remain the sole source of information on the origins and development of this medium. He is currently co-director of the Columbia-Princeton Electronic Center. His music freely includes all sound sources available, especially *musique concrète.*

LUNETTA, Stanley   (b. 1937) was a member of the *New Music Ensemble* and, aside from his work as percussionist (Sacramento Symphony Orchestra), has composed many *avant-garde* works. His music is theatrical and employs multimedia techniques. Through his association and performances with David Tudor and Larry Austin, he has been instrumental in advancing the cause of new music in America.

LUTOSLAWSKI, Witold   (b. 1913, Poland) is both an active conductor and a composer in Poland. Most of his early works were destroyed in World War II but show a marked traditionalism. His works today are a strong fusion of *avant-garde* and traditional techniques. He works very slowly (a large work every two years or so) and has used indeterminate and improvisatory procedures. He attributes much of his current style to a hearing of Cage's *Concert for Piano and Orchestra* (divulged in a conversation with the author).

MacKENZIE, I. A.   (1894–1969) was an early exponent of experimental ideas involved with novel instrument exploration and philosophical concepts of ego and art. His music, though for the most part without notation or significant audience approval, continues to motivate polarization of *avant-garde* ideals: fancy vs. reality.

MADERNA, Bruno   (b. 1920, Italy-d. 1974) was an active conductor of new music (testament are the large number of recordings and premieres of new works he conducted in both Europe and America), as well as a composer. In 1961 he founded the Darmstadt International Chamber Ensemble which he conducted until his death.

MORAN, Robert   (b. 1937) is currently a freelance composer in New York City. His works often involve humor as well as drama. Primarily a composer of mixed-media compositions, Moran has also been active in performing a good deal of new music (such as the puppet operas of Satie and many others when he was director of the West Coast Music Ensemble, 1968–73).

MUMMA, Gordon   (b. 1935) was a member of the Sonic Arts Union (live-electronic music) and is a composer/performer actively concerned with the preservation of live performance and a controlled theatrical/gesture situation. His music is found on the *Music of Our Time* series (Odyssey Records) and Lovely Music. He is currently Professor of Music at the University of California, Santa Cruz.

OLIVEROS, Pauline   (b. 1932) is a composer of electronic, live-electronic, and multimedia compositions and an articulate experimentalist. Her works appear on the *Music of Our Times* series (Odyssey Records) and Columbia Records, and her articles in *Source, The Composer* and Printed Editions.

PARTCH, Harry   (1901–1974) received many grants, including those from the Carnegie Corporation, Fromm Foundation, and the University of Illinois. A virtually unknown experimentalist in new tunings and instruments for many years, his works and ideas have recently gained wide notice, consideration, and success. His book *Genesis of a Music* and his works serve as a storehouse of new concepts and performing techniques. He lived in San Diego and taught part-time at the University of California until his death.

PENDERECKI, Krzysztof   (b. 1933, Poland) has won awards from the Polish Union of Composers and UNESCO (1960) and is a graduate of the University of Cracow. His music explores the vast possibilities of sonic material available within traditional concert bodies (e.g., orchestra, choir). He currently teaches at Yale University.

POUSSEUR, Henri   (b. 1929, Belgium) works at the Brussels electronic music studio and conducts theory classes in Darmstadt. He is a graduate of the Liège and Brussels Conservatories. Most of his music is electronic, and much of it explores the numerous sonic and acoustical possibilities of tape with live performers (especially orchestra).

REYNOLDS, Roger   (b. 1934) was cofounder of ONCE and has received Fulbright, Guggenheim, and Rockefeller Foundation fellowships. He currently teaches at the University of California in San Diego. His works are available from C. F. Peters and are recorded on Nonesuch Records.

ROCHBERG, George   (b. 1918) has, since 1960, been on the staff at the University of Pennsylvania in Philadelphia. He uses "quotes" freely and his more recent music has returned to a liberal approach to serial techniques.

SATIE, Erik   (b. 1866, France-d. 1925) was one of the most influential composers of the *avant-garde*. Composers such as John Cage, Robert Moran, and many others have given Satie the highest plaudits in terms of his influence on new music. These influences take the form of ultra-simplicity, new time concepts (i.e., *Vexations*) and intermedia. A number of biographies are available and have been listed in the appropriate chapter bibliographies.

SCRIABIN, Alexander   (b. 1872, Russia-d. 1915) has been influential in the use of media forms. Biographical information is available in almost any book on twentieth-century music.

STOCKHAUSEN, Karlheinz   (b. 1928, Germany) resides in Cologne. His experiments with electronic music in the mid-fifties, co-editorship of *Die Reihe,* and prolific compositions utilizing electronic sound sources on tape (performed over numerous speakers placed acoustically and compositionally in and around the audience), have placed him at the forefront of the European *avant-garde*. His life and works are discussed at length in *Kontrapunkte #6* (P. J. Tonger-Rodenkirchen/ Rhein). His writings about music are prolific and complex. His recorded works appear on DG. Fascinating books about Stockhausen include: Karl H. Wörner, *Stockhausen,* trans. Bill Hopkins (Berkeley: University of California Press, 1973) and Jonathan Cott, *Stockhausen, Conversations with the Composer* (New York: Simon and Schuster, 1973).

SUBOTNICK, Morton   (b. 1933) teaches at the California Institute of the Arts in Valencia. He was one of the founders of the San Francisco Tape Center and has worked in the Columbia (New York) electronic studio. His more recent compositions involve "ghost" electronics.

USSACHEVSKY, Vladimir   (b. 1911, Russia), together with Luening, presented one of the first American tape music concerts in 1952, and continues to be one of the foremost exponents of *musique concrète* in this country. He teaches at Columbia University in New York, and was recently visiting composer at the University of Utah.

VARÈSE, Edgard   (b. 1885, France-d. 1965) spent the latter forty years of his life working in New York City. His early predictions and pioneering work with tape and electronic sounds, along with his original approach to concepts of music, mark him as one of the major experimentalists and creators of our time. His music is available from G. Schirmer.

WOLFF, Christian   (b. 1934, France) teaches at Dartmouth University. His association in the early fifties with Cage and Feldman led to the development of very personal borderline indeterminate procedures, often notated graphically but sometimes traditionally. His works are published by C. F. Peters and recorded on Time and Odyssey Records.

WUORINEN, Charles   (b. 1938) is an active composer and pianist. Most of his works (recorded on CRI, Nonesuch, and Advance Records) require immense performer virtuosity and are explicit in notation. He has, more recently, explored more non-theatrical and formally complex electronic music than most of his American contemporaries.

XENAKIS, Iannis   (b. 1922, Rumania) until recently taught at Indiana University. He received his early training in science at the Ausbildung am Polytechnikaus in Athens, Greece. From 1947 until 1959 he worked with the famed architect Le Corbusier. His approach to composition is founded primarily on mathematical principles and explores fields of new sounds using traditional instruments and notation. His music is recorded on Columbia, Angel, Vanguard, and Nonesuch Records.

YOUNG, La Monte   (b. 1935) is one of the most highly original composers of the *avant-garde*. He studied briefly with Karlheinz Stockhausen in Germany, and currently resides as a free-lance composer in New York City. His *Dream Houses* and other mixed-media works, as well as the innovative compositions of 1960, have made him along with John Cage one of the most energetic exponents of new music in both America and abroad.

A great deal of further biographical information on these as well as many other contemporary composers listed in this book is available in *Dictionary of Contemporary Music,* edited by John Vinton. New York: E. P. Dutton & Co., 1974 (834 pp.).

III Notations

The objective of this Appendix is to provide a skeleton outline of a few of the new music notations developed over the past fifteen to thirty years which have become somewhat standard. It is just a minimal sketch, intended to illuminate some of the examples in the book. It gives samples of viable solutions to problems posed by *avant-garde* music, and hopefully will stimulate the reader to research this area in greater depth.

Most scores over the past thirty years include "performance instructions" which describe the new symbols evolved by the composer for the work. It is usually separate, sometimes multipaged, and often full of symbols in direct conflict with similar symbols of other composers. Until the late sixties there seemed an almost endless stream of "artistic" endeavors—as numerous as composers and works attempting New Directions. Since the publication of the *Darmstädter Beiträge zur Neuen Musik* in 1965 there has been a slow but steady pull toward codification of symbology. The short bibliography that follows this introduction indicates a host of articles and books dedicated to this ever-changing animal.

One of the most important new[1] *concepts* employed in new music is that of *proportional notation*. In most music since 1600 bar lines serve a variety of purposes:

1. to keep performers together:
2. to provide (in some music) primary and secondary implied accents for *dance suites* and the like;
3. to make the *reading* of music more feasible (even a Clementi *Sonatina* becomes a "nightmare" upon the removal of bar lines).

Contemporary composers often feel that these bar lines conflict with their ideas of freeing musical line, form, drive, and rhythm from imposed "square-ness" and repetition. While some of these composers have solved their problems within a metered structure (i.e., Elliott Carter: *metric modulation;* György Ligeti: involved and intricate rhythmic entrances, etc.) others have felt that the only solution was to dispense with the bar line entirely. *Proportional notation* is a bar-less structure in which the rhythm of the work is derived from the performer "proportioning" left-to-right visual reading speed with the time allotted for the given section. Toru Takemitsu's *Voice* (fig. 4.4) uses small vertical slashes through the upper portion of the staff to indicate approximately 4½ seconds of playing time. Others, like Penderecki (see fig. 3.9—*Threnody*), use large blocks of space which equal a certain duration of time. The performer then reads at a speed *proportional* to the time given for performance (i.e., if an entrance begins about one-third through a 30-second section the performer waits 10 seconds before entering, etc.). This system eradicates the limits and implied accents of bar lines. At the same time, however, it introduces a certain degree of flexibility in that

---

1. The word "new" is used here with caution: indeed proportionality existed *before* metered notations in many medieval works. In fact, it is probably the oldest concept of music notation. However, it is the new *way* in which the term is used that is of interest here.

each performer reads the score differently (therefore giving more "chance" possibilities to the performance).

Some composers, like George Crumb for example (see fig. 11.3), use tempo marks without bar lines. At the same time most of these composers write in a very *thin* soloistic style so that the need for bar lines is minimal (less than, say, trying to perform *Le Sacre du Printemps* without bar lines). In any event, different composers use notations for different reasons. Many mix proportional and metered notations within the same work (see fig. 4.10—Ligeti's *Aventures*), thereby taking advantage of the benefits of both systems. While to the untrained eye these types of scores may appear unnecessarily difficult and/or obscure, they have become standard practice.

Following a short bibliography (completely annotated bibliographies on the subject are available in many other sources) is a list of somewhat standard new music notations. Again, this is a bare outline only, and does not in any way pretend to be comprehensive, or to make any major codifying suggestions (this is the subject of another of this author's books: *New Music Notation,* referred to below).

Brief Bibliography

Bartolozzi, Bruno. *New Sounds for Woodwind.* London: Oxford University Press, 1967 Revised, 1980.

———. "Proposals for Changes in Musical Notation." *Journal of Music Theory* 5, no. 2 (1961).

Behrman, David. "What Indeterminate Notation Determines." *Perspectives of New Music.* (Spring-Summer 1965).

Brindle, Reginald Smith. *Contemporary Percussion.* London: Oxford University Press, 1970.

Cage, John. *Notations.* New York: Something Else Press, 1969.

Cope, David. *New Music Notation.* Dubuque, Iowa: Kendall/Hunt Publishing Company, 1976.

Cowell, Henry. *New Musical Resources.* New York: Alfred A. Knopf, 1930.

Darmstädter Beiträge zur Neuen Musik. Mainz: B. Schott's Söhne, 1965.

Eimert, Herbert; Fritz Enkel; and Karlheinz Stockhausen. *Problems of Electronic Music Notation.* Ottawa: National Research Council of Canada, 1956.

Howell, Thomas. *The Avant-Garde Flute: A Handbook for Composers and Flutists.* Berkeley: University of California Press, 1974.

Karkoschka, Erhard. *Notation in New Music.* New York: Praeger Publishers, 1972.

Kontarsky, Aloys. "Notation for Piano." *Perspectives of New Music* 10, no. 2 (1972).

Pooler, Frank and Brent Pierce. *New Choral Notation.* New York: Walton Music Corp., 1973.

Read, Gardner. *Twentieth-Century Music Notation* (Unpublished as of this writing).

Rehfeldt, Phillip. "Clarinet Resources and Performance." *Proceedings* 7/8, American Society of University Composers (1974).

Salzedo, Carlos. *Modern Study of the Harp.* New York: G. Schirmer, 1921.

Stone, Kurt. "New Music Notation: Why?" *Musical America* 24, no. 7 (July 1974).

———. *Music Notation in the Twentieth Century: A Practical Guidebook.* New York: W. W. Norton, 1980.

Turetzky, Bertram. *The Contemporary Contrabass.* Berkeley: University of California Press, 1974.

Yates, Peter. "The Proof of the Notation." *Twentieth-Century Music.* New York: Pantheon Books, 1967.

New Music Notations
A) Pitch

meaning	symbol	one composer among the many who use this type of notation.

quarter-tones: ↑ ↓ = (¼ up or down)   *Béla Bartók*

♯ ♭ ♮ = (¼ up)   *Mauricio Kagel*

(sharpen) (flatten)

↑ ♯ ♭ ♩   *Krzysztof Penderecki*
(¼) (¾) (¼) (¾)

highest and lowest pitch   *Krzysztof Penderecki*

clusters   ♩♮ or ♩♯   *Henry Cowell*

silent pitches   ◇   *Arnold Schoenberg*

(to be held down on the piano for ring-off of overtones when other tones are struck)

B) Rhythm

half dot   •♩• = (♩ ♪)   *George Crumb*

repetition of whole groups of notes	• — • — • — • — •	*Krzysztof Penderecki*
slow/even speed-up of pitches		*Karel Husa*
slow/even decrease of speed of pitches		*Karel Husa*
long fermata with duration shown in seconds		*George Crumb*
irregular tremolo		*Krzysztof Penderecki*

C) Dynamics

refined dynamic changes		*Henry K. Gorecki*
ad lib dynamics and flux		*John Cage*

D) Articulation

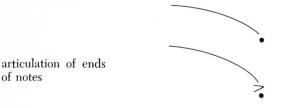

articulation of ends
of notes

Richard Bunger

E) Timbre effects

1. *Winds*

sing while playing

David Cope

multiphonics

Toru Takemitsu

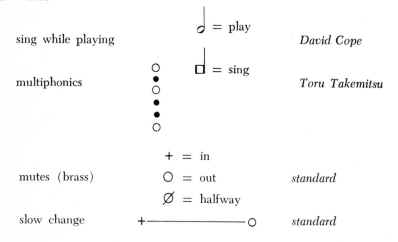

mutes (brass)

+ = in
O = out
Ø = halfway

standard

slow change   + ——————— O   *standard*

2. *Percussion*

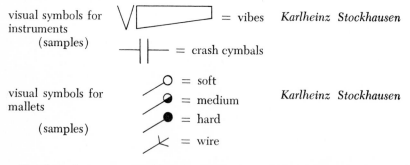

visual symbols for
instruments
    (samples)

= vibes   *Karlheinz Stockhausen*

= crash cymbals

visual symbols for
mallets
    (samples)

= soft
= medium   *Karlheinz Stockhausen*
= hard
= wire

(for these last two see Reginald Brindle's book for complete listing)

3. *Harp*

rolling surf effect *Carlos Salzedo*

(for a complete listing of such effects and notations, see Carlos Salzedo's book in the preceding bibliography)

4. *Piano*

glissando inside over strings   *Henry Cowell*

glissando inside over one string   *Henry Cowell*

mute $\oplus$ *George Crùmb*

5. *Strings*

mute on   *Pierre Boulez*

mute off   *Pierre Boulez*

play between tailpiece and bridge   *Krzysztof Penderecki*

6. *Vocal*

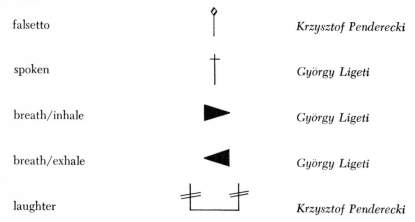

falsetto		*Krzysztof Penderecki*
spoken		*György Ligeti*
breath/inhale		*György Ligeti*
breath/exhale		*György Ligeti*
laughter		*Krzysztof Penderecki*

Note that a number of contemporary scores leave out staves of instruments with empty bars. This contributes to the "new" look of many of the scores of Crumb, Penderecki, and many others shown in this book. Likewise, when non-pitch-related activity is being employed, one-line staves are often used—quite unfamiliar in appearance to those who are used to the standard five-line staff.

IV Source Addresses

The purpose of this appendix is to furnish addresses of record companies, music periodicals, and music publishers, which dedicate a large part of their services to the promotion of contemporary and *avant-garde* music. The lists are provided to aid the reader in these ways:

1. to obtain works for further study and research (since the author has by no means been comprehensive in coverage of *all* works in given areas);
2. to become acquainted with the large number of sources not ordinarily found in record and book stores or even in many university libraries;
3. to help support the dissemination of new music by making the names and addresses of its supporters that much more available.

The lists are by no means complete for a variety of reasons:

1. lack of space (with apologies to all those companies who do support new music yet whose names, for one reason or another, were not included in the list);
2. record availability to the general public (i.e., Columbia Records does indeed support new music, but their name has not been included in this list as their records are available at any retail record store);
3. new music proportion to output: the emphasis here must of necessity be on companies which devote a *major* portion of their production to new music;
4. emphasis on listing those companies from which the examples in the book were taken, thus giving the reader the opportunity to obtain the score, record, or book discussed with comparative ease.

Record Companies

Advance: Box 17072, Rincon Station, Tucson, Ariz. 85731
Advent: 23366 Commerce Pk. Rd., Cleveland, Ohio 44122
AMG: Box 2866, Sta. A, Champaign, Ill. 61820
Avant: Box 65661, Los Angeles, Calif. 90065
Avant-Garde: 250 W. 57th St., New York, N.Y. 10019
Bowdoin College Music: 6 W. 95th St., New York, N.Y. 10025
Brewster: 1822 Monroe St., Evanston, Ill. 60202
CAPRA: 500 Broadway, New York, N.Y. 10012
Chatham Square: 500 Broadway, New York, N.Y. 10012
Concept: 500 Broadway, New York, N.Y. 10012
Cornell University: Lincoln Hall, Ithaca, N.Y. 14850

CRI: 170 W. 74th St., New York, N.Y. 10023
Crystal: Box 65661, Los Angeles, Calif. 90065
Desto: 14 Warren St., New York, N.Y. 10007
Deutsche Grammophone: 810 7th Ave., New York, N.Y. 10019
Earthquack: 500 Broadway, New York, N.Y. 10012
Finnadar: 75 Rockefeller Plaza, New York, N.Y. 10019
Folkways: 43 W. 61st St., New York, N.Y. 10023
Golden Crest: 220 Broadway, Huntington Station, N.Y. 11746
Kama-Sutra: 810 7th Ave., New York, N.Y. 10019
Louisville: 333 W. Broadway, Louisville, Ky. 40202
Mach: 539 W. 25th St., New York, N.Y. 10001
Mainstream: 1700 Broadway, New York, N.Y. 10019
Nonesuch: 15 Columbus Circle, New York, N.Y. 10023
Now: 224 S. Lebanon St., Lebanon, Ind. 46052
Odyssey: 51 W. 52nd St., New York, N.Y. 10019
Opus One: Box 604, Greenville, Maine 04441
Orion: 5840 Busch Dr., Malibu, California 90265
Owl Box: 4536, Boulder, Colo. 80302
Point Park: Wood and Blvd. of the Allies, Pittsburgh, Pa. 15222
Redwood: 8 Redwood Lane, Ithaca, N.Y. 14850
Serenus: Box 267, Hastings-on-Hudson, N.Y. 10706
Trilogy: 723 7th Ave., New York, N.Y. 10017
Turnabout: 211 E. 42nd St., New York, N.Y. 10019
UBRES: P.O. Box 2374, Champaign, Ill. 61020
Varèse: Box 148, Glendale, Calif. 91209
Wergo: 65 Mainz, Postfach 3640, Weihergarten, Germany
WIM: Box 65661, Los Angeles, Calif. 90065

Periodicals

American Society of University Composers: Journal of Music Scores: c/o Joseph Boonin, P.O. Box 2124, South Hackensack, N.J. 07606
Canadian Composer: 159 Bay St., Toronto 1, Canada
Computer Music Journal: MIT Press, 28 Carlton Street, Cambridge, Mass. 02142.
Contemporary Music Newsletter: Dept. of Music, New York University, Washington Square, New York, N.Y. 10003
Darmstädter Beiträge zur Neuen Musik: B. Schotts Sohne, Weihergarten 12, Postfach 1403, 6500 Mainz, Germany
Electronotes: 60 Sheraton Drive, Ithaca, N.Y. 14850
Interface: heerweg 347b Lisse, Netherlands
Interval: Box 8027, San Diego, Calif. 92102
Journal of Music Theory: Yale University, New Haven, Conn. 06520
Konzerte Mit Neuer Musik: Rundfunkplatz 1, 8 Munich 2, Germany
Melos: B. Schotts Söhne, Weihergarten 12, Postfach 1403, 6500 Mainz, Germany
Music in Poland: ZAIKS 2, Hupoteczna Str., Warsaw, Poland
Musical America: 1 Astor Plaza, New York, N.Y. 10036
Nutida Musik: Sveriges Radio, S-105, 10 Stockholm, Sweden
Perspectives of New Music: Princeton University Press, Princeton University, Princeton, N.J. 08540
Proceedings: American Society of University Composers: c/o American Music Center, 2109 Broadway, Suite 15–79, New York, N.Y. 10023

die Reihe (back issues): c/o Theodore Presser Co., Bryn Mawr, Pa.
Sonda: Juventudes Musicales, Madrid, Spain
Sonorum Speculum: Donemus 51, Jacob Obrechtstraat, Amsterdam, Netherlands
Sonological Reports: Utrecht State University, Utrecht, Netherlands
Soundings: 948 Canyon Rd., Santa Fe, New Mexico 87501
Source: Music of the Avant Garde: 2101 22nd St., Sacramento, Calif. 95818
Tempo: c/o Boosey and Hawkes Ltd., 295 Regent St., London, England W1A 1BR
There are a number of other magazines which carry regular columns dealing with new music and/or magazines dealing with more mainstream musical trends. Names and addresses of such magazines can be found in either: *Directory of the Music Industry,* 1418 Lake St., Evanston, Ill. 60204, or *Directory of the World of Music,* Music Information Service, 310 Madison Ave., New York, N.Y. 10017.

Music Publishers

It is very difficult to be complete in this area without filling several hundred pages with addresses. To avoid this, the author has listed only major U.S. music publishers, many of which handle the music of numerous European companies dealing with new music (C. F. Peters, for example, aside from their own nine inner companies, represents forty publishers of new music from around the world). These "umbrella" publishers are noted with an asterisk. Catalogs and lists of music available from almost all new music publishers are available from these "major" companies.

Music distributors are also included in this list and designated by an asterisk. These companies distribute catalogs of publishers around the world.

The Internationales Musikinstitut Darmstädt Informationszentrum für zeitgenössische Musik Katalog der Abteilung Noten (Druck und Herstellung: Druckerei und Verlag Jacob Helene KG., Pfungstadt, Ostendstrasse 10, Germany) is a fairly comprehensive listing of new music and publishers (issued annually).

Along with the listing of major publishers and distributors are a number of smaller companies which deal almost exclusively in new and *avant-garde* music. These companies for the most part are not represented through the distributors. Other such publisher addresses may be obtained from the *Directory of the World of Music,* Music Information Service, 310 Madison Ave., New York, N.Y. 10017, or *Directory of the Music Industry,* 1418 Lake St., Evanston, Illinois 60204.

ASCAP (1 Lincoln Plaza, New York, N.Y. 10023), BMI (40 W. 57th St., New York, N.Y. 10019), and Sesac (10 Columbus Circle, New York, N.Y. 10019) all have publishers' names and addresses (of their own affiliated "performance rights" publishers).

*Associated Music Publishers: 866 3rd. Ave., New York, N.Y. 10022
Augsburg: 426 S. 5th St., Minneapolis, Minn. 55415
*Baerenreiter-Verlag: Heindrich Schutz Allee 35, 35 Kossel, Germany
*B. H. Blackwell Ltd.: 48–51 Broudstreet, Oxford, England OX1 3BQ
*Belwin Mills: 16 W. 61st. St., New York, N.Y. 10023
Bowdoin College Music Press: Brunswick, Maine 04011
Brass Press: 136 Eighth Avenue North, Nashville, Tenn. 37203
*Alexander Broude, Inc.: 225 West 57th St., New York, N.Y. 10019
Composers' Facsimile Edition: 170 W. 74th St., New York, N.Y. 10023
Composers' Press Inc.: 1211 Ditmas Ave., Brooklyn, N.Y. 10018
*J. W. Chester, Ltd.: Eagle Court, London, E.C.1, England
Dorn Productions: P.O. Box 704, Islington, Mass. 02009

Carl Fischer, Inc.: 62 Cooper Square, New York, N.Y. 10003
Galaxy Music: 2121 Broadway, New York, N.Y. 10023
Otto Harrassowitz: Postfach 349, 6200 Wiesbaben 1, Germany
Lingua Press: 6417 La Jolla Scenic Drive South, La Jolla, CA 92037
Edward Marks: 1790 Broadway, New York, N.Y. 10019
Media Press: Box 895, Champaign, Ill. 61820
Mills Music, Inc.: 1619 Broadway, New York, N.Y. 10019
Moeck Verlag: D31 Celle, Postfach 143, Germany
MCA Music: 225 Park Ave. South, New York, N.Y. 10003
C. F. Peters: 373 Park Ave. South, New York, N.Y. 10016
Theodore Presser: Bryn Mawr, Pennsylvania 19010
E. C. Schirmer Music Co.: 112 S. St., Boston, Mass. 02111
G. Schirmer: 866 3rd Ave., New York, N.Y. 10022
Seesaw Music Corp. (also Okra Music): 1966 Broadway, New York, N.Y. 10019
Smith Publications: 2617 Gwyndale Ave., Baltimore, Maryland 21207
Source: 2101 22nd St., Sacramento, Calif. 95818
Universal Edition: 195 Allwood Rd., Clifton, N.J. 07012
Walton Music: 17 W. 60th St., New York, N.Y. 10023
Wilhelm Hansen Group: Gothersgade 9–11, DK 1123 Copenhagen K, Denmark.

Index

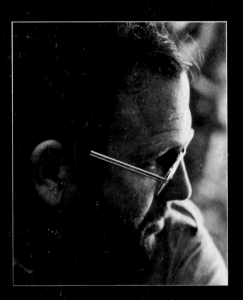

David Cope (born 1941) received his music education at Arizona State University and the University of Southern California and is presently Professor of Music at the University of California, Santa Cruz. Over 60 of his works have been published (primarily by Carl Fischer and Seesaw Music in New York City). Notable performances include those by the Indianapolis, Pittsburgh, Vermont, West Virginia and Santa Cruz Philharmonic Orchestras; complete programs of works in Carnegie Hall, the Kennedy Center for the Performing Arts, and many universities; Autumn Festival of New Music in Como, Italy; Nueva Musica Ensemble of Lima; Composer's forum in New York City; and the IV Festival of New Music in Bialystok, Poland. In addition are numerous performances in the U.S. and abroad. His music is recorded on *Folkways* (2 complete discs), *Orion, Capra, Discant, Redwood,* and *Cornell* labels (the latter with Noel Lee performing his *Variations for Piano and Wind Orchestra* with the Cornell Wind Ensemble).

He has received commissions from the Composers' Theatre of New York City, Harvard University, and the Ensemble MW2 of Poland, among others, and his awards include ten ASCAP Standard Panel Awards and a number of University Faculty Research Fellowships. He has appeared at numerous schools as guest composer and lecturer on aspects of New Music.

Articles by Professor Cope (appearing in numerous magazines on New Music) and interviews (including those with Pierre Boulez, Halsey Stevens, and I. A. MacKenzie) cover the gamut of New Musics. He was, for twelve years, editor of *The Composer* magazine. He has recently completed books on *New Music Notation* and *New Music Composition*.

wcb
Wm. C. Brown Publishers Dubuque Iowa

ISBN 0-697-03607-3